Insecurity and Welfare Regim~ ~~~~~~~~ ~~~~~
and Latin America

. On

Written by a team of internationally respected experts, this book
explores the conditions under which social policy, defined as the
public pursuit of secure welfare, operates in the poorer regions of
the world. Social policy in advanced capitalist countries operates
through state intervention, to compensate for the inadequate welfare outcomes of the labour market. Such welfare regimes cannot easily be reproduced in poorer regions of the world where
states suffer problems of governance and labour markets are
imperfect and partial. Other welfare regimes therefore prevail,
involving non-state actors such as landlords, moneylenders and
patrons. This book seeks to develop a new conceptual framework
for understanding different types of welfare regime in a range of
countries in Asia, Latin America and Africa, and makes an important contribution to the literature by breaking away from the
traditional focus on Europe and North America.

Insecurity and Welfare Regimes in Asia, Africa and Latin America

Social Policy in Development Contexts

Ian Gough and Geof Wood
with Armando Barrientos, Philippa Bevan,
Peter Davis and Graham Room

CAMBRIDGE
UNIVERSITY PRESS

CAMBRIDGE UNIVERSITY PRESS
Cambridge, New York, Melbourne, Madrid, Cape Town, Singapore, São Paulo, Delhi

Cambridge University Press
The Edinburgh Building, Cambridge CB2 8RU, UK

Published in the United States of America by Cambridge University Press, New York

www.cambridge.org
Information on this title: www.cambridge.org/9780521834193

First published 2004
Third printing 2006
This digitally printed version 2008

A catalogue record for this publication is available from the British Library

Library of Congress Cataloguing in Publication data
Gough, Ian.
Insecurity and Welfare Regimes in Asia, Africa, and Latin America: Social
Policy in Development Contexts / Ian Gough and Geof Wood with
Armando Barrientos . . . [et al.].
 p. cm.
Includes bibliographical references and index.
ISBN 0 521 83419 8
1. Developing countries – Social policy.   2. Public welfare – Developing
countries.   I. Wood, Geoffrey D., 1945–   II. Title.
HN980.G68   2004
361.6′1′091724–dc21   2003055171

ISBN 978-0-521-83419-3 hardback
ISBN 978-0-521-08799-5 paperback

Contents

Maps

Figures

Tables

Authors

Ian Gough

Ian Gough is Co-Director of the Research Project on Social Policy in Development Contexts. He is Professor of Social Policy at the University of Bath and editor of the *Journal of European Social Policy*. He is also Co-Director of the five-year ESRC-funded research group Wellbeing in Developing Countries at the University of Bath. He is author of *The Political Economy of the Welfare State* (London: Macmillan, 1979; translated into six languages, including Chinese, Japanese and Korean) and co-author of *A Theory of Human Need* (London: Macmillan, 1991), winner of both the Deutscher and the Myrdal prizes. Other books include *Can the Welfare State Compete?* (London: Macmillan, 1991), *Social Assistance in OECD Countries* (London: HMSO, 1996) and *Capitalism and Social Cohesion* (London: Macmillan, 1999). His latest book is *Global Capital, Human Needs and Social Policies: Selected Essays 1993–99* (Basingstoke: Palgrave Macmillan, 2000). He is a member of the Academy of Social Sciences.

Geof Wood

Professor Geof Wood is Co-Director of the Research Project on Social Policy in Development Contexts on which this book is based. He is Head of the Department of Economics and International Development and Director of the Institute for International Policy Analysis at the University of Bath. He is on the editorial board of the *Bulletin of Concerned Asian Scholars* and the *Journal of International Development*. He also directed the DFID research project 'Systems for Coordinated Poverty Reduction'; co-directed the Urban Livelihoods Study in Bangladesh; re-strategised social development in the Aga Khan Rural Support Programme in Pakistan; participates in the ESRC-funded Wellbeing in Developing Countries research programme; and is part of the World Bank team on social development indicators. Overall research interests lie in social development, agrarian change in South Asia, irrigation and water management, urban livelihoods and micro-finance, with particular focus on Bangladesh, India, Pakistan and Afghanistan. Recent publications include 'Prisoners and Escapees: Improving the Institutional Responsibility Square in Bangladesh', *Public Administration and Development* (2000), 20: 221–37; 'Introduction: Securing Livelihoods in Dhaka Slums', *Journal of International Development* (2000), 12 (5): 669–88 (with S. Salway); 'Desperately Seeking Security', *Journal of International Development* (2001), 13: 523–34; 'Staying Secure, Staying Poor: The Faustian Bargain', *World Development* (2003), 31 (3): 455–71.

Armando Barrientos

Armando Barrientos is Lecturer in Public Economics and Development at the Institute for Development Policy and Management at the University of Manchester, UK. His research interests cover issues of social protection, the interaction of labour markets and welfare production, and ageing, with particular reference to Latin America. Recent publications include: 'Personal Pensions, Pension Reform and Gender Differences in Pension Coverage', *World Development* (1998), 26 (1): 125–7; *Pension Reform in Latin America* (Aldershot: Ashgate, 1998); 'Work, Retirement, and Vulnerability of Older Persons in Latin America', *Journal of International Development* (2000), 12: 495–506; 'Reforming Health Insurance in Argentina and Chile', *Health Policy and Planning* (2000), 15 (4): 417–23 (with P. Lloyd-Sherlock); 'Old Age, Poverty and Social Investment', *Journal of International Development* (2002), 14: 1133–41; 'Health Policy in Chile: The Return of the Public Sector?', *Bulletin of Latin American Research* (2002), 21 (3): 442–59. He has acted as a consultant/adviser for the ILO, IADB, WIEGO and UNRISD.

Philippa Bevan

Philippa Bevan is a Research Fellow in the Sociology of Development at the University of Bath, currently working on a personal ESRC research project 'Towards a Post-Disciplinary Understanding of Global Poverty' and contributing to the University of Bath ESRC research programme on Wellbeing in Developing Countries. In her research activities she uses relevant theoretical and methodological advances in sociology to advance the empirical study of inequality and social change in poor countries. Recent publications include: 'The Successful Use of Consultancies in Aid-Financed Public Sector Management Reform: A Consultant's Eye View of Some Things Which Matter', *Public Administration*

and Development (2000), 20: 289–304; 'Who's a Goody? Demythologising the PRA Agenda', *Journal of International Development* (2000) 12:
751–9; 'Linking Micro and Macro Research: A Sociological Perspective',
Journal of International Development (1997), 5: 761–70; and 'The Perils
of Measuring Poverty: Identifying "the Poor" in Rural Ethiopia', *Oxford
Development Studies* (1997), 25: 315–43.

Peter Davis

Peter Davis is a Lecturer in International Development at the University
of Bath, UK. His research interests cover aspects of the political economy and the political sociology of social policy in developing countries,
particularly in the Indian sub-continent. This includes research into the
conceptualisation and measurement of poverty and social exclusion and
the role of civil society and social movements in the formation of social
policy. He has a particular interest in Bangladesh where he has worked for
a number of years. He has also recently published (with J. A. McGregor)
'Civil Society, International Donors and Poverty in Bangladesh', *Commonwealth and Comparative Politics* (2000), 38: 47–64.

Graham Room

Graham Room is Professor of European Social Policy at the University
of Bath. He has acted as consultant to the European Commission on
the development of its programmes in the field of poverty and social
exclusion, and as Special Adviser to the UK House of Lords Select
Committee on the European Communities, 1994. He is founding editor of the *Journal of European Social Policy*, 1990–2000. Recent publications include: 'Poverty in Europe: Competing Paradigms of Analysis',
Policy and Politics (1995), 23 (2): 103–13; 'Social Exclusion, Solidarity
and the Challenge of Globalisation', *International Journal of Social
Welfare* (1999), 8 (3): 166–74; 'Globalisation, Social Policy and International Standard-Setting: The Case of Higher Education Credentials',
International Journal of Social Welfare (2000), 9 (2): 103–19; 'Commodification and Decommodification: A Developmental Critique', *Policy and
Politics* (2000), 28 (3): 331–51; 'Social Benchmarking, Policy-Making
and Governance in the EU', *Journal of European Social Policy* (2001),
11 (4): 291–307 (with C. De la Porte and P. Pochet); and 'Education
and Welfare: Recalibrating the European Debate', *Policy Studies* (2002),
23 (1): 37–50.

Acknowledgements

This book is the outcome of a research project funded by the Economic and Social Committee for Research (ESCOR) at the Department for International Development (DFID) of the UK government. The award of a substantial grant to us in January 1999 was the result of substantive rationality triumphing over the procedural. When our joint application with the Institute for Development Policy Management (IDPM), Manchester, was lost by the courier, DFID was unable to consider it after the deadline. But wiser counsel prevailed, and more funds were released for researching social policy in development contexts. Geof Wood was convinced of Bath's intellectual claims for support in this area and was invited to re-submit a modified proposal. In this process, the team at Bath is therefore grateful to colleagues at the Institute of Development Studies, Sussex, who led an argument, after our courier disaster, that all proposals should be re-presented. The team is also grateful to colleagues at IDPM who withdrew from the joint application to permit Bath to pursue a Bath-only grant. And we are also grateful to Charles Clift, then head of ESCOR, who supported the revised Bath proposal.

Why was the team at Bath so persistent in seeking this support? In mid-1998, we had launched the Institute for International Policy Analysis (IFIPA) at Bath, which, *inter alia*, brought together colleagues from development studies and social policy into joint postgraduate teaching and research collaboration. We were keen to have a forum in which the hitherto separated traditions of development studies and social policy could converse with and interrogate each other. The DFID grant enabled this, since it bought some of us out of heavy teaching loads in order to think conceptually and collectively. This book is an outcome of that interaction.

In addition to the team members who appear as authors in this book, the research leaders (Gough and Wood) have others to thank for their support in the formation of our arguments and theory – certainly David Collard, a key member of the team focusing upon the inter-generational bargain. He does not appear in this volume, but only because that theme does not fit so readily with the other subject matter. He is publishing elsewhere. However, we did build the 1999 Annual DSA conference at Bath around his focus, and those papers are published in the *Journal for International Development*. Other colleagues from the Centre for Development Studies at Bath, especially Sarah White, James Copestake and Allister McGregor, also contributed to discussions and gave us critical feedback. These broader relations became the platform for forming the cross-departmental ESRC Research Group at Bath on Wellbeing in Developing Countries, led by Allister McGregor, thus continuing and extending the IFIPA collaboration across disciplines. Ian Gough is also indirectly indebted to the Hanse Wissenschaftskolleg at Delmenhorst in Germany, who forced him, when applying for a fellowship, to clarify many of his ideas for the book.

We have also been incredibly well supported administratively. Sue Scull worked with us initially and set up key bibliographic systems, as well as organising workshops at Bath and in Bangladesh. She was followed by Frances Hill, who assisted us further with reference systems and coordinated our regular reporting to DFID. Mark Ellison, the Administrator of the Centre for Development Studies, managed the financial side of the grant.

Geof Wood is aware that he severely tried the patience of co-authors through the extensive distractions of being appointed Head of Department (Economics and International Development) as well as continuing to be Director of IFIPA and completing other research assignments. Thus Ian Gough crucially held us together during that time, before handing production responsibility back to Wood for the final six months. This also means that Gough and Wood had two anxious partners, Margaret Jones and Angela Wood, who lived through the tensions of many drafts, shifts of argument and mutual editing. Our special thanks to them. Finally, Elizabeth Graveling joined us for the last few months to merge the different elements of the book into a single editorial style. She has coped with recalcitrant academics brilliantly!

GEOF WOOD AND IAN GOUGH

Abbreviations

ACP	African, Caribbean and Pacific (countries)
ADB	Asian Development Bank
ADP	annual development programme
AKRSP	Aga Khan Rural Support Programme
ARA	Association for Rural Advancement
ASABRI	Asuransi Sosial ABRI (Indonesian military/police retirement scheme)
ASEAN	Association of Southeast Asian Nations
ASKES	Asuransi Kesehatan Pegawai Negeri (Indonesian civil service and military social security)
BADC	Bangladesh Agricultural Development Corporation
BBV	Banco Bilbao Viscaya
BIDS	Bangladesh Institute of Development Studies
BOLIVIDA	non-contributory pension benefit (Bolivia)
BONOSOL	Bono de Solidaridad (solidarity bond)
BRAC	(formerly) Bangladesh Rural Advancement Committee
BRDB	Bangladesh Rural Development Board
BWDB	Bangladesh Water Development Board
CBI	Confederation of British Industry
CBN	cost of basic needs
CBO	community-based organisation
CDS-Bath	Centre for Development Studies, University of Bath
CELADE	Centro Latinoamericano de Demografía (Latin American Centre of Demography)
CEPAL	Comisión Económica para América Latina y el Caribe (Economic Commission for Latin America and the Caribbean)
CIEDESS	Corporación de Investigación, Estudio y Desarrollo de la Seguridad Social (Centre of Social Security Studies)

CIRDAP	Centre on Integrated Rural Development for Asia and the Pacific
CIS	Commonwealth of Independent States
CLAISS	Centro Latinoamericano de Investigaciones de Sistemas de Salud (Latin American Centre for the Study of Health Systems)
COMECON	Council for Mutual Economic Cooperation
DALE	disability-adjusted life expectancy
DFID	Department for International Development (UK)
DPHE	Department of Public Health Engineering
DRC	Democratic Republic of the Congo
ECLAC	Economic Commission for Latin America and the Caribbean (= CEPAL)
ECOMOG	ECOWAS (Economic Community of West African States) Military Observer Group
EIU	Economist Intelligence Unit
EPF	employee provident fund
EPS	Entidades de Promoción de Salud (health insurance providers)
ERD	Economic Relations Division
EU	European Union
FAO	Food and Agriculture Organisation
FFE	Food-for-Education
FFW	Food-for-Work
FSU	former Soviet Union
GATS	General Agreement on Trade in Services
GATT	General Agreement on Tariffs and Trade
GDI	Gender-Related Development Index
GDP	gross domestic product
GNI	gross national income
GNP	gross national product
GR	gratuitous relief
GSP	global social policy
HCA	hierarchical cluster analysis
HDI	Human Development Index
HDR	*Human Development Report*
HES	household expenditure survey
HIPC	highly indebted poor countries
HPI	Human Poverty Index
IADB	Inter-American Development Bank
IBRD	International Bank for Reconstruction and Development

IDS	Institute of Development Studies
IFI	international financial institution
IGO	inter-governmental organisation
ILAS	Institute of Latin American Studies
ILO	International Labour Office
IMF	International Monetary Fund
IRM	institutional responsibility matrix
IRS	institutional responsibility square
ISAPRES	Institutos de Salud Previsional (healthcare institutions)
ISSA	International Social Security Association
IUSSP	International Union for the Scientific Study of Population
JAMSOSTEK	Jaminan Sosial Tenaga Kerja (Indonesian private sector social security)
JICA	Japan International Cooperation Agency
KCA	k-means cluster analysis
LGED	Local Government Engineering Department
MNC	multi-national corporation
MOHFW	Ministry of Health and Family Welfare
NAFTA	North American Free Trade Agreement
NGO	non-governmental organisation
NHA	National Health Accounts
ODA	official development assistance
OECD	Organisation for Economic Cooperation and Development
OPK	Operasi Pasar Khusus (special market operations for rice, Indonesia)
Pag-IBIG	(Filipino Home Development Mutual Fund)
PAHO	Pan American Health Organisation
PFDS	Public Food Distribution System
PPP	purchasing power parity
PREAL	Programa de Promoción de la Reforma Educativa en América Latina y el Caribe (Partnership for Educational Revitalization in the Americas)
PRGF	poverty reduction and growth facility
PRSC	poverty reduction support credit
PRSP	poverty reduction strategy paper
RD	rural development project
RMP	Rural Maintenance Programme
ROSCA	Rotating Savings and Credit Association
RUF	Revolutionary United Front

SADC	South African Development Community
SEWA	Self-Employed Women's Association
SIDA	Swedish International Development Cooperation Agency
SPLA	Sudan People's Liberation Army
SRL	sustainable rural livelihoods
TASPEN	Tabungan dan Asuransi Pegawai Negeri (Indonesian civil service retirement scheme)
TNC	trans-national corporation
TR	test relief
UDAPE	Unidad de Análisis de Politicas Sociales y Económicas (organisation for the analysis of political science and economics)
ULIMO	United Liberation Movement for Democracy in Liberia
UN	United Nations
UNAMSIL	United Nations Mission in Sierra Leone
UNDP	United Nations Development Programme
UNESCO	United Nations Educational, Scientific and Cultural Organisation
UNICEF	United Nations Children's Fund
UNRISD	United Nations Research Institute for Social Development
USAID	United States' Agency for International Development
VGD	Vulnerable Group Development
VGF	Vulnerable Group Feeding
WDI	World Development Indicators
WDR	*World Development Report*
WEO	World Economic Outlook
WFP	World Food Programme
WHO	World Health Organisation
WIEGO	Women in Informal Employment, Globalising and Organising
WTO	World Trade Organisation

Glossary

bangsho	kinship group (Bengali)
bidhoba bhata	widow's benefit (Bengali)
boyosko bhata	old-age pension (Bengali)
bumiputera	pro-Malay (policies) (Malay)
bustee	urban slum (Bengali)
chaebol	conglomerate (Korean)
equb	rotating savings groups (Amharic)
favelas	slums (Brazil)
fitra	form of Islamic charity (Bengali)
Gemeinschaft	ascribed community (German)
Gesellschaft	purposive association (German)
gosti	kinship group (Bengali)
idir	funeral societies (Amharic)
kajer binimoy khaddo	Food-for-Work (Bengali)
keiretsu	conglomerate (Japanese)
mastaans	gang leaders (Bengali)
matobars	community leaders (Bengali)
obras sociales	social insurance funds
riverain	riverside residents (French)
samaj	community (Bengali)
samiti	committee/cooperative group (Bengali)
sardars	labour gang leaders (Bengali)
thana	police station/administrative sub-district (Bengali)
upazilla	sub-district (Bengali)
zakat	form of Islamic charity (Bengali)

Introduction

Ian Gough and Geof Wood

The improvement of human welfare is now an explicit goal of international development discourse and policy. The Millennium Development Goals commit the UN and other international agencies to: reduce the proportion of people living in extreme poverty by half between 1990 and 2015; to enrol all children in primary school by 2015; to eliminate gender disparities in primary and secondary education by 2005; to reduce infant and child mortality rates by two-thirds and maternal mortality rates by three-quarters between 1990 and 2015; and to provide access for all who need reproductive health services by 2015. These are bold targets, and represent a fundamental shift in global discourse.

The reality is more prosaic and, in many zones of the world, tragic. Few of these targets are on track to be met at the present time. Global inequality has mushroomed to 'grotesque levels' according to the UNDP (2002), thereby increasing the threats to everyone's welfare, even the more wealthy. In parts of Africa especially, HIV/AIDS, famine and war generate intolerable levels of human suffering. In more successful parts of the developing world, rapid capitalist development, which has contributed to the erosion of absolute poverty, has simultaneously heightened insecurity and vulnerability. New risks, threats and uncertainty challenge subjective and objective well-being. This is not to claim that managed development and growth cannot improve human welfare – they clearly can and have done so in much of East Asia, for example – but it is to recognise the new hazards of insecurity and new challenges to well-being, alongside pre-existing ones, in what is essentially still an unregulated international politico-economic system.

Faced with these challenges, the role of social policy is being rediscovered and reappraised in international development discourse. Of course, its relevance to human welfare is hardly news to civil society movements, NGOs, and hard-pressed governmental social sector agencies across the South, let alone to the peoples of these regions. Nevertheless it does represent a sea change in the agenda of powerful international agencies from the fundamentalist neo-liberal decades of structural

1

adjustment and the externally imposed destruction of national social programmes. For example, the recognition of social protection, both as a right and a contributor to development, by the World Bank (2001a) and the UK Department for International Development (DFID 2000) is to be welcomed.

One aspect of this has been a renewed interest in some of the debates and lessons of social policy in the West. What lessons – positive and negative – can be learned from the long experience with national social policy in these richer countries? Can the erstwhile parallel but separate tracks of development studies and social policy studies be integrated in useful ways? How can appropriate social programmes be devised, institutionalised, legitimated and financed within developing countries? What is the role of international agencies in this process? Does social policy need to shift upwards from the national to the global level, as a form of global social policy? Or does it rather need to shift downwards to empower social movements within civil society, as a form of social development? In framing these questions, any comparative analysis has to be sensitive to the history of difference between the two sets of countries as determined by the era of colonial relations and the corresponding variance in the formation and purpose of public institutions. Even in some areas not formally colonised, the combined and unequal organisation of the global political economy has reproduced very different sets of conditions and expectations, with reference to security on the one hand and the respective responsibilities of the state and non-state institutions on the other.

The experience of poorer countries in the South, and now among transitional countries, reminds us of the centrality of personal and family-level security as key to a sense of well-being and as a universal human need.[1] Outside the West this is more starkly observed as a fundamental driver of human survival behaviour both individually and collectively. It is more starkly observed precisely because the formal institutional frameworks for the provision of security are so precarious and fragile. The legitimacy and governance of public institutions are too contested and personalised to guarantee long-term rights to those groups in greatest need. As a result, people have to engage in wider strategies of security provision, risk avoidance and uncertainty management. In Gough's language, the need satisfiers are necessarily much more diverse, and certainly not derived only from the state. This is where the knowledge derived from poverty-focused

---

[1] Wood (2000) would offer 'security' alongside Doyal and Gough's (1991) 'autonomy' and 'health' as a universal human need. For them it is an intermediate need contributing to these basic needs.

studies in poor countries questions the institutional assumptions of Western social policy.

These are some of the questions which prompted the UK Department for International Development (DFID) to fund a two-year plus programme at the University of Bath, entitled 'Social Policy in Development Contexts'. Our particular contribution was to bring together specialists in development studies and social policy to collaborate over an extended period of time. Ian Gough and Graham Room have social policy backgrounds (combining social philosophy and macro-level argument), while Geof Wood, Pip Bevan and Peter Davis come from sociological and anthropological traditions within development studies, with extensive direct fieldwork experience in South Asia and sub-Saharan Africa.[2] This book is one outcome of that collaboration, entailing a critical interrogation of the premises of Western social policy when applied to the different conditions of poor-country political economies. The team at Bath has also been very pleased to associate with Armando Barrientos, now at the Institute for Development Policy Management at Manchester University, who has engaged with our theorising as the backdrop to his regional chapter on Latin America.

Social policy, as an applied field of study drawing on several social science disciplines, has its roots, like so much other social science, in the Western political philosophy of rich industrial and post-industrial countries. It has fundamentally addressed the problem of ensuring security of welfare under the uncertain life-chance conditions of capitalist, market-based societies. In these richer societies, it has been able to rely upon two key assumptions: on the one hand a legitimated state, and on the other a pervasive labour market, as the basis for many people's livelihoods. Another unspoken assumption has been the existence of sophisticated, comprehensive and regulated financial markets providing insurance and enabling savings. In a nutshell it assumes capitalism and a relatively autonomous state. As a result, both the ontological construction of social policy, and the intellectual discipline of social policy studies as a critique of inadequate and ineffective provision for the poor and insecure, focus heavily upon the role of the state in three dimensions: first, the state as an outcome of formal political settlements about government rights to tax and redistribute; second, the state as a regulator of the formal labour market in terms of workers' rights to various forms of social insurance; and, third, the state as a guarantor and direct provider of essential benefits and services to deliver security at socially acceptable minimal standards

---

[2] Another member of the group, David Collard, represented economics. His work on the inter-generational bargain is being published elsewhere (Collard 2001).

of living. In this sense, Western social policy has been associated with particular sets of means (the state) towards the ends of ensuring security of welfare.

These essential principles of Western social policy are encapsulated in Polanyi's 'great transformation', where economic modernisation and the development of liberal capitalism is characterised as the disembedding of the economy from social relations and the consequent realisation of 'self-regulating markets'. But, as Polanyi argued, this principle of the market cannot easily be extended to 'fictitious' commodities like labour, land and money. He argued that capitalism in early nineteenth-century Britain extended insecurity through a process of disembedding the economy from society and the commodification of labour. During the rest of the century 'society' protected itself by re-embedding social relations, mainly via state social intervention. Thus 'the labour market was allowed to retain its main function only on condition that wages and conditions of work, standards and regulations should be such as would safeguard the human character of the alleged commodity, labour' (Polanyi 1944: 177).

These arguments have been strongly developed in Esping-Andersen's notion of a welfare regime (1990; 1999). The concept of a welfare regime contains three elements, not entirely congruent. First, it applies to capitalist societies that have been transformed into welfare states, i.e. not countries that happen to engage in a bit of social policy on the side, but societies so deeply affected by their non-residual, pervasive social policies that they are best defined as welfare states. Second, it denotes a degree of de-commodification through state action – a measure of protection against total dependence on market forces. The OECD countries vary greatly here. Third, the concept denotes the ways in which states, markets and households interact in the provision of welfare to produce and reproduce stratification outcomes. In this way social policies shape political divisions and alliances and, usually, reproduce them through time. On the basis of the second and third dimensions, Esping-Andersen distinguishes three welfare regimes in the OECD world: liberal, conservative and social democratic. The liberal regime reproduces through a dualist politics entailing a strict definition of narrowly targeted residual need; the conservative regime through a strong ideology of family-level responsibility via support for key earners/providers; and the social democratic regime through a universalistic politics. In effect, each regime adopts a different approach to authoritative labelling, reflecting ideological variation in basic political settlements (Wood 1985).

The Bath research programme took this 'welfare regime' paradigm as an heuristic entry point into a debate about social policy in the developing and poor world. Our project was never to apply the welfare regime idea to developing countries *tout court* – that would have made a mockery of the very idea, premised as it is on advanced capitalist societies with relatively autonomous states. Rather, it was about taking that conceptual apparatus and seeing what institutional categories it generated when considering public/private combinations of support for poor people's livelihoods in non-rich countries. This process has resulted in a distinctive approach to regime research, in which Esping-Andersen's OECD model of *welfare state* regime is precisely distinguished from a more generalised conception of *welfare* regime, which embraces the performance of non-state as well as state institutions in the reproduction of security and insecurity. In this way, we offer a framework for comparative analysis, which enables different regions of the world to be broadly classified into different families of regime: welfare state regimes; informal security regimes; and insecurity regimes. The reality is more complicated than such a classification, in the sense that regions or countries within them can combine elements of all three 'families' within a single social formation. Thus different categories of a country's population can experience different primary regimes: some successfully incorporated into state protection; others reliant upon community and family arrangements; and others more excluded from formal or informal mainstream arrangements and reliant upon highly personalised politico-militia patrons, in which a sense of 'in/security' is prevalent. But within that complexity, we are certainly clustering different countries of the world into a primary association with one of these ideal types.[3]

Thus we retain the idea of regime to refer to repeated systemic arrangements through which people seek livelihood security both for their own lives and for those of their children and descendants. Substantively, the notion of a welfare regime embodies the relationship between sets of rights on the one hand and the performance of correlative duties on the other. In Esping-Andersen's approach, notwithstanding his famous delineation of three worlds of welfare capitalism, the state is privileged as the key institutional actor, with the market and family as dependent co-actors. To address this, we transform the triangle into a square by adding a 'community' domain to the other three, and then add a global dimension, recognising that poorer countries have a greater over-reliance in all four domains upon international actors and transfers.

Three further points need to be made in explaining the significance of this theoretical innovation. First, we are explicitly moving on from

---

[3] This method resembles a Marxian approach which associates a social formation embracing several co-existing modes of production with the dominant one in a particular epoch.

a legal discourse about rights and entitlements which sees them only existing in a statutory sense with formal sanctions to ensure the fulfilment of correlative duties. Rather we are adding the possibility that for poor people in poor countries, meaningful rights and correlative duties may be found through *informal* community arrangements. Thus we offer a more sociological rather than only a legal discourse about rights. And we also recognise that rights and correlative duties in all four domains may also become completely degraded and break down. This, alas, is the institutional reality for many of the poorest parts of the world, whether in sub-Saharan Africa or Afghanistan or the West Bank and Gaza. Second, the notion of 'community' has to be deconstructed with subtlety. It is not just a reference to small-scale, homogeneous reciprocity. Rather it represents a wider range of institutional practices between the state and the household involving hierarchy as well as reciprocity: thus inequality and power. It also represents a continuum from immediately local and ascriptive relations (kinship groups, clans, villages and so on) to wider and purposive ones (civil society organisations, including non-governmental organisations). In another language, it represents the range of institutional practices from personal networks to more abstract social capital.

Third, the international dimension connects to the state (international official organisations), market (trans-national capital), community (international NGOs) and household (migratory members and remittances). Within poorer countries with high aid dependency, as well as reliance upon foreign direct investment and household incomes diversified through migration and remittances, the relationship between rights and correlative duties clearly supersedes the domestic arena and should therefore be included within the welfare regime. In effect the international dimension expands the risk pool within which security is sought and uncertainty managed.

Last, our respecification of welfare regime departs from the OECD welfare state regime in one other way. In recognising the significance of a functioning relationship between rights and correlative duties within informal arrangements, we are in effect relaxing the de-commodification principle as the sole instrument and measure of welfare provision. Where the state's performance in this regard cannot be guaranteed or trusted, informal arrangements in the community domain come to the fore: as substitute service provision on the one hand; and as civil society pressure for improved governance on the other. There is yet a further layer of complexity: frequently the informal arrangements within the community domain are themselves problematic, so that improvements in the relationship between rights and correlative duties are required here also. In particular, if informal arrangements within the community are characterised by patron–clientelism, then we must look to *de-clientelisation* as the basis for improving the quality of rights and correlative duties. If we do so, then social movements of empowerment become a precondition for the evolution of a statutory rights-based social policy. The central problem for poor people, of course, is whether they can risk such a process of de-clientelisation if the alternatives are unknown and uncertain. Welfare may be delivered to some extent, and perhaps only precariously and therefore insecurely, through a range of problematic state and non-state relationships.

The focus on welfare has disturbed some of our poor-country colleagues who have associated welfare with the charitable voluntarism of NGOs and religious organisations. In structural reform terms, *welfare* is thus seen as a pale substitute for *development*, which implies more radical change and the achievement of more stable rights, perhaps deriving from grassroots empowerment. Why, therefore, are we deploying a notion of welfare regime in preference to one of development regime? This debate reflects the parallel yet separate tracks of development and social policy studies, with welfare as somehow the lesser and more luxurious agenda of social policy in richer countries but unable to address the conditions of mass poverty. But welfare, in the economist sense of welfare utility, is what people are primarily interested in: namely their own sustainable survival and pursuit of well-being. In that sense, we see welfare as the more generalisable 'ends' term, with development as a 'means' term with varied connotations. Just as the term 'development' should no longer be confined only to policy or change processes in poor countries, since all countries need to develop, so welfare is not just the prerogative of rich countries, but a pervasive adjunct to the universal notion of well-being.

This volume is organised into three parts. Part I comprises three conceptual chapters by Gough, Wood and Bevan, respectively. The first of these by Gough introduces and elaborates the arguments made above. It situates the welfare state regime paradigm in a broader context of human welfare and social policy. It then contextualises it further and generalises the paradigm to make it applicable to countries in the South and transitional countries. Drawing on the subsequent chapters in part I he distinguishes within this paradigm three 'families' of regime: welfare state regimes, informal security regimes and insecurity regimes. This framework is then applied to analyse contemporary data on human welfare and institutional structures across a hundred nations to identify clusters of regimes across the world.

In chapter 2, Wood elaborates the idea of an informal security regime under conditions where a legitimated state and pervasive formal labour markets cannot be assumed. In poor countries all people, but especially the poor, experience greater uncertainty and a higher sense of insecurity. Risk management takes centre stage and all people, but especially the poor, must rely upon a range of informal arrangements for maintaining sustainable and secure welfare. First Wood applies the idea of the 'peasant analogue' in which labour is not 'freed' as a commodity and political rights are correspondingly circumscribed. As a result, he argues that poor people are located in dependent, hierarchical relationships through which survival and welfare have to be sought. While drawing upon extensive field-work experience from South Asia, these arguments have wider, theoretical validity for other regions of the world where significant proportions of labour remain non-commodified, but which are also relatively stable politically (i.e. significantly agrarian alongside large urban informal sectors as in Latin America, parts of Southeast and East Asia, pockets of sub-Saharan Africa and, re-emerging, in transitional countries and countries in Central Asia).

The final chapter in part I by Bevan also starts from the welfare regime approach but proceeds to sensitise it to African realities and by implication to other parts of the world sharing characteristics of high uncertainty and insecurity. She thus develops a generic model of 'in/security' regimes which, she argues, has more relevance to peripheral, dangerous and powerless zones of the world system. Here the very essence of the nation-state is itself contested, partly as a result of colonial history and post-colonial settlements which transgressed other, competing, primordial loyalties and identities. But these are also zones which are not articulated into the global political economy as national economies, and which thereby experience highly unregulated market conditions and collusions with foreign capital, mediated by patron, warlord and *comprador* economic agents. The pursuit of secure welfare in these circumstances can presume none of the institutional labels that apply to the other two families of welfare regime. Insecurity regimes thus exhibit a far more tenuous relationship between rights and correlative duties, seeing survival mechanisms as more transient and contingent upon the particular alliances being made by power-holders. Bevan describes a world of unstable and frequently violent fission and fusion in which the pursuit of secure welfare is virtually divorced from any recognisable sense of social policy. Reaching poor people with weakened personal social resources in these circumstances of dysfunctional social capital and weak public goods becomes more of a relief process than even a rehabilitation one. Of course the crucial question, under these conditions, is whether there are any signs of shifting interests in the intersection between local vested interests and the global political economy which might encourage institutional reform.

Part II comprises three long case-studies which explore, empirically, welfare regimes in three regions of the world: Latin America; East Asia (excluding China); and Africa. Thus several world regions outside the OECD are not formally included for specific attention in this volume: the degrading statist welfare regimes of the ex-Soviet Union (including the Central Asian states) and Eastern Europe; the emerging regimes in China, India and South Asia (though Bangladesh is covered by Davis in part III, chapter 7); and the Middle East.

In the first of these chapters, Barrientos concludes that the Latin American countries outside the Caribbean are transforming into *liberal-informal welfare regimes*. They are welfare state regimes because a countervailing social policy logic, which emerged in the inter-war period, continues to persist. They are liberal regimes because external pressures from global markets and the US and international institutions destroyed the import substitution strategy on which rested a 'conservative-liberal' welfare regime not unlike that in Southern Europe before the 1980s. They are informal because about half the population in rural and urban informal sectors are excluded, thus displaying aspects of Wood's informal security regime. By the end of the twentieth century, Northern hegemony had effectively imposed economic liberalisation and openness, together with a more market-oriented welfare system, on the continent.

According to Gough in chapter 5, the emerging market countries of East Asia (excluding China and Vietnam) are *productivist welfare regimes*. Though the form of capitalism differs between Northeast and Southeast Asia, all the states in the region have prioritised economic over social policy and have taken economic advantage of alliances and trade with the US and Japan. What social policy there has been has invested in basic education and health: i.e. social investment rather than social protection. The combination of social investment, low taxes and favourable economic conditions has permitted relatively successful and sustainable welfare via family and household strategies as major institutional supports protecting against insecurity. The 1997 Asian financial crisis exposed the external vulnerability of this regime, without so far generating significant moves towards a welfare state regime outside Korea and Taiwan.

Much of the continent of Africa, by contrast, constitutes a generalised *insecurity regime* according to Bevan in chapter 6. She takes forward in some empirical detail the arguments that she has developed in chapter 3. Weak states are open to powerful external forces ranging from the world powers, through external governmental organisations, transnational corporations and international NGOs, to criminal networks. These interact with local patrons to reinforce patronage relationships, resulting either in the precarious adverse incorporation and dependence of the population or in the exclusion of groups from any form of livelihood and welfare and their consequent destruction. The result is a combination of: predatory capitalism; variegated forms of oppression; inadequate, insecure livelihoods; shadow, collapsed and/or criminal states; diffuse and fluid forms of political mobilisation reproducing adverse incorporation and exclusion; and political fluidity, if not outright chaos. This picture of generalised insecurity constitutes an unstable institutional landscape in which the relationship between rights and correlative duties is continuously shifting, requiring continuous adaptation by the poor as they negotiate short-term solutions to welfare in the absence of longer-term ones.

In part III we broaden our focus to trans-national factors and actors by first examining Bangladesh, a country with a long history of foreign aid, which displays, *inter alia*, the significance of including external actors within our regime analysis. Welfare outcomes are generally poor and insecurity is endemic. The welfare mix in Bangladesh is much more reliant on family, kinship, community, local government and 'civil society' forms of welfare provision, which together establish some informal but stable claims to entitlement. In addition, the foreign aid community and other bilateral and global actors mediate the welfare mix in critical ways. Aid dependency brings an external discourse about rights and correlative duties into the society, offering the prospect of a welfare state regime via well-governed and targeted state interventions underpinned by a growing economy alongside successful agrarian subsistence. However, that model is difficult to reproduce under conditions of elite capture of aid and continuing economic vulnerability to volatile global markets, in which a new transparent settlement between rights and correlative duties cannot be realised without losing comparative advantage. This is the contradictory fix for many similar societies. Under such conditions, deep structures continue to define the relationship between rights and correlative duties as highly personalised, segmented, preferential, discretionary and clientelist, as patrons of various kinds intermediate between the needs of poor people and the imperfect institutions in the state and market domains. Patron–clientelism provides some security of welfare, but it comes at the cost of adverse incorporation – individual or collective – which blocks more radical reform and the structuring of domestic interests within a welfare state regime discourse. Instead, the informal security regime prevails.

In chapter 8, Room shifts the trans-national focus from countries and nation-states towards a concept of multi-tiered, international welfare systems, thus bringing international-level covenants, treaties and agreements into the regime relationship between rights and correlative duties.

Prompted by Deacon's pessimism that European-style welfare regimes can never develop in the South, Room considers the possibilities that global or regional forms of welfare regime can emerge. His analysis draws on the experience of the most successful regional organisation, the European Union, where growing economic integration has fostered moves towards 'multi-tiered governance' and social interventions. If applied to Southern regional groupings, let alone the global level, this would entail the supra-national governance of economic relationships, aid and debt relief, and social regulation, standard setting and redistribution. Whatever the practical politics of this strategy, the implication is that welfare regimes cannot be conceived solely at the national level. Increasingly they will need to be situated within regional, if not global, systems of governance.

The concluding chapter, first of all, returns to the intellectual and normative foundations of the welfare regime approach developed in this book. It then summarises and situates our findings about welfare regimes in Asia, Africa and Latin America. Third, we outline in some detail the implications of our approach for thinking about social policy in development contexts. Finally, we consider recent arguments about the globalisation of welfare provision and the scope for a global welfare regime.

Part I

Understanding insecurity and welfare regimes in the South: an analytical framework

1   Welfare regimes in development contexts: a global and regional analysis

Ian Gough

Introduction

The purpose of this chapter is to adapt the welfare regime paradigm in order to throw light on social policy and human development in the contemporary world, and to instigate an empirical analysis to map the pattern of regimes across the developing and transitional zones of the global system.[1] It begins from and builds on my background in two fields of study: the political economy of social policy in the advanced capitalist world and the theorisation of human needs as a value base for understanding human flourishing across different cultural contexts. It is organised in eight parts followed by a conclusion.

The chapter begins with a brief discussion of human welfare as the basic goal and purported outcome of social policy and social development. Second, we discuss the emergence and development of social policy in the West – as both a policy discourse and practice, and as an intellectual area of study. Third, it introduces the 'welfare state regime' paradigm initially developed to understand the post-war welfare states of the West, reveals its underlying assumptions and shows that it is less applicable to the less-developed, the developing and the transitional worlds of the South and the East. Fourth, it constructs an alternative paradigm of 'welfare regimes' with some claim to universal applicability. Within this, fifth, it identifies informal security regimes and insecurity regimes: two meta-regime types to stand alongside the welfare state regime model. These are designed to capture basic features and conditions in the poorer and less-developed societies in the modern world system. Following a restatement of our overall framework in the sixth section, the chapter then turns in the seventh section to empirical analysis, applying the techniques of cluster analysis to the rather crude data at hand. The first part of this section conceptualises, measures and maps welfare outcomes, and the

[1] The first half of this chapter draws heavily on previous papers by Geof Wood and especially Pip Bevan. Thanks to Rodney Lowe, Paul Stubbs and Margaret Jones for earlier comments.

second part does the same for the welfare mix or the institutional responsibility matrix. Finally, by combining these two components, I undertake an initial mapping of welfare regimes across the South.

Human welfare

To conceptualise and define human welfare raises profound issues in philosophy, ethics and social science, which cannot be properly aired here. Traditional economics typically conflates well-being with either utility (happiness, satisfaction, desire fulfilment) or resources (income, wealth, command over commodities). Amartya Sen has challenged both these interpretations. On the one hand, wealth and commodities are in most cases a means to achieving welfare, not ends in themselves, and are not the only means. On the other hand, utility measures cannot overcome the way that people typically adjust their expectations and preferences to the reality they face. In much of the world this entails a downward adjustment:

Our mental reactions to what we actually get and what we can sensibly expect to get may frequently involve compromises with a harsh reality. The destitute thrown into beggary, the vulnerable landless labourer precariously surviving at the edge of subsistence, the over-worked domestic servant working round the clock, the subdued and subjugated housewife reconciled to her role and her fate, all tend to come to terms with their respective predicaments. The deprivations are suppressed and muffled in the necessity of endurance in uneventful survival (Sen 1985: 21–2).

As a result, subjective well-being is an unreliable guide to various notions of objective well-being. Cummins and Nistico (2002) observe that people across a wide range of different societies, when asked to rate their overall level of life satisfaction, report a level clustered around 70 on a 100-point scale. The majority of the population lie within a narrow range around this value; when disturbed by crisis or trauma, reported well-being dips but recovers after time to this normal level. Nistico and Cummins argue that such 'positive cognitive biases' are necessary for normal functioning and may have a genetic basis. But such research undermines the usefulness of subjective well-being as a comparative measure of well-being.[2]

In place of wealth and utility, Sen has proposed the linked concepts of human functionings and capabilities, as follows:

Commodities $\rightarrow$ Characteristics $\rightarrow$ Capability to function
$\rightarrow$ Functioning $\rightarrow$ Utility

---

[2] This does not question subjective well-being and happiness as important objects of study in their own right.

A *functioning* is 'an achievement of a person: what she or he manages to do or to be' (Sen 1985: 12). A person's *capability* represents the different functioning vectors (the combination of beings and doings) s/he is *able* to achieve. It is distinct from functioning (bare achievement), in that it reflects a person's real opportunities or positive freedom of choice between possible lifestyles. This has proved to be a fertile paradigm and has fostered a richer understanding of human welfare.

However, Sen has been criticised in turn for failing to provide a systematic list of functionings or capabilities. One well-known attempt to undertake this has been made by Martha Nussbaum (2000). Following in the footsteps of Aristotle, she adumbrates a list of ten 'central human functional capabilities' comprising: life, bodily health, bodily integrity, senses, imagination and thought, emotions, practical reason, affiliation, other species, play, and control over one's environment. According to Nussbaum this 'list isolates those human capabilities that can be convincingly argued to be of central importance in any human life, whatever else the person pursues or chooses' (Nussbaum 2000: 74). While recognising the power and importance of her work, I have questioned (Gough 2003a) the derivation and composition of this list, and continue to advocate the human needs approach developed by Len Doyal and myself (Doyal and Gough 1991). This is brutally summarised below.

We begin by distinguishing between *needs* and *wants*, according to the nature of the goals referred to. Need refers (implicitly if not explicitly) to a particular category of goals which are believed to be universalisable, whereas wants are goals which derive from an individual's particular preferences and cultural environment. The universality of need rests upon the belief that if needs are not satisfied then serious harm of some objective kind will result. We define serious harm as fundamental disablement in the pursuit of one's vision of the good. It is not the same as subjective feelings like anxiety or unhappiness. Another way of describing such harm is as an impediment to successful social participation. Whatever the time, place and cultural group we grow up and live in, we act in it to some extent. We argue that we build a self-conception of our own capabilities through interacting with and learning from others. It follows that participation in some form of life without serious arbitrary limitations is a fundamental goal of all peoples.

This enables us to define *basic needs* as those universal preconditions that enable such participation in one's form of life. We identify these universal prerequisites as physical health and autonomy. Survival, and beyond that a modicum of physical health, is essential to be able to act and participate. But that is not enough. Humans, distinct from other species, also exhibit autonomy of agency – the capacity to make informed choices about what should be done and how to go about doing it. This is impaired, we go on to argue, by severe mental illness, poor cognitive skills, and by blocked opportunities to engage in social participation. At a higher level, we can talk of *critical* participation – the capacity to situate the form of life one grows up in, to criticise it and, if necessary, to act to change it. This more dynamic type of participation requires a second-order level of critical autonomy. Without critical autonomy, human societies would change little, if at all, simply reproducing themselves from generation to generation.

Accepting that these common human needs can be met in a multitude of different ways by an almost infinite variety of specific 'satisfiers', we go on to identify those characteristics of need satisfiers that everywhere contribute to improved physical health and autonomy. These we label 'universal satisfier characteristics', or *intermediate needs* for short. We group these characteristics into eleven categories: adequate nutritional food and water, adequate protective housing, non-hazardous work and physical environments, appropriate healthcare, security in childhood, significant primary relationships, physical and economic security, safe birth control and childbearing, and appropriate basic and cross-cultural education. All eleven are essential to protect the health and autonomy of people and thus to enable them to participate to the maximum extent in their social form of life. We thus end up with a hierarchical list of concepts embracing basic and intermediate needs, all of which purport to be universal and cross-cultural.

Despite differences between the work of Sen, Nussbaum, Doyal and Gough and others the upshot is a non-monetary and multi-dimensional concept of human needs, functionings and well-being.[3] These approaches permit us cautiously to compare well-being across cultures, nations and time. I return to operationalise and apply some of these dimensions of need in the last section of this chapter.

Social policy in the North and the South

Social policy can refer to both a branch of government and an academic field of study. If, according to Alvin Gouldner, modern sociology is the child of the welfare state, so much more so is the academic discipline of social policy. However, the discourses and theorisations differ across countries and eras, making generalisations difficult. This difficulty is compounded because the emergence of social policy as a branch of government has, with rare exceptions, been piecemeal and haphazard, reactive

---

[3] There is in fact a marked congruence between our 'list' and that of Nussbaum (Gough 2003a).

rather than proactive.[4] In large part, as Polanyi explained, it was a spontaneous reaction to the disembedding of the economy from wider social relations occasioned by the spread of capitalist markets in labour and land, initially in Britain.

In Britain, modern social policy can be dated from the New Poor Law Act of 1834 and the 1842 Chadwick *Report on the Sanitary Condition of the Labouring Population of Great Britain*. State intervention in education and social security came much later. The Prussian state introduced compulsory education earlier on, and in 1883 Bismarck introduced the world's first health insurance programme, followed by old-age pensions in 1889. The period before World War I witnessed, in Britain, the introduction of old-age pensions, school meals and the first social insurance scheme. The term *Wohlfahrstaat* first appeared in Germany in the late 1920s and *welfare state* in Britain in the early 1940s. The post-war settlement in many Western countries cemented the place of an extensive and comprehensive social policy in modern polities.[5] Though the form of social policy differs across countries and policy domains, it has been a massive feature of all Northern states in the second half of the twentieth century. Therborn (1983) defined 'welfare states' as those states where more than one-half of all government expenditures are devoted to social policy, as opposed to the economy, the military, law and order, infrastructure and other traditional functions of the state. On this basis even the United States qualified as a welfare state in the last quarter of the twentieth century.[6]

The twentieth century consequently witnessed the emergence of the specialised study of social policy. In Britain, for example, Rowntree's study of poverty in York in 1899, the formation of the Fabian Society and the foundation of the London School of Economics were important landmarks. Richard Titmuss was appointed to the first chair in Social Administration in the LSE in 1950. Social policy as an applied field of study drawing on several social science disciplines is today found in many, though not all, Western countries. It is difficult to define. At a formal level, according to Erskine (1998: 18), social policy studies the welfare of individuals and social groups and analyses the impact of relevant policies

---

[4] It is a paradox that the emergence and consolidation of the so-called 'natural' phenomenon of markets has been continuously aided by the prescriptions of the disciplines of political economy and economics, whereas the development of the conscious, 'unnatural' social interventions of state was broadly spontaneous and untheorised before the event.

[5] Though not in fascist Spain and Portugal, nor in the US-established one-party states of Italy and Japan.

[6] Of course, in other respects it does not. Forty million of its citizens lack health insurance and two million, mostly poor and black, are in prison. Is this a welfare state or a 'carceral state'?

in the context of national institutions and organisations. Yet this hides wide national and ideological variations in its understanding.

Early writings on the emergence of social policy in Britain, such as Dicey's, tended to explain the growing state role in terms of social reformers and their ideas confronting the changing realities of a modernising society. Later on, the role of more collective actors, such as business and trade unions, of governments and policy networks, and of politico-economic structures were stressed. This fed into a critical debate on the very nature of the 'welfare state', which questioned both its beneficial intent and its effects, stressing rather its role as an agent of social control. Confronting these divergent perspectives, I earlier argued that the welfare state in capitalist societies was inherently contradictory: 'it simultaneously embodies tendencies to enhance social welfare, to develop the power of individuals, to exert social control over the blind play of market forces; and tendencies to repress and control people, to adapt them to the requirements of the capitalist economy' (Gough 1979: 12).

This tension still dominates many interpretations of social policy in the West. Writing in the Weberian sociological tradition in Germany, Rieger and Leibfried (2003: 270) claim that social policy has emerged in the West as 'a highly autonomous institutional complex governed by a separate sphere of values and norms. This sphere's development . . . can run expressly counter to the capitalist economic order.' This is reflected in T. H. Marshall's notion of the 'hyphenated society' of democratic-welfare-capitalism (Marshall 1981: 104). It is in large part commonly accepted that social policy can counterpose an alternative set of values to the capitalist economic order and thus contribute to countervailing forces acting to change its welfare outcomes. But the extent of this institutional autonomy is insistently disputed by globalisation theories announcing the renewed disembedding of the economy from social relations on a global scale, and the weakened ability of states to offset the growing structural power of capital.

An authoritative history of social policy in the South is yet to be written. It would need to distinguish to begin with what Therborn (1992) labels the four routes to modernity: the European route which later embraced Eastern Europe and Russia, the settler societies of the New Worlds including both North and South America as well as southern Africa, the colonial zone of Africa and much of Asia, and the countries of externally induced modernisation, where nominally independent states, in the face of Western pressures, undertake autonomous strategies of development (including such nations as Japan, China, Egypt and Turkey).

To take just one part of the colonial zone, that of British colonies, we find early historical analyses representing the development of social policy as part of the civilising imperial mission (e.g. Mair 1944). Even nationalist writers broadly accepted the modernising impulse behind the import of schools, hospitals and orphanages. Following the tide of independence in the post-war period, however, the benevolent despotism thesis was soon challenged by more materialist explanations of colonial social policy. These have interpreted health services, for example, in terms of their security, accumulation and legitimation roles. According to this perspective, environmental hygiene and public health developed to protect European administrators, traders, and public servants from cholera, plague and other epidemics, as in India in the 1860s. Second, the health and welfare of key workers, such as plantation workers and miners, required social programmes such as those instigated in South Africa in the 1870s. Third, when confronted with crises or opposition to colonial rule, social reforms have played a role in reinforcing the legitimacy of colonial governors, as in the Indian famine Commission Report of 1879, or the reforms in Malaya after the Second World War. This sequence of explanations parallels the more critical theories of social policy in the North. In turn they have occasioned a more general critical stance towards 'colonial medicine', 'colonial education' and 'colonial welfare' (Manderson 1987). The negative aspects of social policy in the North, stressed by some critical theorists, are over-determined in the colonial zone of the South by its role as, simply, an agent of imperialism.[7]

But underlying these controversies is an area of agreement. Social policy in the West has been able to rely upon three key assumptions: a legitimated state, a pervasive labour market as the basis for most people's livelihoods, and sophisticated financial markets providing insurance and a vehicle for savings. In a nutshell it assumes a developed form of capitalism and a relatively autonomous state. As a result, both the ontological construction of social policy and the intellectual discipline of social policy as a critique of inadequate and ineffective transfers to the poor and insecure focus heavily upon the role of the state: state policy as an outcome of formal political settlements about government rights to tax and redistribute; and the state as a guarantor and provider of essential services to deliver security at socially acceptable minimal standards of living. In this sense, Western social policy has been associated with particular sets of means as well as ends.

In order to make it relevant to the very different contexts in the South, the Bath research programme 'Social Policy in Development Contexts'

---

[7] This is now being challenged in turn by a new wave of writings which seek to contextualise colonial social policy and to evaluate it in terms of its contribution to the satisfaction of human needs. See Jones (2002, 2003).

took a related but much broader conceptual paradigm, that of 'welfare regime', as our heuristic entry point. As will be explained below, this has many advantages over its alternatives. But our project was never to apply the welfare regime idea to developing countries *tout court*. Rather, it was about taking that conceptual apparatus and seeing what institutional categories it generated when considering public/private combinations of support for poor people's livelihoods in non-rich countries.

As we shall see, this framework requires a wider conception of social policy than the typical state-centric version in the West. The working definition of social policy we use in this book is as follows. Social policy is:

- a *public policy*, i.e. an intentional statement of action within the public sphere to achieve certain goals, not just whatever happens as a matter of course;
- oriented to *social welfare goals*, i.e. some negative conception of avoiding harm and suffering, or some positive conception of human well-being, whether defined in terms of human needs, capabilities, flourishing, participation, equity, justice or whatever;
- which operates through a wide variety of policy *instruments* across a number of sectors, i.e. it may include land reform, work programmes, food subsidies and tax breaks as well as health, education and social protection programmes;
- and is formulated and implemented by a wide range of *actors*, i.e. the public sphere is not confined to the nation-state, but may extend downwards through regions, localities and associations to 'clubs' and communities, and upwards to trans-national and global actors.

This definition is premised on a wider set of concepts, including welfare regimes and the welfare mix, to which we now turn.

The welfare state regime model

'Regime' refers to a set of rules, institutions and structured interests that constrain individuals through compliance procedures (Krasner 1983: 1–3; North 1990: 200–2). Analytically speaking, these rules and norms may be imposed from above using forms of political power, or they may 'emerge informally' out of regular face-to-face interaction. Empirically there is an interaction between the two – regimes are always related to issues of power, conflict, domination and accommodation (O'Connor, Orloff and Shaver 1999: ch. 1). Regimes tend to reproduce themselves through time as a result of the way that interests are defined and structured. In situations of rapid change, disruption or crisis, regimes can break down, to be replaced by a different regime or by regime competition or by institutional breakdown.

In adopting a regime approach we are placing ourselves within the historical-institutional school of social research. This attempts to steer a middle way between teleological or functionalist approaches (both modern and Marxist) on the one hand, and post-modern approaches emphasising uniqueness and diversity on the other hand. It integrates structures and actors within a framework which promises a comparative analysis of socio-economic systems at different stages of development and different positions in the world system (Giddens 1979; Gough 2000a: ch. 2). Similarly it seeks to reconcile the rival 'structural' and 'actor' approaches within development sociology (Buttel and McMichael 1994; Long and van der Ploeg 1994). We recognise that structures are socially constructed, reproduced and changed through the actions of people in real time, but that, at given points in time, actors occupy different interest and power positions within structures, giving them different goals, levels of autonomy and clout.

A *welfare state* regime[8] is at the most general level an institutional matrix of market, state and family forms, which generates welfare outcomes. According to Esping-Andersen's classic text, *The Three Worlds of Welfare Capitalism* (1990: chs. 1, 3), this matrix is shaped by different class coalitions working within a context of inherited institutions. Welfare state regimes are characterised by (a) different patterns of state, market and household forms of social provision, (b) different welfare outcomes, assessed according to the degree to which labour is 'de-commodified' or shielded from market forces, and (c) different stratification outcomes. The last component refers to the role of 'political settlements' in defining the shape of welfare state regimes; for example, the Great Depression of the 1930s and the Second World War were important in shaping new political settlements between capital, labour and the state in many Western countries. The stratification effects generated within this political settlement provide positive feedback, shaping class coalitions which tend to reproduce or intensify the original institutional matrix and welfare outcomes. Thus 'existing institutional arrangements heavily determine, maybe even over-determine, national trajectories' (Esping-Andersen 1999: 4).

Esping-Andersen identifies three welfare state regimes in advanced capitalist countries with continual democratic histories since World War II: the liberal, the conservative-corporatist and the social democratic.

---

[8] I explicitly use the term 'welfare state regime' rather than 'welfare regime' at this stage, for reasons discussed later on.

	Liberal	Conservative-corporatist	Social democratic
Role of:			
Family	Marginal	Central	Marginal
Market	Central	Marginal	Marginal
State	Marginal	Subsidiary	Central
Welfare state:			
Dominant locus of solidarity	Market	Family	State
Dominant mode of solidarity	Individual	Kinship	Universal
		Corporatism	
		Etatism	
Degree of de-commodification	Minimal	High (for breadwinner)	Maximum
Modal examples	US	Germany, Italy	Sweden

Figure 1.1. The three worlds of welfare capitalism

He summarises their characteristics as shown in figure 1.1 (Esping-Andersen 1999: table 5.4). This welfare state regime paradigm has spawned an immense amount of empirical work and has attracted volumes of critical commentary and theoretical reworking, which can be divided into the following critiques (Gough 1999):

- The identification of just three regimes and the allocation of countries between them is disputed. For example, it has been argued that Australia and New Zealand are not liberal, that the Mediterranean countries are different from North European countries, and that Japan cannot be encompassed in such a 'Western' framework (see Arts and Gelissen 2002).
- In concentrating on income maintenance and labour market practices it overlooks critical social programmes like health, education and housing which do not conform to these welfare regime patterns and which, further, often reveal that national patterns of social policies are programme-specific (Kasza 2002). For example, 'liberal' Britain still retains a universal National Health Service.
- In defining welfare outcomes in terms of de-commodification – insulation from market forces – it ignores other components of well-being, in terms of autonomy and need satisfaction, and other sources of ill-being.
- In concentrating on class analysis, it ignores other sources of stratification such as religion, ethnicity and gender.
- In particular, the effects of the gendered division of labour and household forms are ignored at all three levels (social programmes, welfare outcome and stratification effect).
- In emphasising the reproduction and stability of class coalitions, social programmes and welfare outcomes it cannot handle dynamic changes and shifts in welfare regime (such as took place in Britain in the 1980s).

- In focusing on domestic institutions and coalitions it ignores the growing constraints of the global political economy and the growing role of supra-national institutions.

This debate has encouraged modification of the regime approach even in its OECD heartlands. It is not our intention to review these criticisms systematically here, but three issues should be considered and incorporated before we proceed.

First, the dominant emphasis on labour markets and social protection programmes is related to the reliance on de-commodification as the measure of welfare outcomes. But modern welfare states also deliver health and other social services designed to ameliorate harm or suffering caused by illness, accident and frailty – what Bevan calls 'life processes' (see chapter 3). A major result in the West is a gigantic 'health state' (Moran 1999), with interests, institutions and dynamics of its own. Second, the modern state undertakes human investment through education, training, work experience and allied programmes. Heidenheimer (1981) contends that the early development of the mass education state in the US provided an alternative path of social development to the welfare states of Europe. More recently, interest has grown in the OECD in 'active' alternatives to traditional 'passive' welfare programmes. Room (2000a) interprets these activities as 'de-commodification for self-development', thus linking them conceptually to Esping-Andersen's original framework. In what follows we shall follow him and extend the idea of welfare state regime to incorporate provisions that ameliorate harmful life processes and invest in human capacities.

Third, another important absence in Esping-Andersen's original idea of welfare regime, in the eyes of many, is its blindness to gender. The fact that women undertake the vast bulk of unpaid labour across the developed world, that this establishes a gendered division of labour embracing paid work, that caring duties reproduce inequalities between men and women within households and that this in turn entails a sharp split between the public and private spheres of social life – these social facts have contributed to enriching the analysis of welfare regimes in the West. Disputes continue, however, on whether the earlier map of welfare state regimes is much altered when such gender differences are incorporated (see O'Connor, Orloff and Shaver 1999). A related absence in Esping-Andersen's original formula was the family/household.[9] The central place of the state–market–family trinity in his theory was not followed up and in practice the role of the family was neglected. In his recent work (1999) he

---

[9] It continues to ignore the role of communities and voluntary associations, which are of considerable importance historically in the emergence of Western welfare states.

redresses this imbalance by integrating the role of households. In addition he develops the (pre-existing) idea of 'de-familialisation' – the extent to which an individual's welfare is independent of kinship – as a counterpart to de-commodification and independence from the market. The role of households as actors is brought centre stage, but they are portrayed as adapting to different welfare regimes in different ways, which tends to preserve nationally divergent patterns of familialism. We shall assume in what follows that gendered life processes shape the welfare mix, welfare outcomes and stratification effects in all welfare state regimes.

From welfare state regimes to welfare regimes

What contribution can this model make in understanding poverty and social policy in the South? We consider that it offers a powerful framework for studying social policy in development contexts for four reasons. First, the welfare regime approach is precisely concerned with the broader 'welfare mix': the interactions of public sector, private sector and households in producing livelihoods and distributing welfare – a dominant theme in the development literature. Second, it focuses not only on institutions but outcomes – the real states of well-being or ill-being of groups of people. Third, it is a 'political economy' approach which embeds welfare institutions in the 'deep structures' of social reproduction: it forces researchers to analyse social policy not merely in technical but in power terms, and this has much to offer. Fourth, it enables one to identify clusters of countries with welfare features in common; it holds out the promise of distinguishing between groups of developing countries according to their trajectory or paths of development.

In applying this framework to the developing world, however, many adjustments are necessary, beginning with the terminology. As Wincott (2001) observes, Esping-Andersen in his original book *The Three Worlds* refers to *welfare state* regimes, but by the publication of *Social Foundations* in 1999 this had silently shifted to *welfare* regimes. The former tends to privilege the state, notwithstanding its situation within the welfare mix. The latter can encompass settings where the state is only one player among several and not necessarily the most important.

Henceforth I shall use this distinction. Welfare *state* regimes refer to the family of social arrangements and welfare outcomes found in the OECD world of welfare states. *Welfare regime is a more generic term, referring to the entire set of institutional arrangements, policies and practices affecting welfare outcomes and stratification effects in diverse social and cultural contexts.*[10]

---

[10] In an earlier draft of parts of this chapter I referred to 'social policy regimes', which I now think too restrictive and equally state-focused (Gough 2003b).

Thus welfare state regimes form one 'family' of welfare regimes alongside others.

We have encountered objections, notably among scholars in the South, to the phrase 'welfare regime' when applied to less-developed societies. These objections are of several sorts. First, welfare has positive connotations and cannot encompass vulnerability, insecurity, famine and other extreme threats facing many peoples in the South. Second, the pursuit of livelihoods and protection by some peoples frequently involves the 'adverse incorporation' or exclusion of other peoples (see chapter 2). The search for welfare may be a zero-sum struggle. Third, economic development is critical to improving human well-being in the South and the Northern divide between economic and social policy loses much of its meaning. Fourth, and stemming from this, the very idea of a countervailing welfare discourse, of social policy as a 'highly autonomous institutional complex', is invalid when institutions are not clearly differentiated from and 'contaminate' each other, as Wood argues in chapter 2 below.[11]

We recognise these dilemmas but remain attached to the term 'welfare regime'. Welfare in its original English sense means 'faring well' and thus directs our attention to the outcomes of human activity in terms of ultimate goals, whether these are 'social development' or 'social policy'. Similarly, the idea of a welfare regime is grounded on some independent measure of human well-being with which to evaluate different socio-economic systems. This can just as well embrace ill-being. Nor does it necessarily entail the reformist identification of state action as the universally necessary precondition for normatively desirable outcomes; indeed it incorporates a hard-headed power analysis alongside a normative analysis. These analytical benefits apply just as much to poorer countries where what Wood calls 'the peasant analogue' has more relevance.

To tap this potential, we must first stand back and distil its essentials. We contend that the following nine elements are integral to the welfare state regime paradigm.[12]

1. The dominant mode of production is capitalist. There is a division of labour based on the ownership or non-ownership of capital; the dominant form of coordination is *ex post* via market signals; the technological base is dynamic, driven by a never-ending search for profit.

2. A set of class relations is based on this division of labour. The dominant form of inequality derives from exploitation by asset-owners of non-asset-owners.

---

[11] In addition, some critics, notably in East Asia, contend that the term 'welfare' denotes state handouts and charity and is therefore an illegitimate or at least not a helpful term.

[12] This list owes much to an earlier draft of chapter 3 by Pip Bevan.

3. The dominant means of securing livelihoods is via employment in formal labour markets; conversely, the major threats to security stem from interrupted access to labour markets (and from 'life processes').
4. Political mobilisation by the working classes and other classes and 'democratic class struggle' shapes an inter-class 'political settlement'.
5. There is a 'relatively autonomous state' bounded by the structural power of capital but open to class mobilisation and voice and able to take initiatives on its own behalf.
6. These factors, together with inherited institutional structures, shape a set of state institutions and practices which undertake social interventions. This state intervention combines with market and family structures and processes to construct a 'welfare mix'.
7. This welfare mix de-commodifies labour to varying degrees (and provides social services and invests in human capital).
8. Together the welfare mix and welfare outcomes influence the definition of interests and the distribution of class power resources which tend to reproduce the welfare regime through time.
9. Within each regime, 'social policy' entails intentional action within the public sphere, normally intended to achieve normative, welfare-oriented goals.

Each one of these elements must be examined when our attention turns from the North to the South.

Informal security regimes and insecurity regimes

This section draws on and synthesises the detailed analysis by Wood on informal security regimes in chapter 2 and by Bevan on insecurity regimes in chapter 3. I shall initially present a stark contrast between each of the nine elements of the welfare state regime framework with an ideal-type informal security regime model as outlined in chapter 2. Further contrasts are then drawn between these and insecurity regimes, as outlined in chapter 3, to complete a three-way framework.

First, the division of labour is not uniquely determined by a capitalist mode of production. Across much of the world, other forms of production persist, develop and interact with capitalism. These include the direct production of food and other goods and services, employment in informal labour markets, the productive role of community resources, kin connections, smuggling and illegal activities. In Althusserian terms, 'social formations' are more variegated and over-determined than the abstract 'capitalist mode of production'. Furthermore, external capitalism (international market forces and trans-national actors) heavily influences the environment of Southern political economies. The capitalist world system and its actors are of course not without importance in understanding advanced capitalist countries, but in the South there is a lack of congruity – the world system does not necessarily transform them into developed capitalist social formations.

Second, and related to this, two other forms of domination loom large alongside exploitation: exclusion and coercion. *Exclusion* refers to processes of 'shutting out' certain categories of people from major social forms of participation (such as cultural activities and political roles) on the basis of their ascribed identity or other factors. A wide range of exclusionary practices – closure, monopolisation and opportunity hoarding – create alternative sources of disadvantage. *Coercion* refers to 'all concerted application, threatened or actual, of actions that commonly cause loss or damage' (Tilly 1999: 36). It can vary from discrete threats to the full-scale destruction of people and communities. In much of the developing world, class-based exploitation relations are interwoven with other systems of inequality and domination. This is hardly absent from advanced capitalism, but it is qualitatively more important in the South.

Third, the idea of livelihoods replaces that of wages and salaries. Individuals and families use diverse strategies to make a living, involving various types of labour. Standing (2000) distinguishes, alongside wage labour: sharecropping, peasant agriculture, tribal cultivation, nomadic pastoralism, artisans, outworking, family working and bonded labour. In addition, migration for labour, petty trade, begging and petty crime also co-exist. The modern peasant moves between different forms of employment and ways of life; in Kearney's (1996) term they are 'polybians' akin to amphibians moving between aquatic and terrestrial environments. Another important difference from the ideal modern capitalist model concerns the lack of a clear division between production and reproduction and the significance of 'non-productive' activities, including investment in social networks. The feminist critique of the regime literature, alluded to above, has of course brought this centre stage in understanding Western welfare states, but again its qualitative role is greater still in the South.

Fourth, political mobilisation takes different forms. Class power resources and mobilisation can no longer be privileged. Ethnicity, regional origin, religion, caste, age groups, clan or kinship groups and other interpersonal networks can all form the basis of identity and mobilisation. In Parsonian terms, ascribed status remains as important as achieved identity. The complexity of sources of identification, and the existence of excluded groups outside the political system altogether, confound or preclude the emergence of political class settlements, the foundation of welfare state regimes in the West. Where there is political stability, this more often reflects a balance of forces than a negotiated compromise (see chapter 3).

Fifth, 'states' are at best weakly differentiated from surrounding social and power systems. As Wood argues in chapter 2, there is not only a marked 'permeability' between the polity and society, but a 'negative' permeability, wherein private interests dominate public interests. Political relationships are particularistic and diffuse, are based on interpersonal obligations, and mix together economic, instrumental and political elements of exchange, yet are premised on deep inequalities in power between patrons and clients (Eisenstadt and Roniger 1984: 48–9). The result is 'the patron state', which engenders a widespread form of political incorporation of subordinate classes (McGregor 1989). The result is a dependence of the powerless on relationships which may offer a measure of security in the short run but prevent their longer-term liberation and ability to enhance their security and welfare. In Wood's phrase, they are 'adversely incorporated'.

Sixth, the institutional landscape of the welfare mix becomes problematic. At one level, a wider range of institutions and actors are involved in modifying livelihood structures and their outcomes. At the domestic level, 'communities', informal groups and more formal NGOs, figure as informal actors and add a fourth institutional actor to the state–market–family trinity. More important, all four elements have important counterparts at the *supra-national* level: outside economic actors such as trans-national corporations or semi-illegal traders; international governance organisations such as the IMF, the World Bank, the WTO; the arms of powerful nation-states such as the US and international aid bodies; and international NGOs. Even the household sector has an international dimension, through migration and remittances. Thus a broader 'institutional responsibility matrix' emerges as in figure 1.2.

But the complexity does not stop there. To repeat: the peasant analogue model does not presume the degree of institutional differentiation of the classic welfare regime model. On the contrary, the different institutions do not operate independently of each other in terms of rules and pervading moralities. Self-interest is not confined to the market realm, loyalty to the

	Domestic	Supra-national
State	Domestic governance	International organisations, national donors
Market	Domestic markets	Global markets, MNCs
Community	Civil society, NGOs	International NGOs
Household	Households	International household strategies

Figure 1.2. Components of the institutional responsibility matrix

family realm and group interests to the political realm. Instead there is *permeability*. Behaviour is frequently not different when acting within the state, the market, the community or the family. As Wood puts it: 'Markets are imperfect, communities clientelist, households patriarchal and states marketised, patrimonial and clientelist.' Bevan argues that one should refer instead to the 'arenas' of the polity, economy, community and kin networks.

Seventh, 'de-commodification' becomes even less suitable as a measure of welfare outcomes than in the OECD world. The very notion of de-commodification does not make sense when economic behaviour is not commodified and where states and markets are not distinct realms. As already argued, the goal and measure of welfare needs to expand to take on board protection against 'life processes', amelioration of exclusion and active investment for self-development. More than that, the fuzzy distinction between *development* and welfare and the wider range of threats to security (such as from violence and physical insecurity) entail nothing less than an audit of basic and intermediate need satisfaction (Doyal and Gough 1991: ch. 8).

Eighth, the notion of path-dependent development has a broader applicability. Countries dependent on overseas aid or NGO-based provision or remittances from migrant labour or clientelist networks will develop group interests and alliances which act to continue and extend the private benefits these generate. Internal political settlements are harder to establish and less necessary when external funders provide much formal welfare, as Davis argues in chapter 7. This reinforces the informal security regime. Elsewhere in the world, Bevan argues in chapter 6, even societies with persistent civil and cross-border wars may organise livelihoods and develop forms of collective provision which adapt to war and reproduce through time. Yet, in parts of Africa, the vulnerability of poorer countries in the face of an uncontrollable external environment frequently results in uncertainty and unpredictable change. In *insecurity* regimes the likelihood of any stable political settlements is low.

Last, the very idea of social policy as a conscious countervailing force in Polanyi's sense, whereby the public realm subjects and controls the private realm in the interests of collective welfare goals, is thrown into question. Social policy in the West is based on the idea that behaviour in one sphere can be successfully deployed to modify behaviour in another sphere. More specifically, mobilisation in civil society can, via the state, impose collectivist values on the pursuit of individual interests in the market (and the family). Like Ulysses tempted by the Sirens, citizens and voters voluntarily chain and restrict their ability to pursue their short-term desires in the pursuit of longer-term collective needs (Elster

	Welfare state regime	Informal security regime	Insecurity regime
Dominant mode of production	Capitalism: technological progress plus exploitation	Peasant economies within peripheral capitalism: uneven development	Predatory capitalism
Dominant social relationship	Exploitation and market inequalities	Variegated: exploitation, exclusion and domination	Variegated forms of oppression, including destruction
Dominant source of livelihood	Access to formal labour market	A portfolio of livelihoods	A portfolio of livelihoods with extensive conflict
Dominant form of political mobilisation	Class coalitions, issue-based political parties and political settlements	Diffuse and particularistic based on ascribed identities: patron–clientelism	Diffuse and fluid, including flight
State form	Relatively autonomous state	'State' weakly differentiated from other power systems	Shadow, collapsed and criminal states with porous, contended borders
Institutional landscape	Welfare mix of market, state and family	Broader institutional responsibility matrix with powerful external influences and extensive negative permeability	Precarious: extreme negative permeability and fluidity
Welfare outcomes	Varying degrees of de-commodification plus health and human investment	Insecurity modified by informal rights and adverse incorporation	Insecurity: intermittently extreme
Path-dependent development	Liberal, conservative and social democratic regimes	Less autonomous path dependency with some regime breakdown	Political disequilibrium and chaos
Nature of social policy	Countervailing power based on institutional differentiation	Less distinct policy mode due to permeability, contamination and foreign actors	Absent

Figure 1.3. The three meta welfare regimes

1979). However, if negative permeability rules and the principles of different domains 'contaminate' each other, then social policy cannot act as an independent countervailing force, or will reinforce privilege, private short-term gain, exclusion or domination. In this situation 'all are prisoners' (Wood, chapter 2).

These nine contrasts with the welfare state regime model delimit what Wood calls the 'informal security regime'. Like the concept of welfare state regimes it is an ideal type. Figure 1.3 summarises these contrasts.

But we are not yet finished. Bevan, in chapter 3, drawing on research and evidence from parts of sub-Saharan Africa, identifies a third meta-regime: an insecurity regime. This is also represented in figure 1.3. It depicts a harsh world of predatory capitalism, variegated forms of oppression including the sporadic destruction of lives and communities, inadequate, insecure livelihoods, shadow, collapsed and/or criminal states, diffuse and fluid forms of political mobilisation generating adverse incorporation, exclusion, and political fluidity if not outright chaos, and extreme forms of suffering. This is the nightmare of absent security structures, where even informal arrangements would mark a qualitative improvement in conditions of life. It forms the opposite extreme of the global worlds of welfare and illfare.[13]

Restating the welfare regime framework

We thus conceptually distinguish three broad groups of *welfare regimes*: welfare state regimes, informal security regimes and insecurity regimes.

A welfare state regime reflects a set of conditions where people can reasonably expect to meet (to a varying extent) their security needs via participation in labour markets, financial markets and the finance and provisioning role of a 'welfare state'. This regime family is premised upon capitalist economies, formal labour markets, relatively autonomous states and well-entrenched democratic institutions. On the back of broad political settlements they establish rights-based claims to a range of social services and cash benefits and back these up with extensive tax-funding and public provisioning. This mitigates economic insecurity and diminishes poverty to varying degrees. It also reinforces different class coalitions and interest groups (e.g. taxpayers and pensioners), which reproduce social policies through time in a path-dependent manner.

An informal security regime reflects a set of conditions where people rely heavily upon community and family relationships to meet their security needs, to greatly varying degrees. These relationships are usually hierarchical and asymmetrical. This results in problematic inclusion or adverse incorporation, whereby poorer people trade some short-term

[13] Bevan argues in chapter 3 that her broad framework of *in/security* regimes applies at diverse levels and does not solely focus on the nation-state, as does the framework of welfare regimes. Outside Europe, she claims, there are not national regimes but 'differently balanced regime mixes', such that the very rich rely on international markets, the next tier use government services and domestic markets, a third group rely on informal security arrangements, while a fourth group try to combat gross insecurity with no help outside their own efforts. This is, of course, a common recognisable pattern across much of the world, even within some heartlands of the West. However, the idea of welfare regime can accommodate, indeed begins with, unequal access to different components within the welfare mix. A welfare regime typically embraces multiple welfare *systems*. I would disagree with her argument that the in/security regime concept can be applied at all levels from the household to the global. However, her warning that stable national boundaries and cohesive states cannot be taken for granted – are the exceptions rather than the rule in contested zones of the world – is of first-rate importance, and is integral to the arguments of this chapter.

security in return for longer-term vulnerability and dependence. The underlying patron–client relations are then reinforced and can prove extremely resistant to civil society pressures and measures to reform them along welfare state lines. Nevertheless, these relations do comprise a series of informal rights and afford some measure of informal security.

An insecurity regime reflects a set of conditions which generate gross insecurity and block the emergence of stable informal mechanisms to mitigate, let alone rectify, these. These regimes arise in areas of the world where powerful external players interact with weak internal actors to generate conflict and political instability. Insecurity regimes are rarely confined within national boundaries. The unpredictable environment undermines stable patterns of clientelism and informal rights within communities and can destroy household coping mechanisms. In the face of local warlords and other actors, governments cannot play even a vestigial governance and security-enhancing role. The result is a vicious circle of insecurity, vulnerability and suffering for all but a small elite and their enforcers and clients.

These are ideal-type constructs at a high level of abstraction: adopting the biological hierarchy they are *family* ideal types. Within them we may then go on to identify *genus* and *species*. For example, we have seen that within the OECD family of welfare state regimes Esping-Andersen continues to identify three genuses – liberal, conservative and social democratic – though this has spawned an immense research industry in which claims are made for four, five or more distinct 'worlds of welfare capitalism' (for a thorough survey see Arts and Gelissen 2002). Part II of this book studies in detail the regime genuses and species in three continents. Before that, however, let me briefly survey some research into whether the welfare state regime framework applies outside the OECD.

Esping-Andersen's edited book (1996) contains studies of Latin America, East Asia and Central and Eastern Europe, alongside those on Western countries. Before they collapsed, the socialist welfare systems of Central and Eastern Europe exhibited full employment and state services alongside welfare services provided by state enterprises. Latin America resembled Southern Europe with extensive labour market regulation and clientelist social insurance programmes for the core labour force.[14] Both regions faced fierce external pressures to adapt to global economic pressures in the 1980s and 1990s, respectively. The common form of welfare state adaptation was a liberal strategy of labour market

---

[14] Compared with the clientelist features of the informal security regime, this is a clientelism adapted to democracy and state welfare, involving, for example, the trading of votes for state jobs and benefits.

deregulation, privatisation and targeting (though Huber, one of the contributors, argued that Brazil and Costa Rica were developing a quite different universalistic strategy). The dynamic East Asian economies, on the
contrary, faced the need to move beyond Confucian familialism and were
beginning cautiously to graft a social investment approach alongside a further extension of existing policies. Democratisation and nation-building
are likely to generate welfare state-building in this region in the future.

Another collective work edited by Alber and Standing (2000a) studied the impact of globalisation and 'social dumping' on welfare states
and labour market regulation in the same three regions. It recognised the
alternative paths such countries faced: a race to catch up with the Western welfare state model, or avoiding this path altogether. The results of
the regional studies reconfirmed some of the Esping-Andersen analyses
but were more favourable to further welfare state development. Central
Europe, if not the former Soviet Union, showed few signs of social cuts or
other indicators of social dumping – rather some measures of increased
compensation. The same pattern was evident in the Southern Cone of
Latin America where domestic political coalitions defending status-based
social policies appeared to outweigh external economic pressures for cuts.
In East Asia social security, far from being backward, has been inau-
gurated at lower levels of national income than in Western countries a
half-century earlier.

Both studies suggested that in the 1970s Central and Eastern Europe
and Latin America exhibited identifiable welfare state regimes: the state
exerted an explicit social policy role within the welfare mix, certain levels of security were guaranteed for most workers (in Eastern Europe) or
core workers (Latin America, at least in the Southern Cone), and these
shaped domestic preferences and interests which acted to try and preserve
the welfare system even in the face of overwhelming external pressures.
Dynamic (North) East Asia revealed a quite different, far less state-
centric, regime with an extensive family role based on savings, transfers
and services. However, it was suggested that these countries were in a
process of transition towards something like a welfare state regime.

According to these and other studies, the welfare state regime family
thus extends beyond the West and includes further distinctive genera.
Northeast Asia may even resemble a transitional form between two families, a mixture of informal security regime and welfare state regime.
Chapters 4 and 5 explore these issues in much more detail. It would be
safe to conclude from this literature, however, that these regions mark the
outermost bounds where the welfare state regime model can be applied.
Much of the rest of the world, notably South Asia and much of Africa,
cannot be understood within this paradigm. Chapters 6 and 7 explore the

applicability of our notions of insecurity and informal security regimes, respectively.

Regimes in the developing and transitional world: an empirical cluster analysis

In order to situate the regional analysis in part II of the book, this section introduces a statistical analysis of welfare regimes across the developing and transitional world. The aim is to explore patterns of welfare mixes and welfare outcomes: unlike much regression analysis, the goal is to reveal patterns of difference as much as relations of similarity. To this end, the main statistical technique employed is cluster analysis. We rely on commonly available data covering all the transitional, underdeveloped and developing countries outside the OECD, though inevitably their validity, reliability and comparability are open to question. (Details are presented in the appendix to this chapter.) Nevertheless, some empirical analysis is necessary to prepare the ground for the regional analyses in this book.

Welfare outcomes

We have seen that de-commodification is peculiarly ill-suited as a conceptualisation of security in less-developed countries and contexts, and alternatives are needed. These must include more direct measures of human well-being and ill-being, security and insecurity. In the light of our earlier discussion on human welfare, I consider measures of poverty, need satisfaction and human development in what follows.

Poverty is the immediate target of much overt international discourse and action (World Bank 2001a: ch. 1). Since Rowntree's (1901) study of poverty in York in 1899, this has been defined and measured as lack of sufficient monetary income or consumption. Rowntree developed a quite complex and rigorous method of estimating sufficiency, beginning with the scientific calculation of the minimum nutrients to maintain 'merely physical efficiency'. Various combinations of foodstuffs (in the York of his day) which yielded these nutrients were then costed and the very cheapest chosen irrespective of cultural standards. To this sum was then added the costs of the minimum amount of housing, heating, clothing and other essential sundries, to yield an overall monetary poverty line. It is clear that Rowntree attempted to abstract from social and cultural contexts in calculating such a minimum; it is also clear that he failed to do so, when including, for example, a daily newspaper in his list of sundries. This recognition has inspired many subsequent studies of 'relative poverty', broadly defined as that income or consumption-bundle necessary to enable a minimum socially acceptable level of participation in one's social form of life (Townsend 1979).[15] Compared with this ideal the only extensive comparative data is crude. Though the World Bank collates data using national poverty lines, its own poverty standard measures the numbers with incomes or expenditures below $1 per person per day and $2 per person per day.

Non-monetary concepts of human needs, functionings and other welfare outcomes are, as argued above, essential complements to these monetary measures, but face additional problems of their own. In particular their inherent multi-dimensionality makes comparisons between people, groups and time periods difficult. There are two broad solutions. The first is to adopt a deliberately disaggregated approach, as, for example, in *A Theory of Human Need* (Doyal and Gough 1991: part III). This proposes a variety of cross-cultural measures of the satisfaction of basic needs for health and autonomy, such as life expectancy, prevalence of disabilities and child developmental deficiencies, prevalence of severe mental illness, lack of culturally relevant knowledge, illiteracy, exclusion from significant social roles and severe lack of 'free time'. At the level of intermediate needs, the wide range of (negative) indicators proposed includes: nutrition and stunting, access to safe water, homelessness, exposure to hazardous workplaces and environments, absence of basic healthcare, abandoned and neglected children, absence of support groups, gross physical and economic insecurity, lack of access to safe contraception and safe births, and inadequate education. There is growing reliable international data on some of these dimensions of well-being.

The second solution is to construct a composite measure of two or more dimensions of welfare, of which the best-known example is the Human Development Index (HDI) developed by the UNDP. Indirectly based on Sen's concept of capabilities, this provides a composite index of average achieved capabilities in three dimensions: longevity, knowledge and standard of living. These are measured using life expectancy at birth, educational attainment (literacy and enrolment ratios) and a logarithmic function of GDP per capita.

In what follows I use three main indicators of welfare outcomes: first, the recent computations of disability-adjusted life expectancy (DALE) by the WHO, calculated using national and regional estimates of the burden of non-fatal diseases combined with life tables for each nation-state (WHO 2000: 146–7); second, the usual index of adult illiteracy, which provides a reasonable first approximation to the cognitive dimension of

---

[15] This relative poverty approach thus laid the ground for a subsequent shift to a more general concept of 'social exclusion' (Room 2000).

Final clusters and standardised cluster centres	(1) DALE* high (0.7), Literacy high (0.7), Poverty gap low (−0.5)	(2) DALE average (−0.2), Literacy low (−1.3), Poverty gap average (0.1)	(3) DALE low (−1.0), Literacy average (−0.1), Poverty gap high (1.0)	(4) DALE low (−1.7), Literacy low (−1.9), Poverty gap high (1.4)
East Asia	China, Indonesia, Korean R., Malaysia, Philippines, Thailand			
South Asia	Sri Lanka	Bangladesh, Nepal, Pakistan	India	
Eastern Europe and Central Asia	Belarus, Bulgaria, Czech R., Hungary, Kazakhstan, Kyrgyz R., Lithuania, Moldova, Poland, Romania, Russia, Slovak R., Turkmenistan, Ukraine, Uzbekistan			
Middle East and North Africa	Algeria, Jordan, Tunisia, Turkey	Egypt, Morocco, Yemen R.		
Sub-Saharan Africa		Ivory Coast, Senegal	Kenya, Madagascar, Nigeria, Rwanda, South Africa, Tanzania, Uganda, Zambia, Zimbabwe	Burkina Faso, Ethiopia, Guinea, Mali, Mozambique, Niger, Sierra Leone
South and Central America	Bolivia, Brazil, Chile, Colombia, Costa Rica, Dominican R., Ecuador, El Salvador, Honduras, Mexico, Paraguay, Peru, Uruguay, Venezuela		Guatemala, Nicaragua	

Notes: $n = 65$; all countries with population > 3m for which data available; k-means cluster analysis, $k = 4$; ANOVA F-scores: DALE 90.5, literacy 136.8, poverty gap 30.5 (see Gough 2001b for further details).

∗ disability-adjusted life expectancy

Figure 1.4. Cluster analysis of welfare outcomes by world region

autonomy; and, third, the World Bank measure of national poverty gaps at $2 a day, which takes into account the extent to which poor people fall below this level.

Using these three variables a cluster analysis shows developing and transitional countries clustering into four groups, presented in figure 1.4 according to world region. The first and largest group of countries exhibit above-average levels of healthy life expectancy, literacy and freedom from poverty (compared with the average of all low- and middle-income countries). These are spread across all regions except for sub-Saharan Africa and South Asia (apart from Sri Lanka). Every country for which we have data in East Asia, Eastern Europe/Central Asia and South (though not Central) America falls into this group. The fourth cluster lies at the opposite pole, with poor outcomes in all three dimensions, and comprises only countries in sub-Saharan Africa. The third cluster exhibits poor health, high poverty but average literacy. This is centred on South and East Africa

Table 1.1. *Welfare and insecurity measures for selected countries, 1997–99*

	Population (m)	HDI	HPI %	DALE (years)	Literacy %	Poverty gap ($2 pp per day)
China	1,275	0.72	19.0	62.3	83.5	21.0
Indonesia	212	0.68	27.7	59.7	86.3	22.6
Thailand	63	0.76	18.7	60.2	95.3	7.1
Bangladesh	137	0.47	44.4	49.9	40.8	31.8
India	1,009	0.57	35.9	53.2	56.5	42.9
Russian Federation	146	0.78		61.3	99.5	8.7
Ethiopia	63	0.32	55.8	33.5	37.4	32.9
Nigeria	114	0.46	38.2	38.3	62.6	59.0
South Africa	43	0.70	19.1	39.8	84.9	12.4
Argentina	37	0.84		66.7	96.7	
Brazil	170	0.75	15.8	59.0	84.9	6.3
Colombia	42	0.77	10.5	62.9	91.5	11.6
Unweighted average, 101 countries		0.62	30.8	53.1	74.5	20.3

Sources: see appendix.

(plus Nigeria), where the impact of the AIDS pandemic is undoubtedly reflected by the WHO's disability-adjusted life expectancy index. India is a member of this group, albeit as an outlier. The second cluster comprises the remaining countries of South Asia plus five others, and shows another mixed pattern of average health and poverty standards but low literacy.

It is not possible for reasons of space to present data on more than one hundred countries. But in order to illustrate these patterns, table 1.1 provides data for nine countries from the four regions featured in this book plus India, China and Russia. The countries have been selected from among the most populous in each world region.

The welfare mix

When we turn to the welfare mix or the map of institutional responsibilities in different countries, the problems in operationalising and measuring the concepts increase still further. Of the eight components of the welfare mix identified in figure 1.2, we can compile reasonably valid and reliable comparative statistics on two domestic components (public and private social expenditures) and two international components (overseas remittances and foreign aid). This means that the role of the third sector and

NGOs and of intra-household savings, transfers and care cannot be reckoned in what follows. Of the remainder, available data severely restricts any attempt to be inclusive.

To measure public social expenditure we have fairly comprehensive data on public health and education spending but less systematic data on expenditure on social security, let alone items like welfare and community services and housing. We must therefore use state expenditure on education and health as a proxy for public sector institutional responsibility in much of what follows. This is unfortunate since these services perform distinct social investment functions compared with the social protection functions of social security, Food-for-Work programmes and the like. Nor are the two functions closely correlated. For example, Uruguay exhibits relatively low education and health spending (4.8 per cent of GNP) alongside high social security spending (19.1 per cent of GNP), whereas in Morocco the pattern is reversed (6.9 per cent and 2.3 per cent respectively). In the case of private welfare spending we are restricted still further to data on private (out-of-pocket and insurance) *health* spending. For the international dimension of the welfare mix we use World Bank data on overseas development assistance and recent ILO data on worker remittances to their home countries.

Table 1.2 presents data on these components expressed as percentages of GDP for the selected countries. Across all countries in the South, including the transitional states, public spending on health and education combined averages 6.5 per cent of GDP. Private spending on health treatments and drugs accounts for another 2.5 per cent. Thus the average total domestic resource commitment to the welfare mix which we can measure is 9 per cent of GDP. However, this excludes social security, which accounts for 8.6 per cent in those fifty-two countries for which the ILO supplies data. This cannot simply be added to the preceding public spending figure because the ILO data includes expenditure on health insurance and thus double-counts some health spending. If this figure is added to education spending alone, we arrive at a figure of 12.6 per cent of GDP, almost doubling the relative scope of state responsibilities. This makes the absence of comprehensive information on social protection programmes doubly unfortunate; however, the data tends to follow the programmes: the remaining countries will have much lower commitments than this. For these fifty-two countries the total domestic commitment is thus nearer to 15 per cent of GDP.

The table shows that these domestic flows (excluding social security) are roughly matched in the South by international flows from governments via foreign aid and by household members via remittances. For all countries, unweighted by population, remittances contribute 4.5 per cent of GDP and overseas aid 6 per cent. Esping-Andersen's sole focus on

Table 1.2. *The welfare mix in selected countries, 1996–2000*

	Public expenditure health + education	Private expenditure health	Total domestic expenditure	Remittances	Aid	Total international expenditure	Total expenditure
China	4.3[a]	1.5[a]	5.7[a]	0.5	0.2	0.7	6.4
Indonesia	2.1	0.8	2.9	0.9	1.0	2.0	4.9
Thailand	6.6	4.1	10.7	0.3	0.6	0.9	11.8
Bangladesh	4.0	1.9	5.9	4.9	2.7	7.6	13.5
India	4.6[a]	4.2	8.8	2.8	0.4	3.2	12.0
Russian Federation	7.2[a]	1.2	8.4	0.1	0.5	0.6	9.0
Ethiopia	6.0	2.4	8.4	7.4	10.8	18.2	26.6
Nigeria	1.6[a]	2.0	3.6	4.5	0.6	5.1	8.7
South Africa	9.4	3.8	13.2		0.4	(0.4)	(13.6)
Argentina	8.6	5.4	14.0	0.1	0.0	0.1	14.5
Brazil	7.5	3.7	11.2	0.3	0.0	0.3	11.5
Colombia	8.7	4.2	12.9	0.7	0.2	0.9	13.8
Unweighted average, 101 countries	6.5	2.5	9.0	4.5	5.8	10.2	19.2

Sources: see appendix.
Notes: () some data missing; [a] 1992–7.

domestic welfare commitments cannot survive when analysing the developing world. Thus, on average, and accepting the numerous inadequacies in this data, domestic and international resources contribute roughly one-tenth each to the welfare mix, totalling about one-fifth in all.

Interestingly, nearly all the individual countries portrayed in table 1.2 reveal much lower aid receipts and even remittances than this Southern average. This reflects the pattern for larger countries' international receipts to represent a lower proportion of GDP than smaller countries' (since the average is not weighted by population size, the smaller countries dominate). Ethiopia, and to a lesser extent Bangladesh, rely significantly on both, while Nigeria has a significant remittances flow. South Africa, Russia and the three South American countries have significant public social sectors. The same countries, minus Russia, but plus Thailand and India, also exhibit substantial private spending, at least on health services and drugs, presumably reflecting relatively large and long-established middle classes.

To investigate cross-national patterns of welfare responsibility in any more detail we must again use cluster analysis. Figure 1.5 shows the clusters that emerge when we run three components: state education and

Final clusters and cluster centres (standardised)	East Asia	South Asia	Eastern Europe and Central Asia	Middle East and North Africa	Sub-Saharan Africa	South and Central America
(1) Public spending low (−0.6), Private spending low (−0.5), International flows high (0.9)	Laos		Kyrgyz R.		Benin, Burkina Faso, Burundi, Central African R., Chad, Ethiopia, Ghana, Madagascar, Mali, Mozambique, Senegal, Tanzania, Togo	
(2) Public spending high (1.2), Private spending low (−0.6), International flows low (−0.6)			Belarus, Bulgaria, Czech R., Kazakhstan, Lithuania, Moldova, Poland, Slovak R., Ukraine, Uzbekistan	Algeria, Tunisia		Bolivia
(3) Public spending medium-low (−0.3), Private spending high (1.7), International flows average (0.0)	Cambodia, Thailand, Vietnam	Nepal	Armenia	Lebanon	Kenya, Sierra Leone, Uganda	Argentina, Colombia, El Salvador, Honduras, Uruguay
(4) Public spending low (−0.5), Private spending medium (0.0), International flows low (−0.6)	Indonesia, Philippines	Bangladesh, Pakistan, Sri Lanka		Iran, Morocco, Syria		Brazil, Chile, Dominican R., Ecuador, Guatemala, Paraguay, Peru
(5) Public spending high (1.0), Private spending high (0.8), International flows high (1.7)				Jordan	Malawi	

Notes: $n = 59$; k-means cluster analysis, $k = 5$. ANOVA F-scores: public spending 18.3, private spending 33.4, international flows 24.9.

Figure 1.5.   Cluster analysis of the welfare mix: institutional responsibility across the South

health expenditures, private health spending and the combined international inflows of aid and remittances. Initial testing for four clusters revealed extensive intra-cluster variation; this attenuated when we moved to five clusters and the two outliers of Jordan and Malawi (in which the values of all three variables were high) were separated out. Absent data hinders an overall generalisation, but the following patterns are clear.

Cluster 1 represents countries dependent on international resources, whether aid or remittances or both, and predominantly embraces sub-Saharan Africa. Cluster 2 represents countries with extensive public commitments to welfare, and primarily covers the ex-communist world of Eastern Europe and Central Asia. The third cluster identifies countries with high levels of private spending (on health): these are found patchily across all regions of the world (and probably include India). Last, the fourth cluster represents countries with low values for all resources – foreign, public and private: these are predominantly located in Latin America and parts of South and East Asia (it is probable that China would fall into this category). In terms of regions, we find that Eastern Europe and Central Asia rely predominantly on states, and African countries on overseas flows. Countries in East Asia, South Asia and Latin America tend to exhibit low levels of resourcing from all the sources shown – which suggests greater reliance on households or community institutions. The Middle East and North Africa is the most varied region with a wide range of welfare mixes.

Mapping welfare regimes

As a first step towards empirically identifying welfare regimes we can cluster measures of both welfare mix and welfare outcomes. This is not easy, due to the number of variables plus the consequent loss of cases. To keep the analysis simple, the exercise in figure 1.6 uses just two indicators of welfare mix – public spending and international flows of aid and remittances combined – and one indicator of welfare outcomes – the HDI. Around 1997 this yields four main clusters with three country outliers, shown in figure 1.6.

At a very crude level of interpretation we may label these clusters as follows:

1. *Actual or potential welfare state regimes*: with high state commitments and relatively high welfare outcomes. They include much of Central Europe (with some representatives in Eastern Europe); the Southern Cone of Latin America; Kenya, Algeria and Tunisia in Africa; and Thailand.
2. *More effective informal security regimes*: with relatively good outcomes achieved with below-average state spending and low international flows. They include parts of Southeast Asia (probably including China); Sri Lanka; the remaining countries of Latin America for which we have data; together with parts of the Middle East.
3. *Less effective informal security regimes*: with poor levels of welfare coupled with low public commitments and moderate international

Final clusters and standardised centres	Countries (grouped by region)
(1) HDI high (0.8), public spending high (0.9), international flows low (−0.7)	Thailand Belarus, Bulgaria, Czech R., Hungary, Lithuania, Poland, Slovak R., Ukraine, Uzbekistan Algeria, Tunisia Kenya Argentina, Bolivia, Brazil, Chile, Colombia
(2) HDI medium-high (0.5), public spending low (−0.6), international flows low (−0.3)	Indonesia, Philippines, Vietnam Sri Lanka Armenia Iran, Lebanon, Morocco, Syria Dominican R., Ecuador, El Salvador, Guatemala, Honduras, Paraguay, Peru, Uruguay
(3) HDI low (−0.9), public spending low (−0.8), international flows medium (0.0)	Cambodia Bangladesh, Nepal, Pakistan Cameroon, Central African R., Madagascar, Tanzania, Togo
(4) HDI very low (−1.4), public spending low (−0.5), international flows high (1.1)	Laos Benin, Burkina Faso, Burundi, Chad, Ethiopia, Ghana Malawi, Mali, Mozambique, Senegal, Uganda
HDI medium-high (0.5), public spending very high (1.8), international flows very high (2.1)	Jordan
HDI medium-high (0.5), public spending very high (3.5), international flows medium (0.1)	Moldova

Notes: n = 61; *k*-means clustering, *k* = 6. ANOVA *F*-score: HDI 60.5, public spending 42.1, international flows 28.6.

Figure 1.6. Cluster analysis of welfare mix and welfare outcomes, *c.* 1997: towards welfare regimes

inflows. This cluster comprises South Asia (excluding Sri Lanka but probably including India) and certain countries in sub-Saharan Africa.

4. *Externally dependent insecurity regimes*: heavily dependent on aid and/or remittances with very poor welfare outcomes. This cluster comprises the bulk of sub-Saharan Africa for which we have data.

The variables used in this analysis can of course be criticised as inadequate and additions and alternatives suggested. The inclusion of *private* welfare spending would differentiate Latin America, where its role is considerably greater (see figure 1.5) from Central and Eastern Europe. These caveats illustrate the gulf that exists between our conceptualisation of the welfare mix and our ability to operationalise it at present. This gap becomes a chasm when we turn to the richer, more complex concept of the welfare regime. The only option is to undertake detailed regional analysis, qualitative as well as quantitative, guided by these crude initial clusters. That is the purpose of part II of this book.

I do not proceed further here to analyse the economic, social, political and cultural structures correlated with and causally implicated in these varying regime patterns across the world. On the one hand this entails a large programme of research. On the other hand, there is already a range of good research which indirectly addresses these issues. In an earlier paper, I have undertaken a statistical path analysis of 128 countries to discern what factors account for the great disparities of human welfare across the contemporary world, using indicators of both basic and intermediate needs (Gough and Thomas 1994; Gough 2000a: ch. 5). The study concludes that level of development is only one of several factors explaining cross-national variations in need satisfaction: the degree of economic and political independence of nations, the extent of democracy and human rights, the capacity and dispositions of the state, and relative gender equality all impact positively and independently on a nation's level of welfare.

There is growing empirical support for this perspective. For example, Mehrotra (2002), in adumbrating an alternative framework for development to that of the dominant 'growth is good for poverty reduction' one, postulates 'two synergies'. One is between interventions in health, nutrition, family planning, water and sanitation, and basic education. The other is between interventions which are the basis of income growth, the reduction of poverty and improved health and educational status. The first synergy is actually a subset of the second, argues Mehrotra. This establishes a link, with growing empirical support, between capabilities/need satisfactions and equitable growth. The resulting virtuous (and vicious) circles point to a more socially embedded notion of the economy. Unfortunately, the present stage of globalised capitalism is generating rising inequality between nations and within most nations and may be reducing the power of public authorities and networks in civil society in developing countries to counteract these pressures. It is a 'sad irony', says Stewart (2000), that our understanding of the synergies within embedded economies has emerged at a time when global capitalism is heading in the opposite direction. This dilemma constitutes a major structural constraint for the developing countries and poor communities in our study.

Conclusions

This chapter has presented a conceptual model of welfare regimes applicable, we contend, to all areas of the developing and transitional world, and a preliminary empirical classification. Following an account of social policy in the West it adumbrates a wider definition to suit the South. In subsequent sections it modifies the 'welfare state regime' paradigm, constructing alongside it families of 'informal security regimes' and 'insecurity regimes'. All three comprise different forms of welfare regimes. The chapter then operationalises two basic concepts of the regime framework: welfare mix and welfare outcomes. Using available international data for 101 countries, it maps country variations in both using cluster analysis. The chapter concludes with an initial empirical categorisation of welfare regimes across the South. This prepares the ground for the more detailed, qualitative and contextualised studies in part II.

We contend that the welfare regime framework moves forward the analysis of social policy and human welfare in development contexts. In particular, it enables us to begin synthesising the insights of social policy in the North with development studies in the South. The welfare regime paradigm situates social policy and public action within the broader institutional context of the welfare mix. It relates policies to contexts and outcomes. It exemplifies a materialist approach which explains welfare outcomes in terms of the deep structures of the domestic and international political economy, yet recognises the role of actors' goals and mobilisations. Last, by charting a middle-range theory, it permits the identification of clusters of countries sharing regime characteristics. In part II we put some of these claims to the test.

Appendix

The predominant statistical technique used is cluster analysis. This measures the distance between cases (countries) on a combination of dimensions and uses this to identify groups of cases within which there is considerable homogeneity and between which there are clear boundaries. The idea of welfare regime entails disjuncture and difference, and hence requires a classificatory approach such as cluster or factor analysis, rather than statistical techniques such as regression. There are two main clustering techniques: hierarchical cluster analysis (HCA) and k-means cluster analysis (KCA), and both are employed here (see Gough 2001b).

HCA is the simpler technique: it begins by finding the closest pair of cases (normally using squared Euclidean distance) and combines them to form a cluster. The algorithm proceeds one step at a time, joining pairs of cases, pairs of clusters or a case with a cluster, until all the cases are in one cluster. The steps are displayed in a tree or dendrogram. The method is hierarchical because once two cases are joined in a cluster they remain joined. KCA, on the other hand, permits the recombination of cases and clusters over repeated iterations. It requires the researcher to specify a priori the number of clusters (k) and thus provides a preliminary testing of alternative typologies. The clustering begins by using the values of the first n cases as temporary estimates of the k cluster means. Initial cluster centres form by assigning each case in turn to the cluster with the closest centre and then updating the centre, until final cluster centres are identified. At each step, cases are grouped into the cluster with the closest centre, the centres are recomputed, and so on until no further change occurs in the centres. It offers a good range of information to help interpret the results, and for these and other reasons it is the technique favoured here. Since cluster analysis is a tool of descriptive statistics, sources of error and variation are not formally considered.

The database excludes the rich industrialised countries of the West, but includes transitional countries and newly industrialised countries alongside developing countries. Initial cluster analysis consistently reveals that OECD member states in 1995 (i.e. before the recent enlargement) formed a distinct and relatively homogeneous group. Given the focus of our research project, and the extensive research already available from the OECD, little is gained from including them. Another data problem arises from the large number of states with very small populations in the present world system. The UNDP *Human Development Report* reports data for 175 countries including those such as the Bahamas and Malta with populations of less than half a million. The World Bank *World Development Report* excludes sixty countries with populations of less than one million from its basic series and ends up with 133 countries. In order to simplify the analysis I have decided on a higher cut-off population of 3 million, leaving us with 101 countries.

As explained in the text, we use disability-adjusted life years, literacy and the $2 a day poverty gap as prime measures of welfare outcomes. When requiring a single index, we use the HDI. One particular drawback of the HDI is that it is an average index and says nothing about the *distribution* of health, education and income within any country. To improve on this the UNDP has subsequently developed two further indices – the Gender-Related Development Index (GDI) in 1995 and the Human Poverty Index (HPI) in 1997 (UNDP 2002). The latest HPI for 2002 combines the percentage of people not expected to survive to age forty, the percentage of adults who are illiterate, the proportions without access to safe water, and the percentage of underweight children under five. The weighting formula places greater weight on those dimensions in which deprivation is larger, thus approaching a more 'Rawlsian' measure of welfare. Unfortunately, HPI is not calculated for all developing countries. However, it is very closely correlated with HDI and GDI (Pearson coefficient 0.96), so little is lost by using HDI which is calculated for all countries.[16]

---

[16] In contrast, insecurity remains under-theorised and its relation to poverty and other dimensions of welfare obscure. We return to this issue in the conclusion to this book.

Indicators and sources

Welfare outcomes
HDI, 1997: UNDP (1999)
HPI most recent years: UNDP (2002)
Literacy, 1999: UNDP (2001)
DALE 1999: WHO (2000)
Poverty gap, $2 a head, recent years: World Bank (2002a)
Human rights: Freedom House scores for political and civil liberties, mean of 1988–9 and 1998–9: Freedom House (NB: 1 = highest, 7 = lowest): http://freedomhouse.org/ratings/

Welfare mix
Public expenditure on education/GDP, 1996–8: World Bank (2002a)
Public expenditure on health/GDP, 1998: World Bank (2002a)
Public expenditure on social security/GDP, 1996: ILO (2000a)
Private expenditure on health/GDP, 1998: World Bank (2001a)
Overseas remittances/GDP, 1996–2000 average: World Bank (2002a) ('net current transfers from abroad')
ODA receipts /GDP, 1996–2000 average: World Bank (2002a)

2   Informal security regimes: the strength of relationships

Geof Wood

Introduction

This chapter argues that the poorer regions of the world do not comfortably conform to the two key assumptions upon which the OECD model of welfare state regime relies: a legitimate state; and a pervasive, formal sector labour market. This immediately sets up the two key interactive issues of governance and the socio-economic circumstances of the common man (and woman). These circumstances are understood in this chapter through the metaphor of the *peasant* (to capture the significance of reproduction, family and household-level inter-generational transfers) and the analysis of *clientelism* as pervasive adverse incorporation (comprising hierarchical rights; meso-level intermediation with the national-level polity and economy; and quasi-public goods social capital, organised through unequal relationships). These political, economic, social and family dimensions are brought together in this book, for policy analysis purposes, as the institutional responsibility matrix with global as well as domestic dimensions. These four institutional domains are presented as permeable, which can have positive or negative outcomes for different societies. The world's poor regions are characterised by negative permeability in which the level of personal objectives penetrates the level of public aims to produce poor governance and insecurity for the majority of their populations, thus removing any prospect of the corrective principle, in which the state regulates the market for social objectives. Only partial compensation for this absence of the corrective principle is offered by global discourses, conditionality and debt remission leverage. The problem of insecurity thus looms large in the analysis, with a focus on its implications for time preference behaviour[1] at the level of personal as well as social investment. Indeed the short span time preference behaviour of the poor, which reinforces their dependency and reduces long-range choice, thus clashes with the creation and maintenance of long-term social capital and

---

[1] This means the periods of time (present and future) to which people wish to give priority and thus allocate resources: for example, present spending versus future spending.

improvement of governance: a Faustian bargain under conditions of no exit, little voice and tainted loyalty (Wood 2003b).

Faced with this scenario, the chapter argues within the framework of a 'poor' actor-oriented epistemology, which emphasises how the poor negotiate a complex, and hostile, institutional landscape dominated by severe inequalities of power which reproduce their poverty. This position entails a view of the state as not impartial, but working for dominant classes and segments, including a bureaucratic and political class, which sees state control as a crucial means of their own accumulation and reproduction. Since this is a familiar view of the state, it is obvious that social policy as a discipline derived from critical sociology cannot rely upon a benign, liberal, pluralist view of the state, especially under poor-country conditions. This is why any social policy of poor countries very quickly moves onto the agenda of 'civil society compensating for the inequities of the state' instead of the OECD welfare state regime principle of 'the state compensating for inequities of the market'. But given the inherent problem of the state, and the issue of permeability, there cannot be a naïve optimism about the role of a 'progressive' civil society as compensating for the state.

This chapter argues for a more universal conception of social policy that does not exclusively focus upon the role of the state, but rather surveys the efficacy of relationships between different elements of an institutional landscape (characterised by the institutional responsibility matrix) through which all people have to pursue livelihoods and survival. In this way, we offer a more generalised approach to social policy in which significant institutional actors other than the domestic state feature. Within this framework of a more generalised institutional landscape, comprising state, market, large-scale community and family/household, this chapter offers the concept of an informal security regime, to be contrasted with other welfare regimes, which might be mapped onto the generalised landscape.

Specifying the informal security regime

An informal security regime reflects a set of conditions where people cannot reasonably expect to meet their security needs via accessing services from the state or via participation in open labour markets. Thus they have to rely more heavily upon community and family relationships of various kinds. In many poor societies, characterised by significant inequality, these relationships are hierarchical and asymmetrical, leaving only some space for reciprocal support for welfare within and between family groupings. And while, in these discussions, there is a legitimate concern about social exclusion, the more pervasive relationship which dominates poor people's lives is problematic inclusion in these hierarchical relationships. In other words, the provision of security informally comes at the price of adverse incorporation, or clientelism.

In a stylised manner, the basic steps for conceptualising an informal security regime are as follows. A crucial aspect of poverty is uncertainty, and therefore more risk to manage. Risk for poor people is typically co-variant and experienced, as well as managed, in small pools. Thus risk is concentrated upon the poor rather than being spread more evenly across the society. While everybody, rich and poor, is vulnerable to shocks, people are differentially vulnerable to hazards (i.e. more predictable life-cycle or environmental events), since the poor have less room for manoeuvre to prepare for them. The actors in this version of the welfare regime comprise formal agencies (governments, donors, formal employers, financial institutions and so on) and the agency of poor people living real community-based lives: but both operate within inequality and a hostile political economy and thus reproduce it. The poor (in the sense of voice as well as income) have less control over the formal and informal institutions through which they must seek their livelihoods. Thus, in contrast to richer people who act out relatively autonomous security-maintaining behaviour, the poor experience dependent security. While relatively autonomous security 'enables', dependent security 'disables' and forecloses future options for autonomous security by reproducing limited room for manoeuvre and limited voice. This process of reproducing dependent security is stimulated by greater uncertainty and therefore higher discount rates for the poor. For survival, risk has to be managed in the present. Thus poor people have a time preference option for the present which induces foreclosure of choices and investment for the future. Poor people in poor countries, in overall insecurity conditions, are less able to manipulate problematic arenas in their institutional landscape (i.e. state, market, community and household) to their advantage, compared to richer people. Such conditions represent weak social capital for the poor, inducing greater reliance upon personal social resources at community and household level, even though the latter also remain problematical.[2] Poor people with some capacity for social action to improve their personal circumstances,[3] as a counterpart to agency intervention, nevertheless require forms of social protection to alter their time preference behaviour

---

[2] A distinction is made here between the concept of social capital and that of personal social networks on the basis of subtractability. Social capital is not sensitive to the 'subtraction' of individuals (i.e. withdrawal, death, deviance, etc.), whereas personal social networks are.

[3] As distinct from the chronically poor who may not have this capacity.

in order to encourage their investment in the future, and thereby increase their own capability and that of subsequent generations. However, present realities dictate that poor people have to find that social protection informally through relationships and institutions which work more predictably for them. These relationships comprise a series of informal rights, even if they are subject to adverse incorporation or low-value reciprocity. These informal rights, the reliance upon them and the need to reproduce them through dependency behaviour, thus become an 'informal security' version of the generic welfare regime. We might then argue, within the framework of a modernist welfare regime, that the policy agenda in response to such an informal security regime is: altering time preference behaviour; enabling preparation for hazards; formalising rights; de-clientelisation; enlarging choice and the risk pool; improving the quality and predictability of institutional performance, partially via poor people's agency (empowerment and voice); and strengthening membership of well-functioning collective institutions, which reduce adverse incorporation.

Understanding regimes: limits of the welfare state regime approach to poor countries

What institutional categories are generated by Esping-Andersen's conceptual apparatus when considering public/private combinations of support for poor people's livelihoods in non-rich countries? First, we can identify a strong version of 'welfare regime' as comprising the state's role in de-commodifying the labour market. We have referred to this as a 'welfare state regime'. A weaker version sees 'welfare regime' as a political settlement between the major competing interests in society.[4] However, second, even the weaker version does not adequately deconstruct the institutions through which those interests compete, nor does it easily contend with societies where the poor are effectively disorganised by those institutions. We have argued in chapter 1 that the 'welfare regime' paradigm in both its strong and weak versions retains considerable validity in the richer, middle-income countries of Southeast Asia and Latin America, and is clinging to relevance in CIS and transitional countries of Eastern Europe. However, even its basic categories of analysis such as state and market are deeply problematic as descriptions of conditions elsewhere, where the great transformation in the Polanyian

---

[4] This distinction thus corresponds to the one made in the previous chapter between welfare state regime and welfare regime.

sense of disembeddedness might be considered not to have occurred. At the same time, wherever peasant systems are being transformed by the global restructuring of capital, with its flexible labour markets, then, even as peasants enter labour markets through migration and urbanisation, so they continue to be disempowered and insecure in those markets. Thus they have little prospect of recourse to state protection even where legal rights formally exist.

This obliges us to argue for an approach to social policy that does not conceptually privilege either the state or the market; and which treats them both as problematic alongside civil society or community and the household. These institutions also have to be understood as operating at different levels from the local to the global. Thus insecure, vulnerable people have to negotiate secure livelihoods through these imperfections and consequent uncertainties.[5] These imperfections and uncertainties reflect both the general principle of embeddedness within social relations and culture as well as the specific issues of power, inequality, class relations and other 'identity' aspects of fission and fusion which constantly disturb the landscape (Castells 1997). Thus the critical social policy, as expressed through a generic notion of 'welfare regime', has to be the understanding of rights and responsibilities as actually articulated in the institutional universe faced by the poor in developing contexts.

This standpoint enables us to conceive of the practice of social policy as a combination of the social, cultural and political arrangements through which poor people supplement their weaknesses in economic arrangements, partially but not exhaustively framed as markets (whether labour, product or service). This formulation puts some distance between the assumptions underpinning the welfare state regime paradigm and the institutional conditions prevailing in many parts of the poorer world. The key difference is represented by the welfare state regime principle of 'de-commodification': i.e. the state acting as a regulator and redistributor of otherwise unconstrained outcomes of market economic behaviour – organising equity, in other words (Schaffer and Lamb 1981). The principle of de-commodification simply does not make sense in societies where economic behaviour is not commodified; where general commodity

---

[5] It seems reasonable to distinguish the business of social policy, as a critical but applied multi-discipline, from its less applied, more detached social science equivalent: namely, the analysis of political economy. In the latter, we may shrink even from terms like 'state' and 'market' and substitute 'polity', 'economy', 'society' and 'family' as more neutral terms (Bevan, chapter 3). However the study of policy, and especially social policy in the service of poverty eradication, entails a normative disposition towards the principles of rights and responsibilities. This would seem to necessitate the more normative terminology of state, market, civil society/community and household within an institutional responsibility framework.

relations do not prevail as even imperfect markets; and/or where the social embeddedness of markets limits any prospect of their purity.

Given poverty eradication as the point of departure, our central task then becomes how to characterise these non-OECD conditions and thereby to assess their implications for rethinking the basic principles of social policy. In particular, these conditions bring centre stage the significance of social and cultural resources at 'community' and family levels for pursuing secure livelihoods, displacing states and markets. However, it may be that the answer to the question 'how do people presently survive?' does not lead to an adequate social policy answer, since a policy of strengthening present informal arrangements may amount to strengthening adverse incorporation and clientelism. If so, then prescriptions almost inevitably take the form of improving both governance and the operation of markets (i.e. the realm of rights and responsibilities). While these prescriptions appear to conform to the agendas of the World Bank and other international organisations and donors, our analytic conclusions are likely to differ in three ways: first, with respect to the value of present social resources; second, with respect to the territorial space within which governance and markets might flourish; and, third, with respect to the socio-political methods by which institutional conditions for a favourable social policy can be created. That is to say: the means of social policy have to be specified differently.

The way into this understanding can be described as the phenomenology of insecurity, supported by a 'poor-actor-oriented' epistemology.[6] In another language, we have to be more 'emic' in our methodological approach[7] with a stronger questioning of the present language and discourse of normative social policy which is captured by an economics discourse of levers, incentives and responses and a political discourse of citizenship, unmediated by actually existing institutions.[8] In a counternarrative, poor people in the poorer parts of the world can be characterised by other discourses such as 'peasant' and/or 'client', reflecting the particular embedded nature of livelihood options in a non-commodified socio-political economy. Countries in South Asia and sub-Saharan Africa remain predominantly agrarian and pastoral, and even though this will demographically change over the next quarter-century, the associated principles of social organisation will persist perhaps indefinitely, since we

---

[6] That is: the presumption that actors' perceptions explain their behaviour, which gives us knowledge about outcomes.

[7] That is: gaining insight through empathising with the way choices and options appear to the objects of our analysis.

[8] See the papers in Conway *et al.* (2000) for an example of a non-emic narrative, especially the one by Jorgensen and Holzmann from the World Bank.

cannot equate urbanisation with a linear route to commodified modernisation (see, e.g., Roberts 1978). At the same time, while these countries have operating nation-states (just), their problems of governance and effectiveness remain (World Bank 2002b; Wood 2000; UNDP 2000). In sub-Saharan Africa, continuing to be agrarian is only part of the understanding since the general conditions of insecurity through wars, famines and AIDS challenge the very conception of nation-state as a valid territorial entity. Bevan characterises these situations as 'insecurity regimes', with large-scale political clientelism (i.e. not just localised socio-economic clientelism) as the main framework of social inclusion (Bevan, chapter 3).

This analysis can be expressed through the analogue (or model) of the peasant. The principles of being a peasant extend for poor people and their patrons into urban, industrial and informal sector life – i.e. into urban as well as rural labour markets, and into urban as well as rural lifestyles (Roberts 1978; Wood and Salway 2000; Loughhead, Mittal and Wood 2000). This 'peasant' analogue could be described as the phenomenology of insecurity: risk aversion, discounting, co-variance of risk, emphasis upon reproduction (physical and social), significance of the domestic/life cycle, inter-generational forms of transfers and provision, intra-family dependency ratios, significance of social resources in the context of weak social capital. Pervasive clientelism takes this phenomenology a step further by emphasising loyalty over voice in the absence of exit options (Hirschman 1970), but therefore the kind of loyalty which extends and compounds the problem of governance.

What is distinctive about developing countries?

As a precondition for developing a more contextualised policy model, we have to engage with the distinctiveness of developing countries. The intellectual project of transferring 'social policy' into a developing-country context has to be done explicitly, acknowledging some basic problems in the transfer attempt.

Returning to the central problematic of 'de-commodification', this principle drove Esping-Andersen's North Atlantic work on post-industrial societies. It reflects long-established assumptions in social policy as well as moving it forward in terms of a large-scale, comparative model. However, the welfare state regime idea,[9] derived from it, relies upon the state regulation of markets to achieve more equitable social

---

[9] It is recognised that Esping-Andersen uses the term 'welfare regime', but the more global comparative analysis of this book requires us to distinguish between Esping-Andersen's variants of welfare state regimes, on the one hand, and a plurality of welfare regimes on the other, in which the positive role of the state is not over-privileged.

outcomes. But in any attempt to generalise this principle to poor countries in South Asia and sub-Saharan Africa, several objections instantly loom large:

- The economy is not commodified and free of other major social and cultural objectives which determine both its functioning and outcomes.
- The state has so widely 'failed' both in competence and legitimacy that it cannot feature as a corrective to class-creating markets.
- And, more linguistically, 'welfare' in poorer countries is perceived in contrast to 'development' as a combination of relief and charitable transfers, occurring within kin and other social relationships where the culture sustains such morality.

These objections to the welfare state regime as a universal policy model have led us to introduce the institutional responsibility matrix (IRM),[10] in which the institutional domains at national and global levels, comprising the social policy landscape, are deliberately problematised from the outset. The IRM thus represents a more universalistic, abstract conception to embrace the notion of welfare and development mixes, enabling us to distinguish between the welfare state regime and other forms of welfare regime. Its composition, *around the normative principle of 'responsibility'*, reflects that we are analysing policy frameworks rather than insecurity and political economy per se. In chapter 1, we have presented the IRM through linking domestic to global domains. The first step was to extend the Esping-Andersen triangle of state–market–family to include 'community'. This refers to the multitude of sub-societal organisational forms, including NGOs, and the related notion of civil society. The result is the domestic 'institutional responsibility square' (IRS). Second, a variety of international components feature strongly in the institutional landscape of poor countries. These include supra-national equivalents of the four domestic components: official donors and other international governmental organisations; global markets; international NGOs and other 'voice' organisations; and the 'internationalised household'. The latter operates through a combination of migration, remittances and global risk aversion through access to international welfare (Deacon 1999; Room 2001) and finance institutions (Sharif and Wood 2001). We have set out the eight-component institutional responsibility matrix (IRM) in chapter 1.

A crucial feature that the IRM shares in common with Esping-Andersen's analysis is that *these institutions do not operate independently from the others in terms of rules and pervading moralities*. In other words, there is permeability. However, in a more problematised world, we have

---

[10] As outlined in chapter 1.

to distinguish between the quality and therefore outcomes of this permeability – positive and negative. This in turn sets limits in different contexts to *the possibility of one set of institutions counteracting or compensating for the dysfunctional effects of another*. It is through this distinction that contrasts can be made between different types of society and their respective welfare regimes. Let us explore the significance of these permeable relations between institutions as the basis for classifying different welfare regimes.

The assumption that underpins the de-commodification basis of Esping-Andersen's welfare state regime approach is that the state can compensate, in distributional terms, for the market. In order for this to happen, North Atlantic societies and corresponding social theory seem to be premised upon Isaiah Berlin's incommensurate principle,[11] in which behaviour (and presumably morality) in one sphere can be successfully deployed against countervailing behavioural principles in another. Thus humans in such situations habitually live and function in opposite, incompatible and contrasting categories of thought, commitment and behaviour, and accept that imperfections in one arena can always be corrected by another. It represents a kind of moral free ride, rather like Catholic confession, in which sin is always possible because absolution and external restraint are likewise on perpetual offer. This is a fundamental tenet of Western liberal philosophy, in which there is an expectation that freedoms and excess will be constrained by the activation of other freedoms. The conceptual device which brings this about is permeability rather than complete fusion or compatibility.

Deploying Berlin's principles further, we need to understand permeability in such confessional societies at a higher meta-level (i.e. at the level of public aims rather than personal objectives). Thus, in developed societies, we might acknowledge a formal consistency between the *publicly* espoused principles and aims of fairness, equity, transparency and trust as they operate in all domestic institutions of the IRM. However, at the level of *personal* objectives, people are selfish and engage in tax evasion, avoidance and cheating, but not to the point of allowing anarchy and chaos to prevail over order. Furthermore, it is as if people know their own predilections for selfishness in their private 'market' and 'community' corners and deliberately accept the obligations of citizenship enacted through the state corner. So can we really say with this analysis that the state is 'compensating' for the market, when those operating in the market are simultaneously committing a degree of their personal autonomy to the state because they do not trust their own autonomy to deliver the public

---

[11] Enunciated, *inter alia*, by Isaiah Berlin in his famous essay 'The Hedgehog and the Fox' (see Michael Ignatieff's biography of Berlin, 1998).

goods of social order based on equity and sharing? Furthermore, they accept the state because they acknowledge their own propensity along with those of others to otherwise free-ride.[12]

The problem arises when the permeability functions with the opposite effect – i.e. when *public* principles and aims are indistinguishable from *private, personal* ones: of privilege; of natural superiority of rights and entitlements; of selfishness; of private short-term gain; of fission; of social closure; and other risk-averse behaviour under conditions of high uncertainty associated with the peasant analogue. Here all components of the IRM exhibit dysfunctional degrees of failure. Markets are imperfect, communities clientelist, households patriarchal and states marketised, patrimonial, partial and based on political clientelism. In most developing countries, with non- or partially commodified markets and a more ascriptive basis to the acceptance and exercise of authority, such core values prevail across the different spheres of relationships with greater certainty. One's behaviour is simply not different whether inhabiting the state, market, community or household. Under such conditions, how does it make sense to expect the state to disentangle itself from deep structures in order to compensate for them? To bend a famous phrase of Poulantzas: the state is a condensate of *social* relations. In this situation all are prisoners (Wood 2000). In other words, we have the negative principle of *permeability* between the arenas of social and economic behaviour, and public and private action, guided by dominant and cohering sets of values and accompanying norms, thus removing any prospect of the corrective principle being applied.

Methodological limits of Western social policy

In chapter 1, the OECD-centric 'welfare state regime' has been replaced with a more generalised, comparative institutional framework.[13] This replacement comparative framework has important methodological implications, especially in framing the relationship between people's behaviour and institutional performance. In particular, below, we argue for a 'meso'-focus, which links poor people as social actors to the problems of governance and markets, as a necessary element of extending the analysis of social policy to poor countries.

---

[12] This argument sets severe limits to the Doyal and Gough assertion of autonomy as a universal human need (Doyal and Gough 1991).

[13] Within that framework, two substantive issues were considered: the basic critique of the institutional components of the domestic square; and the significance of the global dimension of the IRM as representing the corrective principle through aid and conditionality (such as structural adjustment in the past, and PRSPs today).

In this comparative framework, there remains a methodological tension between those seeking generalising statements (laws, patterns and grand theory) and those more micro-empiricists who are concerned to emphasise the specificity of particular countries, regions and cultures. Writers like Esping-Andersen and Fukuyama (cf. Fukuyama 1995) teeter on the edge of banality in the attempt to erect comparative theory involving empirical generalisation about institutions such as the family, the composition of business, and attitudes towards the state. So does our quest for a typology of 'regimes'[14] commit the same offence to the micro-empiricists?

As noted above, in confronting the discourses and language of OECD-centric social policy with the reality check of poorer countries with large-scale poverty, the same basic assumptions cannot be made about legitimated states and pervasive labour markets. As revealed in the permeability discussion above, the negative permeability critique entails a basic challenge to the unproblematised, large-scale categories through which social policy as a social science assembles data and makes argument, such as:

- the state acts . . .;
- the market behaves . . .;
- the poor need . . .;
- the family functions . . .;
- the voluntary sector can . . .;
- the globalised economy offers . . .;

and so on.

Does our replacement comparative framework offer a convincing challenge to the utility of such epistemology implied in the expressions above? The real test of our consistency is whether we can combine an analysis of the classic categories of social policy (e.g. pensions, social insurance, social protection, safety nets and social sector spending on health and education) with an *embedded* analysis of the state (i.e. governance) and the labour market. An embedded analysis of the state requires attention to basic issues of governance. An embedded analysis of the labour market requires attention to the circumstances of peasants (as metaphor) and clients, with high proportions excluded altogether from the labour market, and with others experiencing various forms of adverse incorporation and exploitation within them. However, in this quest for *embeddedness*, micro, highly context-specific, perspectives also have limited utility, as the trees take over from the wood in the quest for nuanced subtlety and

---

[14] Embracing, for example, welfare, development, growth, growth through equity, informal security and insecurity.

holistic analysis. Such contextualised detail would be useful only so long as the corresponding resources were also at hand at that micro-level in terms of analytic expertise as well as capacity to follow up with finely honed policy, requisite resource transfers and commensurate institutional strategies.[15]

This is how we reach the meso-domain in our epistemology as well as the scale of generalisation and level of engagement with policy. The macro is out simply because we cannot presume the state or the generalised morality in the society as a whole that enables strangers to exchange in the de-personalised market over time and space. But, empirically, the meso does enable us to say why Ethiopia and Zimbabwe share similarities and are different from Uganda or Zambia on, for example, dimensions of security or governance (Bevan and Sseweya 1995). Epistemologically, the meso enables us to connect an actor-oriented perspective to institutions through the exploration of negotiation, choice, room for manoeuvre, opportunity and iterative redefinition of the landscape itself. In other words it connects people's actual livelihood strategies to the institutional, policy and ideological landscape which shapes their options, prompting acceptance, compliance or struggle.

In establishing this methodological focus upon the meso, we also have to be more alert to the mediating contexts through which livelihood strategies are pursued. Western-derived social policy relies very heavily upon mature labour and financial markets when considering the boundary between people's own behaviour (and options) and compensatory intervention by the state. Labour markets, with corresponding thinking (Room 2000b) about personal investment in human capital development (i.e. de-commodification for personal development), are presumed to be the major ingredient of private livelihood strategy, supported by financial markets that enable: saving and borrowing; liquidity management over family domestic cycles through loans and savings access; longer-term security via pensions and personal equity plans. The business and entrepreneurial sector is located as a feature of the labour market. The dominant assumption is formal sector employment, whether self-employed or salaried. Thus the labour and financial markets are conceived as the major mediating context for pursuing livelihoods in urbanised, industrial and post-industrial societies.

---

[15] In the context of micro-diversity, exacerbated by dynamic social and economic opportunities, that is precisely the approach developed by micro-empiricists such as Wood and Bevan in northern Pakistan (Wood 1996). But the situation is unique, with a generously funded technical agency (the AKRSP) still able to commit human resources at such intensity to the grassroots. Such conditions are simply not replicable on a grander scale elsewhere in Pakistan, let alone further afield.

Leaving aside the social embeddedness and imperfections of such markets,[16] over-reliance on mature labour and financial markets as a basis for defining the public and private content of social policy is too ethnocentric when considering poor, developing countries. We simply cannot make the same kind of assumptions about commodification (Esping-Andersen) or generalised commodity relations (Marx) under capitalism. People are not 'freed' in the Marxian sense to treat their labour or that of anyone else as a commodity, disentangled from other relationships: the Polanyian argument. Exchange is not single transactional in single periods, but multi-transactional in multi-period games: interlinked, and for the most part interlocked. Although such exchange can be reciprocal, and frequently is in very poor, pastoral societies, in the inequality of agrarian societies where control over land is paramount to understanding its structure, exchange is hierarchical, patriarchal and clientelist: within and between families.

This leads us to incorporate the following principles into our analysis:

- a recognition of the social, political and economic conditions of agrarian, subsistence, semi- and fully pastoral societies;
- acknowledgement that urbanisation in the poorer countries is not co-inciding with the development of mature, disembedded labour markets connected to formal sector industrial, manufacturing or services growth;
- the cultural significance of gender in structuring labour markets and household-level subsistence activity;
- a more balanced emphasis between productive functions (via a labour market focus) and the reproductive ones associated with the peasant metaphor;
- less analytic and therefore policy emphasis on human capital investment maintenance (including migration for health and education) where many of the current capability arguments take us (e.g. Sen or Nussbaum 2000) and correspondingly more emphasis on informal, family-based activity connected closely to immediate survival contexts (e.g. farming and risk-averse cropping decisions, livestock management, infrastructure maintenance, storage and rationing, induction into kin and community cultures, marriage arrangements, nurturing the young and caring for the elderly);
- an understanding of inter-generational transfers (Collard 2001 and the special issue of the *Journal of International Development* 2000) which embraces these realities;

---

[16] The former should be intrinsic to any concept of market, while the latter can always be found.

- a more creative conceptualisation of social protection and the range of informal as well as formal instruments of social protection which actually engage with such lives (see Conway, de Haan and Norton 2000 for an exposition of the Western-derived donor discourse);
- and a more realistic and embedded notion of rights not just at the level of universal morality but in terms of institutions, which can meaningfully perform correlative duties in the absence of supportive state action.

Actor-oriented epistemology

At the same time, our comparative framework challenges the whole technocratic approach to social policy (in which nice rich people do nice things to nice poor people) through problematising structure and action. Thus any comparative policy analysis has to be influenced by an actor-oriented methodological perspective located within a political economy appreciation of power and inequality which significantly places the political onus of pro-poor institutional change upon the poor themselves, often at the meso-level of action. This leads to four key presumptions:

- that only the poor will ultimately help themselves to the point of structural significance in relation to the basic terms of control over key societal resources;
- that the poor will act according to their perceptions of options, but that these perceptions can be enlarged by their own and others' actions to expand room for manoeuvre;
- that individual acts can be significant at the level of the graduating individual, but come up against the usual social mobility arguments in which only a few change status and only in steps rather than jumps;
- so that collective action can be structurally significant for wider units of solidarity with many gains on the way to full structural re-formation (which may never happen).

Thus collective social action becomes the key ingredient of a policy stance where poverty eradication relies upon the principle of structural change, with individual action relegated to a secondary, though significant, principle offering individual routes to improved livelihoods through personal graduation. In other words, poverty eradication is about *cohorts* confronting power and inequality, whereas poverty alleviation is about reducing the incidence of poverty via *individual* processes of graduation and successful *individual* incorporation into existing social arrangements and patterns of distribution.

The key to a comparative understanding of social policy is, then, identifying what is conducive to structurally significant social action as well as individual, graduating action within an institutional landscape that circumscribes options and their respective meanings. Conduciveness is a function of the conditions experienced by the poor. Thus there are individuals, social collectivities and institutions operating iteratively upon each other in a continuous process of redefinition of possibilities. Giddens called this 'structuration'. Put in our present language, we envisage a fluid, institutional responsibility matrix (IRM), with global as well as domestic aspects, as the main vehicle through which all social actors (i.e. including, crucially, the behaviour of the non-poor) shape positive or negative permeability across the institutional spheres and therefore stratification outcomes within the social space occupied by the matrix (i.e. not just local or national, but regional and global).

Thus we are arguing for a perspective in which individuals and social collectivities have to negotiate their way through a complex landscape which continually alters shape as a result not just of their own actions but those of others as well. 'Others' are sometimes remote. In this way we have a policy model which is intrinsically about structure, relationships and conditions under which people have constrained choices due to the poverty of the institutional landscape which is thus partly responsible for reproducing their own poverty in the process. Such a policy model must therefore logically include, as an object of policy, institutional reform. In this way, the policy agenda is about institutional reform, not just strategies towards the conditions of being poor. In another language, it is about improving the capacity of institutions to perform the correlative duties of honouring the rights claimed by or offered to the poor as the basic condition of poverty eradication. Since such institutions are themselves inhabited by people, implicated as classes, races or genders in the subordination of others, institutional reform itself cannot be just a matter of prescription. By necessity it has to be about conflict and struggle; hence the limitations of the technocratic perspective. Our expertise (as technocrats?) lies in analysing why positive outcomes are so difficult to achieve, not because solutions do not exist, but because they are mediated through relationships of power and inequality, which define the performance of the very institutions through which we expect outcomes.

Characteristics of the informal security regime: peasants and clients

Mindful, therefore, of context and actor-oriented epistemology, a phenomenological account of security and insecurity represents the central link between livelihood aspirations and the precarious social conditions through which they have to be realised (including, crucially in a policy context, the problem of governance). This account links conditions, perceptions and family/domestic life cycles very closely together. When considering livelihood strategies, the key decision-making points are: individual; nuclear family; and extended family (sometimes brothers living together with their respective wives and children, but increasingly less so). We must always recognise that individuals and families see themselves as dynamic not static. They intrinsically operate within a strong sense of life cycle. This comprises the domestic cycle of the family with its notions of stewardship and shifting dependency ratios over time, perpetually threatened by events, requiring continuous trade-offs between present consumption (the more poor, the higher the necessity) and future investment (the more poor, the less certain the conditions for any investment).

Given the concerns, expressed above, about overemphasis upon labour markets in our point of departure, we therefore need more of the 'peasant' in our basic understanding of these decision-making levels. This remains true even when we acknowledge structural change in the direction of: marketisation and commodification; wage employment; industrialisation and the new service economy; urbanisation; rising incomes; and the nucleation of families (see Kearney 1996 on reconceptualising the Mexican *campesino*). In poor countries, we cannot assume that these changes will inexorably lead us towards commodified modernisation. Contemporary survival options include seeking to reproduce 'peasant' behaviour and client status under conditions of urbanising labour markets, characterised by segmentation and informal sector attributes (Opel 2000) as well as increasingly unstable families (Jesmin and Salway 2000).

This peasant mentality, perforce, has to focus more upon reproduction than production as the central motivation for managing the domestic cycle, whether annual or inter-generational. The peasant, with low technological control over the environmental conditions for production, and always a price-taker rather than a price-maker, is pervaded by a sense of market insecurity. But since the peasant is rarely, if ever, self-sufficient, then any exchange, as a prerequisite for survival, is fraught with danger. And with the state historically functioning more as a predator-protector than as a market compensator and enabler, the state represents part of the problem of insecurity rather than a moderator of it. Thus the peasant has to rely for survival more upon those institutions where membership is more complete, acknowledged and legitimate: i.e. community and kin. This, arguably, is where the peasant has more chance of controlling events and reducing insecurity. This only works up to a point. Where the community level is itself characterised by severe inequality, then class or other exclusions undermine the value of these institutions to the excluded as a basis for dealing with uncertainty and insecurity.

Certainly, under such conditions, any notion of reciprocity has to give way to hierarchical, adverse incorporation: i.e. the embracing of client status and a consequent reinforcement of clientelism as the pervasive political settlement.

Within the peasant analogue it is important to reflect upon wider conditions of insecurity derived loosely from a country's poverty status as well as the family-level life-cycle conditions. The wider conditions also contribute to the uncertainty at the local, community and family level and undermine the viability of institutions at that level to perform secure reproduction functions. These points are made more with reference to contemporary Africa than South Asia or elsewhere. But, when considering them, let us not forget Afghanistan, Kashmir, Burma (and the border areas with its neighbours), East Timor, other parts of Indonesia and the Philippines, parts of Colombia,[17] and the Balkan region. Recent history would add a few more examples outside Africa too.

The first set of conditions surrounds the problem of the state as socially embedded, producing discretionary, even arbitrary outcomes with legitimacy based upon authority rather than accountability, and sometimes straightforward coercion as a substitute for legitimacy. With large clan and ethnic factions capturing such states and excluding others from rent-seeking opportunities, any opposition quickly escalates into violent challenge and civil war. Political culture reflects intense, all-or-nothing competition over scarce and valuable natural resources (such as minerals and watersheds) as well as rent-seeking opportunities in trading and production, especially through preferential access to bank credit with high default rates. War, or the constant threat of it, alongside continuous tension and low-level fighting, has to be acknowledged as a pervasive dislocation, negatively impacting upon the family life cycle in three different time periods: short-term potential damage to the cropping season; medium-term asset damage such as livestock theft and destruction of shelter; and, in the longer term, as any predictable basis for investment in human or productive capital is undermined. Such dislocation also undermines the incentives for large-scale, long-term public investment (especially if it also involves collective action and voluntary labour), which might, for example, manage water more securely and reduce cropping risk.

Second, historical, often colonial, legacies have been significant in reproducing insecurity. For example, the colonial restructuring of agrarian and pastoral economies in northern Uganda undermined the traditional flexibility of response to climatic conditions. By mapping a notion of

---

[17] Despite Colombia's overall paradoxical progress on economic and social indicators (Barrientos, chapter 4).

tribal rights onto a defined physical space, herdsmen could not respond to drought by moving stock to remoter water holes in 'another's territory'. This was a powerful explanation of the Karamoja famines during the 1980s. More generically, we have witnessed the enforced mobility of populations as refugees from war zones, which has frequently been caused by the imposition of arbitrary colonial borders dissecting other forms of identity. Sometimes these colonial boundaries have trapped significant ethnic minorities, leaving them vulnerable to long-term oppression by dominant national groups who have captured the state, for example in southern Sudan, or parts of Afghanistan. These legacies have also left whole regions within these 'nation'-states highly vulnerable to natural disasters, such as crop failure. Such populations incur two layers of insecurity: neglect by the hostile state in the first place; and increased vulnerability as such populations are forced to migrate into hostile areas through desperation, losing the value of many of their personal networks on the way. Alongside these territorial legacies are the contrary legacies of indentured labour (especially in Southern Africa, but also connecting South and East Asia), stimulating migrant male cultures and machismo gender outcomes, interacting with trade routes to socially underpin pandemics like HIV/AIDS, now a major source of insecurity at all societal levels and in all institutional arenas.

Third, the value of community-level institutions is threatened, especially in Africa,[18] through these periodic severe crises of food security and market collapse. Under such conditions, we can observe a shrinking morality of care as the corollary of the breakdown of public trust. As social capital in general declines, so poor people become more reliant either upon ever-decreasing circles of more immediate kin, thus reducing the size of the risk pool, or upon intensifying their client dependency upon locally richer patrons (as, for example, in Bangladesh or Pakistan), quasi-military commanders (as, for example, in Afghanistan, Angola, Congo) and guerrilla leaders (as, for example, in Colombia).

Under these conditions, it is hardly surprising that the poor in poor countries have a high discount rate.[19] The demands on the present are too extreme to warrant sacrificial investment in a highly uncertain future. This can be exacerbated by global economic conditions as well as thoughtless domestic macro-economic policy which removes certainty from skill-based labour markets, and thereby removes the propensity for

---

[18] But not exclusively, if we think again of Afghanistan.

[19] That is: with the future being so uncertain, they discount or reduce the value of it for preparation and investment purposes in favour of survival and the use of scarce resources in the more immediate present.

private or public human capital investment in them.[20] Better, therefore, for the poor to operate in the spheres of the known, familiar and controllable. The survival algorithm is stronger than the optimising one (Lipton 1968).

It is argued, therefore, that under these conditions of prevailing insecurity summed up through the analogue of the peasant and corresponding contexts of state capture, market collapse and shrinking risk pools, the welfare regime is dominated by particular institutional conditions of risk management in which neither the state nor the market are reliable, and in which the resort to community-level options (as an informal security regime) is at best problematic. In these circumstances, social policy as practice cannot rely upon regulatory, de-commodification instruments. It has to consider other, community-level, collective action entry points which might offset the shrinking morality of care, and restore the value of wider personal social networks and social capital which extends the risk pool. To develop this argument, the issue of risk management has to be explored further.

Institutional options for risk management

As stated above, when understanding the poor in a poor-country context, the *peasant* is a stronger analogue than that of *employed worker*. Insecurity and uncertainty induce risk-averse behaviour, by leaving poor people more exposed to livelihood-threatening risk. This insecurity and risk is partly an issue of time and partly an issue of social capital and social resources. Time is the discounting issue, noted above, and is elaborated elsewhere in Collard (2001) and Wood (2001b). Certainly the 'snakes and ladders' analogy is useful here (Room 2000b). Across the tenuous uncertainty of time, precarious families are stretching out a survival strategy, but always dominated by a hand-to-mouth reality, which prevents the necessary preparation for the future. Room presents endowments of resources and relationships which can offer ladders to bliss if aided by passports, or which offer only snakes leading to social exclusion unless inhibited by buffers. Passports and buffers are created through the public/ private partnerships of social policy, but unfortunately the institutional prospects of achieving them are lowest where the need is greatest, hence the need to be innovative about points of institutional entry for social policy as practice.

---

[20] See Kanbur (2001) for the all-important distinction between growth, which is always positive for poverty reduction, and particular growth-oriented economic policies, which maintain poverty where it might otherwise have been reduced.

We have already noted the overall problem of institutional failure in the IRM (see Wood and Salway 2000, and Wood 2000), in which states and markets are especially problematical for everyone in such societies. Under such conditions, everyone suffers a problem of social capital, but not everyone suffers a problem of social resources and power to control or manage events, which flows from such resources. Thus social capital has to be conceived more as a public good (or 'bad' if functioning in highly partial ways – see Khan 2000), whereas social resources can be seen more as a private good which operates to offset the weaknesses of social capital. Weaknesses of social capital constitute a lack of faith by social actors in a range of institutions, from formal political organisations and their civil bureaucratic counterparts on the one hand, to informal, community and kin organisations on the other. Such weaknesses ultimately derive from uncertainties about membership and stakeholding, and accompanying ambiguities about rights and entitlements.

A lack of social capital breeds a lack of social capital in the sense that the moral universe shrinks to the irreducible unit of the family, producing Banfield's 'amoral familism' (1958) and intensifies a sense of distrust in the community-level institutions. Without trust (Fukuyama 1995), there is insecurity in almost any imaginable arena of social interaction. However, those with social resources (clearly a dimension of power and an expression of superiority in the political economy) recreate trust through a labyrinth of interlocking networks in order to introduce greater security and predictability in transactions, especially over time. They are actively involved as dynamic actors in creating a structure that works for them.[21] When such processes become institutionalised, we call it 'civil society' and expect its features to act upon the state and market as a reforming angel. However, such origins of 'civil society' are themselves reflections of power and unlikely to be representative of the interests of the poor. This is how Gramsci could see the emergence of civil society as a pillar of the unrepresentative state (Gramsci 1976) – acting out the observed principle of negative permeability.

With social resources so unevenly distributed within the society, the problem for the poor is that they are exposed to the weaknesses of social capital, without any prospect of meaningful social resources to compensate. Their claims across the IRM are weak as a result. Therein lies their major source of risk. And without the social options to manage that risk, they have to rely more heavily upon their family and less upon transactions with others; hence the shrinking moral universe, hence the validity of the peasant analogue.

---

[21] As Long and van der Ploeg (1994) remind us, actors are active, structures are fluid.

This exposure to risk is multiple and co-variant. The *World Development Report* (*WDR*) *2000/1* discusses risk in various places, distinguishing between micro, meso and macro levels of risk in chapter 8, and co-variant risk, particularly induced by conflict, in chapter 3 (see especially box 3.2) and chapter 7 (World Bank 2001a). The *WDR* claims to encompass the risk terrain by also distinguishing between co-variant and idiosyncratic risk (chapter 8), such as illness, injury, old age, violence, harvest failure, unemployment and food prices (p. 136). However, nowhere does the discussion acknowledge the structural aspects of risk induced by inequality, class relations, exploitation, concentrations of unaccountable power and social exclusion as absence of 'community' membership. In other words, an institutional and relational account of risk is missing. This is a key objection to much of the contemporary livelihoods discourse (see below in this chapter): it fails to explain the micro circumstances of poor people in terms of meso and macro institutional performance, which express political economy and culture.

A 'resources profile' approach to vulnerability (see Lewis *et al.* 1992 for the original discussion by the CDS-Bath group), wherein households are understood as having a range of material, human, social, cultural and political resources to deploy, is basically a framework of non-idiosyncratic co-variance, with weakness on one dimension triggering weakness on another with an unravelling effect on livelihood security as a whole. Some elements of this co-variance are more familiar than others. For example, we expect poverty, seasonality of incomes and food availability, nutrition levels, morbidity, acute illness and loss of employment to go together, leading to loss of assets and further spiralling decline. Until recently, we might not have connected strength in social resources to human resources such as health and education; or labour participation[22] to common property access where an ability to contribute labour constitutes membership.

It is this co-variance of risk which needs to define policy process and content: understanding in context which type of intervention or entry point offers the most leverage on strengthening the livelihood portfolio as a whole via the identification of key risk linkages. Clearly the *WDR 2000/1* addresses this partially in its chapter 8, box 8.3 'Mechanisms for Managing Risk' (p. 141), where it distinguishes between reduction, mitigation and coping objectives and response categories divided between informal (individual/household and group-based) and formal (market and publicly provided). But since the *WDR* is derived from and therefore limited by its prior antiseptic, de-politicised treatment of the issue, it continues to be naïve about social and political institutions and the

----

[22] Under a 'material resources' heading representing income flows.

constrained opportunities for positive action via the rules embedded in those institutions. Thus physical incapacity of male adults for the labour market might not matter if there is no labour market, or if access is heavily segmented ethnically and culturally. Prices of essential agricultural inputs, or a levelling out of seasonal fluctuations in local-level food prices, could be much more significant for local peasants and casual, agricultural wage labourers. And, of course, prices are themselves outcomes of an only partially commodified political economy, characterised by segmentation and embedded interlocking.

These arguments set up a proposition. The imperatives of risk aversion in the present may deliver short-term security while reproducing the conditions for long-term insecurity in the future. This causation exists particularly strongly in the social domain. The individual and household needs for functioning social resources in the context of overall weak social capital require either over-strong reliance upon internal family relations (which may be reciprocal or hierarchical) or allegiance to other providers (hierarchical) at the cost of dependent and sometimes bonded loyalty (adverse incorporation). But such risk avoidance extends to other behaviour which has to favour meeting immediate needs over future ones within a peasant analogue. Examples might be crop diversification and subsistence preferences regardless of prevailing prices; or debt acquisition foreclosing future investment options (e.g. raising dowry capital versus investment in education); and so on (Wood 2001b). Thus, when poor social actors are negotiating their institutional landscape, their cognitive maps comprise: discounting; managing immediacy within severely constrained choices; awareness about long-term loss for short-term gain; and frustration about never being able to get ahead of the game for long enough to really commit resources for the future.

How can policy alter these time preferences? How can it convince poor people of sufficient present security to invest in their future? These questions lead us to a view of social protection, safety nets and welfare more generally as having a fundamental development function by altering time preferences. To elaborate: if development is understood, *inter alia*, as enabling people to prepare and plan for their futures, social protection and safety nets are not only justified as providing short-term welfare, but as securing the conditions under which poor people are more inclined to invest forwards. This point reflects concern about de-linking the discourses of social protection and social investment, and shifting the policy emphasis towards the latter with the onus on poor people to help themselves. But how far is it appropriate and ethical to shift the balance of effort in social policy *from* the stance of intervention to compensate for market outcomes (social protection) *to* the stance of supporting poor people's higher level of entry point into labour, commodity and services markets (social investment)? The wider institutional implication of this shift is that the performance of real markets will improve poor people's lives simply because poor people have entered them! This is to be over-optimistic about structuration!

In response to this policy choice dilemma (if it is a choice), it is useful when considering vulnerable livelihoods to distinguish between shocks and hazards. The sustainable livelihoods literature has recently been critiqued in Wood and Salway (2000) for: over-privileging social agency; unrealistic assumptions about poor people's social action; confusion between social capital and social resources; an inadequate account of political economy and power; and having a stochastic approach to shocks as a de-contextualised rather than chronic (i.e. continually hazardous) feature of poverty. Given that people must always be understood dynamically as somewhere along their domestic cycle experiencing troughs and peaks of financial and other security, Room's 'snakes and ladders' offers a more obvious framework for understanding the dynamic 'careers' of people in contrasting trajectories of poverty: improving or graduating; coping; and declining through irreversible ratchets/traps (unless assisted by social protection in general and safety nets in particular). Although 'snakes and ladders' offers only limited additionality to its predecessors,[23] its importance to our composite approach is:

- it tracks individuals and groups through gateways of opportunity and disaster, with some indication of what happens to them on the way (it is a 'career' approach);
- it is thus consistent with a poor actor-oriented epistemology of agency negotiating structure, expressed as a hostile political economy;
- and it therefore offers a model for understanding both how people negotiate the institutional responsibility matrix, and how social policy might assist in the improvement of that negotiation – e.g. not just 'individual graduation' passports but 'institutional reform' passports for whole societies, with different contents and meanings for different people and situations.

The rationale for social policy in this kind of poverty scenario is assistance to people who face chronic rather than stochastic insecurity. The basic conceptual issue here is that shocks are not shocks but hazards.[24] This then becomes the basis of a distinction between social policy as 'relief'-type interventions (when shocks are shocks, whose unpredictability requires rapid mobilisation of short-term response) and social policy

[23] Given that R. Chambers (1983) discussed 'downward ratchets'.
[24] I am grateful to Sarah White at Bath for pointing this out.

as 'preparation' for the more predictable hazards which affect subsets of the population chronically or structurally. Thus 'relief' responds to situations where security has broken down in surprising ways: e.g. flash floods in Italy. But 'preparation' should be in position for the predictable hazards of flooding in Bangladesh, in a well-functioning, non-hostile political economy (i.e. one with good governance, economic growth, public revenues and policies of redistribution via state instruments). This notion of 'preparation' is thus directed at improving the capacity of poor people to negotiate their institutional landscape, which features hazards more significantly than it does shocks. It consists of the creation and maintenance of security, especially when that security is predictably threatened by life-cycle events.

So, we have social policy in poor countries as essentially comprising: preparation; improving negotiating capacity; and the creation and maintenance of security in the context of hazards. And to this conception of policy we must add two other dimensions: the prevailing context of rights; and the significance of the household and other kin/clan units as security providers over time. The efficacy of such informal security provision is itself determined by the surrounding character of rights and the corresponding performance of institutions beyond kin, clan and ethnic identities into the other IRM domains of 'non-familial community', market and state, along with their global attributes. This moves our discussion from the metaphor of the peasant (male and female) at the social level of reproduction, production and exchange to those circumstances affected by the problem of governance: i.e. the whole question of rights and correlative duties.

Rights and correlative duties

Thus, as a dimension of insecurity and risk management, people's cognitive maps include ideas about rights and entitlements, which reside deeply at different levels of community and kin. The key question for poor people in poor countries is: where do rights and entitlements most securely reside in the institutional landscape? This is the key to evolving an account of social policy in a developing-country context. Where can rights possibly come from in the context of the peasant analogue and associated widespread social and political clientelism? Can they meaningfully reside in the state and market arenas? Our argument is that in the context of societies with poor governance, non-legitimate states and political insecurity, we have to look for (in shorthand) a *Gemeinschaft* rather than a *Gesellschaft* basis of rights. Herein lies the essence of this chapter: i.e. an argument for the concept of informal security regimes and forms of social policy, which acknowledges this reality for the time being.

When examining rights dimensions in the market, we have the classic debates[25] about the capacity of emerging societies to evolve moralities of exchange, and therefore trust, *beyond* face-to-face personalised transactions with perfect information *towards* generalised exchange between strangers under conditions of imperfect, asymmetrical information. Clearly the issue of rights and entitlements in the market incorporates a notion of fairness into the relationship between scarcity, quality and price. And as we know from Sen (1981), the principle of fairness can break down catastrophically for the poor, as sudden scarcity, whether real or manipulated, dominates the exchange equation. Under such conditions, as entitlements collapse, there are no 'moral economy' restraints to speculation or concern over disastrous outcomes for some, since there is a low level of moral proximity between the gainers and losers in distant markets. Rights in markets beyond those circumscribed by the moral economy are contingent and precarious. The prevailing political conditions of insecurity in many parts of Africa reflect such fragility. But in the peasant analogue, applicable to other parts of Africa as well as South Asia and other poor regions and pockets, poor people have significant proportions of their economic transactions within more localised, moral arrangements where a residual sense of fairness persists and therefore rights to entitlements exist.

Turning to the state as a repository of correlative duties for the poor, we have already critiqued the 'welfare state regime' assumption of the legitimated state compensating for the amoral market as a de-contextualised view of the state, benignly de-linked from the morality of the prevailing political economy. It is a position which normatively asserts positive permeability where the reality is negative. This is a fortiori even more so in societies where questions about the legitimacy of the state are combined with critiques of democracy and governance. It is therefore difficult to sustain a universalist account of formal rights and citizenship, based in effect upon Western liberal philosophy, in societies where even the incorporationist version of civil society[26] was underdeveloped through colonial behaviour; and nowhere more so than in Africa. Thus the idea of rights emanating from the legitimated state, serviced by intermediary organisations (social capital in the Putnam sense, 1993) constituting civil society, is almost laughable as a responsible description of the evolution of political institutions of power and authority in sub-Saharan Africa. South

---

[25] For example, involving Scott (1976), Granovetter (1985) and Platteau (1991), and now Putnam (1993) and Fukuyama (1995), as well as dozens of others.

[26] As in the Gramscian critique of civil society as a countervailing force to the state.

'd differently, with respect to civil society, with a longer and
_ted basis to an organised critique of the colonial state, along-
an incorporated set of intermediary institutions. But even in South
Asia, the tradition of an expected set of rights defined by the state, realised
and maintained through civil pressure, is much stronger in contemporary
India than in its neighbours Bangladesh and Pakistan.

Thus the idea of rights enshrined in the state remains a weak and
contestable phenomenon in the cognitive maps of social actors (rich and
poor alike). Rights have a tenuous position in the state and market arenas
of the domestic institutional landscape, and thus limit severely a view of
social policy as state intervention, or 'remedies by the state'. Even looking
for that position commits the sin of ethnocentrism and ignores the real
history of actually existing social capital instead of the one foisted onto
such countries by contemporary modernisationists. The fact that people
may be in a prison does not prescribe, unrealistically, the form of escape
(Wood 2000).

Our social policy agenda thus has to be sensitive to variation in means
by which correlative duties can be performed, even if we continue to accept that a universal approach to the definition of rights and needs can be
upheld.[27] Given this critique of the formal-legal discourse about rights
and correlative duties, where do they actually reside most securely in the
minds of social actors in poor countries? Where are the universal rights
and needs most nearly provided for in the domestic, and sometimes globalised, institutional landscape? If the domestic state and market domains
continue to be problematic, then clearly we have to look to the 'community' and household, kin and clan domains.[28]

Outside the domain of the state and therefore law, such rights and
entitlements are usually referred to as 'informal' in contrast to formal.
Within the overall presentation of the institutional responsibility matrix
(see chapter 1), the alternative institutional domains to the state and
the market have been designated as 'community' and household. There
can be many ambiguities in words such as community and household.

---

[27] As Doyal and Gough would argue (1991) as well as the *Human Development Report 2000*
(UNDP 2000).

[28] Before exploring these further, there is a logical point to be made. It is axiomatic that
we cannot conceive of society without some established acknowledgement of need, and
a notion of rights to ensure the meeting of need. In other words, rights and perceptions
of need have to reside somewhere to fulfil the conditions for calling a collectivity of
people 'a society'. Otherwise, we are only looking at anarchy and war; i.e. such a state of
insecurity that no one's interests can be met, so that there is no reason for that particular
collectivity to exist. Bevan (in chapters 3 and 6) gets close to that position when being
pessimistic about Africa, though of course she is arguing that the insecurity conditions
support the interests of a few powerful people and some of their followers for a while.

Both are heavily contested terms. 'Community', for example, can stretch from imagined ones (Anderson 1983) to closed, locational and residential ones, with other variants in between. Some communities can be more moral than others (Bailey 1966) and can be characterised by reciprocity and hierarchy, sometimes simultaneously. For social actors, the experience of community is variable, according to circumstances of conflict and unity, of fission and fusion. In other words, they are fluid not fixed, and our understanding of them has to depend upon an actor-oriented epistemological perspective. Sometimes, the construction of community reflects kin structures, thus blurring the distinction between community and household. Indeed, we have preferred the term 'household' over the term 'family' so that broader kin relations can appear under a community heading, while reserving the term household to refer to much closer, hearth-bound, interdependencies and senses of responsibility.[29] Thus, within 'community' we can include clans and lineages which offer social actors crucial identities as well as the social frame within which rights of allocation of scarce resources occur, such as land, water, access to pasture, places to build homesteads, and so on. This would apply with equal force to, say, northern Pakistan and rural East Africa.

Kin dimensions of community also offer a key basis of 'membership', and with membership goes rights, which are connected to prevailing presumptions about needs and entitlements. To lose 'membership' is to be excluded. People lose membership under various conditions: migration; resettlement; urbanisation (until 'membership' is regained, or re-established); failure to conform or perhaps contribute; being elderly or infirm (e.g. in the West); being cast as a minority in the context of larger-scale events (e.g. Jews in Germany in the 1930s and 1940s); or being outcast in various ways in South Asia and Africa.

Apart from the usual list of scarce resources associated with the peasant analogue, such as land or water, what broader needs are usually recognised within a universalist concept of 'social policy'? These may partly refer to an improved quality of basic needs, consistent with the peasant analogue, such as food security and sanitation. But crucially, in a changing, modernising world, these also refer to the development of people's talents, aspirations, cognitive maps and therefore opportunities beyond the peasant analogue. From the welfare regime perspective, this is

[29] Of course there are many different forms of 'household', characterised by the classic terminology of anthropology: patrilineal, patriarchal, patrifocal, virilocal, matrilineal, matrifocal, monogamy, polygamy, polyandry, and so on. There are some clear stylised differences between a South Asian patrifocal polygamous household sharing the same hearth and a sub-Saharan African patrilineal, polygamous, matrifocal extended family with scattered matrifocal hearths.

where Room's 'de-commodification for self-development' applies (Room 2000a). By defining social policy as 'moving the agenda forward' for poor people in poor countries, the policy agenda becomes a combination of improving present conditions attached to peasant forms of survival and a process of self-development that moves poor people into wider forms of livelihood choice. If this is so, then we need to understand what appreciation of needs, and supporting sense of rights, currently obtain.

Let us take an extreme example: that is, 'extreme' to us Westerners, but also capable of raising the eyebrows of others in northern Pakistan. Women in Kohistan[30] suffer from vitamin D deficiency due to culturally induced non-exposure to the sun.[31] Their bone strength deteriorates quickly in their twenties after several pregnancies. They develop gynaecological complications, which not only undermine their quality of life, but threaten it. What are their rights, since their needs seem to be clear? Very limited indeed, when males argue that the cost of visits to health clinics/hospitals compares unfavourably to acquiring a new wife. Neither the household nor the community offer any kind of security; there is no market freedom for women to purchase curative care; and the state simply does not operate in such an area. Even within the peasant analogue, as recognised by other peasant societies elsewhere (even close to Kohistan), such basic needs are not acknowledged.

Let us now take the condition of men in the same society. Outsiders, especially feminists, might hold the men wholly responsible for the sad condition of their women. This must be partly true, even from the most relativist of analytical perspectives. However, it is reported by men from the region that approximately 60 per cent of young men (certainly of marriageable age) dare not go out of their homesteads after sunset for fear of feuding reprisals; that a resolution of inter-family conflict involves a man taking a woman/girl as a wife from the opposing family's near kin; and that for a man to treat his women with respect, as defined locally, requires extreme purdah without which the man himself has no honour locally. Without honour there is no membership, and without the latter no rights for either the man or his women. Wives and daughters are then at risk from more predatory interest, and further rounds of feuding ensue. What is the process by which social policy extends the rights of women and men, under these conditions, let alone moving the agenda on to self-development? It would require confrontation with the locally powerful mullahs who define the present ideological agenda: that is, the prevailing definitions of right and wrong, or, in other words, rights.

---

[30] The remote mountainous region, traversed by the Karakoram highway, between Islamabad and Gilgit-Hunza (see Wood 2003a, for a further description of this area).
[31] They are strictly secluded, not only within the compound of the household, but mainly indoors.

Clearly this is an extreme, though real, example. But it helps to reveal contexts more subtle than this, but which nevertheless contain the basic challenge to the extension and formalisation of rights and a recognition of the value as well as the limitations of the informal ones. Within the political economies of poor countries, especially in the poorest ones of South Asia and sub-Saharan Africa, what general informal rights pertain whether at some abstract societal level of values and beliefs or at a more specified community level? Given the vested interest of the rich in prevailing structural inequalities, we need to distinguish between rights realised through hierarchical relations and through reciprocal relations.

Rights through *hierarchical* relations basically operate within relations of adverse incorporation and clientelism. They can be classed more as welfare than developmental ones. That is to say, clientelist relations will offer relief to clients but rarely invest in long-term security through, for example, education or capital transfers on easy terms. Relief or welfare transfers, for example through tied labour, long-term debt or interlocked tenancy agreements, occur in return for loyalty and other 'dependent' favours which contribute to the reproduction of the initial inequality. Such relations are as likely to occur between close kin as between others more distant.[32] With market penetration and a widening of economic opportunities, the shrinking of moral ties further reduces the community sense of responsibility for others. Indeed, with the ideology growing, in the minds of the rich, that poor people are the responsibility of their aid-supported governments, community-level rights about welfare are correspondingly threatened. At the same time, especially in rural contexts, community leaders/elders and stronger classes are reluctant to see whole poorer families or poor relatives completely outcast or cast out. Where, in northern Pakistan for example, access to common property remains an important part of the family livelihood portfolio, then those unable to fulfil the conditions for membership are often assisted to that effect: for example, widows and the elderly or infirm (including the mentally infirm).[33]

Other basic needs might also be guaranteed locally:
- allocation of homestead land;
- allocation of agricultural and pasture land (where the community or extended kin group traditionally disposes of it);
- access to drinking water (but much less so to irrigation water);
- access to materials (wood and mud) for building construction;

---

[32] See Wood (1994) for descriptions of this process in villages in Bangladesh.

[33] I have recently written a report (as yet unpublished) for the Aga Khan Rural Support programme on informal social protection in the Northern Areas and Chitral district of northern Pakistan: 'AKRSP Poverty Policy for 2003–8 Phase: Issues, Strategies and Dilemmas', mimeo, 21 pages, 9 March 2002.

- access to fuel-wood or peat; access to wild fish stocks and forest products (i.e. gathering and hunting rights);
- a share in communally engineered new land (via forest clearing, new irrigation channels, and feeder roads opening up new physical access);
- and access to primary healthcare and even education facilities, possibly with some means-tested adjustment to expected cost recovery.

Where the provision of these rights, in the sense of correlative duties to honour them, are hierarchical via the collectivity of richer, dominant families in the community, then we observe a collective version of adverse incorporation. This entails a strong expectation that poorer, aided, families express gratitude by not challenging the basic arrangements of the political economy which reproduces the poverty in the first place. In this way, we observe institutional and plural clientelism at the community level, alongside the more private, individualised form which emphasises intense personal loyalties and dependencies. Thus we have collective and individual patronage, with the former offering more long-term security than the latter.

Rights through *reciprocal* relations can be problematic in other ways. Basically rights offered and guaranteed by those with little power in the society or local community are not worth much in longer security terms. Thus the poor do not have much to offer each other beyond very micro, immediate transfers plus sympathy. However, such a dismissive remark needs to be qualified in at least two opposing directions. First, the value of reciprocal relations, offering rights between the poor, are further limited by the structural conditions of poverty which place the poor in competition with each other for scarce resources, including the social resources of patronage. Solidarity is not necessarily natural. But, second, movements to build solidarity among the poor have precisely emerged from the interrelated analysis of structural inequality and the need to overcome the 'within poor' competition that results from it. Such movements are intended to create the social resources for the poor that are naturally lacking, and thereby contribute to the formation of social capital (i.e. institutions) more conducive to their long-term interests. Proshika in Bangladesh would be a good example of this approach.[34] So reciprocal relations can be enhanced, and this has to be a major ingredient of any poverty-focused social policy in poor conditions. However, it is these socio-political characteristics of poverty, as revealed through the

---

[34] A large, social mobilisation NGO, currently organising in excess of 80,000 landless groups (both men's and women's), with a federated structure increasingly significant at district level.

discussion of rights and correlative duties, which have to be interwoven into a conception of poverty-relevant social policy.

Framing social policy within the peasant analogue and clientelism

We are arguing that poor men and women lack confidence in states and markets, as a reflection of prevailing conditions of uncertainty and insecurity. If social policy is confined to a compensatory manipulation of the market by the state (i.e. de-commodification), such a conception has limited value or relevance to the poor experiencing this insecurity. Thus the poor have to resort to 'community' and 'household', albeit under various types of adverse conditions. This has compelled us to adopt, heuristically, the principle of the 'peasant analogue' and to acknowledge pervasive, accompanying clientelism. Once we do so, we see within the peasant analogue the significance of the inter-generational transfer processes of: welfare to deal with present insecurity; and investment in capacity to deal with future insecurity. And, with clientelism, we see the significance of informal rights in the absence of formal governance.

This analytical stance must make us wary of the welfare state regime options of de-familialisation and de-clientelisation,[35] since both 'families' and 'the rights of adverse incorporation' represent key lifelines, and indeed key aspects of social inclusion. Although households are gendered, and frequently non-altruistic along gender lines, they continue to represent the most reliable retreat option for most of their members and thus offer security over time. The inter-generational bargain is acted out more strongly at the family level when other institutions cannot be trusted. But as the basic element of security within the peasant analogue (i.e. secure usufruct over land as the principal means of production and own consumption) steadily disappears as economies transform, so the hazards of land management under low technological conditions are replaced by the hazards of amoral labour markets with poor men and women facing, instead, the hazards of globalised market conditions (i.e. adverse terms of trade, shifting comparative advantage, currency fluctuations and an enlarged reliance, for some countries, upon food imports). Under these conditions of autonomy loss, reliance upon the household retains its significance for risk management. This is why we have adopted the peasant analogue, as a guide to perception and behaviour in relation to insecurity.

---

[35] That is 'de-clientelisation' as a logical, contextualised alternative to de-commodification, in principle offering statutory rights to social protection in order to de-link clients from dependence upon their patrons.

It takes a long time to fade, precisely because of the untrustworthiness of the remaining elements of the institutional landscape. For this reason, the analogue is more than just heuristic.

By adopting this perspective as a 'reality check'[36] we can also assess more critically the impact of certain prescriptions within the global and universal rights agendas. Let us go the heart of the matter: marriage as the essential *rite de passage* in the reproduction of the immediate family (household) and therefore security. Universal rights prescriptions, with a strong emphasis on liberal concepts of freedom and moral individualism, raise questions about child betrothal, arranged marriages, dowries and control over sexuality as refuting the fundamental rights of choice for girls and women. Without over-elaborating the point here,[37] each of these marriage practices can be seen as essential to the rationality of the peasant analogue in the context of an otherwise uncertain institutional landscape. Without such practices, the security of all individuals within the household is threatened, especially that of children. With such practices, hazards are minimised, especially at later stages in the life cycle when inheritance becomes a key inter-generational transfer issue. With urbanisation and other aspects of the proletarianisation of labour, some may argue that the peasant analogue recedes in significance, thus permitting a weakening of reliance upon inter-generational transfers within the family and, consequently, a more justified intrusion of a universal rights agenda as a corrective function. But such assumptions presume a social replication of rich-country labour markets in poor countries, whereas what we observe is a 'peasantisation' of cities (Roberts 1978) through the characteristics of what others have termed the informal sector and maintenance of strong family traditions.

Clientelism and adverse incorporation are key aspects of peasantisation and the informal sector. But clientelism extends well beyond economic relations into social and political ones as preconditions for physical and material security. While I characterised the whole of Bangladesh as a prison in this respect (Wood 2000), we have to be wary of simply advocating de-clientelisation as the process of escape. Ultimately it must be, even if I stand accused of ethnocentric modernity. However, the transition must be defined so as to avoid cutting the poor off from their present institutional lifelines without adequate substitutes. To continue the metaphor, if escapees or released inmates have nothing to go to they

---

[36] That is: against the assumptions of 'freed' men and women operating in open labour markets, protected by benevolent governments.

[37] For example, the social requirement for unambiguous paternity when property is being transferred in a patrilineal society to the designated bloodline, and its consequent restraint upon female mobility and access to non-incestuous males.

quickly become recidivists – which is probably as good a description of the turmoil in Russia and the FSU states as any.

Challenging the meso domain of the institutional landscape

This leads on to another observation about means. Institutional failure in the state and market arenas of the institutional landscape (with adverse incorporation and clientelism prevailing in the absence of pervasive, formal sector, labour markets) severely constrains some of the classic instruments of social policy. The instruments for engaging with the needs of people as atomised individuals in formal sector labour markets are not applicable for dealing with the needs of people characterised by the peasant analogue. In formal sector labour markets, the principle of incentives through altering the price of things and services can operate more strongly. Policy can therefore be far more fiscal on both the demand and supply side. It can operate within the loop of the state via tax revenues and direct employment of service providers (like social workers, teachers and health staff). Or it can operate within the quasi-market via targeted subsidies to enable the poor and needy to purchase services from private sector providers. Or it can operate through tax relief as an incentive: to invest in financial markets for old-age security or educational trusts for one's children; or even to purchase elite services beyond the state's basic, direct provision in the health, care and education sectors. In the West, such policy is basically residualist and concessionary. It is more about alleviation than eradication, and committed to a retention and reproduction of the capitalist market as is. That is to say, it is about compensating for the market, improving it as a vehicle for livelihoods, but not destroying it.

By contrast, in many poor countries, the weakness and partiality of market penetration limits the efficacy and coverage of fiscal instruments. The relation between the state and people in poor countries with agropastoral, feudal and colonial histories has always relied heavily upon intermediate institutions, which deliver limited services in return for loyalty and quiescence. This is the meso domain referred to earlier in the chapter. In the context of the peasant analogue, the problem is that this meso domain is occupied by highly problematic elements of the institutional landscape, broadly performing the functions of adverse incorporation – where time preferences clash with social capital. At best, these intermediate institutions might be regarded as incorporated civil society, performing hegemonic duties outlined in the Gramscian critique. At worst, they are mafia-type, clientelistic social arrangements, acting out prevailing class relations and power at the local level with the outcome of entrapping the poor into short-term security at the cost of their own long-term personal development.

Thus, since social policy, almost by definition, cannot engage with poor men and women under these conditions via fiscal instruments, so it has to develop other passports and buffers for the poor (as collectivities, not just graduating individuals) via institutional reform. This cannot be done top-down, both because the inclination to do so cannot be assumed in a hostile political economy, and because rights given are worth much less and are much less secure than rights gained. Hence the focus upon support for agency (i.e. social movements and their action) has to be correspondingly much stronger. The presently problematic intermediate institutions, currently occupying the meso domain of the institutional landscape, therefore have to be challenged as a precondition for extending support to poor people. That is, the means and instruments have to be different from the fiscal ones of welfare state regimes. Some examples follow below.

An obvious example is *micro-finance*, which challenges the banking sector (see Sharif and Wood 2001) and can offer welfare support (small loans and savings for liquidity management and consumption smoothing), as well as development opportunities through deepening with larger-scale finance, connected to wider capital markets, even global ones. Another is *land reform*, including urban tenure rights, but this has to rely on mobilisation for social agency, as in West Bengal, not just legislation. Another might be *public/common property partnerships* for sanitation and clean drinking water. Another has been the highly pragmatic work of SEWA in Gujarat, India, on *labour standards*. Another has been to challenge local municipalities in Dhaka, Bangladesh, *not to evict* without replacement. Another has been *drop-in centres* for female victims of violence, organised by a very local NGO in Gilgit, north Pakistan. Another has been the widespread introduction *non-formal primary education* in Bangladesh by BRAC, Proshika and others as a challenge to the state education service. Another has been the development of *labour-contracting societies of poor people* to circumvent the corruption of local contractors and local government engineers in collusion to defraud the state and the labourer. Another has been to *enter product and service markets with higher productivity technologies* than those offered by traditional micro-credit. There are many other examples of the under-performing meso domain which can be challenged, deploying agency, social movements and social action which do not expose the poor to the organised repressive retaliation of the state and its privileged beneficiaries. What they have in common, ironically, are pre-existing notions of membership (and therefore rights and entitlements) derived precisely from 'common law' assumptions about inclusion in relationships of reciprocal and hierarchical rights.

Conclusion

This chapter has argued that neither the weak version of the welfare state regime (political settlement) nor the strong version of the welfare state regime (de-commodification) can appropriately be applied to conditions prevailing in the poorest regions of the world, such as countries in South Asia and sub-Saharan Africa. The poorer regions of the world do not comfortably conform to the two key assumptions upon which the OECD model of the welfare state regime relies: a legitimate state; and a pervasive, formal sector labour market. This immediately sets up the two key interactive issues of governance and the socio-economic circumstances of poor men and women. These circumstances have been understood in two main ways: first, through the metaphor of the peasant (to capture the significance of reproduction, family, household-level intergenerational transfers and reciprocal interdependencies within kin and clan structures); and, second, through the analysis of clientelism as pervasive adverse incorporation (comprising hierarchical rights, meso-level intermediation with the national-level polity and economy, and quasi-public goods social capital). Together, these dimensions comprise the informal security version of a welfare regime.

These political, economic, social and family dimensions have been brought together, for policy analysis purposes, as the institutional responsibility matrix with global as well as domestic dimensions. These four institutional domains are seen as permeable, which can have positive or negative outcomes for different societies. The world's poor regions are characterised by negative permeability in which personal objectives penetrate the domain of public aims to produce poor governance and insecurity for the majority of their populations by removing the corrective principle. Only partial compensation is offered by global discourses, conditionality and debt remission leverage. The problem of insecurity thus looms large in the analysis, with a focus on its implications for time preference behaviour at the level of personal as well as social investment. Indeed the necessarily short-term time preference behaviour of the poor is seen to clash with the creation and maintenance of long-term social capital and improvement of governance – a Faustian bargain of dysfunctional structuration under conditions of no exit, little voice and tainted loyalty.

Faced with this scenario, this chapter has argued for a 'poor'-actor-oriented epistemology,[38] which emphasises how the poor negotiate a complex and hostile institutional landscape dominated by severe inequalities of power which reproduce their poverty. This position entails a view of the state as not impartial but working for dominant classes and segments, including a bureaucratic and political class, which sees state control as a crucial means of its own accumulation and reproduction. Since this is a familiar view of the state, it is obvious that social policy as a discipline derived from critical sociology does not rely upon a benign, liberal, pluralist view of the state. Thus the issue of 'governance' as contemporary 'development-speak' is intrinsic.

This is why any social policy of poor countries very quickly moves onto the agenda of 'civil society compensating for the inequities of the state' instead of the OECD welfare state regime principle of 'the state compensating for inequities of the market'. But given the inherent problem of the state, and the issue of permeability, there cannot be a naïve optimism about the role of a 'progressive' civil society as a compensation for the state. The reality of poor-country political cultures is that we have to distinguish between civil societies (i.e. in the plural): between the Gramscian civil society incorporated into the elite project of unaccountable state power; and the critical civil society of de Tocqueville. However, the critical civil society is never completely autonomous of prevailing culture and permeability because it consists at best of renegade elites with personal positions to defend and to reconcile with more radical, public agendas – the tense relation between personal objectives and public aims again (Devine 1999).

Thus social policy, from an actor-oriented perspective, has to include struggle and movements (i.e. collective action) which impact upon the institutional landscape itself to secure a formalisation of informal and precarious rights. Such social action can be distinguished from approaches to social policy which emphasise the creation of enabling environments (by the benign among the powerful) within which individual action for graduation can occur. That 'methodological individualism' is again premised upon the notion of the liberal, pluralist state, acting as a market adjuster, so that individuals can invest in their own human capital development (de-commodification for self-development). Methodological *collectivism*, on the other hand, is a structuration process in which the potential instruments of policy are themselves reformed through large-scale political action. In such societies, where the issue of governance is central, how can

---

[38] Of course such an epistemology applies to the rich as well, and is implied through the analysis of adverse incorporation and clientelism in which the rich are the defining actors.

one conceive of social policy in any other way? Social policy, as practice, has always reflected (and must definitionally reflect) political settlements. The point is whether such settlements, when they work against the poor, can be de-stabilised. But is it always a zero-sum game between classes?

Although OECD social policy does rely heavily upon the concessionary principle,[39] it has also been acknowledged that economic elites had increasing interests in the development of a skilled and educated labour force to manage technological advance, including the organisation of industry itself (i.e. management roles). That was how apartheid was eventually undermined in South Africa, by the expanded reproduction interests of white capital. Thus, in the context of globalisation, we should not presume a zero-sum game clash between a global rights discourse and the interests of poor-country domestic economic elites. Much of the global social policy agenda is about universalising rights and creating level playing fields, as if domestic elite resistance is to be expected. However, there has been insufficient consideration of national-level elite interests in creating an educated, skilled labour force, which sees itself as committed, therefore, to the capitalist project, as in Taiwan, South Korea (see chapter 5), and especially now in India with its neighbours nervously adopting similar ideas. Indeed, these were the classic, anti-communist strategies supported strongly by the US from the end of the Second World War. The rural equivalent has always been about creating petty landholders (petty commodity peasants) to offset the communist mobilisation of disaffected, expropriated rural labour – hence land reform as a long-established instrument of social policy: i.e. giving some classes of poor people a stake in the elite project. *Thus we have social policy, under these circumstances, as essentially incorporationist.*

However, this chapter has focused, conceptually, on poorer societies: where the incidence of poverty is highest; where the agrarian basis of poor people's livelihoods remains dominant, both as a continuing though finite reality, and as a metaphor of poor people's psychology and cognitive maps; and where the peasant analogue (even under conditions of significant rural landless labour) refers to risk-averse behaviour under conditions of high insecurity (i.e. much of South Asia and Africa). The prospects for win-win political settlements under these conditions are more remote. The political economies are just too hostile to the poor, with everyone desperately searching for security (Wood 2001b) through the pursuit of personal objectives rather than public aims. *Under these conditions, the action agenda for social policy has to be different: less incorporationist,*

---

[39] That is: elite-dominated states recognising the costs of not making concessions to an increasingly organised working class.

more oppositional. But, at the same time, we have to remember that para-doxically the various factors to be overcome also operate to foreclose more ambitious individual and collective action. These are: the discounting behaviour of the poor; short-term liquidity management; the uncertainty of the future; and the induced acceptance of adverse incorporation and clientelism (as the predominant form of non- and pre-commodified economic relations). But we cannot naïvely rely upon the benign among the powerful to alter these conditions. What changes such time preference behaviour?

In a resources profile framework, the mutual interdependence between different sets of resources (material, human, social, cultural, etc.) is emphasised. In policy terms, it is necessary to identify for different contexts which set of resources is key, in the sense of altering the status and functioning of the others. It might be individual self-development via education and vocational training in some circumstances (parts of East and South Asia). It might be overcoming adult male morbidity in others (e.g. urban Bangladesh). It might be social action around common property management in north Pakistan. And it might be struggle-based social action on wages, rents or family law in rural India. And so on. In other words, more social policy needs to be based on a 'horses for courses' approach, rather than assuming a universal agenda everywhere. Not everyone's basic needs are the same, because the jugular problem for them is not the same. Thus we need to distinguish between a 'universalist' stance with respect to overarching needs for secure welfare, and a 'relativist' approach which specifies precise, contextualised inter-linkage between variables, and identifying, among the non-idiosyncratic co-variance, which is the key entry point for *whose* action.

The point about 'whose' action does not therefore presume the state (of course! given negative permeability and problematic governance). It does not presume countervailing forces in the civil society. It does not presume the poor themselves either as individuals or collectively (trapped as prisoners in adverse incorporation). It does not presume the efficacy either of aid or universal discourses about rights. And it certainly does not presume technocratic responses. What it does presume is a meso approach to understanding room for manoeuvre for action; but which actors and what agendas will vary according to meso context. And we are strategically privileging meso over micro. We are ruling out micro (methodological individualism and personal graduation) as structurally insignificant under conditions of hostile political economies, and arguing that meso-level encounters, entailing collective mobilisation, carry the best medium-term prospects for bringing about structural change in the institutional landscape.

Thus, this chapter concludes by re-emphasising the need to understand three processes: the way in which different groups and classes negotiate problematic institutional landscapes, domestic and global; what they can get out of existing political settlements (the access/participation agenda); and how their social action can effect changes in that landscape to offer more security in the future (the political action/struggle agenda).

3   Conceptualising in/security regimes

Philippa Bevan

Introduction

This chapter is one result of our dialogue between European social policy and the sociology of development. I was charged with the task of exploring how the concepts of 'welfare regime', 'social exclusion' and 'social policy' might be usefully adapted for understanding African realities in the context of a growing interest in the notion of 'global social policy' and the increasing merger of development and (military) security (Duffield 2001). My starting point was to 'sensitise' the welfare regime model to African realities using selected studies by political scientists, historians, social anthropologists and others working in the 'African studies' and development traditions. This process led to the design of a more abstract and encompassing model which I am calling the in/security regime model.[1] This is an analytical model which identifies general mechanisms, processes and relationships to guide the collection and analysis of information in *any* empirical 'welfare' context. As explained below, the model can be used[2] to explore and compare welfare regimes, informal security regimes and insecurity regimes (see chapter 1), and has a variety of other possible uses. In the concluding section of this chapter I use it in a brief examination of the global in/security regime mix.

It is important here to draw a distinction between (1) abstraction and (2) generalisation as a result of empirical comparison. In this chapter I use some existing empirical studies to explore some of the ways in which, and the reasons why, as it stands, the European welfare regime model does not fit African realities, in order to develop a more abstract conceptual model, with less empirical content, which can be widely used as a research tool. This chapter does not draw any empirical conclusions about in/security regimes in Africa[3] although it makes use of relevant empirical

---

[1] The '/' indicates that empirical regimes can vary from the extremely insecure and harmful to the extremely egalitarian and inclusive.
[2] And implicitly or explicitly has been in other chapters in the book.
[3] The in/security regime model could have been developed through a similar sensitisation of the welfare regime model to many other current and past political economy structures

88

evidence. Africa is a large continent with a diversity of political economy structures and cultures at different levels of economic development which are differentially interacting with wider regional and global structures. Current Eurocentric social science knowledge about these structures and cultures, which are embroiled in huge and diverse processes of change involving considerable contention, is thin, patchy and unintegrated, and we are not yet in a position to draw properly founded general conclusions about similarities and differences among all in/security regimes in Africa. While in chapter 6 I use the research tool developed in this chapter in a further empirical exploration of African in/security regimes, I regard that chapter as a preliminary and inconclusive first step.

This chapter begins with a critical discussion of three European social policy concepts: welfare regimes, social policy and social exclusion. In the second section I sensitise the regime model and the concept of 'social policy' to some current African structures, actors and dynamics. In the third section the in/security regime model is described, a more detailed methodology is developed, and there is some discussion of how the model might be used to analyse meso-level regimes and their articulation with other meso structures and with larger structures at macro and global levels. In the fourth section I use the model to explore the current stratified and segmented global in/security regime, with a particular focus on a major element of the global welfare mix and an important 'stratification outcome', namely the emerging and complex system of global liberal governance (Duffield 2001) with its burgeoning development, humanitarian and conflict resolution 'industries'. I conclude by considering some implications for 'global social policy'.

European social policy concepts

Welfare regime model

I have isolated five important elements, or 'spaces of comparison', from the definitions of 'welfare regime' in Esping-Andersen (1990) and Gough (1999).

1. *The generation of insecurity and illfare*: A division of labour (between capitalists and workers) in terms of activities based on differential control over the means of production (capital and labour) which produces livelihoods involving the exploitation of wage labour by capital.

and dynamics; for example, a number of Latin America countries (e.g. Peru, Columbia), recent Afghanistan, mediaeval Europe.

2. *Political mobilisation*: A set of class relationships (involving exploitation) based on this division of labour, and the interests and power associated with it, which are supported (and challenged) by ideologies and form the basis for political mobilisation.

3. *Political settlement and welfare mix*: As a result of the mobilisation of labour in the context of multi-party democracy there is 'a political settlement' between capital and labour involving a degree of de-commodification of labour. This settlement entails a set of institutions (socially constructed norms and rules), supported by a set of values, identifying how, and who is, to deal with the insecurity which would be generated by the unfettered operation of the pursuit of capitalist interests. The form of political settlement varies between countries, resulting in a 'welfare mix' of provision by a combination of state (social assistance/social insurance/universal citizenship), market (e.g. private insurance, fringe benefits), family/household, and, in some versions, 'community' or third sector.

4. *Path dependence and stratification outcomes*: These institutions create a further set of interests or 'stratification outcomes'.

5. *Welfare outcomes*: These relate to the degree of 'de-commodification' achieved – the extent to which the standard of living and 'self-development' (Room 1999) of an individual are insulated against their position in the market.

In the European welfare regime model the first two spaces of comparison tend to be ignored, and it is usual to compare welfare regimes according to variations in welfare mix and related welfare and stratification outcomes, the most usual distinction being drawn between liberal, conservative and social welfare regimes. It is assumed that (1) there is no variation between regimes in the underlying source of insecurity and illfare, which is identified as industrial capitalism, and (2) the key mobilising political group is the working class.

Social policy

I have not been able to find a clear definition of 'social policy' even in the European social policy literature. There is first a distinction between intentional actions and what actually happens in practice, the latter being socially constructed by all participants through the dynamic interaction of intentional policy actions and their consequences with other actions and their consequences. Second, in the realm of intentional actions, there is a distinction between the more or less clearly articulated set of ideas and intentional practices guiding what *is being* done to meet welfare needs, and alternative ideas about what *ought to be* done to meet welfare needs.

Thus we can distinguish at least 'mainstream social policy', 'critical social policy' and 'social policy in practice'. In the European social policy literature these ideas, intentional actions, and total practices are usually seen as occurring 'within the public sphere' and as 'oriented to some positive conception of human wellbeing' (Gough, chapter 1). Government regulation and/or resource provision is key. Policies analysed under the heading of 'social policy' involve instruments relating to social security (income maintenance), housing, health, education, family welfare[4] and (sometimes) law and order (Marshall 1998: 619). There are other key areas of national policy which, intentionally or not, have important impacts on 'welfare' including macro-economic policy, micro-economic policy and (sometimes) foreign policy, but these are regarded as the prerogatives of other ministries (intentional actions) and academic disciplines (ideas).

Social exclusion

Within European welfare regimes it became clear in the later decades of the twentieth century that exploitation was not the only process leading to insecure livelihoods; the phenomenon of social exclusion was recognised – a process which generated an 'underclass' of people who were not de-commodified/exploited by, but irrelevant to, the capitalist project. In the context of (post-)industrial capitalist societies it has been suggested that these people have experienced a 'catastrophic break' from society (Room 1999).

Key issues

Before attempting to sensitise the model to African conditions it is worth considering a number of relevant problems associated with the application of the welfare regime model to advanced capitalist societies.

Welfare outcomes   In the welfare regime model de-commodification involves the reduction of insecurity in the context of industrial capitalism and is a *social* rather than an individual measure. However, it is difficult to operationalise, especially in contexts where de-commodification in relation to position in the labour market might be achieved by commodification in relation to insurance and investment markets. As an alternative 'individualising' approach, Gough has suggested that welfare is a positive conception of human well-being 'defined in terms of human

---

[4] Including family benefits, paid leave for childcare, free education, child health services, playgrounds, etc.

needs, capabilities, flourishing, active participation, equity, justice,[5] etc.'
(Gough, chapter 1), which can be measured using a range of nationally
generated statistics about individuals (or sometimes households). This
approach opens the way to a more complex understanding of illfare and
the mechanisms which generate it, to which income insecurity is only one
of a number of contributors. It also encourages a focus on individuals,
and, if these are recognised to be embodied, opens a space for studying variations in need based on age, sex, health and habitus. However,
as Peter Davis argues in his chapter, it is important not to lose sight of
the quality of the underlying economic and political relationships; commodification is a social relationship/mechanism/process which defines
some people as 'means', rather than as ends in themselves (Nussbaum
2000).

The generation of insecurity and illfare   In recent modern cap-
italistic contexts this is seen as resulting from two mutually exclusive
processes: exploitation and exclusion. Exploitation involves the extraction of surplus labour from workers through the cash nexus. There are
three main reasons why 'workers' need to be de-commodified: low pay,
temporary unemployment and inability to work as a result of life processes. Life processes generate variations in dependency/autonomy and
include life-cycle features (e.g. babyhood, pregnancy, old age), and variations in health resulting from disease, accident or war. 'Workers' are
often implicitly assumed to be males with responsibility for family dependants, while work (employment) for women is seen as secondary to
family responsibilities (which are not regarded as 'work'). Unemployment
depends on the supply of jobs (an economic policy issue) as well as the
ability of the potential worker to perform the jobs available (an education
policy issue). In contrast to exploitation, exclusion is seen in terms of the
long-term structural unemployment of an 'underclass'.

Analyses of the ways in which capitalism generates insecurity and illfare
in particular contexts can usefully lead to the consideration of economic
policies for reducing them in conjunction with social policies to reduce
and/or compensate for them. However, the welfare regime model only
focuses on social policy, and the emphasis on labour and insecurity often
(1) lends itself to male bias, (2) crowds out discussion of the generation of
illfare outcomes among the non-employed – for example, the particular
plights of poor old people, unemployed single parents and poor children –
and (3) ignores other illfare generators: for example, violent conflict, as in
Northern Ireland. Also, in many contexts, processes of exclusion, defined

---

[5] These last two are, in fact, indications of social rather than individual well-being.

as 'an ubiquitous social process' involving various types of 'opportunity hoarding' (Tilly 1999), create categories of people with subordinate and marginalised identities, who are then easily exploited. It is analytically useful to recognise various degrees of exclusion: marginalised exploitative inclusion, marginalised non-exploitative inclusion,[6] 'expulsion' (as with refugees and internally displaced people) and 'extermination' (for example, ethnic or religious 'cleansing'). Even in advanced capitalist settings, a model which links analysis of the generation of different forms of exploitation and exclusion and life processes to livelihood and quality of life outcomes would be useful.

Mobilisation The focus here is on the working classes, capitalists and the government. However, there are other economic and political actors mobilising to reduce/increase the exploitation and exclusion involved in particular instances of modern capitalism. It is useful to analyse the ongoing mobilisations of those playing key roles in the maintenance, management and challenging of the 'political settlement' and related welfare mix and welfare outcomes. Some of these are domestic (for example the CBI, National Health Service managers, etc.) but increasingly there are regional (e.g. EU) and international (e.g. WTO) players. In recent years national and trans-national companies involved in private insurance, pensions, health and education have been increasingly mobilising in search of profit rather than the reduction of exploitation and exclusion.

Political settlements and welfare mix It is important to remember that the context of the political settlement is a Western democratic political system involving political parties with political programmes and election manifestos, regular changes of government, loyal oppositions, and interest group lobbying. Also, given that 'social policy' includes a range of practices, there may be different welfare mixes (more or less liberal/conservative/democratic) for different policy arenas. The allocation of government/market/community/family responsibility may vary depending on whether the issue is livelihood promotion (macro/microeconomic policies, company employment policies), livelihood protection (pensions, children's allowances, insurance, social assistance), care (housing, health services, social services) or self-development (education, training). Furthermore, given the underlying social inequality to be found

---

[6] These two forms of inclusion are both contained in the notion of 'adverse incorporation'. The former is harder to counter since, in addition to time preference problems (Wood, chapter 2 this volume), the exploiter has an interest in maintaining the relationship.

in all modern capitalist societies welfare regimes are informally stratified, with poorer people having no access to expensive market provisions and access to poorer government facilities across all the social policy dimensions, and very rich people depending almost totally on the market. And, while responsibility may be allocated to particular institutions, in practice they may fail to meet those responsibilities.

Stratification outcomes   Stratification outcomes are usually analysed in relation to the government, private sector and family interests created within particular welfare regimes. However, globalisation and regionalisation[7] processes are affecting both economic and social policy systems in advanced capitalist countries and allowing increasing roles in country welfare regimes for trans-state and inter-governmental actors who also develop their own interests.

Sensitising the welfare regime model to African conditions

For use in the African context (see chapter 6) the five headings identified above have to be 'sensitised' to African realities. In this section I describe this process and use it to generate a conceptual model, the in/security regime model, which can be used to analyse any regime which involves the generation of insecurity and illfare and mobilisations to reduce them. This involves exploring the major challenges that the welfare regime model faces and adapting it to take account of them. The key issues raised in the last section provide some assistance here.

In many discourses, sub-Saharan Africa is distinguished from 'Arabic' North Africa (grouped with the Middle East) and a special exception is made of South Africa. In chapter 6 I argue that it is useful to maintain a continental view that includes all countries in the land mass, while acknowledging the diversities found as a result of empirical research (rather than prior judgements), and the trans-continental networks and nodes which play important political economy and ideological roles. However, most of the evidence presented in this chapter comes from sub-Saharan Africa, and there is none from South Africa, although there are resonances with the experiences of sub-populations in both South and North Africa. The necessary focus on insecurity and illfare results in a highlighting of the problematic instances and aspects of African economies, polities, societies and cultures at the expense of their 'light sides'. The empirical conclusions described in this section come from a small deliberately

---

[7] See Room's chapter.

selected sample of critical social science studies. They are used to expose some extreme features of African regimes which any aspiring universal conceptual model must be able to handle and should not be interpreted in a simplistic way as applying to the whole continent all of the time.

Welfare outcomes: insecurity and illfare

Some evidence In the wider African context it is possible to identify states and processes of non-commodification, commodification and de-commodification which in specific contexts may be associated with greater or lesser insecurity and illfare. For example, sometimes commodification improves welfare and sometimes de-commodification reduces it. The same is true of states and processes of clientelisation and de-clientelisation. It is also necessary to consider insecurity and illfare generated by states and processes of 'conflictualisation' and 'deconflictualisation'. In other words there is a wider range of underlying economic and political relationships involved in the generation and amelioration of insecurity and illfare. Risks resulting from life processes are also greater as a result of a more dangerous environment and limited resources and material and organisational technologies to mitigate and compensate for them.

Adopting the Gough needs approach described above, it is possible to use statistics to provide outcome evidence at the individual level. The following 'approximate estimates' (World Bank 2001b: xiii) are taken from a recent report called *African Poverty at the Millennium*. It should be emphasised that the authors have considerable reservations about the quality of the data on which these estimates are based.[8]

The estimated total population of (sub-Saharan) Africa in 1995 was 580 million. Of these:
- 291 million people had average incomes of below $1 a day in 1998;
- 124 million of those up to the age of thirty-nine years were at risk of dying before forty;
- 43 million children were stunted as a result of malnutrition;
- 205 million people were estimated to be without access to health services in 1990–5;
- 249 million were without safe drinking water in 1990–5;
- More than 2 million infants die annually without reaching their first birthday;
- 139 million youths and adults were illiterate in 1995.

---

[8] Problems relating to the poor quality of African statistics are discussed further in chapter 6.

These outcomes are generated by poor livelihood chances, life processes occurring in a context of poor service provision, and the activities of other people seeking to secure or improve their own livelihood chances, in some cases through violent conflict. Personal suffering is often compounded in situations of conflict.

Child soldiers were treated very harshly. The boys were inducted through a process of initiation by which they were drugged and forced to commit some atrocity such as raping, killing or throwing someone into a well or river, on pain of being shot themselves for disobedience. At other times, they would be lined up by force to witness the execution of members of their family or friends, and if they refused or failed to applaud the executions, or cried or screamed, they were themselves executed (Abraham 2000: 10).

The HIV/AIDS pandemic is also causing considerable suffering, including the pain of related illnesses, fear of death, stigma and shame, threats to serious sex relationships, infection of babies, fears for children's futures, orphans, pain of bereavement, and new responsibilities for grandparents.

Sensitised definition of welfare outcomes   Social processes and relationships involving commodification, clientelisation, and in some cases conflict have darker and lighter sides for poor people depending on the context. There are good and bad markets, good and bad clients, conflict with good and bad resolutions. So, for example, in some contexts the absence of a patron increases insecurity and illfare, and at a social level a relatively peaceful patrimonial structure usually produces less illfare than a warlord structure.

At the individual level personal insecurity is defined as the danger of harm, while security involves protection from harm. 'Harm' is a bodily concept entailing death, physical and psychological damage, and anticipation of these in the future. A person may suffer harm as the result of exploitation and other forms of adverse incorporation, exclusion, or loss of or damage to (1) her body/psyche, (2) material 'things' she values and/or uses to generate income, (3) other people on whom she depends or whom she loves, and (4) her way of life and 'community', territorial and/or imagined. The content and relative salience of each of these sources of harm varies through gendered life cycles. In the model I use the concept of 'suffering' (Kleinman *et al.* 1997) to focus on the enormity of many of the personal experiences of harm generated by informal security and insecurity regimes in Africa and elsewhere, which cannot be captured in, or understood through, measures such as life expectancy or mortality rates. The concept of 'livelihood' focuses attention on a range of income-generating activities which are described below, and replaces the concept of the labour market.

The concept of *in/security outcomes* replaces 'welfare outcomes'. There are three types of outcome, related to (1) quality of underlying relationships, (2) suffering/subjective quality of life and (3) livelihoods.

The generation of insecurity and illfare

Some evidence African economies cannot be described as capitalist, although, in different ways, and with different levels of engagement, capitalism is a key player in these economies. Outside North and South Africa[9] there are relatively few indigenous African capitalists; most African 'economic actors' are relatively poor[10] and 'households' and people in many urban and rural areas are involved in a mixture of diversified livelihood activities, often crossing urban–rural spaces (Ferguson 1999; Francis 2000). Many of these activities are neither 'productive' nor 'human reproductive', and relatively few are found in competitive labour markets. They involve investment in social networks, rent-seeking, and/or 'primitive accumulation' which may involve violence. Those marketed and non-marketed activities which are productive include subsistence farming, pastoralism, cash-cropping, agricultural wage labour, house-building and maintenance, petty trade, petty manufacture including handicrafts, transport and other wage labour, while human reproductive activities include both unpaid[11] and marketed petty and professional services. Other sources of income include begging, theft and petty corruption. Most 'formal sectors' are small and employ relatively little wage labour. Governments employ soldiers, bureaucrats, other white-collar workers, university teachers, other teachers, health professionals and support staff. They often pay very low and irregular salaries, forcing occupants to seek additional sources of income. There are relatively good income opportunities for private education and health professionals, some of whom combine public and private work.

A few Africans, mostly political leaders, are very rich, and there are opportunities for wealth in politics (through access to government revenues,

---

[9] Regional and other diversities are discussed in chapter 6.

[10] Though there is considerable structured inequality among 'the poor' involving relationships of exploitation, exclusion, domination, destruction and rectification *among* them.

[11] These occur within and across 'households'. However, while most development economists using household surveys are prepared to put a value on non-marketed agricultural products, their unwillingness to put a value on non-marketed non-agricultural products and services (mostly performed by women and children) leads to the exclusion of much economic activity from the formal statistics. Non-market economies in Africa are discussed further in chapter 6.

including aid, and bribery opportunities), mining, timber exploitation, larger-scale manufacturing and trade, 'capitalist' farming, the higher levels of the bureaucracy, military and NGO world, as well as the worlds of warlords, militias, smugglers and scams. African regimes also include important non-African economic actors among whom are: international migrants and diasporas; the World Bank, the IMF, the WTO and regional financial institutions; finance capitalists; bilateral donors; international NGOs; academics; trans-national corporations (TNCs) mining oil, gold, copper, and other minerals; diamond dealers; arms dealers; drug dealers; money launderers; mercenaries; TNCs growing or buying tea, coffee, chocolate and tobacco, etc. and selling pharmaceuticals, fertiliser, machinery, etc.; consumers and private investors (including pension funds) from developed countries. In this context exploitation, or the extraction of surplus labour, is only one of the mechanisms involved in the generation of insecurity and illfare, while control of 'the means of production' is rarely based on legal ownership in the European sense. Also, while processes of exclusion are heavily implicit in the generation of insecurity and illfare, they often do not produce a 'catastrophic break' with a larger society. Relationships between these economic and political actors seeking livelihoods and influence at different levels involve complex mixes of exploitation, exclusion, coercion and redistribution. Insecurity and illfare are also generated by problematic life processes, many of which are left to run their course in the context of 'government failure' and 'market failure'.

Furthermore, political and military activities, much of it by people who control the government (or the 'state'), often generate illfare rather than welfare, including mass violent deaths and injuries. Most African states are 'bifurcated' (Mamdani 1996), 'hybrid' or 'rhizome' (Bayart 1993), and neo-patrimonial (Medard 1992). Many are 'weak' (Jackson and Rosberg 1983), and 'lame Leviathans' (Callaghy 1987), and some are collapsed (Zartman 1995), fictitious (Sandbrook 1985), 'shadow' (Reno 1995), 'shows', 'vampire' (Attiyeh 1999), 'alimentary spaces' (Mbembe 1992), and 'criminal' (Bayart *et al.* 1999). None are welfare states and few can make a serious claim to be developmental. Economic policy management has often been poor and driven by personal or internal political considerations, and while there have been multi-party elections in many countries since the early 1990s, these have not led to democratic accountability in the way Westerners understand the term (Joseph 1999). In addition, real economies, polities, societies and cultures often do not coincide, and are not described by country borders; in some instances they overlap borders, while in others they do not include the whole country. The major legitimation of African states has come from the international political system rather than inhabitants (Clapham 1996), and internal politics have always interacted with wider international political structures, processes and events (e.g. the Cold War and Islamism). Violence and coercion play an important role in most polities and economies, often supported by resources and actors from outside the continent.

'Communities' and 'households' are probably as much involved in the generation of insecurity and illfare as they are in rectifying it. In fact, there are huge problems in using these concepts to describe local African structures, and researchers working in local languages frequently find it difficult to find appropriate translations. As used in donor development discourse they usually come with inbuilt Western assumptions: for example, that communities are found in villages that offer their members 'a fairly comprehensive universe' (van Binsbergen et al. 1986: 283). While this is sometimes the case, research in Central African villages has found them to be 'the scene of an uneasy truce between strangers, only temporarily constructed into community' (ibid.: 284). Comparative Ethiopian research in fifteen 'villages' (Bevan and Pankhurst 1996), revealed a range of community structures and livelihood strategies. For example, one settlement, where people shared history, religion and subculture in a grain-surplus locality, was geographically and socially well integrated and rich in livelihood- and welfare-enhancing institutions. This can be contrasted with a fairly recent and expanding peri-urban settlement of people from four 'ethnicities' (of differential status) and three religions, which, while it offered improving diversified livelihood opportunities 'on average', also offered visible conflict, exploitation and exclusion. Most of the 'villages' depended on external economic and political players, with those in famine-prone areas locked in a relation of aid dependency with donors/NGOs/government. In many African contexts people networked in economic and social relationships are increasingly involved in 'straddling' urban and rural economic spaces.

Throughout the continent there is also a huge variety (1) in household structures (as figure 3.1 illustrates), (2) in the stability of household structures,[12] (3) in gender relations within households and communities, and (4) in the salience of household boundaries for the sharing of production and service activities, assets, income, food consumption, roof, sexual relationships, and responsibility for children. Furthermore, in many places 'traditional' structures are having to adapt to migration, war, displacement and HIV/AIDS. The terms 'community' and 'household' do not describe well the networks of relationship to be found in African societies

---

[12] Among the Amhara of Ethiopia it is not uncommon to find older people who have been 'married' more than ten times and sometimes more than twenty.

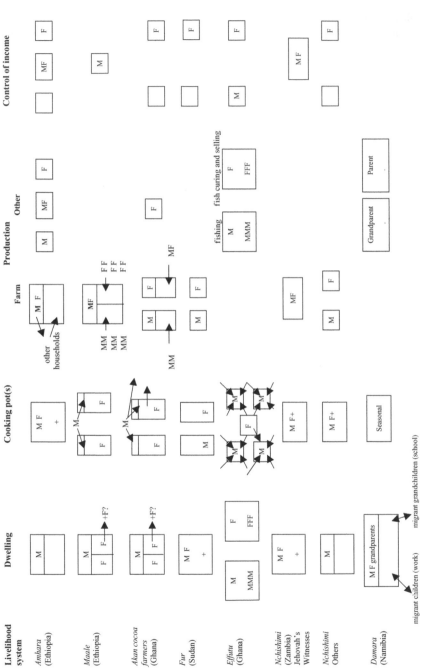

Figure 3.1. Some examples of variations in 'ideal' African household structures

which have always been flexible and dynamic, and which, in the past thirty years (and more in some cases), have been subject to huge and ongoing changes as a result of war, insecurity, political and 'developmental' interventions, economic decline or restructuring, and HIV/AIDS. Both 'community' and 'household' are dynamic, socially constructed, unequal structures (the latter nested in different ways in the former) which themselves need to be analysed as in/security regimes involving relationships of exploitation and exclusion based on sex and age, as well as class, caste, ethnicity, bodily state[13] and any other locally salient status base.

Sensitised definition of the generation of insecurity and illfare   In/security results from divisions of labour in terms of activities based on differential access to/control over livelihood resources[14] which involve a range of exploitative, exclusionary, dominating, destructive and rectification mechanisms, and a range of sub-national, trans-national, international and global structures, actors and dynamics. These activities generate livelihoods at various levels, many of which are inadequate. Suffering also results from political violence and from life processes which are not insured against, or compensated for by public action.

There are six major processes, often working simultaneously, involved in the generation of personal insecurity for those Africans on the receiving end: exploitation, exclusion, domination, destruction, economic failure, decline or collapse, and 'natural' life processes, calamities and diseases. The first four of these processes[15] also generate benefits to those in the superior power position. They are managed, and challenged, through coercion[16] and the social construction of institutions, and cultural meanings in a context of unequal power. The major, interpenetrating, arenas where these relationships are played out are polity (replaces 'state'), economy (replaces 'market'), society (replaces 'community') and kin networks (replaces 'household'). Within these arenas, in different empirical contexts, 'state', 'market', 'community' and 'household' are variably constituted and have variable importance. In all empirical contexts it is necessary to explore the particularities of their constitution, as well as the constitution of other organisations and institutions involved in the particular in/security regime under study.

---

[13] Particularly disabilities of all kinds and in many cases HIV/AIDS infection.
[14] Including the means of domination, the means of production and exchange, the means of relationship and reproduction, and the means of persuasion.
[15] Which may also usefully be seen as relationships and/or mechanisms.
[16] '[A]ll concerted application, threatened or actual, of action that commonly causes loss or damage' (Tilly 1999: 36).

In the in/security regime model we are interested in the *generation of insecurity and illfare* which includes the generation of inadequate livelihoods and incomes as a result of exploitation, exclusion and economic decline, the inability to deal with natural vicissitudes, and the generation of individual suffering and social destruction resulting from political domination and violent conflict.

Responses of affected actors: political mobilisation outcomes

Some evidence   In this context we do not find a working class mobilising to ameliorate the problems produced by capitalism. The many kinds of actor described above are 'mobilising' in diverse but interacting economic, social, cultural, and political directions. These mobilisations involve combinations of loyalty, exit and voice. In the process new forms of agency and legitimacy are socially constructed (Duffield 2001: ch. 6).

Sensitised definition of political mobilisation outcomes   An in/security regime is one where the activities and relationships governed by the regime's institutions generate (1) benefits to those in power and (2) suffering to those who are exploited and/or dominated, excluded from opportunities and/or physically attacked. Those with power engage in activities designed to maintain and enhance their benefits, to keep power, and (sometimes) to promote social improvement. They have three main (non-exclusionary) routes for mobilisation in relation to others: (1) seeking loyalty through, for example, patron–client networks[17] (which may be more or less exploitative), charisma, ideological legitimisation and persuasion, and/or responding to 'voice' with action to improve livelihoods and/or services generally; (2) the exclusion of competing groups from resources and opportunities, in some cases to the point of 'extermination'; and (3) repression of opposition or 'voice'. They also have the option of seeking external relationships and resources. The 'sufferers' have three major 'mobilisation' options: loyalty, exit and voice. These strategies take a variety of interacting political, economic, social and cultural forms. When the exploited exercise voice they are trying to change vertical structures of inequality. When the excluded exercise voice they are sometimes seeking some or greater inclusion and sometimes to wrest control of resources from those who have excluded them – to change the regime elite rather than the regime itself.

[17] Over time these can 'solidify' into 'informal security regimes'.

In the in/security regime model, we are interested in all forms of *mobilisation* in response to the generation of insecurity and the search for security.

Political settlements and the welfare mix

Some evidence   At times the interacting mobilisations of the actors involved in a particular situation generate periods of political equilibrium (a more appropriate word than 'settlement' which implies some level of agreement and acceptance of some shared norms and values); at other times situations are marked by slow change, rapid change or 'chaos'[18] so that it is impossible to identify a 'regime' with a relatively predictable future trajectory. The characterisation of institutional 'responsibility' for 'welfare' using the differentiated concepts of 'state', 'market', 'community' and 'household', which are problematic in many developing contexts, are magnified in the African context. To an extent they relate to the relative lack of development of the division of labour, and the consequent socio-cultural interpenetration of kin, wider social networks, economy and polity. Political structures are 'marketised' and 'familialised'[19] and economic structures are politicised (in patron–client structures) because the same people, or their relatives, cronies or clients are operating throughout. Many of these structures are also 'violentised'. Another problem is the considerable amount of production and exchange that goes on outside 'the market' through barter or longer-term social exchange arrangements, or is 'informal', i.e. takes place beyond the formal jurisdiction of the state.[20] For example, smuggling is a regular response to attempts at state regulation and trade taxation (see chapter 6).

Figure 3.2 shows the main analytic components of what I have called the current African 'rectification mix'. I am using the word 'rectification' since the adjective 'welfare' seems inappropriate to describe some of the activities in the mix, which, while they generate livelihoods and social protection for the perpetrators and their households, involve the adverse incorporation[21] or exclusion[22] of some or all of the members and/or directly

---

[18] 'Under the right circumstances, the slightest uncertainty can grow until the system's future becomes utterly unpredictable – or, in a word, chaotic' (Waldrop 1992: 66).

[19] There is a lot of intermarriage between the families of political leaders, and it is noticeable that the recently murdered president of Congo, Dr Laurent Kabila, was replaced by his son.

[20] In Mozambique it is thought that the conventional economy only accounts for half of the country's GNP; in Kenya (and Russia) it is estimated at 40 per cent (Duffield 2001: 141).

[21] For example, the sale of a child into slavery.

[22] For example, the starving of a child to gain access to food aid.

Analytic arena	Roles for domestic actors[a] (examples)	External actors
Polity	*'Formal government'*: Ministries pursuing formal social policy, e.g. government schools and health service providers; food aid; regulators *'Informal government'* (through patronage): government politicians, bureaucrats, military, professionals *Non-government political actors* Legitimate and illegitimate opposition party members; chiefs/kings; religious leaders; guerrillas; militias	International development and humanitarian organisations, regional organisations, national 'donors'
Market	*'Formal'*: Private employers, insurance companies, private schools, private health services providers *'Informal'*: Pharmacists, traditional medical practitioners, 'witches' and 'witchfinders'	TNCs as employers or providers of insurance, education, pharmaceuticals, health services, etc.
Society	Neighbours, Big Men, clerics, congregations, religious schools, religious health services, community-based organisations including women's groups, hometown associations, secret societies, trade unions, development NGOs, burial societies, ROSCAs, other local organisations, altruists, bandits	International development and 'humanitarian' NGOs
Kin	Lineage members, clan members, 'households', extended family (including domestic migrants)	International migrants and diasporas
Self	Self as domestic resident	Self as international migrant

[a]Some actors play more than one role.

Figure 3.2. Main components of the current African rectification mix

damage or remove the livelihoods, life chances and lives of others.[23] It is important to recognise the extent to which poor African individuals fail to access resources for survival through state, market, community *or* household; some find other sources while the fate of others is visible in the high morbidity and mortality rates. It is also important to acknowledge the large number of external members of 'the mix', including international migrants and diasporas, the international financial institutions, UN organisations concerned with development and humanitarian aid, international development and humanitarian NGOs, and bilateral and regional donors.

At the level of rhetoric, there is a donor-driven Eurocentric 'social policy' agenda for aid-dependent African countries in which welfare outcomes are chiefly defined in terms of consumption, poverty, life expectancy and formal education. This rhetoric is increasingly driving aid policy and practice. This relatively new social policy agenda matches the

---

[23] For example, the military hijacking of humanitarian aid.

longer-running economic policy agenda of the World Bank to promote economic growth through 'commodification': liberalisation and privatisation in the context of 'sound macro-economic policies' geared to produce low inflation rates and economic stability (World Bank 2001a: 49) to encourage international trade and inward foreign investment. Government expenditure should be pro-poor, guided by a government-owned poverty reduction strategy paper (PRSP).[24] Access to concessional aid in the form of highly indebted poor countries (second round) (HIPC2) funds, IMF poverty reduction and growth facilities (PRGFs) and World Bank poverty reduction support credits (PRSCs) depends on international financial institution (IFI)[25] approval of the PRSP. Most bilateral donor aid also depends on this approval. One feature of approved PRSPs is an emphasis on formal primary education and primary (cosmopolitan) healthcare. While there is increasing discussion of 'social protection' there are few established formal arrangements in sub-Saharan Africa, mostly confined to government employees,[26] and the current donor emphasis is on 'productivist' social policy.

The *World Development Report* (World Bank 2001a) also proposes a political agenda to make state institutions more accountable and responsive to its citizens, especially poor people. This involves support for 'civil society', local government reform, and programmes, implemented by NGOs, aimed at changing the beliefs, attitudes, behaviour and social relationships of poor people through 'participation' and 'empowerment'. Many involve the provision of micro-credit (more 'commodification'). There is also a separately organised and funded 'humanitarian' agenda to assist those caught up in 'complex emergencies', which often combine violence and famine. In recent years the development and military security agendas have grown closer (Duffield 2001). Roles that some of these external players have played in particular African in/security regimes are examined in chapter 6, and the networks and discourses of the donor contributors to the 'welfare mix' in poor countries are discussed below.

Sensitised definition of political settlements and the welfare mix   In all regimes we find partial countervailing pressures and processes towards the reduction of insecurity, which include idiosyncratic mixes of redistribution, reciprocity (including patronage and 'inter-generational bargains'[27]) empowerment, inclusion, pacification, economic growth and/or formal and informal market[28] insurance. As a result of recent

---

[24] In the African context often written by international consultants contracted by donors.
[25] I.e. the IMF and the World Bank.
[26] South Africa and Namibia are partial exceptions here.
[27] Which, in the event, are not always able to be kept.
[28] For example, the *idir*, or funeral societies, which have spread in rural Ethiopia.

globalisation processes and changes in international political structures we must be conceptually prepared to deal with new kinds of actors, structures and dynamics.

Thus, in any empirical context, we have to identify the set of institutions (socially constructed norms and rules) identifying how, and who is, to (try to) deal with the insecurity generated by the unfettered operation of the pursuit of interests by other people, particularly the powerful. The institutions guiding the activities of the actors create a further set of interests and only sometimes represent a 'political settlement' between powerful exploiters and those they exploit and/or partly exclude, although periods of political equilibrium or stability can be identified. In these diverse and complex situations processes of rectification can involve a range of different 'internal' and 'external' actors, meaning that different rectification mixes need to be identified empirically.

Political dis/equilibria and rectification mix replaces 'political settlements and welfare mix'.

Stratification outcomes

Some evidence   These involve complex structures of exploitation and exclusion socially constructed by a range of social actors, and multiple 'political equilibria' and episodes of 'disequilibria' embedded in empirically varying, stratified *and* segmented, dynamic economic, political, social and cultural structures with varying relationships to physical territory. The key point about African in/security regimes is that the institutions of 'state', and 'market', which many development theorists propose are, or should be, the leading responsible elements in the 'welfare mix', actually are, in many cases, the active generators of the insecurity that requires rectification. Also, as figure 3.2 shows, many of the contributors to African in/security regimes are not African, and the interests created as a result of their contributions to the 'welfare mix' are often powerful.[29] Furthermore, since politics and violence often take precedence over economic production for access to resources and income, relationships of domination and destruction must also be taken into account.

Sensitised definition of 'stratification outcomes'   The institutions/ organisations which create a new set of interests as a result of their welfare provision may include government, market and family (kin rather than household), and also 'community'. However there are a range of other 'providers' with interests (see figure 3.2), key among whom are

---

[29] The interests and discourse of what Duffield describes as 'an emerging system of global governance' (2001: 2) are described below.

military organisations of various kinds and members of the development and humanitarian aid industries.

There is no need to change the concept of *stratification outcomes*; however, there is a need for a wider definition of the 'stakeholders' involved in in/security regimes.

Dynamic insecurity regimes in Africa

Regime dynamics involve path-dependent upward and downward trends and spirals as well as 'natural', economic, political, military, social and cultural 'shocks' or sudden changes. The 'macro-level' insecurity regimes and contentious episodes (McAdam *et al.* 2001) that can be identified in Africa since the 'independence decade' of the 1960s have rarely been spatially bounded (since they usually contain at least one powerful external player) or socially closed, and what boundaries exist are not often those of the nation-state; while societies, cultures, economies and polities are often 'overlapping sets' in spatial terms, they rarely all coincide with each other or with the nation-state as defined by the international political system. Many of these regimes have been involved in one or more social reconstructions and suffered periods of disequilibrium with knock-on effects for the 'meso-level' in/security regimes at 'household' and 'community' levels contained within them.

The in/security regime model

This is a conceptual model for thinking about the structures, relationships, actors, activities and dynamics involved in the generation and alleviation of insecurity and illfare. Its origins in the welfare regime model are described above, but it can also be seen as the bringing together of two erstwhile 'rival' development sociology approaches, involving structures (Buttel and McMichael 1994) and 'actors' (Long and van der Ploeg 1994), recognising that structures are (dynamically) socio-culturally constructed (reproduced and changed) through the activities of actors in real time, but also that, at points in time, different actors occupy different interest and power positions within structures, giving them different goals and different degrees of autonomy and clout. The playing out of the relationships of power constituted in these structures underlies the distributions of consumption and life chances[30] captured in the statistics collected by international organisations. A regime can only be identified

---

[30] See Goldthorpe and Bevan (1977) for an analysis of social stratification in Britain in these terms.

in retrospect when there has been a reasonable period during which the rectification mix and related stratification outcomes remain in rough equilibrium. Shorter periods of equilibrium are better described as 'episodes', with periods of disequilibrium identified as transition episodes. These are often 'contentious' (McAdam *et al.* 2001).

European welfare regimes had their birth in the Second World War and, because of fairly linear path dependence and stable stratification outcomes, it is often argued that in terms of welfare mix and relative welfare outcomes they have remained identifiably the same since then (i.e. conservative, liberal or social democratic).[31] Over the same period in/security regimes in other parts of the world have been more volatile, and in many places mix and outcomes have been hugely affected during rapid transitions and longer episodes of insecurity. The trajectories of many country regimes have not been linear, a key example being the countries of the former Soviet Union, and path dependence has involved complex interactions between revivals/inventions of 'tradition' and 'modernity', and punctuated equilibria. The in/security regime model can be used to explore periods of equilibrium and periods of transition and fits well with analyses based on complexity and chaos theory metaphors (Byrne 1998; Eve *et al.* 1997; Duffield 2001).

This model has five key elements: the (economic, political and life process) generation of inadequate livelihoods and suffering; mobilisation outcomes; rectification mix; in/security outcomes; and stratification outcomes. This allows potentially for five 'spaces of comparison'. While much of the analysis in this book focuses on comparisons across the rectification mix / in/security outcomes spaces, an understanding of what is going on in the generation/mobilisation/stratification spaces is key to understanding insecurity and illfare in poor developing country contexts.[32] The model can be used to analyse and compare regimes in any social context where there are interacting economic and political structures and dynamics entailing mixes of relations of exploitation, domination, exclusion, and/or destruction (plus life processes producing dependency) which potentially produce poverty and suffering which are more or less rectified through counteracting relationships involving regulation, reciprocity, redistribution and the maintenance of social order.

There are two key ways of looking at in/security regimes, both of which should be used together.[33] The first involves the identification of

---

[31] See, for example, Barrientos' chapter 4 in this volume.

[32] This reflects the fact that global, international and national economic policies and political strategies are much more important for the welfare of people in poor countries than social policies at equivalent levels.

[33] The need for both wave and particle approaches to the analysis of light provides an analogue.

a particular type of regime on the basis of the dominant underlying economic and political relationships which generate insecurity and illfare. We have identified three: commodification, clientelisation and political contention which are associated with welfare regimes, informal security regimes and insecurity regimes. Under current conditions of globalisation such regimes are not typically uniquely contained and/or totally diffused within nation-state boundaries. This is most likely to be the case for full-blooded welfare regimes which depend on powerful well-functioning states, and least likely to be the case for insecurity regimes, since the state is usually a focus for contention, and the regime usually includes powerful external players.

The second approach involves analysis at country level which, depending on empirical context, will identify differently balanced 'regime mixes', with welfare regimes for one section of the population, informal security regimes for another section, and insecurity regimes for the remainder. In European contexts the overwhelming majority of the population residing within national boundaries belong to a national welfare regime and only very tiny minorities are involved in informal security regimes (e.g. illegal immigrants) and insecurity regimes (e.g. a few in Northern Ireland). However, I would argue that this is not the case for a number of Latin American countries, and that rather than Latin America having a 'liberal-informal' welfare regime (Barrientos, chapter 4), different Latin American countries have differently balanced regime mixes of (liberal) welfare, informal security and insecurity regimes. In chapter 6 I suggest that most African countries have quadri-furcated regime mixes: the very rich rely heavily on the burgeoning international liberal (market-based) welfare regime; the next tier use a mix of government services and domestic market provision depending on the quality of the former (national-level welfare regime); the third group relies on informal security regimes similar to those described by Wood in chapter 2; while the fourth group are embroiled in violent crisis situations involving the failure of state, market, community, and often family welfare institutions. The exact mix in different country contexts can only be established through detailed empirical research. In/security regimes, which need not be territorially contained, nor include everyone living within a territory,[34] can be identified at global, regional, country, cross-country and sub-country levels;[35] they range from the relatively benevolent (welfare regimes) to

---

[34] The increasing non-territoriality of regimes under current conditions of 'globalisation' poses problems for traditions of analysis which prioritise states and national economies; however, as this book shows, the model can be fruitfully used in a number of different ways so long as the desire to overgeneralise is controlled.

[35] Households, wider kin organisations, farms, villages, formal and informal enterprises, mafias, NGOs, universities, etc.

the actively destructive (insecurity regimes). In practice real regimes have varying lifespans with periods of regime transition often associated with increased insecurity and suffering.[36] The five headings of the in/security regime model can be used to produce detailed methodologies designed to analyse particular regimes. The following schedule, designed for the African context, is used in a number of ways in chapter 6.

1. *In/security outcomes*
   - Quality of underlying relationships
   - Suffering
   - Livelihoods
2. *The generation of in/security*
   - World context: economic, political and socio-cultural structures, actors and ideologies
   - Regime context: economic, political and socio-cultural structures, actors and ideologies
   - Life processes
3. *Mobilisation*
   - Internal elite mobilisation
   - Mobilisation by external regime members
   - Non-elite mobilisation
4. *Political dis/equilibria and rectification mix*
   - 'Government' policies and actors
   - 'External' policies and actors
   - 'Market' opportunities and actors
   - 'Other societal' policies and actors
   - 'Family/household' policies and actors
   - Self
5. *Stratification outcomes*
   - Internal interests
   - External interests

The in/security model can be widely applied (so long as the model is 'sensitised' to local conditions and meanings) in a comparative way in a range of empirical contexts to gain understanding of the generation and alleviation of insecurity and related path-dependent stratification outcomes. For example, applied at 'household' level it focuses attention on: (1) the distribution of harm among people seen as being 'within the household' and the quality of relationships between males and females, between older and younger people of all ages, and between family and non-family members; (2) the role of relationships with external players, the cultural values and beliefs within and outside the household which uphold or undermine the

---

[36] As in the transition from socialism in the former Soviet Union and Eastern Europe.

relationships; (3) the location of the 'household economy' in the wider local, national and global context; (4) the status of the 'household' in the 'wider community/society'; and (5) the ways in which wider economic and political changes have impacted on differently located household-based regimes. The analysis also recognises that 'household' regimes have dynamics. Use of the model at local, 'imagined community', and internal regional levels generates information on the wider structures of power that are socially constructed by, and simultaneously constrain, the actions of members of differentially located households. There is also scope for using the model to analyse the different ways in which different households, villages, imagined communities, and other small structures relate to each other and fit into wider in/security regimes. The model opens up a research programme for analysing the interacting global-to-local structural generation of livelihood failure and suffering and the real effects of attempts to counter them.

The global in/security regime

In this section, relying heavily on the work of Manuel Castells, I use the model to explore very briefly some of the features of the global in/security regime which contains an extremely unequal regime mix of welfare regimes, informal security regimes and insecurity regimes, some of which are described in this volume

In/security outcomes

In the mid-1990s, taking as the extreme poverty line a consumption equivalent to one US dollar a day, 1.3 billion people, accounting for 33% of the developing world's population were in misery. Of these poor people 550 million lived in South Asia, 215 million in sub-Saharan Africa, and 150 million in Latin America . . . The largest concentration of poverty was, by far, in the rural areas (Castells 1998: 82).

However, there are also growing pockets of poverty in the advanced economies; for example, the US 'has displayed, in the past two decades, a substantial increase in social inequality, polarisation, poverty and misery' (*ibid.*: 129). In 1994 there were 38 million Americans living below the national poverty line. A considerable amount of poverty in advanced countries is associated with inner-city and suburban ghettos where the form social exclusion takes indicates the 'catastrophic break' with the wider society described by Room (1999). The collapse of socialism in the late 1980s and subsequent economic and political restructuring in the countries of the former Soviet Union and Eastern Europe have produced considerable poverty and suffering. There has also been widespread suffering associated with violence and war. UNICEF estimated that between 1985 and 1995 2 million children were killed, between 4 and 5 million were disabled, over 1 million were orphaned or separated from their parents, 12 million were left homeless, and over 10 million were psychologically traumatised (Castells 1998: 157). Death and disability from infectious diseases and malnutrition are strongly associated with poverty and/or war.

The generation of in/security

The relationships and processes underlying these outcomes vary, depending on the way in which (changing) local economic and political structures articulate with (changing) wider national and trans-national networks and structures. Pakistani children sewing footballs for sixteen hours a day are exploited through commodification; child slaves in Sudan are exploited through domination; excluded children in the *favelas* of Brazil die from lack of food and disease; children in Angola die through treading on landmines; etc.

At the roots of children's exploitation are the mechanisms generating poverty and social exclusion throughout the world, from sub-Saharan Africa to the United States of America. With children in poverty, and with entire countries, regions, and neighbourhoods excluded from relevant circuits of wealth, power, and information, the crumbling of family structures breaks the last barrier of defence for children (*ibid.*: 159).

In the later decades of the twentieth century, capitalism took on new forms with the spread of information technology. Following Castells (1996: 147), it is possible to identify a new international division of labour constructed around four different positions in the global economy: the producers of high value, based on 'informational labour'; the producers of high volume, based on low-cost labour; the producers of raw materials, based on natural endowments; and 'the redundant producers, reduced to devalued labour'. This level of exclusion involves economic production and exchange of no international value. 'Informationalism does create a sharp divide between valuable and non-valuable people and locales' (Castells 1998: 161). There is a cross-cutting dimension relating to legality and 'formality'; the activities of international criminal and shadow economies are hidden.

In all countries there is a mix of these economies; the size of each element of the mix varies according to the way in which the country's economic structures articulate with the wider global economy. Position in the international division of labour depends on the characteristics of a country's labour and technology which 'are enacted and modified by governments and entrepreneurs' (Castells 1996: 147). Non-valuable people and locales fall into the 'black holes of informational capitalism' (*ibid.*: 147). The global economy is currently organised around three major economic regions: Europe, North America and the Asian Pacific. Around each centre an economic hinterland has been created and some countries are gradually being incorporated into the global capitalist economy. 'However, the intertwining of economic processes between the three regions makes them practically inseparable in their fate' (*ibid.*).

Politics and war also play a role in the generation of illfare and insecurity. The transformation of capitalism has had profound effects on the international political system. Socialist structures could not adapt to the information revolution and subsequent restructuring has involved conflict and war in many areas, including former Yugoslavia, Tajikistan, Azerbaijan, Chechnya, Albania, etc. The collapse of the Soviet Union has left the US in a hegemonic position as a result of its technological superiority, particularly in armaments. US foreign policy appears largely driven by the interests of US-based capital, including the oil industry. The main political enemy is now 'terrorism' mostly arising out of Islamist networks with bases in Afghanistan, Pakistan, Saudi Arabia and Iran, and threats from 'rogue states' such as Iraq and North Korea. The US has a history of militarised intervention in Latin America, related to the threat of socialism and the drugs trade. With little economic interest, conflicts in Africa have tended to be ignored, particularly after the problems that the US experienced in Somalia in 1993.

At the level of static analysis, a key distinction is that between those welfare and developmental states where governments have control over national territory, and authority that depends on a political bargain which involves economic and social development, and those states where this is not the case. Within this category there is a second distinction: between those states which have been (stably) captured by elites for their own patrimonial purposes and those where aspiring elites are in violent competition for economic resources and/or control of state resources. This last group has recently included regimes in transition (particularly from socialism), as well as regimes where such conflict appears to be becoming endemic.

Mobilisation

The social dynamics of what Castells calls 'the network society' includes state apparatuses, global networks of various kinds, self-centred individuals, 'resistance identities' based both on traditional values (e.g. God, nation, family) and new ones (e.g. feminism, environmentalism), and, potentially, project identities 'able to reconstruct a new civil society of sorts, and, eventually, a new state' (Castells 1997: 356). In this context bottom-up mobilisation against exploitation and exclusion takes a wide variety of exit and voice forms including migration, political activity based on organisation and solidarity, and the social adaptation and construction of local institutions. Some mobilisation leads to violent conflict that generates its own insecurity and illfare. Disagreeing with some aspects of Castells' characterisation of the 'fourth world' as excluded and redundant, Duffield has recently argued that 'coming from the South there has been an expansion of transborder and shadow economic activity that has forged new local–global linkages with the liberal world system and, in so doing, new patterns of actual development and political authority – that is alternative and non-liberal forms of protection, legitimacy and social regulation' (Duffield 2001: 2).

In the face of these 'emerging political complexes' the North is responding to the threat 'of the excluded south fomenting international instability through conflict, criminal activity and terrorism' (*ibid.*) Duffield identifies an 'emerging system of global governance' with the goals of 'riot control' and poor relief. This system, which he describes as constituting 'liberal peace' (rather than 'new imperialism'), includes international financial institutions, UN organisations, inter-governmental organisations, international NGOs, bilateral donors and influential thinktanks, working in multi-disciplinary and multi-sectoral networks. It is bringing together a network of people and organisations from the 'development industry', the 'humanitarian aid industry' and an emerging 'conflict-resolution industry'. 'Emerging from the North, the networks of international public policy have thickened and multiplied their points of engagement and control. Many erstwhile functions of the nation state have been abandoned to these international networks as power and authority have been reconfigured' (*ibid.*: 9). The encounter of this emerging system of global governance with the emerging political complexes has formed a new and complex development–security terrain with a fluctuating border and in many places involving relations of accommodation and complicity.

Rectification mix for poor countries

The aim of liberal peace is to transform dysfunctional war-affected states into cooperative, representative stable entities (*ibid.*: 11) using resources to shift the balance of power between groups and to try to change attitudes and behaviour. In conflict situations 'old humanitarianism' responded directly to the needs of the people adversely affected by it. The 'new humanitarianism' is based on consequentialist ethics: 'do no harm' (Anderson 1999). In poor countries without 'war' the international financial institutions and donors move in with advice, technical assistance and resources to restructure governments to enable them to pursue the macro-economic policies which are now seen as required for success in the Northern-controlled global economy. In this context policies are no longer designed to produce a national economy: countries must fit into the wider global economy on the basis of 'comparative advantage' established through exposure to global markets. Economic growth is expected to result from liberalisation and privatisation. As described above for Africa, all countries bidding for concessional aid (HIPC2 debt relief, IMF poverty reduction and growth facilities, and/or World Bank poverty reduction support credits) must produce a poverty reduction strategy paper describing their anti-poverty programme.[37] While this paper should be developed in consultation with local 'civil society' it also has to be approved by the IMF and the World Bank. For example, it is expected that government social policy expenditure will focus on primary education and primary healthcare (a 'productivist' agenda). Superficial acknowledgement of problems associated with patrimonial structures and corruption has led to a programme for 'building civil society' and establishing 'multi-party democracy'.

Stratification outcomes

The 'liberal way of war', which involves a blurring of the distinction between people, armies and government, has constructed emerging non-liberal political complexes which are socially exclusive, exploitative and destructive. Furthermore there is a blurring of 'war' and 'peace'. 'In many parts of the South, countries at war, recovering from war, or indeed, with no experience of war can all appear remarkably similar'[38] (Duffield 2001: 188). Duffield argues that these conflicts should be seen as sites of innovation and reordering rather than breakdown and chaos. The liberal peace

---

[37] In November 2002 the following countries were engaged in the PRSP process: Albania, Armenia, Azerbaijan, Benin, Bolivia, Burkina Faso, Cambodia, Cameroon, Cape Verde, Central African Republic, Chad, Democratic Republic of the Congo, Ivory Coast, Djibouti, Ethiopia, The Gambia, Georgia, Ghana, Guinea, Guinea-Bissau, Guyana, Honduras, Kenya, Kyrgyz Republic, Lao People's Democratic Republic, Lesotho, Macedonia (former Yugoslav Republic of), Madagascar, Malawi, Mali, Mauritania, Moldova, Mongolia, Mozambique, Nicaragua, Niger, Pakistan, Rwanda, São Tomé and Príncipe, Senegal, Sierra Leone, Tajikistan, Tanzania, Uganda, Vietnam, Yemen, Yugoslavia, Zambia: (www.imf.org/external/np/prsp/prsp.asp).

[38] In peacetime El Salvador in 1995 there were 8,500 murders, compared with a yearly average of 6,250 during the conflict. In South Africa 27,000 people were murdered in 1997 compared with 12,000 in 1989.

reflects the normalisation of violence and acceptance of instability in some parts of the world (*ibid.*: 17) as a result of de-bureaucratisation and the attenuation of nation-state competence in parts of Africa, Afghanistan and the former Soviet Union.

As contributors to the international welfare mix, the development, humanitarian and burgeoning conflict-reduction industries are sites of considerable interests and power. The ostensible purpose of these industries is the transformation of the poor economies and societies of the world, but, as a result of political and disciplinary differences, there are ongoing struggles[39] about (1) what kind of transformation should be the goal and (2) how social change can be engineered. There are few thorough studies of the aid industry, but it is arguable that the chief beneficiaries have often been members of the industry rather than those they were contracted to assist.

Global social policy

In this very short concluding section it is not possible to deal properly with the complexities of the idea of a 'global social policy'. However, there are a few points to be made arising out of the above analysis. Earlier in this chapter I distinguished three definitions of social policy: (1) mainstream social policy – the set of ideas actually guiding current intentional actions to improve human well-being; (2) critical social policy – a set of ideas and proposed related intentional actions suggesting what ought to be done, further or differently, to improve human well-being; and (3) social policy in practice – the policy practices and outcomes socially constructed in dynamic interactions by 'policy suppliers', 'policy recipients' and other interested parties.

Mainstream 'global social policy' as reflected in the rhetoric and actions of key global policy-makers with resources to disburse is accepting of the underlying economic and political relationships which generate the different kinds of insecurity and illfare found in different parts of the world. There are different mainstream 'global social policies' for different parts of the world. In relation to those parts suffering most insecurity and illfare the mainstream policy (described above) has not been developed out of analyses of political economy and socio-cultural realities and it therefore contributes to policy-in-practice which is far removed from what was intended. Current analyses of poverty and conflict are largely conducted in a language coming out of 'the imaginary world of aid' (Duffield 2001: 252). Concepts such as social capital, civil society,

---

[39] Some ongoing in this volume.

market, state, community, household, social protection, (consumption) poverty, primary education, primary healthcare, etc. are related to the development industry goals of societal transformation: to what they want poor countries to *become* rather than to what they actually *are*. Research and practice organised around these concepts usually fails to engage with the ways in which social actors from both North and South actually construct the structures, cultures and dynamics of power which generate the unacceptable levels of insecurity and illfare found in our world today.

The development of an alternative set of ideas and related intentional actions requires in-depth understanding of political economy and sociocultural contexts, and of how 'policy' actually works in practice in the different contexts. This should be one of the contributions coming from critical social policy. However, towards the end of the twentieth century the critical global social policy/development agenda suffered two setbacks: the collapse of socialism associated with the end of the Cold War, and the undermining of structural analyses and universalist approaches to welfare under the influence of post-modern ways of thinking. The in/security model and similar approaches[40] offer an intellectual foundation for a revived critical global social policy. One great advantage of such approaches is that they 'endogenise' the global social policy makers (including the authors of this book as generators of ideas) and reveal that there is more to 'mobilisation' than top-down policy design or NGO programmes.

The analysis in this chapter suggests that an effective global social policy must be about mobilisation and coalition-formation by/of social actors located in many different positions in the global social structure or 'network society'. In response to the emerging 'liberal networked system of global governance' there is an emerging, though less powerful, 'international welfare network' with a different vision of how the world economy and polity and its different parts might be organised. Members of this network need to network and organise more seriously. There are roles for the 'well-intentioned' exploited and excluded in every country, for local 'escapees' (Wood 1999b) from consumer, patrimonial and warlord structures, for members of the development and humanitarian industries, for academics, interested Northern politicians, trade unionists and businessmen, for journalists, religious figures at all levels, etc. as well as for a variety of brokers, mobilisers and organisers. The (very long-term) goal of a global welfare regime requires the global challenging of the liberal peace system of global governance which is based on badly controlled

---

[40] For example, Hugo Slim's suggestion of 'stakeholder analyses of violence' covering leaders and followers directly responsible for war (primary stakeholders) *and* the secondary stakeholders who in different ways contribute to it.

capitalism and a poorly regulated international political system. It also requires functional 'families', 'communities', 'economies' and 'states' or their equivalents, demanding a search for ways of assisting in the struggle for the social re/construction of culturally appropriate and politically viable institutions which meet universal human and social needs for security. This requires informed action at all levels from individual to local, internal regional, national, external regional, international and global.

'The new power lies in the codes of information and in the images of representation around which societies organise their institutions, and people build their lives, and decide their behaviour' (Castells 1997: 358). There is a particular role for research 'as a moral force' (Duffield 2001: 264). Recently the international development research that predominantly informs international public policy for very poor people has mainly fallen into two camps. Policy economists, using mathematical modelling techniques and econometric analyses of survey data, usually operate in a generalising mode, feeding the bureaucratic preference for top-down blueprint approaches to policy intervention. 'Qualitative' researchers from various backgrounds tend to work at local levels and produce detailed but 'anecdotal' evidence that feeds the NGO preference for 'grassroots mobilisation'. Both these projects are 'de-politicising' and fit well with the aims of 'liberal peace'. The in/security regime approach requires in-depth empirical analysis of the global, national and local structures, actors and dynamics involved in the generation and rectification of insecurity and illfare in particular contexts. Such analyses depend on research from all the social science disciplines including history, political science and geography as well as social anthropology, sociology and economics. They can provide the information required to pursue a 'horses for courses' approach[41] to mobilisation and intervention, which is the only approach likely to lead to a convergence between policy intentions and policy in practice. They also come with a critical edge.

[41] See Wood's chapter in this volume.

Part II

Regional regimes

4   Latin America: towards a liberal-informal welfare regime

Armando Barrientos

Introduction

Esping-Andersen (1990; 1999) has developed a typology of welfare regimes for developed countries. His analysis focuses on the production of welfare, understood as the articulation of welfare programmes and institutions – including the state, markets and households – insuring households against social risks. In his later book he notes that understanding welfare regimes, and their change over time, involves '(a) a diagnosis of the changing distribution and intensity of social risks, and (b) a comprehensive examination of how risks are pooled between state, market, and family' (Esping-Andersen 1999: 33). This chapter[1] undertakes this task for Latin America. The welfare regime approach can provide a much-needed framework enabling a comprehensive analysis of changes in welfare production in Latin America, including the study of the linkages existing between social protection and labour market institutions, and an evaluation of the outcomes of these changes. There is important research on specific programmes or institutions, but few have attempted to compare and integrate their findings.[2] Extending this framework beyond its original focus on industrialised nations can provide a valuable new dimension, and the chapter will consider whether the fundamental change in economic and social institutions undergone by most countries in Latin America provides a rare example of a welfare regime shift.

The chapter is organised as follows. The next section identifies welfare systems in Latin America and the Caribbean. The following section considers the welfare mix prior to recent social protection and labour market reform and identifies a welfare regime for Latin America. A third section argues that recent reforms amount to a welfare regime shift. Further

---

[1] I am grateful to Ian Gough and Stephen Kay for detailed comments on a previous draft; the errors that remain are all mine.
[2] Exceptions are Mesa-Lago and Bertranou (1998).

sections consider welfare outcomes and stratification effects, respectively. The following section looks at political economy issues associated with the welfare regime shift. The penultimate section discusses the dynamics of welfare mix change in three countries. A final section provides some conclusions.

The welfare regime approach and Latin America

It is possible to distinguish two broad welfare systems in the Latin American and Caribbean region. In Latin American countries, formal welfare programmes developed during the first half of the twentieth century around social insurance institutions for specific groups of workers, providing insurance against specified contingencies in exchange for earnings-related contributions (Mesa-Lago and Bertranou 1998). Over time, the range of contingencies and the labour force covered expanded. In addition to social insurance, Latin American countries have extensive employment protection regulations and public provision of education and healthcare, but social assistance is very rare. In Caribbean countries, except for Cuba of course, welfare provision developed after independence in the 1960s and 1970s along the lines of Anglo-Saxon countries, with a contributory social insurance system covering basic contingencies, and universal social assistance providing basic income maintenance (ISSA 1995; ISSA 1996). Employment protection is rare, rudimentary and of recent origin (Downes, Mamingi and Antoine 2000). In contrast to Latin American countries, Caribbean countries have not pursued fundamental welfare reform in the last two decades. The chapter focuses on Latin American countries (Spanish-speaking countries of Central and South America, and Brazil). As will be shown, there is enough commonality in welfare provision across Latin American countries to argue that they share a common welfare regime. Country differences in individual programmes and institutions, some of which will be considered below, should not obscure the fact that the overall articulation of state, market and household shows considerable similarity in Latin America.

In the welfare regime approach, the articulation of these welfare-producing institutions constitutes the welfare mix, which is associated with specific welfare outcomes, and these in turn reinforce the welfare mix through stratification effects. The following sections will identify the key features of the Latin American welfare regime, trace the welfare regime shift which has taken place in the last two decades, and then move on to discuss welfare outcomes and stratification effects. A summary of the key points is presented in figure 4.1.

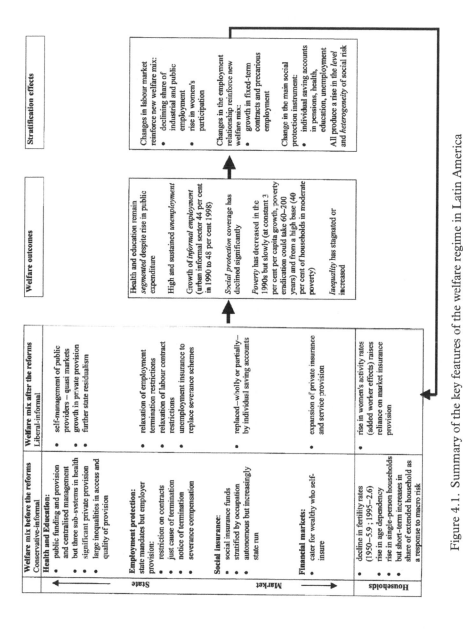

	Welfare mix before the reforms Conservative-informal	Welfare mix after the reforms Liberal-informal	Welfare outcomes	Stratification effects
State	**Health and Education:** • public funding and provision and centralised management but three sub-systems in health • significant private provision • large inequalities in access and quality of provision	• self-management of public providers — quasi markets • growth in private provision in health • further state residualism	Health and education remain *segmented* despite rise in public expenditure	Changes in labour market reinforce new welfare mix: • declining share of industrial and public employment • rise in women's participation
Market	**Employment protection:** state mandates but employer provision: • restriction on contracts • just cause of termination • notice of termination • severance compensation	• relaxation of employment termination restrictions • relaxation of labour contract restrictions • unemployment insurance to replace severance schemes	High and sustained *unemployment* Growth of *informal employment* (urban informal sector 44 per cent in 1990 to 48 per cent 1998)	Changes in the employment relationship reinforce new welfare mix: • growth in fixed-term contracts and precarious employment
	Social insurance: • social insurance funds stratified by occupation • autonomous but increasingly state run	• replaced—wholly or partially—by individual saving accounts	*Social protection* coverage has declined significantly	Change in the main social protection instrument: • individual saving accounts in pensions, health, education, unemployment
	Financial markets: • cater for wealthy who self-insure	• expansion of private insurance and service provision	*Poverty* has decreased in the 1990s but slowly (at constant 3 per cent per capita growth, poverty eradication could take 60–200 years) and from a high base (40 per cent of households in moderate poverty)	All produce a rise in the *level* and *heterogeneity* of social risk
Households	• decline in fertility rates (1950–5.9 ; 1995–2.6) • rise in age dependency • rise in single-person households but short-term increases in share of extended household as a response to macro risk	• rise in women's activity rates (added worker effects) raises reliance on market insurance provision	*Inequality* has stagnated or increased	

Figure 4.1. Summary of the key features of the welfare regime in Latin America

The welfare mix in Latin America before the reforms

The starting point in characterising a Latin American welfare regime is to examine its welfare mix: the specific articulation of household, market and state welfare production. The main components of the welfare mix are examined below. The section ends with a full characterisation of the Latin American welfare regime. A dominant feature of Latin American countries before the recent reforms was the role of social insurance and employment protection for workers in formal employment, and its counterpart, the restricted coverage of formal welfare production, resulting in the exclusion of wide sections of the population, and especially poor and vulnerable groups.

Household welfare provision

The household is an important source of insurance against social risk, and for many low-income groups it constitutes the primary means of protecting household consumption.[3] The capacity of households to provide insurance against social risk can be investigated along two important dimensions: household size and structure, and intra-household transfers or support.[4] These will be examined in turn below, but first it is important to sketch longer-term demographic trends.

Compared to developed countries, Latin America is undergoing an accelerated demographic transition.[5] This results from the combination of a decline in fertility rates and a rise in life expectancy, but the very pronounced decline in fertility rates in Latin America is the driving force behind these changes. For Latin America as a whole, the fertility rate fell from 5.9 in 1950–5 to 2.66 in 1995–2000, and is forecast to decline more gently to 2.1 by 2050. This will ensure rapid population ageing

---

[3] Although in this chapter I use the terms 'family' and 'household' interchangeably, there are important differences existing between them. Households may contain more than one family unit (defined by kinship), each with varying degrees of autonomy. In analysing responses to social risk in Latin America, households, and not families, are the appropriate unit. Because of widespread housing supply constraints and cultural norms, households with multiple family units are common. Even without joint residence, household support and transfers are an important locus of responses to risks such as illness, unemployment and changes in the family unit arising from births and deaths. It is also common for households in Latin America to include non-kinship-related members, or *allegados*, as well as domestic workers (ECLAC 1995).

[4] The efficiency with which households use their resources to insure against social risk is an important fourth dimension.

[5] As the World Bank's *Averting the Old Age Crisis* noted, while in Belgium it took more than a century for the share of population over sixty to double from 9 to 18 per cent, this demographic change was compressed into only twenty-two years in Venezuela (World Bank 1994).

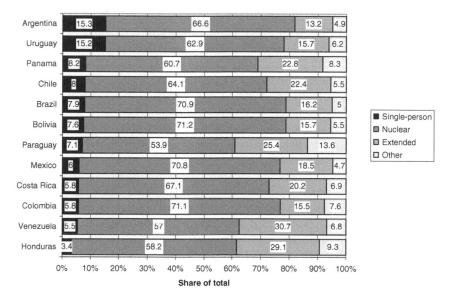

Source: ECLAC (1997).

Figure 4.2. Household types for selected Latin American countries 1994

in the region in the first half of this century. The old-age dependency ratio, measured as the population over sixty-four as a proportion of the population aged 20–64, is predicted to reach 0.41 for Uruguay, 0.36 for Chile and 0.33 for Mexico by 2050. Population ageing will have a strong impact upon existing mechanisms for inter-generational transfers, and therefore on households (Sorrentino 1990). Rising activity rates among women, up from 34 per cent in 1990 to 44 per cent in 1998, will reinforce demographic trends and ensure sustained change in household size and composition in Latin America (CELADE 1996; IADB 1998).

As regards household size and structure, a useful classification distinguishes single-person, nuclear and extended households. Nuclear households include one or two adults and children, while extended households include, in addition, other adult relatives.[6] Figure 4.2 summarises information on the share of household types in selected Latin American countries. The nuclear household is dominant, accounting for around two-thirds of all households (ECLAC 1998). The share of single-person

[6] The residual 'Other' group includes nuclear or extended households with non-relatives, and non-nuclear households in which a head lives with others (relatives or non-relatives) but without the spouse or children.

households is higher for countries like Argentina and Uruguay (around 15 per cent in 1994) with older populations and longstanding pension schemes. In other countries, the share of single-person households ranges from 5 to 8 per cent. Trends show a rise in the share of single-person households for most Latin American countries. The share of extended households ranges from one-sixth to one-fifth of all households.

Poverty incidence appears to be greatest among extended households, and lowest among single-person households, although this finding is sensitive to assumptions used to infer individual income from household income.[7] Household size can be positively correlated with economic vulnerability, especially where the incidence of extended households among lower-income groups reflects a strategy to insure against social risk. A recent Inter-American Development Bank report notes that the poor may live in larger households 'in order to improve income stability, avoid vulnerability, and reduce the costs of transferring resources to other members of the family' (1998: 67). Falling back on the extended household may constitute a response to macro-economic risk. In figure 4.3 a scatter plot of a measure of macro-economic risk, the coefficient of variation of GDP growth, and a measure of changes in the share of extended households suggests a positive correlation. Countries experiencing greater variation in GDP growth rates also appear to have experienced a rise in the share of extended households. This is true even for those countries well advanced in their demographic transition such as Argentina. The figure also shows that countries with more stable GDP growth experienced a decline in the share of extended households.

It is worth noting the relatively high proportion of consensual unions in Latin America compared to other regions. The share of consensual unions is below 15 per cent in Chile, Argentina, Uruguay, Brazil and Mexico, but above 30 per cent in Honduras, El Salvador, Panama, Cuba, Guatemala and Venezuela, and above 50 per cent in Nicaragua, the Dominican Republic and Haiti. Consensual unions are more common among low-income groups, and are less stable. Changes in economic conditions impact on the incidence of unions in general, and in the share of consensual unions within the total. Studies suggest the incidence of new unions declines in periods of economic crisis, and the share of consensual

---

[7] Lanjouw and Ravallion (1995) argue that the positive correlation of household size and poverty is sensitive to assumptions concerning economies in consumption within the household. In addition, assumptions concerning the relative cost of children are also important, because larger households generally have more children. When individual income is measured as total household income divided by the number of household members, this is likely to underestimate well-being among larger households relative to smaller households, because it implicitly assumes identical costs for all household members, and because it fails to take account of economies in consumption.

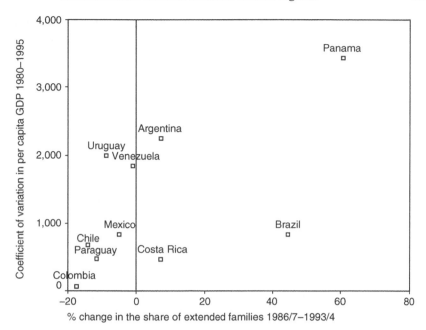

Source: ECLAC (1998) and IADB (1996).

Figure 4.3. Household size and macro-economic risk

unions rises in periods of economic crisis (Bravo 1992). The 1980s and 1990s economic crises experienced by Latin American countries have also made unions less stable.[8] The capacity of nuclear households to provide adequate insurance against social risks is restricted by instability in consensual unions.

There is very little evidence on patterns of intra-household transfers in Latin America and the Caribbean. Cox and Jimenez (1998) use a sample of 369 households in Colombia to investigate private transfers in an urban setting. Economic models of private transfers question whether insurance-motivated private transfers could work in an urban setting due to the difficulty in monitoring risk-related behaviour and therefore in precluding moral hazard. Households can play an important role in sustaining informal insurance networks. Cox and Jimenez found that one-third of the sample were transfer recipients, and that transfers amounted to 15 per cent of the private income of recipients. The direction of

---

[8] There is scant evidence on the incidence of union dissolution and marital breakdown, but a study by CELADE argues that existing measures for Latin America and the Caribbean significantly underestimate their incidence (CELADE 1996).

the flows appears to be from better-off older households to worse-off younger households. Their findings support the view that private transfers are, to an important extent, insurance motivated, and also that they are significant.

Barrientos (2000) examined sources of income for older households (households with a head aged fifty-five and over) in 1994 in Chile. As a proportion of total household income, private transfers were marginal even for those households in the lowest quintile of income (around 1.3 per cent). The contribution to household income of public transfers was comparatively more important (around 8 per cent). This would suggest that intra-household monetary transfers, at least for older households, are less significant. However, the data does not cover in-kind intra-household transfers (accommodation, food, etc.) that may be important. Another proviso is that Chile is unusual in having social assistance pensions for those over seventy with no other sources of income. To the extent that public transfers crowd out private transfers,[9] this finding cannot be safely extrapolated to other countries in the region.

On the issue of intra-household distribution of welfare, only indirect evidence is available. Cutler, Knaul *et al.* focus on the impact of the 1994 crises in Mexico on mortality rates. They find that 'mortality rates have increased with economic crisis, particularly among the elderly, and possibly among the very young' (Cutler, Knaul *et al.* 2000). For example, they find that mortality rates were 5–6 percentage points higher than longer-term trends during the crises for those over sixty. This can be taken as evidence that the intra-household distribution of income fails to provide adequate insurance against social risk for all its members.[10] They find that the higher mortality rates for older and younger household members were associated with declines in household consumption, and especially out-of-pocket healthcare spending. The decline in private healthcare spending was significantly more pronounced in households with older members than in households without them. There is also evidence that the impact of economic crisis on the provision of public healthcare may have been responsible for some of the rise in mortality rates. These findings suggest that households may not provide adequate cover against social risk for the young and the old.

The household is an important source of insurance against social risk, but both secular changes and recent economic conditions suggest the capacity of households in Latin America to insure against shocks to household consumption is in decline. Households are an important source of

---

[9] See Murdoch (1998) for a review of the evidence for developing countries.

[10] This is in line with findings for other developing countries that intra-household resource allocation is skewed towards productive members of the household (Kochar 1999).

insurance against social risk among low-income groups. Evidence discussed above suggests that changes in the share of the extended household are associated with macro-economic instability – faced with unemployment and poverty, Latin Americans move in with their extended households. There is also evidence suggesting that intra-household transfers reflect insurance motives, that among older households monetary private transfers are not significant compared to public transfers, and that intra-household resource distribution is skewed towards productive members. In sum, households are an important source of insurance against social risk in Latin America, but on their own they are a less than effective insurance device for low-income and vulnerable groups.

State and market welfare production

In contrast to other developing regions, by the 1980s Latin American countries had longstanding, and in some cases well-developed, formal welfare production institutions and programmes. It is useful to distinguish three main ones. First, there was a set of occupationally stratified social insurance funds providing pensions, health insurance, unemployment and family benefits, and in many cases housing loans. Second, a raft of employment protection measures and employer-provided family wage supplements constituted an important component of welfare provision in the region. And, third, there was an aspiration to secure public universal provision of education and healthcare.

A hard and fast distinction between state and market welfare production does not apply to Latin America, because of its complex mix of government mandates and regulation on the one hand, and public and private provision on the other. A key feature of Latin American countries is the intertwined roles and responsibilities of the state, employers and private providers in formal welfare production institutions. In fact, each of the components of formal welfare production identified above exhibits a mix of public and private inputs. Social insurance funds began life as autonomous institutions, but with a strong measure of state support and supervision. The state had a role in mandating affiliation for salaried workers, and defining minimum contributions and benefits. State involvement become more important in the 1970s and 1980s, due to the financial problems experienced by social insurance funds, and as a means of consolidating and homogenising provision. While this trend is dominant, autonomous social insurance funds have survived in many countries in the region. Employment protection also shows a mix of private and public inputs. Employment protection has always been government-mandated but employer-provided. Minimum standards of entitlement and coverage are set by the state, but employers are usually free to decide on providers. The same applies to health insurance and healthcare. The state requires affiliation to social health insurance for formal sector workers, but health insurance is provided by employers, unions and private insurance; and public healthcare provision co-exists with extensive private healthcare provision. It is therefore more appropriate to place the relevant welfare programmes and institutions on a continuum, with 'purer' state institutions at one end and 'purer' market institutions at the other.

Figure 4.1 shows the key components of state and market provision in Latin America. These are discussed in more detail below.

Social insurance funds

Social insurance developed for selected groups of workers in the form of social insurance funds (e.g. *cajas de previsión*). Mesa-Lago (1991) distinguishes three groups of countries. In the first group, the pioneer countries, stratified social insurance funds developed in the 1920s. This group includes Chile, Uruguay, Argentina, Cuba and Brazil. A second group of intermediate countries includes Colombia, Costa Rica, Mexico, Paraguay, Peru and Venezuela. In this group, social insurance developed after the 1940s, encouraged by the ILO. A distinguishing feature of social insurance within this group is that a central social insurance agency was set up from the outset, resulting in a lower level of stratification than in the pioneer group. A third group of mainly Central American countries, the latecomers, developed social insurance institutions in the 1950s and 1960s.

Broadly, three stages in the development of social insurance funds can be identified. Initially, the social insurance funds grew out of workers' mutuals, and covered a few contingencies such as funeral expenses and survivor pensions. Affiliated workers and their employers made payroll contributions to the fund from which benefits covering specific contingencies were paid. As public sector employees and the military were usually among the first groups of workers to be covered by a social insurance fund, the government was involved from the outset. A second stage typically involved the extension of social insurance funds to cover a wider range of contingencies, and of workers. The new contingencies covered included old-age and service pensions, unemployment, sickness and disability, maternity and family benefits, and housing loans. The social insurance funds were originally partially funded, but the expansion of coverage and increasing government involvement led to their becoming pay-as-you-go. Governments were keen to expand the range of mandated benefits, and became increasingly involved in both the governance and financing of the social insurance funds. The piecemeal development of the social insurance funds, together with the heterogeneity in the social risks affecting different groups of workers, meant considerable fragmentation in social insurance welfare production.[11] There was considerable diversity in governance, contributions and benefits across social insurance funds, and the funds reinforced existing social and economic inequalities. A third stage in the development of social insurance is currently unfolding. The economic crisis of the 1980s in Latin America, and particularly its impact upon labour markets and fiscal deficits, ensured rising financial imbalances among the social insurance funds. This in turn led to their consolidation and reform in the 1990s (Schulthess and Demarco 1993; Barrientos 1998).

Employment protection

A feature of Latin American countries has been their extensive employment protection legislation. This includes restrictions on non-standard employment contracts, restrictions on cause of dismissal, a period of notice, and a range of compensation payments including tenure-based severance payments (IADB 1996; Lora and Pages 1996). Employment protection also covers maternity leave and benefits. In Latin America, employment protection legislation is the nearest equivalent to income maintenance social protection programmes in the developed world, with two important differences. First, in common with social insurance programmes, they cover workers in formal employment only and, second, employment protection rules protect jobs rather than workers.

The majority of Latin American countries have government mandates on severance compensation in the event of employment termination. Normally, employers are required to pay compensation in cases where the employment termination is involuntary, and where the employer cannot claim to have a just cause for the dismissal of the worker. Labour legislation establishes what is considered to be just cause for dismissal. It is usually restricted to breach of contract or misconduct on the part of an employee, but in some countries it has been extended to include the economic needs of the firm and political activities. In addition, employers are required to give a minimum period of notice before termination. Severance compensation is normally a lump sum calculated as a multiple of monthly earnings per year of service. The severance compensation rate ranges from one-quarter of monthly salary to two months' salary per year of service. Figure 4.4 shows, in index form, a

---

[11] Queisser (1998) reports that before the 1994 pension reform in Colombia there were over 1,000 social insurance funds in the public sector alone.

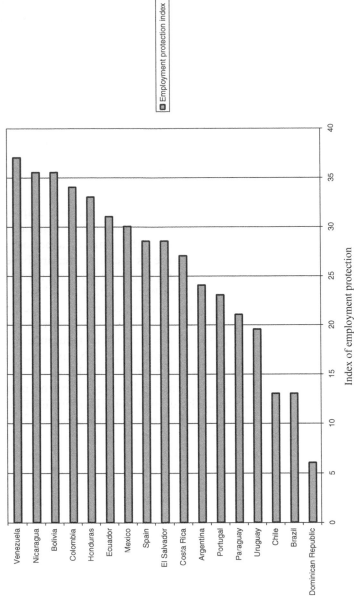

Index of employment protection

Source: Márquez and Pagés (1998). Index includes information on definition of just cause, severance payments, probationary period, severance after twenty years tenure, probability of reinstatement.

Figure 4.4. Employment protection index for Latin American countries and Spain and Portugal

composite measure of the strictness of employment protection for Latin American countries and Spain and Portugal computed by Márquez and Pagés (1998).

Employment protection also applies to work absences due to maternity. In this context, government mandates specify a maximum period of leave and an earnings-related maternity benefit. These are restricted in coverage to workers affiliated to social insurance schemes with a minimum tenure. Figure 4.5 shows an index of maternity protection for Latin American countries. The index is the sum of the standardised scores for each country's qualification period leave period and benefit replacement rate.[12] Higher index values show greater generosity of maternity schemes. Maternity benefits are restricted to employees, although eight Latin American countries provide maternity benefits for the self-employed. Maternity benefits include leave with the mode at thirteen weeks, and earnings-related replacement rates ranging from 50 to 100 per cent. Some countries provide additional benefits in the form of maternity grants and allowances, birth grants, nursing allowances and in-kind benefits.

In some Latin American countries government mandates extend to family wage supplements. Usually, dependants include children below the age of eighteen, and spouses and elders without other sources of income. Both maternity leave and benefits and family supplements reflect a concern with supporting household welfare provision (typical of conservative welfare regimes), rather than a concern with facilitating women's continuous employment (typical of social democratic welfare regimes).

Public provision of education and health

In Latin America, access to basic education and healthcare is an entitlement enshrined in relevant legislation, sometimes in the constitution itself. The state is given responsibility for securing this universal entitlement, for formulating and implementing national health and education policy, and for promoting the integration of services offered by public and private providers. Latin American countries share the aspiration to provide universal, integrated health and education programmes, but this is just that – an aspiration. While significant strides have been made to extend access to health and education to the population over a long period of time, significant gaps and inequalities in provision remain. The

[12] The value of the index for each country is calculated as the average for each variable of the difference between the observed value for a country from the minimum for all countries as a fraction of the range (the difference between the maximum and minimum value observed for that variable). The resulting index is bounded between 1 and 0.

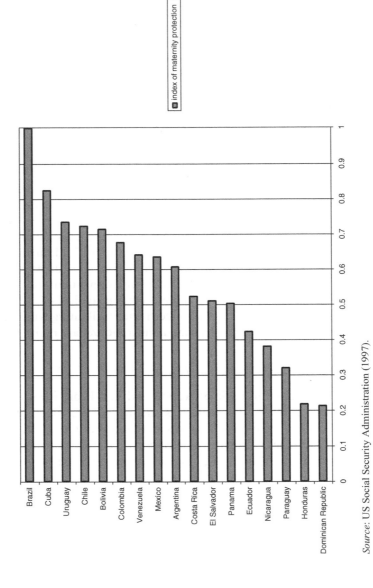

□ index of maternity protection

Source: US Social Security Administration (1997).

Figure 4.5. Index of maternity protection for Latin America

adverse economic conditions prevalent in the 1980s led to cuts in public funding on education and health, and many countries have introduced reforms to their health and education systems that encourage decentralisation in provision management and the expansion of private provision. An outline of the basic features of the pre-reform health and education systems is provided below.

Health The establishment of health insurance and care provision began early in Latin America, especially by comparison to other developing regions. By 1950, 47 per cent of countries in Latin America and the Caribbean had established health and maternity social insurance programmes, compared to 5 per cent in Africa, and 16 per cent in Asia and the Middle East (Mesa-Lago and Bertranou 1998).

Health insurance and healthcare developed over time into three main sub-systems, stratified by income level (Londoño and Frenk 1997). A first sub-system includes high-income groups who largely self-insure, in the sense that they rely on out-of-pocket purchase of healthcare from mainly private sector healthcare providers. A second sub-system covers workers in formal employment and their dependants. These participate in social health insurance plans which developed within social insurance funds. Health insurance plans are largely financed from earmarked payroll contributions, and partially refund affiliates' health expenditures. In some countries social health insurance programmes developed their own healthcare infrastructure, but the norm is for social health insurance to be restricted to monetary compensation for care obtained from a mixture of public and private providers. A third sub-system includes low-income groups, who are rarely covered by health insurance and access basic healthcare, where available, from public providers.

There are many links existing between these sub-systems. Private healthcare providers service both the high-income groups and social health insurance affiliates, whilst the public sector provides preventive medicine for all, primary healthcare for low-income groups, and secondary healthcare for low-income groups and those covered by social insurance. Private health insurance and care would not prosper without the public sector training health professionals and taking responsibility for the high-risk groups. Private health insurance, and to a large extent social health insurance, focuses on secondary healthcare, while the public sector focuses on primary and hard-to-insure high-cost secondary care (e.g. catastrophic and congenital conditions and long-term care). The logic of each of the sub-systems reinforces a segmentation precluding optimal healthcare outcomes. Costa Rica is alone, among Latin American countries, in having managed to establish a fully integrated healthcare

Table 4.1. *Health expenditure by sub-system for Latin America, 1980*

	Health expenditure as a proportion of GDP (%)				
	Public including social insurance	Public excluding social insurance	Social insurance	Private	Total
Argentina	3.64	1.24	2.40	2.76	6.40
Bolivia	3.41	2.11	1.30	3.25	6.66
Brazil	2.35	0.82	1.53	3.81	6.16
Chile	2.06	2.06		3.44	5.50
Colombia	2.20	1.10	1.10	3.86	6.06
Costa Rica	7.20	1.27	5.93	2.22	9.42
Dominican Rep.	1.57	1.14	0.43	3.26	4.84
Ecuador	1.31	1.12	0.20	2.28	3.60
El Salvador	2.27	1.54	0.73	3.53	5.79
Guatemala	2.01	1.41	0.60	1.59	3.60
Honduras	1.23	1.23		4.85	6.08
Mexico	3.40	3.40		2.57	5.97
Panama	3.09	0.39	2.70	1.98	5.07
Paraguay	0.36	0.36		3.95	4.31
Peru	0.87	0.87		3.51	4.38
Uruguay	1.51	1.07	0.44	4.56	6.07
Venezuela	1.94	1.19	0.74	4.84	6.78
Region average (weighted by population)		1.52	0.98	3.35	5.86

Source: PAHO (2000).

system. This was achieved by transferring public healthcare to a single social insurance institution, with the state subsidising low-income groups.

A measure of the size of the sub-systems before the reforms can be gauged by considering healthcare expenditure for Latin American countries for 1980. This is done in table 4.1.

The figures show that, as expected, more developed countries have higher total health expenditure as a proportion of GDP. The average for the region was just below 6 per cent, above that of other developing regions. There is significant variation in the contribution of sub-systems to health expenditure across countries, reflecting the structure of their health system and their level of development. Overall, private health expenditure is dominant – more than twice as much as public health expenditure – and over three times as much as social insurance health expenditure. More developed countries show a larger share of public health expenditure.

The sub-system shares of health expenditure bear little relationship to their population coverage. The majority of the population is covered by the public sector, while the private sub-system includes a very small minority of the population but concentrates the largest share of health expenditure.[13] Health insurance and healthcare are therefore not only heavily segmented in Latin America, but also highly unequal in terms of access and outcomes.

Education   Education in Latin America is universal in provision and largely publicly funded. Before the recent reforms, private provision mainly focused on elite education for wealthy groups. Central government was responsible for determining the curriculum, funding and management of all education sectors, and it supervised private providers. A key objective for education policy was to improve coverage and standards. By the 1980s the objective of expanding enrolment among the relevant age groups had been largely met, although access to education for the rural and urban poor remained a problem (Puryear 1997). Inequality in the quality of provision and in educational outcomes is the key issue in the region, especially in comparison to developed countries and to Southeast Asia (Duryea and Székely 1998). There is evidence that poor groups have a higher incidence of repeating years and lower rates of completion of educational stages. Gajardo (1999) remarks that with similar enrolment rates for low- and middle-income groups, by the fifth year of primary school, only 63 per cent of children of low-income backgrounds remain at school in South America, and 32 per cent in Central America. This compares badly with the same figures for high-income groups at 98 and 83 per cent respectively. By the ninth year of schooling only 15 per cent of children of low-income backgrounds in South America, and 6 per cent in Central America, are at school.

Expenditure on education shows some dispersion across sub-regions, and a positive relationship between economic development and public educational expenditure. The 1980s economic crisis led to deep cuts in state funding for education, and sparked off reforms aimed at decentralising management and financial control over schools and colleges, together with measures to increase co-financing by local authorities and parents. Table 4.2 shows regional trends in public education expenditure. Despite the recovery in education expenditure in the 1990s, educational provision and outcomes are highly segmented by income level (ECLAC 2000).

---

[13] Private health expenditure includes out-of-pocket expenditure by households (including poor households), so that the figures may overstate the concentration of health expenditure on wealthy groups. With this in mind, the general conclusion stands.

Table 4.2. *Trends in public expenditure on education per student (US$ 1992)*

Sub-region	1970	1980	1988	1993
Andean	227	281	246	293
Brazil	184	388	384	479
Southern Cone	498	612	307	496
Central America	200	212	184	196
Mexico	134	349	275	446
English-speaking Caribbean	461	545	714	588
Regional average	234	370	308	411

Source: Gajardo (1999).

The provision of basic public services, including education and health, is far from achieving universality. In practice, public provision of education and health excludes large segments of the population in the region, and especially the poor and vulnerable groups. Psacharopoulos and Patrinos (1994) use household survey data to examine the social and economic conditions of indigenous people in four Latin American countries. They found that indigenous people have a higher incidence of poverty and poorer health and educational outcomes than non-indigenous populations. In Bolivia, for example, the share of indigenous people in the population was 51.3 per cent in 1988, and they had on average three fewer years of schooling than non-indigenous people. In Mexico indigenous people are a smaller share of the population (7.4 per cent in 1990), but years of schooling decline as the share of indigenous people in a municipality rises. Average schooling was seven years in municipalities with a 10 per cent share of indigenous people, but only 3.5 years in municipalities with a 40 per cent share of indigenous people. Similar findings apply to access to healthcare and health status. Access to public services in rural areas is limited, and ECLAC (2000) reports large differences in educational outcomes across the urban and rural sectors.

In conclusion, in the period up to the 1980s, state and market welfare provision had three main components: social insurance, employment protection and publicly financed education and healthcare programmes. In the two decades up to 1980, social insurance funds expanded in both the range of contingencies covered and the share of the labour force covered. Employment protection legislation has been traditionally strong in Latin America, consonant with the conservative-corporatist goal of stable male employment. Social public expenditure, including health and education, was lower in the region than in industrialised countries, but higher than in some Southeast Asian economies. On paper, public health and education programmes have the goal of universal coverage, but this remains an aspiration. Health insurance and healthcare are segmented into three sectors: a self-insurance/private provision sector for high-income groups, a social insurance sector for workers in formal employment and their dependants, and a public sector covering the basic needs of the poor. There is some variation in sub-system health expenditure, but private health expenditure is dominant in the region. Education provision was almost universal by the 1980s, but strongly segmented in access, quality of provision and particularly outcomes. The economic crisis of the 1980s radically changes this picture. After 1980, coverage rates of social insurance stagnated and declined, employment protection legislation was diluted, and public social expenditure contracted. These trends will be discussed below.

Characterising Latin America's welfare regime

A useful starting point in characterising the welfare regime in Latin America is to compare its key features with those of the welfare regimes identified by Esping-Andersen for developed countries. At the beginning of the 1980s, and before the recent reforms, Latin American countries showed elements of all three welfare regimes identified by Esping-Andersen. The absence of significant, or inclusive, state welfare provision reflects an underlying liberal welfare state residualism. Social insurance funds, employment protection and family benefits reflect conservative welfare regimes. Finally, public, universal provision of education and healthcare – even if it is only an aspiration – reflects the developmental and equity features of the social democratic welfare regime.

Focusing initially on the formal institutions and programmes of welfare production, there are important similarities between these and the Southern European branch of conservative welfare regimes. A parallel with the Southern European welfare regime variant is suggested by history and culture, and can be framed within Castles' analysis of a 'family of nations' (Castles and Mitchell 1993). However, the minimal presence, and in some cases complete absence, of a welfare state sets Latin American countries apart. The stratified nature of social insurance and employment protection, as well as the presence of family wage supplements and the specific design of maternity protection, all parallel key features in the conservative welfare regime. This also applies to the segmentation in health insurance and healthcare provision, and to the important role of employers in welfare provision. Outside the household, these are the main institutions of welfare production, and dominate the welfare mix.

In the context of Esping-Andersen's typology, Latin America's welfare regime is predominantly conservative.

Before accepting this characterisation of the welfare regime in Latin America, it is crucial to consider that these formal institutions and programmes of welfare production apply to only a fraction of the labour force and population. Formal welfare institutions mainly cover workers in formal employment and their dependants, but these are increasingly a minority in Latin America. For all practical purposes, a majority of the population in Latin America are excluded from social insurance and employment protection, and their access to public provision of basic services is limited. Groups with limited access to market production, such as the elderly, find themselves outside the cover of formal welfare institutions. Workers in informal employment are seldom covered by social insurance funds, the self-employed and workers in precarious employment are not covered by employment protection legislation, and both the urban and the rural poor find it difficult to access basic services such as education and health. In practical, rather than institutional, terms, Latin American countries are characterised by an informal welfare regime. This informal welfare regime shares with Esping-Andersen's liberal welfare regime a very narrow identification of social risks, and the primacy of the market as a source of insurance against social risk. A key difference with Esping-Andersen's liberal welfare regime is the fact that social assistance programmes are largely absent in Latin America and that for the large segment of the labour force in informal employment, and their households, the sources of insurance against social risk are restricted to relatives and friends, employment, and a patchwork of informal networks linked to national and international NGOs. Characterising a welfare regime for Latin American countries in terms of Esping-Andersen's typology is impossible without reference to this segmentation in welfare production and particularly the presence of a large informal segment.

A Latin American welfare regime is best characterised as informal-conservative, or conservative-informal depending on whether the emphasis is placed on existing, or absent, institutional features. If the emphasis is placed on the type and structure of formal welfare production institutions in Latin America, the welfare regime could be characterised as conservative-informal. Here the informal component is a residual reflecting the large segment of the population who depend mainly on household and market welfare production. Referring to the informal component as a residual accurately describes widely shared expectations in the period up to the early 1980s that the gradual formalisation of informal employment, together with the extension of public sector service provision, would eventually cover the great majority of the population in the region. On the other hand, due recognition of the very restricted population coverage of formal welfare institutions in the region suggests that an informal-conservative welfare regime is a more accurate characterisation. The 1990s have 'resolved' this dilemma by pushing Latin American countries firmly in the direction of a liberal welfare regime. This is the subject of the next section.

A welfare regime shift in Latin America?

Welfare production in Latin American countries has undergone fundamental change and reform in the 1990s.[14] The driving force behind the reform was the acute economic crises suffered by the economies of the region in the 1980s and early 1990s, and the structural reforms these provoked. Structural reform encompassed trade liberalisation, macro-economic stabilisation, privatisation, and labour and capital market liberalisation – broadly in that order. These amounted to a switch in development strategy from import substitution industralisation to export-oriented growth (Edwards 1995). Trade liberalisation drastically reduced the barriers preventing the integration of the economies of the region within the global economy. It enforced extensive employment restructuring, and encouraged de facto de-regulation in the labour market, which in turn resulted in rising levels of poverty and inequality (Altimir 1997). Macro-economic stabilisation strengthened efforts to reduce rising fiscal deficits which compounded pressures on existing welfare provision (Huber 1996). Structural reform inevitably led to proposals for the reform of welfare and labour market institutions, seeking to introduce changes which reinforced the new export-oriented growth strategy, for example by strengthening labour supply incentives, reducing fiscal deficits, and facilitating worker mobility and labour market adjustment.

Multi-lateral lending institutions such as the World Bank and the Inter-American Development Bank have played an important role in shaping welfare reform in the region. The welfare programmes and institutions predating structural reforms had been criticised on the grounds that they imposed significant restrictions on economic growth. Framed within a 'distortionist' view of welfare and labour market institutions (Freeman 1993), these criticisms provided the rationale for fundamental welfare reform. It was argued that the redistributive impact of welfare programmes generated large distortions upon incentives to work and save. Redistribution introduced a wedge between welfare payroll contributions and

---

[14] Chile underwent welfare reforms at the beginning of the 1980s, following earlier structural reforms in the late 1970s.

benefits, resulting in weaker work incentives. High welfare payroll taxation was held to be responsible for higher labour costs, which in turn reduced employment creation and encouraged evasion and avoidance, and therefore the growth of informal employment. It was also argued that social insurance had a 'crowding' effect upon private insurance, and resulted in small and imperfect financial markets. The redesign of welfare and labour institutions was therefore aimed at removing these distortions and improving market operation and efficiency.

The reforms have affected all three components of state and market welfare production: social insurance, employment protection and public provision of healthcare and education. Table 4.3 summarises information on the incidence of reforms to the welfare mix. The changes are briefly reviewed below.

The reform of social insurance, and especially the reform of social insurance pension programmes, has received the most attention. Chile's 1980 reform of social insurance is paradigmatic in this respect. Before the 1973 military coup which brought neo-liberal policies to dominance, Chile had a large number of social insurance funds providing a range of benefits including unemployment and industrial injuries compensation, family allowances, housing loans, old-age, retirement and disability pensions, and health insurance. These were consolidated by the military regime in the 1970s, and radically reformed in 1980. The reform split off health insurance from pensions, and from a set of residual programmes. Pay-as-you-go pensions in the social insurance schemes were replaced by individual capitalisation pension plans, in which workers contribute a fraction of their earnings to a retirement savings account with a private pension fund manager (Barrientos 1998). Health insurance has also been reorganised on the basis of workers contributing a fraction of their earnings to either a public health insurance fund, or a number of private health insurance plans. The residual programmes remained the responsibility of the government (CIEDESS 1994). The Chilean social insurance reform became a model for similar reforms in other Latin American countries in the 1990s, and especially pension reform.[15]

The reform of labour market institutions needs to be studied at two levels. At a formal level, few countries have overhauled their employment protection and employment legislation. Lora and Pagés (1996) bemoan the fact that whereas twenty-six Latin American and Caribbean countries had completed trade liberalisation, twenty-four had reformed the financial sector, and fourteen had implemented extensive privatisation,

---

[15] Pension reform along these lines has been implemented in Chile, Peru, Argentina, Uruguay, Colombia, Costa Rica, El Salvador, Bolivia and Mexico (Barrientos 1998).

Table 4.3. *Summary information on changes to the welfare mix in Latin American countries ('x' means reforms adopted or implemented)*

Country	Pension reform introducing retirement saving accounts	Relaxation of labour contract regulations	Relaxation of employment termination regulations	Introduction/ changes to unemployment insurance	Health – changes in the public–private mix	Education – introduction of demand subsidy
Argentina	x	x	x	x	x	
Bolivia	x	x				
Brazil		x		x	x	
Chile	x	x	x	x	x	x
Colombia	x	x	x	x	x	x
Costa Rica	x		x		x	
Dominican Republic	x		x		x	
Ecuador						
El Salvador	x				x	
Guatemala					x	
Honduras						
Mexico	x				x	
Nicaragua					x	
Panama						
Paraguay	x		x		x	
Peru	x	x	x		x	
Uruguay	x			x		
Venezuela	x		x			

Sources: ECLAC (1997 and 2000); Gajardo (1999); Barrientos (1998).

only five countries had implemented significant labour reforms.[16] They explain the slow pace of labour reforms on the grounds that widespread informal employment made labour markets highly flexible, thus heavily discounting any potential gains from labour market reforms. The reforms have reduced the costs to employers of terminating workers, relaxed the range of employment contracts sanctioned by law, and reduced non-wage labour costs to employers (Marshall 1996). At an informal level, there has been extensive labour market liberalisation, reflected in the growth of informal employment in the 1980s and 1990s, and enforced by high and persistent unemployment in the region (Márquez 1998). The share of workers on fixed-term or temporary contracts increased in Peru, a country which has implemented labour market reform, from 30 per cent in 1985 to 50 per cent in 1995, and in Bolivia from 11 per cent in 1985 to 30 per cent in 1990, despite not having reformed its labour legislation. There has been a significant de facto liberalisation of employment protection and labour institutions in the region.

Reforms in health and education have decentralised the operational and financial management of providers, encouraged private provision, and changed the financing mix by lowering government contributions (ECLAC 2000). Broadly, the scope for universal public provision has been restricted to compulsory primary and secondary education (Birdsall and Sabot 1996), and the provision of a basic healthcare package for low-income uninsured groups and the elderly.

In healthcare, governments in the region have encouraged self-management of public healthcare, by transferring managerial and financial decision-making to providers. In some countries, the reforms aim to establish a quasi-market in healthcare by allowing healthcare providers to charge directly for services provided to the different groups (those insured privately, affiliates to social health insurance, and the poor subsidised by government) (Barrientos and Lloyd-Sherlock 2002). The government retains overall responsibility for national health policy, preventive medicine and health education, and the financing of primary healthcare for the poor and the uninsured. In health insurance, healthcare reforms have opened up health insurance provision to private providers (Barrientos and Lloyd-Sherlock 2000). In Chile, the reforms in the early 1980s established private health insurance providers, the ISAPRES (Institutos de Salud Previsional) in direct competition with the public health insurance provider. In Colombia, reforms in 1995 created the EPS (Entidades de Promoción de Salud). In Argentina, legislation implemented

---

[16] These are Argentina (1991), Colombia (1990), Panama (1995), Peru (1991, 1995) and Guatemala (1990).

at the beginning of 2001 gave workers the choice of affiliation to the previously dominant *obras sociales* or emerging private health insurance providers (*pre-pagas* and *mutuales*). Reforms in Peru and Mexico will provide the conditions for the expansion of private health insurance providers (CIEDESS 1998). In poorer Latin American countries, NGOs have given a boost to micro-insurance projects in healthcare, which are targeted on groups excluded from existing health insurance programmes (CLAISS 1999). The health system reforms in Latin America have resulted in an expansion of private health insurance and care provision, strengthening the private and social insurance sub-systems.

In education, the reforms also aim to decentralise and encourage self-management by providers, and to increase the private financing of education. The decentralisation reforms are now quite extensive in Latin America, and the model has been to shift overall responsibility for schools and colleges to local authorities (Gajardo 1999). On financing, the shift to demand subsidies has only been implemented in two countries so far: Chile and Colombia. The education reforms have been strongly opposed by the teachers' unions which are strongly committed to public education and are concerned at the erosion in pay and conditions associated with the introduction of local management. Private finance and provision in tertiary education has substantially expanded.

A key feature of welfare reforms in the region has been the increased reliance on market welfare provision. In principle, markets can provide insurance against social risk. Financial markets provide a means to create buffer stocks of assets to be used when needed, and also credit. Insurance markets provide cover against a range of contingencies threatening household consumption. These markets are relatively underdeveloped in Latin America, with private providers largely focused on middle- and high-income households. Recent welfare reforms in Latin America are creating a new set of financial and insurance institutions, and encouraging the modernisation of financial and insurance markets (Barrientos 1999). Pension reform, for example, has established pension fund managers providing a range of financial services. These collect workers' contributions, invest them in a range of permitted assets, and manage individual retirement saving accounts. Pension reformers have circumvented existing financial and banking institutions because of their poor record on access and financial probity. The new pension fund managers are set to provide a wider range of additional services, such as voluntary saving and unemployment compensation accounts. These exist in Chile and Colombia, and provide affiliated workers with access to financial markets and to a wider range of financial and insurance products.

To sum up, all three components of formal welfare production have been subject to fundamental reform. The emerging model of welfare production in Latin America relies to an increasing extent on individuals and households making provision for themselves, through saving and insurance instruments managed by private providers. Service provision has been opened up to competition between decentralised providers, both public and private. In terms of employment protection, the reforms are associated with a substantially reduced level of worker protection, and a fluid labour market. These changes are shifting the Latin American economies away from social insurance and employment protection institutions associated with a conservative welfare regime, and further towards a residual state welfare production. Together with an increasing reliance on market welfare production, these changes constitute a firm shift towards a liberal welfare regime. As the emerging welfare mix in Latin America lacks a basic safety net, it would be accurate to describe the emerging welfare regime as liberal-informal.

Welfare outcomes

Latin American countries suffered an acute recession in the 1980s, to the extent that this is referred to as 'the lost decade'. All countries in the region showed negative rates of GDP growth, falling real wages, and rising unemployment, poverty and inequality. This ushered in structural adjustment programmes, which began with trade liberalisation and macro-economic stabilisation and progressed to labour and capital market liberalisation and welfare reform. Deficits in public finances led to deep cuts in government programmes, including health, education and social security. The economic crisis paved the way for a welfare regime shift. In the 1990s there has been a modest recovery, with some economic growth, but punctuated by further economic crises. An improvement in growth performance has led to some reduction in poverty levels back to the levels before the 1980s, but unemployment has remained high, and inequality has not improved. Public funding of health and education programmes has recovered, but only to the levels of the 1980s. This section reviews the welfare outcomes associated with the welfare regime shift.

Unemployment, poverty, inequality and social protection

Table 4.4 shows trends in unemployment, income inequality and social insurance coverage for selected Latin American countries. Unemployment has risen in the majority of countries in the region, currently

Table 4.4. *Welfare regime shift and welfare outcomes for selected Latin American countries*

Country	Unemployment rate (%)			Inequality (Gini coefficient)		Social insurance coverage		
	1980	1985	1998	1980s	1990s	1980	1990	1998
Argentina	2.3	6.1	12.9			69.1	24.9	20.2
Bolivia	4.5	5.7	4.4					
Brazil	2.8	5.3	7.6	57.6	60.9	87	38.7	34.5
Chile	10.4	17.0	6.4	55.5	56.4	61.7	59	51
Colombia		13.8	15.2	48.3	49.2	22.4	25.7	35.5
Costa Rica	5.9	7.2	5.4	46.2	46.8	68.3	51.7	50.3
Ecuador		10.4	8.5			25.9	17.8	16.2
El Salvador	12.9	10.0	7.6					
Honduras		11.7	5.8	59.9	55.5			
Mexico		4.4	3.2	44.9	47.6	42	12.7	8.2
Panama		15.7	15.5	52.1	57.4			
Paraguay	4.1	5.1	13.9					
Peru		10.1	8.2	42.7	44.8	37.4	22.1	14.3
Dominican Republic			14.3	46.8	49.0			
Uruguay		13.1	10.2			81.2	63.6	57.9
Venezuela	5.9	14.3	11.3	46.0	46.3	49.8	9.2	8.6

Sources: World Bank (1994); ILO (1999b and 2000a); Mesa-Lago (1994); Kanbur (1999).

averaging 10 per cent, with larger increases more noticeable in those countries that have implemented structural adjustment. The rise in unemployment in Latin America is mainly due to modest economic growth performance, coupled with extensive job destruction resulting from structural adjustment. A sizeable growth in the population of working age coupled with a rise in labour force participation by women imply that employment growth rates of between 2 and 3 per cent are needed just to keep unemployment from rising. Poor growth performance has directly resulted in high and persistent unemployment, and unemployment rates in Latin American countries are similar to those in Europe.

Unemployment is not evenly distributed. Rates of unemployment are higher among younger and older workers. They are also lower for both the unskilled and the highly skilled than for workers with secondary school education. The probability of becoming unemployed is higher for low-income groups, but very similar across middle- and high-income groups. Unemployment duration is short, with long-term unemployed constituting usually less than 10 per cent of the unemployed. This is in part because of the scarcity of support for the unemployed, but also

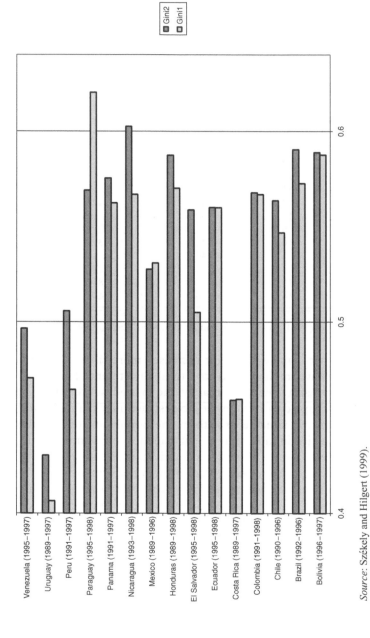

Legend: Gini2, Gini1

Source: Székely and Hilgert (1999).

Figure 4.6. Urban household income inequality changes in the 1990s

because of the high incidence of 'job churning' in liberalised labour markets.

Poverty increased markedly in the 1980s, and remained stagnant in the 1990s. The proportion of households categorised as poor – that is, those with incomes below twice the monetary value of a subsistence basket of goods – has been estimated at around 40 per cent for the 1990s, the same level as in the 1970s. The proportion of households categorised as indigent – that is, having incomes below those needed to purchase a subsistence basket of goods – was estimated at 18 per cent in the 1990s. Marginal improvements in poverty levels in the 1990s for some countries are explained by a better growth performance, but they show significant heterogeneity across sectors and income groups. A recent Inter-American Development Bank review of poverty reduction prospects for the region concluded that 'growth alone may not be enough. If income distribution remains unchanged, the pace of poverty reduction might be quite slow even with sustained growth. For example, at yearly growth rates of three percent per capita, depending on the country it would take close to 60 years to over two centuries to completely eradicate poverty' (Lustig and Deutsch 1998: 3).

The economic recovery in the 1990s has not produced noticeable reductions in inequality. Across countries, inequality trends are very mixed.[17] Figure 4.6 profiles trends in inequality measured by the Gini coefficient of urban household labour income for two data points for fifteen Latin American countries. Only Mexico and Paraguay show some improvement in the coefficient, but this may be a factor of the scope of the data. For the majority of Latin American countries, inequality increased in the 1990s. Compared to other regions, Latin American countries traditionally have higher levels of inequality, mainly explained by concentration of land ownership, unequal distribution of human capital, political instability and poor governance. The rise in inequality in the 1990s is a matter of concern because it reflects systemic change in labour and welfare regimes.

As indicated in the previous section, social insurance and employment protection regulation cover only a fraction of the labour force. Figure 4.7 shows trends in social insurance coverage of the labour force. The 1960s and 1970s were decades of growth in social insurance both in terms of the range of contingencies and of the share of the labour force covered. The 1980s brought a retrenchment – a direct consequence of the deterioration in labour market conditions and government finances, leading to reforms

---

[17] As Atkinson suggests for OECD countries, it may be more accurate to speak of episodes rather than trends (Atkinson 1997).

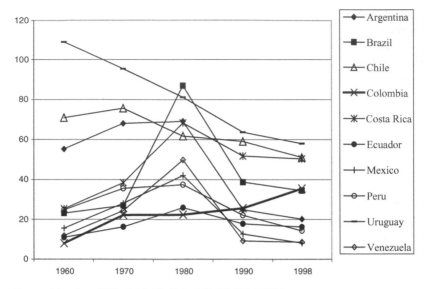

Sources: Mesa-Lago (1991, 1994); World Bank (1994); ILO (1999b).

Figure 4.7. Percentage of the employed labour force contributing to social insurance

in the 1990s (Uthoff 1999). The reform of social insurance schemes has been associated with a decline in coverage (Barrientos 1996). The fall in coverage is understated by the figures for 1990 and 1998 because these measure coverage among salaried workers only, leaving out the large numbers of self-employed workers. It is clear from the data that social protection in the 1990s declined for Latin American countries, the only exception being Colombia (Queisser 1995). Underlying this trend are changes in labour market and economic conditions, and changes in the employment relationship which will be discussed in the next section.

Health and education

The health and education reforms in Latin America are, apart from Chile's, too recent to allow a full outcome evaluation. At an aggregate level, expenditure and outcome indicators on health and education in the region are in line with those of other developing countries. The share of GDP spent on health and education in Latin America is lower than in developed countries, but higher than in many developing countries. The indicators for education outcomes and health status in Latin America also look reasonable in a comparative context. Latin America has almost universal rates of enrolment in primary education, and patterns of morbidity and mortality in line with developing countries' standards. Moreover, public expenditure in education and health has risen in the 1990s, although from a trough in the 1980s caused by the economic crisis and structural adjustment.

The key issue is the acute segmentation and inequality in access and the quality of provision in health and education. A study of the distributive effects of public social expenditure in Latin America in the 1990s concludes that the rise in public social expenditure was not sufficient, nor sufficiently well targeted, to undo the adverse effects of the 1980s economic crisis (Mostajo 2000). Even for those areas of social public expenditure which are progressive in their distribution effects, such as education and health, there is evidence that their progressivity is a factor of higher-income groups opting for better-quality private provision, thus reinforcing a regressivity in the quality of service.[18] The highly segmented nature of health insurance and care will be deepened by the recent reforms because they favour private provision of health insurance and provision, and undermine the aspiration to universal coverage of basic health risk (Lloyd-Sherlock 2000). This also applies to education, as the quality of education provision to poorer groups in Latin America remains an acute problem. Although the reforms have ostensibly targeted improvements in quality for poorer groups, decentralisation and changes in financing have not produced a marked improvement in the quality of education available to these groups. As a recent evaluation of education reform observes, in Latin America education has worked to reinforce existing patterns of inequality, instead of developing into a powerful mechanism for social mobility and advancement (Gajardo 1999).

In sum, an evaluation of welfare outcomes suggests that the shift in welfare regime in Latin America in the 1990s has not produced an improvement in the capacity of the components in the welfare mix to insure against social risks. Consideration of a range of indicators shows that, on the contrary, changes in the welfare mix in the 1990s have increased

[18] The analysis identifies the share of public social expenditure going to household income quintile groups using household data for Argentina, Brazil, Chile and Colombia for the 1990s. It finds that, measured as the ratio of public expenditure going to the poorest quintile to that going to the wealthiest quintile, primary education is the most progressive in terms of its redistributive effects, followed by public expenditure on health. At the same time, indicators for the quality of education (measured as pupil/teacher ratio, for example) had deteriorated for public education. In Peru, for example, this ratio had increased from 29 in 1990/1 to 30 in 1994/5 for public schools, but declined from 26 to 21 for private schools (Mostajo 2000).

exposure to social risk, and that this is particularly marked for low-income and more vulnerable groups.

Stratification effects and the labour market

Stratification effects provide a feedback device through which welfare outcomes reinforce the welfare mix: that is, the articulation of household, state and market welfare production. In Esping-Andersen's account of welfare regimes, stratification effects are important in reproducing the welfare mix, and therefore help explain the persistence of the welfare regime. In short, stratification effects enforce path dependence in welfare regimes. In the context of a change in welfare regime, as, it is argued, happened in Latin America, stratification effects become all important in reproducing and reinforcing changes in the welfare mix. This section considers stratification effects in the region, focusing on labour market segmentation as the key stratification filter.

The focus on the labour market is explained by two factors. First, it is explained by the dominant role of the labour market in the welfare mix in the region. The labour market is key to household strategies to reduce and diversify social risks. This applies equally to those groups excluded from formal welfare institutions and to those covered by them. For the latter group, labour market participation provides not only labour income, but also a range of insurance against social risks (such as industrial injuries, disability, family-related inactivity, earnings variation, longevity, health conditions, etc.). Second, it arises because the development of social insurance is closely tied up with the nature of, and change in, the employment relationship. This is discussed in more detail in the next sub-section. The discussion that follows will examine how changes in the employment relationship and the labour market, and in the main social protection instruments, help reinforce the new welfare mix.

Social insurance, social risks and segmented labour markets as stratification filters

Atkinson (1995) argues that the origins and later development of social insurance can be traced back to the nature of the modern employment relationship. This generates a demand for social insurance as a device for pooling social risks across workers. Both governments and employers, who are keen to facilitate the growth and development of the modern sector, support this demand for social insurance. Social insurance provides a popular institution through which employment in the modern sector can be supported and subsidised.

Social insurance is not, however, an inclusive or comprehensive device for risk pooling. To the extent that labour markets are segmented, occupational and social risks are heterogeneous across workers. The development of inclusive social insurance has less chance of success where the risks of unemployment, or the risks of work-related sickness or injury, are systematically different across occupational groups. Within segmented labour markets, the demand for social insurance is bound to vary across segments. It is usually restricted to certain categories of workers, and normally excludes high-risk workers such as the unskilled, temporary workers and the self-employed. This perspective fits very well the development of social insurance in Latin American countries. Social insurance coverage is focused on public sector workers, white collar private sector workers, and workers in protected sectors of the economy (under import substitution industrialisation these included workers in medium and large-scale manufacturing). These were also the workers most likely to be unionised and to exercise political clout. Pensions and health insurance were well developed for these workers. Few countries set up unemployment insurance schemes. Instead, employment protection regulations and severance compensation schemes provided the main support for unemployed workers. In most Latin American countries, social insurance explicitly excludes bad-risk groups in the labour force.[19] Segmentation in welfare provision constitutes a reflection of the segmentation in the labour market. This illustrates the role of the employment relationship and the labour market as stratification filters, ensuring the persistence of welfare outcomes and, through them, the specific articulation of the welfare mix.

Stratification filters and the welfare regime shift in Latin America

In view of this, it is important to consider the main stratification filters which have supported a welfare regime shift in Latin America. In this section three key stratification filters are identified: changes in the labour market, changes in the employment relationship, and changes in the welfare production instruments.

Labour market changes – including employment restructuring, rising unemployment, rising activity rates among women, and rising wage inequality – have significantly reinforced changes in the welfare mix. Thus employment restructuring enforced by trade liberalisation has produced a large and rapid decline in employment in industries that benefited from

---

[19] Except for Argentina which had a social insurance fund for own account workers, and Brazil which explicitly includes rural workers.

import barriers under import substitution industrialisation, and in public sector employment. At the same time there has been an increase in the share of employment in services and in non-traditional exports (agriculture and primary products). The changes in employment have contributed to a reduction in the labour force coverage of formal social insurance and employment protection institutions. Unemployment has helped enforce a weakening of organised labour, and of employment protection, and has encouraged growth in non-standard forms of employment. Rising activity rates among women have produced the same effects, due to the fact that women work predominantly in the tertiary sector, and have lower rates of unionisation. Furthermore, the increase in involvement in market work reduces their non-market work, thereby leading to an increase in the use of market services such as childcare and the care of older relatives. The steep rise in inequality of labour earnings (ECLAC 1997) increases the variance of the returns to education, and it therefore raises the risks associated with human capital investment. The changes in the labour market in Latin America move over whelmingly in this direction, and have a significant impact upon the pattern and level of social risk.[20]

Changes in the employment relationship brought in by the relaxation in employment protection legislation, and the growth in informality and in non-standard forms of employment, reinforce changes in the welfare mix, because workers with low earnings and irregular employment cannot expect much protection from reformed social insurance, and have largely remained outside it. It is an important issue whether other forms of social protection, i.e. the household, informal insurance arrangements or social networks, can replace the contribution of social insurance and employment protection to the welfare mix. As regards informal insurance arrangements, at least, the evidence for developing countries suggests that it is unlikely these will replace formal insurance (Murdoch 1998).

Changes in welfare production instruments also act as powerful stratification filters, reinforcing the changes in the welfare mix. A key feature of the emerging approach to welfare production is the reliance on individual saving as the preferred instrument to replace social insurance and employment protection.[21] Individual savings accounts constitute the main model of protection against social risk adopted in the area of pensions (World Bank 1994; Brooks and James 1999), but also in health insurance,

---

[20] In the absence of compensating institutions, rising wage inequality will reduce human capital investment (Robbins 1994).

[21] Proposals to replace social insurance programmes wholesale with individual savings plans in developed countries (Folster 1999) are less likely to work effectively in Latin America due to the segmented and fragmented nature of welfare production.

unemployment and education. Individual saving reinforces the emerging welfare mix by encouraging the development of private insurance provision. In the context of pensions, for example, the requirement that retirement savings are invested in life annuities has the effect of strengthening private insurance provision, thus reinforcing the emerging welfare mix. The same applies to health and unemployment insurance, which encourage private insurance providers and reduce the role of government provision. The partial, or in some cases complete, withdrawal of government provision associated with the introduction of individual saving instruments reduces the scope for wider risk-pooling while strengthening market welfare (insurance) provision. The introduction of individual savings accounts as the main instrument of social insurance in Latin America has had the effect of reducing insurance against social risks. With the introduction of compulsory saving against unemployment, for example, workers with irregular employment will be unable to save sufficiently to cover their consumption while unemployed, whilst workers in regular employment will end up with large compulsory savings.

There has been a rapid expansion of private provision in pension fund management, health insurance and unemployment insurance. Table 4.5 provides some indicators of the extent of private welfare production for selected Latin American countries in these sectors. A measure of the assets held by pension fund managers provides an indication of both their economic significance and their rapid growth. With the exception of Brazil, the pension fund management sector developed from scratch in the 1990s. A measure of regular contributors, on the other hand, shows that these cover only a small fraction of the labour force (Barrientos 1999). Private health insurance is much less developed, in part because of stronger public alternatives. The private insurance sector is very undeveloped in Latin America compared to industrialised countries, but it is set to expand due to the introduction of private pension and health insurance. The life annuity market, in particular, will need to grow to complement the growth of private pensions, as is shown by a comparison of the size of insurance premiums as a proportion of GDP in Chile with the same measure in other countries. A feature of private welfare provision is the dominance of foreign investors, both in the health sector (Jost 1999; Stocker, Waitzkin and Iriart 1999) and in the pension fund management sector (Yermo 2000).

In sum, Latin American countries have implemented far-reaching welfare reforms, with changes in the labour market providing the driving force. The 1980s recession brought in rising unemployment, employment restructuring, and a significant change in the employment relationship. These undermined the capacity of social insurance to provide the

Table 4.5. *Indicators of private pension and healthcare providers in Latin America*

	Pension fund assets as % of GDP (1998)	Contributors to individual retirement plans (millions in 1999)	Private pension fund managers (number in 1999)	Private health insurance providers (number)	Insurance premiums as % of GDP (1997)
Argentina	3.3	7.0	15	290 (1999)[a]	1.5
Bolivia	3.9	0.4	2		1.7
Brazil	10.2				2.3
Chile	40.3	3.1	8	26 (1999)[b]	3.3
Colombia	2.1	1.6	8	24 (1996)[c]	2.7
Costa Rica		0.08	8		
El Salvador	0.4	0.3	5		
Mexico	2.7	9.0	14		1.2
Peru	2.5	2.1	5		0.8
Uruguay	1.3	0.5	6		1.2
Venezuela					1.5

[a] Refers to *obras sociales*, and does not include private insurance providers.
[b] Sixteen are open to all, and ten are closed with membership restricted to those working for particular firms.
[c] These refer to the contributory regime only.
Sources: Yermo (2000), Barrientos (1999).

required social protection, even to the minority of workers it covered. The retrenchment of social insurance provision of welfare, the weakening of employment protection, and the replacement of government social programmes with individual savings and private provision have changed the welfare mix in Latin America. Increasingly, the welfare mix can be characterised as liberal-informal, with a narrower specification of social risks, individual saving replacing social insurance, and increased reliance on private provision, without any attempt to develop safety nets.

The discussion in this chapter demonstrates the important role of stratification effects in supporting welfare regime shifts. Changes in the labour market and the employment relationship, and the introduction of individual savings accounts as the preferred welfare instrument, have had the effect of transferring primary responsibility for social risks to the workers themselves, and away from employers and the state. These changes have encouraged the replacement of social insurance and government provision with the private provision of insurance. These changes have also increased the level of social risks for workers, and at the same time they have increased heterogeneity in the distribution of these risks. These changes reinforce the transformation of the welfare mix, and help to shift the Latin American economies firmly towards a liberal-informal welfare regime.

The political economy of the welfare regime shift

The presence of a welfare regime shift in Latin America needs examination. In the context of the welfare regime approach, it would be useful to identify and discuss the conditions under which a welfare reform shift is made possible: in other words, to determine the political economy of welfare regime transformation. In the context of Latin America, what needs to be explained is why Latin Americans would consent to a radical change of the existing welfare mix? And why would they be prepared to countenance a dismantling of existing social insurance structures in the aftermath of an acute economic crisis, when the need for social protection against social risk is greatest?

A key to answering these questions lies in the constraints on social insurance coverage imposed by the developmental model in place in Latin America before the reforms. Social insurance and employment protection covered only formal sector workers in Latin America. As noted above, this was in part a consequence of underdevelopment, but also a direct consequence of the development model itself. The import substitution model of industrialisation was sustained by a political alliance of industrial interests, urban industrial workers and groups attached to the public sector. This development model in turn reinforced this alliance through political mechanisms for capturing and distributing economic rents. Among these, state support for occupational social insurance funds constituted an important device both in enabling the development of the modern sector, and in ensuring sustained support for the development model among workers in formal employment. The crisis of the 1980s in Latin America brought to an end the hegemony of this development model, and replaced it with an export-oriented growth model. This change in the development model aggressively curtailed the political influence of industrial and public sector workers, and undermined support for social insurance among its natural supporters.

Social insurance aimed to provide insurance against life-cycle and ill-health risks, and compensation for family costs to workers with long-term, regular employment. The exclusion of high-risk groups embedded in social insurance and employment protection institutions precluded support for these institutions among workers in vulnerable or informal employment. Under the new development model, employment growth was stronger precisely among those groups usually excluded from social insurance, such as women, workers in micro-enterprises, the unskilled and the self-employed. Employment restructuring following structural adjustment, and the associated steep rise in unemployment, fostered employee mobility and non-standard employment. Changes in the employment relationship, and employment, undermined the constituency of social insurance and employment protection institutions, and transformed the pattern of social risk. This can be observed in the sharp rise in the incidence of unemployment and precarious employment faced by younger entrants to the labour market, who could find little help in social insurance institutions. At any event, the increasing heterogeneity of social risk precluded any collective action in support of social insurance institutions.

Why could beneficiary groups not successfully resist the welfare regime shift? The mechanisms for political representation in Latin America were muted at the time of the reforms to the welfare mix. In an interesting paper, Mesa-Lago investigates the relationship existing between the political environment and the outcomes of pension reform in Latin America. He constructs an index of democratisation reflecting civil and political rights at the time of the legislative approval of pension reform, and an index of the private–public mix of the resulting pension systems. He finds there is an 'inverse relationship existing between the degree of democratisation and the degree of privatisation [in pension reform], so that the least democratic regimes at the time of the reform introduced [pension] systems with a more private mix and the more democratic regimes retained [pension] systems with a more public mix' (Mesa-Lago 1999: 136). A detailed country analysis of pension reform shows that, with the exception of Uruguay, pension reform was pushed through by governments supporting a neo-liberal agenda, and with a majority in parliament, or, as in the case of Chile and Peru, governing by decree (Mesa-Lago 1999). The absence, partial or total, of democratic processes enables far-reaching reforms.

Kay (1999) suggests that pluralist models of political decision-making are not very useful in the Latin American context, especially as neo-liberal governments, supported by multi-lateral lending institutions, could impose their agenda for reform of the welfare regime. Instead, he argues that the observed diversity in pension reform across Southern Cone countries can be explained by the extent to which beneficiary groups could veto the reform agenda. In his view, the absence of pension reform in Brazil, and the nature of the pension reform in Argentina and Uruguay, are explained by the extent to which opponents of pension reform could articulate and make effective their opposition to the reforms. Economic crisis and restructuring greatly diminished the veto power of labour unions and left-of-centre political parties, rates of unionisation fell, and centralised wage bargaining weakened. Changes in employment further weakened the political influence of workers in formal employment.[22] The absence of strong political representation mechanisms and the weakness of labour and political organisations go some way towards explaining the muted opposition to the reforms of social insurance.

Concerns over the sustainability of social insurance institutions also played a part in neutralising opposition to the reforms. Social insurance funds showed large deficits as a consequence of the 1980s crisis, at the same time as government financial support was restricted by fiscal deficits (Mesa-Lago 1989). In unfunded social insurance schemes, restoring financial balance requires a rise in contribution rates and/or cuts in benefits. These undermine credibility in the longer-term survival of the funds, further compounding the problem. By the 1970s, the main social insurance funds in Argentina had already accumulated significant deficits, and this situation became acute in the 1980s. Failure to provide the retired with their full entitlements led to legal actions against the funds. The government acted to consolidate the debt with the funds' beneficiaries and instituted payment of the debt partly in cash and partly in ad hoc bonds. By 1991, the funds debt was estimated at US$5,800 million and involved 2.9 million beneficiaries (Schulthess and Demarco 1993). In Chile, the burden of adjustment fell on contribution rates. The combined employee–employer social insurance payroll contribution rate in 1970 was 25 per cent for public sector white-collar workers, 57 per cent for private sector white-collar workers, and 47 per cent for blue-collar workers. The macro-economic stabilisation package introduced by the military in 1973 led in 1974 to the combined payroll contribution rates increasing to 58, 68 and 60 per cent respectively, gradually declining to around 30 per cent in 1980, and to 23 per cent under the social insurance reform in 1981 (Cheyre 1991). Whether benefit or contribution rates adjustments were used to restore the financial balance of the social insurance funds, these had the effect of undermining credibility in the long-run sustainability of the social insurance funds.

It is interesting to pose the question whether the welfare regime shift could possibly reflect changed voter preferences for the welfare mix.[23]

---

[22] Banuri and Amadeo comment on the importance of a 'centre of gravity' in the development of labour institutions, and argue that under import substitution industrialisation this was, in most cases, constituted by the export sector (Banuri and Amadeo 1992).

[23] There is very little evidence on this for Latin America, and a radical change of this sort is not likely. In Chile, the country with the most radical and earliest structural reform, the political allegiances of voters in the late 1990s broadly mirror, remarkably, the political preferences of the early 1970s, with the right, left and centre parties roughly polling an equal third of the electorate. It is remarkable that the political and economic rollercoaster which Chile experienced in these two decades failed to make a deeper imprint on the political map.

Esping-Andersen attributes the resilience of welfare regimes in developed countries to an increasingly older median voter who has an interest in the stability of the welfare regime. The median voter model assumes a single peaked distribution of voter preferences more likely to reflect the stable and consensual politics in the developed world. In the context of Latin America, the preferences of voters regarding the welfare mix can be better described by a three-peaked distribution of preferences. This would describe, for example, the pattern of health insurance coverage under social insurance presented above. Broadly, wealthy groups self-insure, middle-income groups of skilled workers rely on occupational social insurance and state-supported welfare programmes, and the majority low-income groups rely to a certain extent on limited public healthcare provision, but mainly on out-of-pocket health expenditure financed from labour earnings and family support.[24] When the distribution of voter preferences has more than one peak (the Arrow paradox), there is a strong likelihood that democratic processes may not succeed in aggregating preferences.[25] Furthermore, in Latin America, political institutions show important weaknesses in preference aggregation as well as instability. A three-peaked distribution of preferences, in the context of weak political institutions, may allow for a radical shift in the welfare regime without an equally radical transformation in welfare mix preferences as a necessary precondition. Compared to the situation described by Esping-Andersen, the political institutions and voter preferences in Latin America make a welfare regime shift more likely.

In sum, the constraints on social insurance and employment protection imposed by the development model paved the way for a welfare regime shift in Latin America. Instead of developing towards universal coverage, social insurance and employment protection reinforced the segmentation in the welfare mix by excluding more vulnerable groups of workers. Even health and education programmes, which aspired to universal access and provision, were afflicted by large inequalities in access and quality of provision. The change in the development model from import substitution to export-led growth undermined support for social insurance and employment protection institutions from key stakeholders: the state and employers. The beneficiaries of social insurance and employment protection – workers in formal employment – were weakened by structural reform and proved unable to resist the change in welfare mix. Instability

---

[24] There is an important literature in public economics concluding that voters' preferences for the level of public provision of private goods may lead, under certain circumstances, to the emergence of three broad coalitions (Stiglitz 1974 and Gouveia 1997).

[25] Furthermore when voter preferences are strong on issues which overlap political platforms, democratic institutions may deadlock (the Hillinger paradox) (Chakravarty and Hojman 1999).

and fragmentation in the political mechanisms for preference aggregation, together with the rule of authoritarian regimes in the 1980s, facilitated a welfare regime shift even in the absence of a significant change in voter preferences. In contrast to the experience in developed countries, the distribution of voter preferences regarding the welfare mix, and the weaknesses of political institutions, facilitates welfare regime shifts.

Convergence and divergence: case-studies on social reforms in Bolivia, Argentina and Chile

It will be useful at this stage of the argument to consider the process of change in the welfare mix for specific countries. The welfare regime approach seeks to draw out common traits in welfare production, but at the cost of downplaying country-specific development. It has been established that there is enough commonality in welfare production in Latin America to justify focusing on a single welfare regime for the region as a whole, and that this commonality extends to the changes in the welfare mix and stratification effects leading to a welfare regime shift. At the same time, there are important residual cross-country differences in welfare mix,[26] and it would be interesting to assess whether the dynamics of change in the welfare regime will weaken or strengthen these residual country differences. This would clarify whether the welfare regime shift is associated with divergence or convergence trends.

This section includes short outlines of the social sector reform process in Bolivia, Argentina and Chile. These three countries provide contrasting experiences. This focus on processes will also contribute more detail on the political economy conditions needed for a welfare regime shift. Chile's welfare mix reforms took place under a military dictatorship, but in Argentina and Bolivia the reforms were adopted under democracy. The evolution of Argentina's reforms reflects the interplay of powerful actors in overcoming strong path dependence. Bolivia's experience is interesting, both because it sought to package social reforms with the privatisation of state-owned enterprises, and because of its failed attempt at overcoming the perceived weaknesses of social reforms elsewhere in Latin America.

Chile

Welfare reform in Chile has played a paradigmatic role in Latin America's welfare regime shift. Compared to other countries in the region,

---

[26] The cross-country differences in the welfare mix can only be described as residual in the context of the welfare regime approach, but are primary in other contexts pitched at different levels of abstraction.

Chile's economic restructuring happened earlier and was much deeper. The military coup in 1973, which deposed President Allende and brought to power General Pinochet, was followed by the suspension of political processes and the repression of organised labour and political organisations on the left and centre. Macro-economic stabilisation was followed by far-reaching trade and labour market liberalisation. In 1979, the government began considering an ambitious programme of modernisation of the public services, including health, education and training, labour legislation and welfare. The design of the reforms and their adoption were unencumbered by political scrutiny.[27] The only two groups capable of vetoing the proposals were the military and businesses, and initial opposition from the military was overcome by leaving them out of the reforms.

Reform of employment protection had been implemented de facto, reflecting the weakness of organised labour in a repressive environment, but a new labour code consolidated the changes in the late 1970s. At the same time, public provision of education and healthcare was decentralised financially and administratively. In 1980 the surviving social insurance schemes were radically reformed. Pension schemes were consolidated and closed to new members. Individual retirement plans were introduced instead. In 1981, health insurance was split off from social insurance and newly established private providers were encouraged to attract contributors, in competition with a reformed public health insurance provider. The other social insurance programmes were reformed or wound down and transferred to the government. The thrust of the reforms aimed to change the role of government from provider to regulator, and to encourage private welfare provision. Despite widespread opposition, the reforms took root on the back of an acute recession in 1982, accelerating the rapid decline in public services, and increasing government support and subsidy to the private providers. Individual retirement pension plans accumulated high initial returns, helping to attract a majority of workers in formal employment. The reforms imposed a fundamental shift in welfare production towards a liberal welfare regime.

The return of democratic governments in 1990 has not reversed the reforms, but some important differences in approach can be observed. There has been a greater willingness to regulate private providers and reconsider public subsidies to private provision. There is a stronger commitment to public provision in healthcare, with a substantial injection of resources (Barrientos 2002). Together with the elimination of subsidies to the private sector, it has produced a marked shift from private to public

---

[27] An insider's account of the process can be found in Piñera (1991).

health insurance – to the extent that the continued presence of private provision is threatened. There has been a strengthening of employment rights, but this has been as much the consequence of improved economic conditions as of the introduction of a reformed labour law. Overall, the return to democracy has brought about some changes to the welfare mix, with a rebalancing in favour of public provision and regulation in some areas, but no structural change in the mix. Chile's welfare mix retains its strong liberal features.

Argentina

Welfare reform in Argentina has been a much more complex process than in Chile or Bolivia. This is in part because social insurance institutions were considerably more developed in Argentina prior to the reforms, and are based on political constituencies, especially trade unions, with strong political influence. In the language of Esping-Andersen, Argentina's welfare mix shows stronger path dependence. To an important extent, welfare reform in Argentina is still unfolding, but the direction of the reforms is clearly towards a liberal regime. Argentina provides a good example of the transition from a mainly conservative welfare regime to a typically liberal one, in a relatively open political environment.

Argentina had well-developed welfare provision based around social insurance schemes for specific sets of workers, trade-union-provided health insurance, and state provision of education and healthcare. These showed strong growth during the Peronist dominance in the 1950s and 1960s. The political settlement gave considerable power to the trade unions, and fostered a corporatist consensus on social protection, which survived the political instability and dictatorship of the 1970s and 1980s (Lo Vuolo 1997). In the meantime, economic problems in the shape of unemployment, inflation and fiscal deficits continued to mount. The rise to power of President Menem, a Peronist, in 1989 produced a radical change in policy. He began a far-reaching structural adjustment programme, which included the privatisation of state-owned enterprises, the opening up of the economy to world markets, dollarisation with a strict convertibility plan, and a substantial weakening of employment protection legislation and payroll taxes.

The reforms extended to welfare provision. Changing conditions in the labour market led to a significant weakening of employment-based social protection, and both de facto and de jure flexibility in employment. A reform of the pension system was introduced in 1994, while a reform of health insurance, started in 1995, is still in progress. Administrative and financial decentralisation of education and healthcare has replaced the aspiration to universality in provision and has encouraged the expansion of private provision, especially in secondary healthcare and higher education.

The reform process has been complex and slow, as the political influence of trade unions and other constituencies remained strong. The Menem government took extraordinary economic emergency powers which neutralised some of these power groups, but it has also fragmented opposition by involving some unions in the reform process. Pension reform is a good example. It initially aimed to provide a two-pillar system with a basic safety net pension complemented by individual retirement plans. Opposition from trade unions, the retired and social insurance institutions forced amendments in parliament which required employer contributions to finance the basic safety net pension, retained defined-benefit complementary pensions in competition with individual retirement plans, and included a public pension fund manager. After the implementation of the reform in 1994, subsequent changes have scaled down entitlements to the basic safety net pension, and limited transfers from the private individual retirement plans to the public defined-benefit pension scheme (Barrientos 1998). Health insurance reforms followed a similar pattern. Initial reforms aimed to consolidate and financially strengthen union-dominated *obras sociales*, but subsequent changes have encouraged competition from private health insurance providers (Barrientos and Lloyd-Sherlock 2000).

Welfare reforms in Argentina have followed, as in other Latin American countries, structural changes in the economy, with far-reaching repercussions on the labour market. These have weakened the key groups likely to lose in the process of welfare reform: trade unions, public sector workers, the old and the poor (Ghilarducci and Ledesma 2000). The emergency powers of the Menem government, and the acquiescence of some unions, helped to fragment and diffuse opposition to the reforms, and ensured a transition to a liberal welfare mix. The recent crisis in Argentina threatens this transition. When the Argentine government was forced to abandon parity with the dollar and devalue the peso at the end of 2001, accumulated pension balances lost one-third of their value at a stroke. The government's subsequent attempt to raid pension savings to finance its debt unleashed a deep political and financial crisis which, at the end of 2002, remained unresolved.

Bolivia

Bolivia's reform of pension provision provides an interesting dimension of welfare regime shift in Latin America. Bolivia embarked upon pension reform later than other countries in the region. Pension reform designers in Bolivia attempted to emulate the Chilean model of pension reform by transforming the existing unfunded social insurance pension plans into individual retirement plans, but with special features imposed by country-specific structural adjustment (von Gersdorff 1997). Pension reform formed part of a package of 'second-generation' reforms[28] instituted in the mid-1990s, including administrative decentralisation, education, land reform and capitalisation of state-owned enterprises (Gray-Molina 1999).

Three key features are unique to the Bolivian pension reform: the link between pension reform and capitalisation of state-owned enterprises, the introduction of a universal basic pension benefit financed from the dividends from capitalisation, and monopoly in private provision. First, in its design, motivation and implementation, pension reform was directly linked to the capitalisation of state-owned enterprises. Capitalisation involved the incorporation of state-owned enterprises, with one-half of shares offered to private investors, and the other half kept as a Collective Capitalisation Fund (Fondo de Capitalizacion Colectiva) financing pension benefits (UDAPE 1997). Second, a universal pension benefit, the BONOSOL (Bono de Solidaridad), was to be financed by dividends from the Collective Capitalisation Fund, paying a fixed monthly benefit to all citizens over sixty-five.[29] Third, the government split the territory into two, and tendered pension fund management to international financial institutions, eventually selecting two Spanish banks (Argentaria and BBV). These managed the individual retirement accounts of pension affiliates and the Collective Capitalisation Fund.

Opposition to pension reform came from the many pension funds predating the reforms, from trade unions, and from organisations of the retired. Linking together the capitalisation of state-owned enterprises and pension reform, and including a universal pension entitlement, helped defuse opposition from the retired, and to a lesser extent from trade unions. More importantly, it helped defuse opposition to capitalisation.

Financial constraints on the one hand, and political instability and instrumentalism on the other, led to the unravelling of the pension reform soon after its implementation. The incorporation of state-owned enterprises began in 1993, extending to enterprises in the transport, telecommunications and petrochemical sectors. The BONOSOL began to be

---

[28] 'Second-generation' because they followed on from 'first-generation' structural adjustment in 1985.

[29] Entitlement was restricted to those aged twenty-one and over on December 1995, on the grounds that these cohorts had contributed to building up state-owned enterprises, but younger cohorts had not.

paid in May 1997 (just before the June 1997 general election), but was quickly suspended in January 1998. The rapid rise in take-up (reaching 364,000 beneficiaries compared to an estimate of 200,000) left the scheme in deficit from the start. In June 1998, the government introduced legislation to replace BONOSOL with BOLIVIDA, scaling down entitlements.[30] Payment of the BOLIVIDA started in December 2000 at US$60 a year (less than a quarter of the BONOSOL's US$248 a year) (Muller 2001), but was suspended soon after. The merger of Argentaria and BBV, the two banks selected to manage pension funds, removed even potential competition in the management of the new pension plans.

Bolivia provides an example of a social sector reform introduced to ensure the success of the privatisation of state-owned enterprises, a link implicit in social sector reforms in other Latin American countries, but made explicit in Bolivia's. The attempt to graft universal entitlements onto this helped line up sufficient support for these reforms, but it unravelled soon after implementation. In the process, existing social insurance institutions built around formal employment have given way to self-insurance and private provision.

The brief case-studies show a strong commonality in social sector reforms, and in the direction of the changes to the welfare mix in the region. There is considerable similarity in the design of the reforms, supported and orchestrated by international organisations. There is a strong convergence trend in the welfare mix of Latin American countries. The emerging welfare regime shows an important measure of path dependence, as indicated by the evolution of social sector reforms in Chile after the return to democracy. The reforms to the welfare mix differ mainly with regard to the political economy conditions required for the adoption, design and implementation of the reforms (Grindle 2001). These explain country differences in the speed and extent of social sector reform. A key issue remains how to integrate solidarity objectives into the reforms, and many of the potential divergence trends are associated with the way different countries in Latin America respond to this issue.

Conclusion

This chapter has investigated whether the welfare regime approach developed by Esping-Andersen can be usefully applied to Latin American countries. The broad conclusion is that the exercise has been productive. The welfare regime approach can provide an effective and fruitful

---

[30] Only those aged fifty on December 1995 are entitled; the younger groups will receive one-off 'people's shares' (*acciones populares*), though this has not yet been finalised.

framework for a comprehensive analysis of welfare production in Latin America, and the changes experienced in the late 1980s and 1990s. The welfare regime approach proved to be particularly useful in exploring the linkages between social protection and labour market institutions, and their change in the region.

The welfare mix in Latin America prior to the recent reforms could be best characterised as conservative-informal. It exhibited many of the key features of the Southern European variant of the conservative welfare regime identified by Esping-Andersen in developed countries. It relied on stratified social insurance and employment protection as the core of welfare production. In contrast to conservative regimes in developed countries, in Latin America these applied to workers in formal employment only. Workers in informal employment relied instead on the household and the labour market as sources of insurance against social risk. Welfare production as it applied to them exhibited some similarities with Esping-Andersen's liberal welfare mix, especially a very narrow specification of social risks and residual state welfare programmes, but in contrast to liberal welfare regimes, Latin American countries did not develop means-tested social assistance programmes.

In the late 1980s and 1990s, fundamental welfare and labour market reform successfully redefined the welfare mix, scaling down employment protection, replacing social insurance with insurance schemes based on individual savings offered by private providers, decentralising education and health provision, and encouraging private provision and private financing. As these conservative components of welfare production fall away, the emerging pattern can be best characterised as liberal-informal.

The changes to the welfare mix have been facilitated and reinforced by changes in the labour market and the employment relationship, and also by the development of individual saving as a key insurance instrument. These have further undermined existing social insurance institutions, have ensured the concentration of risk on the workers themselves, and have reinforced a greater heterogeneity in the distribution of social risk. The acute economic crises experienced by all countries in the region in the 1980s and early 1990s led to a change in the development model. Structural reform, against a background of stratified and restrictive social insurance and political instability and fragmentation, paved the way for the implementation of the shift in the welfare mix.

The main welfare outcomes of the shift in welfare regime have been largely negative. Unemployment is high and persistent. Inequalities in income, and especially labour income, have risen. Poverty incidence has stagnated or declined marginally, despite economic growth. Social protection coverage has fallen significantly for all countries except Colombia.

Despite advances in access, the coverage and quality of the public provision of education and health programmes remains highly unequal. The welfare regime shift in Latin America has resulted in a rise in the level and heterogeneity of social risk.

Fundamental change in economic and social institutions in Latin America provides a rare example of a shift in welfare regime. The resilience of welfare regimes, observed by Esping-Andersen for developed countries, is largely absent in Latin America, and arguably in other developing countries. The welfare regime shift in Latin America can be explained by the political economy conditions associated with a change in development model from import substitution industrialisation to export-oriented growth, which strengthened authoritarianism and weakened opponents to the reforms. Weak mechanisms for preference aggregation, sharp inequalities of income, and rising heterogeneity in social risk all contributed to facilitate changes in the welfare mix. A brief examination of the process of welfare mix change in three contrasting countries points to a growing convergence in welfare production in the region towards an already dominant liberal-informal welfare regime.

5   East Asia: the limits of productivist regimes

Ian Gough

Introduction

Benedict Anderson identifies a common post-war pattern of development in the 'long strip of coastal capitalist states stretching down from
South Korea to the eastern edge of the Indian Ocean' (Anderson 1998:
300). This definition of East Asia excludes the two regional powers, Japan
and China, alongside North Korea. It embraces ASEAN, the Association
of Southeast Asian Nations, but leaves Myanmar in limbo, and extends
northwards to include South Korea, Taiwan and Hong Kong. The major
countries are shown in table 5.1, in order of economic affluence. All the
countries, except Thailand, were colonised up to and including the twentieth century but by a variety of different powers: Portugal, Spain, the
Netherlands, France, Britain, the US and Japan. The region also en-
compasses vast differences, from rich Singapore to very poor Laos and
Cambodia – country variations wider than those in any other part of
the world. To make our task manageable, this chapter will ignore the
richest – the city-states of Singapore and Hong Kong – and the poorest – the newly emerging economies of Vietnam, Cambodia and Laos.
The remaining group are all classified by the World Bank as 'middle income', though Indonesia hovers on the borderline of low-income
countries.

Within this group, I concentrate on five countries: Indonesia, South
Korea, Malaysia, the Philippines and Thailand. These are of interest for
three reasons. They have all been participants in the 'East Asian miracle' and beneficiaries of the alleged benefits of economic openness and
market-friendly policies (World Bank 1993). They have in common a very
restricted range of social protection measures combined with relatively
good welfare outcomes. And they were all notable victims of the Asian
financial crisis of 1997–9, which exposed the risks of globalisation and
the precariousness of existing social protection. Despite these similarities
they differ in many ways, not least in economic development. Korea's
income per head is roughly double that of Malaysia, the next richest,

Table 5.1. *East Asia, major countries: basic data*

	Population (millions)		Income per capita (GNP) ($)			Income per capita PPP (GNI) ($)	Labour force in agriculture (%)	
	1970	2000	1970	1997	2000	2000	1970	1998
Singapore	2.1	4.0	960	32,810	24,740	24,910	3	0.2
Hong Kong	3.9	6.9	890	25,200	25,920	25,590	4	0.3
Taiwan	14.0	22.2	390	13,560	14,087	N/A	37	8.6
Korea	31.9	47.3	260	10,550	8,910	17,300	49	18.1
Malaysia	10.9	23.3	390	4,530	3,380	8,330	54	27.3
Thailand	35.8	60.7	190	2,740	2,000	6,320	80	64.1
Philippines	37.5	75.6	240	1,200	1,040	4,220	58	45.8
Indonesia	117.5	210.4	90	1,110	570	2,830	66	55.2
Vietnam	39.5	78.1	300	310	390	2,000	77	68.9[a]
Lao PDR	3.0	5.3	120	400	290	1,540	81	N/A
Cambodia	7.5	13.1	130	260	260	1,440	79	73.7[a]
Total/ weighted av.	303.6	546.9	234	4,198	3,224	9,339	61	42.1

Note: [a] percentage of the employed.
Source: World Bank (2002a); ADB, http://www.adb.org/statistics/ default.asp.

and is ten times that of Indonesia, the poorest (in terms of purchasing power parity the difference is six to one – see table 5.1).

Our focus in this chapter is thus on four major countries of Southeast Asia plus Korea. This chapter[1] analyses the regimes in this region using the framework set out in chapter 1 in five stages. First, I describe in some detail the welfare mix or institutional responsibility matrix of the five countries, covering the role of states, markets, communities, households and international actors and institutions. Second, welfare outcomes in the region are briefly sketched. The third section then identifies a unifying East Asian policy regime, and goes on to present a political economy analysis and explanation of this, focusing on the stratification effects and internal and external determinants in Northeast Asia and Southeast Asia respectively. I conclude that East Asia exhibits a novel form of productivist social development regime. The fourth section then considers the impact of the economic–financial crisis of 1997 and the unmitigated sources of insecurity which this revealed. Finally, I speculate about the likely future development of social policy and ask whether the crisis is the harbinger of a regime shift in the region.

[1] Thanks to my doctoral students, Shin Dong-myeon, Kim Jin-wook, Choi Young-jun and Jerick Aguilar, for valuable research assistance, and to Peng Ito and colleagues in the Bath research group for helpful comments on an earlier draft of this chapter.

Table 5.2. *Public expenditure, percentage of GDP*

	Total govt revenue 1997–98	Total govt expenditure 1997–98	Education 1995–97	Health 1997–98	Social security 1990–97	Total education health, SS 1990–98
Japan	31.9	29.4	3.7	5.3	6.7	15.7
Singapore	24.5	16.8	1.8	1.2	0.8(2.2)[a]	3.8(5.2)[a]
Hong Kong	20.9	14.5	2.6	1.7	1.2	5.5
Taiwan	26.1	22.7	5.0	3.5	2.2	10.7
Korea	20.0	17.4	3.7	2.2	3.0	8.9
Malaysia	23.1	19.7	4.7	1.3	1.4	7.4
Thailand	16.4	18.6	4.7	1.7	0.7	7.1
Philippines	19.0	19.3	3.6	1.7	2.8	8.1
Indonesia	16.8	17.9	1.3	0.6	1.1	3.0
Average	19.1	18.6	3.6	1.6	2.2	7.4

Notes: [a] Including social-related withdrawals from the central provident fund.
Main Sources: World Bank (2002a).
ADB (1998: figs 2.7, 2.8).
http://www.stat.go.jp, http://www.taiwanheadlines.gov.tw, http://www.info.gov.hk,
Social security: Korea: OECD 2001; Philippines: ILO
www.ilo.org/public/english/protection/socsec/publ/css/phil93e.htm

Social policy and the welfare mix in East Asia

State social policies

Public social expenditure in East Asia is very low on a world scale (see table 5.2). Total spending on education, health and social security varies with level of development, ranging from 3 per cent of GDP in Indonesia, 7–8 per cent in Malaysia, the Philippines and Thailand, to 11 per cent in Korea. Less than half of total government spending is devoted to all social spending. However, rapid economic growth means that real resources devoted to the social sector have expanded faster than in most countries. There is a generalised hostility to Western ideas of the 'welfare state' except paradoxically for employees of the state – social provision for civil servants, the military and police, teachers, and others is everywhere extensive and generous.

East Asian governments have consistently emphasised the central role of *education* in economic development, though this is not matched by a higher-than-average expenditure for middle-income countries. The general verdict is that the allocation of resources is more effectively targeted on basic education than in other developing countries (World Bank

Table 5.3. *Education enrolment indicators*

	Primary		Secondary		Tertiary		Average years
	1970	1995	1970	1995	1970	1995	of study 1992
Korea	103	101	41	101	8	52	13.1
Malaysia	89	91	30	61	2	11	9.3
Thailand	81	89	17	55	2	20	8.9
Philippines	108	117	46	79	20	27	11.6
Indonesia	80	113	16	48	2	11	9.0

Sources: Mingat (1998: table 3); World Bank (1997).

1993: 192–203). Most villages (and urban neighbourhoods) across these vast territories have a working school with teachers who turn up to teach each day. Nevertheless, there have been significant differences in educational development across the region according to the colonial legacies of the different countries. The Japanese occupation of Taiwan and Korea resulted in a remarkable expansion of educational opportunities. 'No other colonial power in Asia or elsewhere approached native education with anything like the seriousness of purpose of Japanese educators in Taiwan'. The other exception is the US legacy of high schools and college education in the Philippines. As a result, these three countries had achieved near-universal primary education in the early post-war period. The colonial record elsewhere in the region was meagre. However, by the 1980s Malaysia, Thailand and Indonesia had achieved near-universal primary education. The development of secondary, not to speak of tertiary, education is far more patchy. The Philippines, Taiwan and Korea had enrolled over one-half of children in the 1970s and Malaysia had done this same in the 1980s, whereas Thailand and Indonesia lagged far behind. 'Singapore, Malaysia, Thailand and Indonesia all had lower levels of educational attainment [in the 1990s] than Taiwan or South Korea in the 1960s'. In terms of standards of achievement, Korea and Taiwan stand out with levels above the international norm, contrasting sharply with lower-than-average standards in Southeast Asia (Mingat 1998: tables 5, 8). Higher education is expanding but remains remarkably undeveloped in Malaysia and Indonesia, resulting in education overseas or in sub-contracted campuses at home. The absence or poor quality of tertiary education probably reflects the fear felt by authoritarian regimes for volatile student bodies (Anderson 1998: 306).

Health expenditure is low in East Asia compared with other middle-income countries and actually fell as a share of GDP in the 1990s in all countries except Thailand (Ramesh 2000: table 4.5). Since private spending accounts for over one-half of the total, public health expenditure is remarkably low – between 0.6 per cent of GDP in Indonesia and 2.5 per cent in Korea. Not surprisingly, all health inputs (doctors, nurses, hospital beds) are very scarce on a world scale. Yet governments are heavily involved in all countries, and there is reasonable access to basic and preventive health care, with Korea and Malaysia as the best performers. 'The widespread availability of public health care in Southeast Asia suggests that most sick people have some access to health care' (Ramesh 2000: 113). In all five countries governments provide an infrastructure of health centres and hospitals, yet almost two-thirds of the cost is paid directly by individuals.

Beyond basic healthcare countries diverge, except for the ubiquitous and superior provision for civil servants and state employees. All countries, apart from Malaysia, now have some form of public health insurance for organised workers, though with widely different levels of coverage and quality. The Philippines has a long-established health insurance system, but with low coverage and erratic provision of services. (The 1995 National Health Insurance Act plans to provide universal healthcare by 2010.) Taiwan and Korea introduced limited health insurance for privileged groups which was slowly extended. In 1995 Taiwan moved towards a fully fledged national health insurance scheme. From a later start Korea has also moved, in little over a decade, to a national health insurance system – universal and integrated but with high co-payments and not yet redistributive. Indonesia has a minimal system of health insurance for limited sections of the population and Thailand legislated in 1990 a Social Security Act which is intended to provide free medical care and income compensation, though it is unclear how this is progressing (Phananiramai and Hewison in OECD 2002). All countries except for Malaysia also have free and subsidised healthcare programmes or other forms of medical assistance for lower-income groups. Malaysia has a more British-style national health service, backed up by personal medical accounts within the employee provident fund and a growing private sector. In conclusion, Korea, Taiwan and Thailand appear to be following the Philippines into national health insurance, Malaysia exhibits public provision with a growing private sector, and Indonesia is yet to develop a coherent health plan (figure 5.1).

Social security across the region has a low salience, extremely low public spending and low coverage (Asher 1998; ADB 1998; Ramesh and Asher 2000). This applies to pensions, with the exception of pensions for civil servants, the military and teachers. For the rest of the population, the national pension systems divide into two main types: social insurance

	Public	Medical assistance	Social insurance	Provident fund
Korea	Public health services	Medical assistance (1977)	Medical insurance programme (1977), universal medical insurance plan (1989), National Health Insurance Act (1999)	
Malaysia	National health service, rural health service			EPF: Account III
Thailand	Public health services, medical benefits for civil servants	Free medical care for poor, aged, and children, community health card, public assistance	Social security system (1992)	
Philippines	Public hospitals	Free services for indigent	Medicare	
Indonesia	Public health centres	Means-tested free services	ASKES (Asuransi Kesehatan Pegawai Negeri): civil servants and military; JAMSOSTEK (Jaminan Sosial Tenaga Kerja): private sector	

Sources: Ramesh (2000: table 4.3); Shin (2000).

Figure 5.1. Healthcare systems in East Asia

in the Philippines, Korea, Taiwan and Thailand, and provident funds in Malaysia and Indonesia. The Filipino scheme is more than forty years old and continues to expand its coverage, including voluntary membership for Filipinos working overseas. Replacement rates are high at around 60 per cent, but employer compliance is low, with up to two-thirds of the paper members not contributing at any one time (Ramesh and Asher 2000: 71). From a late start in 1988, the national pension scheme in Korea is extending its coverage and building up a transitory fund over a twenty-year period – full pensions will not start until 2008. Thailand, in January 1999, added an old-age pension element to the Social Security Act of 1990. This is a defined-benefit pay-as-you-go scheme but will not pay out full pensions until 2014 and non-compliance is high.

The Malaysian employee provident fund (EPF) founded by the British in 1951 – the first in the world – is a developed, expensive and savings-effective fund. Since 1994, members have been able to opt for an annuity instead of a lump-sum pay-out. Reforms have established separate accounts for education and health and have encouraged more flexible individual investment. However, the EPF provides weak protection against poverty in old age, offers insecure returns and, through tax exemptions and other features, redistributes to the wealthy. Despite an almost

	Social assistance	Social insurance	Provident fund	Mandated occupational	
				Defined benefit	Defined contribution
Korean Republic	Public assistance programme (1969)	National pension scheme (1988), universal coverage (1999)		Schemes for civil servants, military, and private school teachers	Company severance pay schemes
Malaysia	Social assistance programme		Employees' provident fund (1951, 1991, 1995)	Civil servant and company schemes (lump sums)	
Thailand		Social Security Act (1990, implemented 1998)		Government pensions and provident fund for state and some private employees	Large corporations: voluntary Provident Fund Act (1987/96)
Philippines		Social security system (1957, 1997)	Pag-IBIG fund 1998	Government service insurance system	Company pension schemes
Indonesia			JAMSOSTEK (1951/92)	TASPEN: civil servants; ASABRI: military and police	Large-company schemes

Source: Stanton and Whiteford (1998: tables 4.2, 4.3); World Bank (1999a: 70); Ramesh (2000: 65).

Figure 5.2. Old-age/retirement programmes in East Asia

equally long history, the JAMSOSTEK fund of Indonesia has a small coverage, uneven record-keeping, tiny reserves and poor governance (figure 5.2).

Formal *safety nets* can be defined as public programmes targeted to the poor with the objective of raising living standards to a specified social minimum. They can take the form of cash transfers, public works employment and subsidies for important need satisfiers, such as food and housing. Before the crisis they were limited in scale, coverage and cost throughout the region, but they have been expanded in response to the crisis and are thus considered later in this chapter, pp. 195–7.

Market

Access to the *labour* market is a major resource in East Asia, as in the OECD, and the expansion of wage labour in the region has been remarkable. Over the two decades until 1997 the labour force grew by 2 per cent per annum. The regional participation rate is high: ranging from 89 per cent in Thailand to 66 per cent in Malaysia. This labour force is becoming feminised, but, with the exception of Thailand where it is higher, the overall share of women at about 40 per cent is roughly the world average. Unemployment rates were consistently low, except in the Philippines, until the crisis of 1997–8 (World Bank 1999a: 14). Despite remarkably extensive labour protection legislation, the practice is poor due to weak government agencies, official corruption and weak trade unions (Deery and Mitchell 1993; Rigg 1997: 223–7). Nevertheless, growing access to the formal labour market – commodification – has been a critical feature of East Asian welfare regimes.

The private market for *social services* is substantial and fast-growing. One-half of all education spending and almost two-thirds of all health spending is privately financed (Gough 2003c: 508), while life insurance premiums equal state social security spending in all countries except the Philippines. Korean households spend 10 per cent of their income on education and 5 per cent on health, compared to 1.4 per cent and 1.3 per cent in the UK (Shin 2000). Much of this is reactive and unorganised, comprising out-of-pocket expenditure, book purchases and self-medication. Government regulation of private providers is typically weak. There is as yet little development of private life insurance or pensions. Boundaries between the public and private sectors are 'shallow' (Jacobs 1998).

In Japan and Korea, *enterprise welfare* is also notably important. This non-statutory welfare provided by firms, especially larger firms, can include severance pay, housing benefits, assistance with the costs of weddings, births and funerals, and (a fast growing area) assistance with private education expenses and fees. Initially pushed by the state to economise on public spending, and by more paternalist and anti-union firms as a means of social control, it emerged as an increasing site of union demands following the democratic turn in Korea in 1987. However, it has been steadily declining in Japan since the 1980s (Peng 2000). It is insignificant across the rest of the region.

Community, civil society and NGOs

Non-profit and non-governmental organisations active in the field of human development and welfare are a very recent phenomenon in East Asia, where in the past they have been discouraged by authoritarian regimes (Yamamoto 1995). The one exception is the Philippines where they have a longer history due to the American and Catholic legacy. The Marcos martial law period encouraged radical voluntary organisations, based mainly on churches and universities, to challenge abuses and human rights violations and eventually to contribute to his overthrow. With the arrival of the Aquino government, NGOs entered the mainstream and were recognised in the new constitution. However, with recognition has come dependence, incorporation and fragmentation. There are now an estimated 59,000 NGOs embracing membership-based organisations, development and advocacy agencies, traditional charitable and welfare organisations, and government-run and business-organised NGOs (Luna 2000). Some of these are integrated in the nine 'flagship programmes' of the 1994 social reform agenda. The dynamism, commitment and creativity of the Philippines' third sector is self-evident, but so are its failures. These include confusion and duplication at local levels, a wide gap between rhetoric and policy substance, poor targeting and administration and an inability to dent mass poverty (May 2002).

The remainder of East Asia has had a different history but is witnessing some resurgence of civil society and NGO activity. Following democratisation community development is now a burgeoning part of social policy across the region. The role of developmental NGOs varies from high-profile activism in Thailand through a more moderate role in Indonesia and Malaysia to persistent controls in Singapore. Thailand appears to be following the Philippines in promoting NGOs in social welfare and development issues (there were an estimated 8,000 in 1997) (Godement 2000). However, the total amount of funds disbursed by community health NGOs is small relative to Thailand's total health expenditure. Moreover, all NGOs remain heavily dependent on external sources for funds, notably official overseas aid organisations, US philanthropic funds and Japanese corporate funds. The third sector appears to have a poor record in provisioning social welfare (as opposed to organising the poor and campaigning for welfare): even *zakat* raises significant sums of money in countries like Malaysia only because the state endorses and regulates the practice and promotes a streamlined administration through the 1986 Zakat Act (Ghazali 1991). Rodan (1997) concludes that the prospects for civil society in Southeast Asia are of extended forms of state co-option and of dominance by privileged business and professional groups.

Family – household

Throughout East Asia, the extended family persists as a provider, saver and redistributor, despite rapid economic development and urbanisation. The level of savings is extremely high in East Asia, the Philippines excepted, which should permit more families to mitigate risk by 'self-insuring': saving in good times and dis-saving in bad times (World Bank 2000a: chapter 5). However, despite the substantial development of micro-finance and credit schemes, the unequal distribution of incomes undermines this in Southeast Asia. On the other hand, calculations of private transfers show high levels in the Philippines, Indonesia and Malaysia, adding between 9 and 20 per cent to the average incomes of recipient households. These outweigh public transfers by several orders of magnitude. In the 1980s, the majority of people over sixty years were receiving income from family members and an even higher proportion lived with children or family – between 75 per cent and 95 per cent in the Philippines and Thailand. These remarkably high proportions are now falling in Korea, from 78 per cent in 1984 to 49 per cent in 1994.[2]

International components of the welfare mix

No world region received more US 'aid', military, economic and political, in the third quarter of the twentieth century, when it was the leading zone of Cold War contestation. Following the US–China rapprochement this rapidly tailed off, but was replaced in part by burgeoning private investment flows. Before the Asian financial crisis, Korea and Malaysia received no ODA, but it remains of some significance – between 0.4 and 0.8 per cent of GNP – in the other three countries. Short-term crisis aid to countries such as Indonesia since 1997 has raised this share but it remains a marginal contributor to the East Asian welfare mix.

In contrast, international firms see the region as a growing market for a variety of health products, ranging from drugs to health maintenance organisations. This is mainly the result of gaps in public provision, but is increasingly being sponsored by governments. For example, Indonesia permitted for-profit hospitals in 1988, extended this to foreign investment in large hospitals in 1994 and, in 2003, will permit unrestricted foreign investment in all healthcare (EIU 1999: 115). There is also a growing market for overseas health treatment for the rich, notably in regional centres such as Singapore, Hong Kong and Australia.

The dominant international household strategy is labour migration and remittances of money, especially in the Philippines. By 1995 1.5 million Filipinos lived abroad as permanent immigrants and a further 2 million at least worked temporarily abroad or at sea (Woodiwiss 1998: 101). The remittances they send home amount to 6.4 per cent of Filipino GNP, and 10 per cent if unrecorded cash and goods brought home by workers are included (ILO 2000b: tables 2, 4). These flows, together with the household flows within the country discussed above, constitute a

[2] World Bank (1994: 63) and www.worldbank.org/poverty/safety/design/choosing2p28. htm: table 1.

% of GDP (% of total social expenditure)

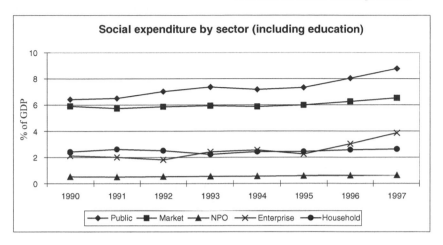

Source: Gough and Kim (2000).

Figure 5.3. The welfare mix in Korea

significant element of the Filipino welfare regime. There is also evidence that overseas workers from the same village or neighbourhood fund improvements to community facilities back home, such as schools and health centres. Illegal Indonesian migration is also important, notably in Malaysia, as is migration to Thailand from Mynamar, and onward migration of Thais to Singapore, Malaysia and Taiwan (Oberndorfer and Berndt 2000).

The overall welfare mix

It is difficult to construct comparative measures of these different elements. However, we have managed to produce estimates for Korea in figure 5.3 (Gough and Kim 2002). Alongside public expenditure, this includes estimates of market spending (households' market purchases of education and health services), non-profit organisations' spending on health, social welfare and education, enterprise welfare (all non-statutory welfare as well as mandatory severance pay) and private transfers between family members in different households in the form of both regular gifts and lump-sum transfers. When all such items are included, 'welfare' expenditure accounted for 22.4 per cent of Korean GDP in 1997. This figure is not far removed from the size of the social budget in the USA. However, the contrast between the scale of the Korean 'welfare state'

(9 per cent of GDP) and the Korean 'welfare society' (22 per cent of GDP) shows the importance of considering functional equivalents of the welfare state in less-developed and non-Western settings. The most important components of the welfare mix in Korea are state and market, with 39 per cent and 29 per cent of the total in 1997, followed by enterprise welfare (17 per cent) and family transfers (12 per cent). The non-profit sector is of little significance. Over time, the most notable change has been the rising share of enterprise welfare after 1995, though the overall stability of each component of the welfare mix is evident. Excluding education, the shares of state, market, enterprise and family are even more similar. Korea has a remarkably mixed welfare mix.

A summary of the welfare mix in the rest of the region must be less precise. It comprises low public responsibility (in terms of expenditure and provision if not regulation), extensive family provision and redistribution, and growing private markets and community-based organisations. Until the 1997 financial crisis, the countries had been curtailing their dependence on aid, but they increased their openness to commercial penetration from abroad. Within the public sector priority is given to social investment in health and education, notably basic healthcare and primary education, with very little attention to social protection.

Welfare outcomes

We pointed out in chapter 1 the necessity to take a broad view of welfare outcomes in order to capture the range of threats to human welfare and security in the developing world. 'De-commodification' has less meaning in societies with significant agricultural and informal labour and is not systematically measured in East Asia, but we may be confident that it is low. Labour in Southeast Asia in particular is either pre-commodified, working in subsistence agriculture, or it is commodified – reliant on the labour market with few statutory protections or substitutes. Indeed, opportunities to participate in the labour market are a key feature of the East Asian welfare regime.

Let us begin, then, with 'poverty' and 'human development'. For a decade or more the East Asian record in poverty reduction has been recognised as exemplary in the international community. The absolute numbers of East Asian people (excluding China) living on less than $1 a day more than halved in the decade 1987–97, while the share of the poor in the total population fell to one in ten from a rate some four times higher in the 1970s. Taking a relative poverty line, the record is less good, showing 23 per cent living on less than one-third of the average national consumption in 1996 (World Bank 2001a). Many groups continue to

Table 5.4. *Welfare outcomes: human development, poverty and inequality*

	Human development index			Human poverty index (%)	Poverty: national measures	Poverty rates <$1 a day	Poverty rates <$2 a day	Poverty gap at $2 a day	Gini index
	1975	1997	2000	Latest	1987–2000	1994–6	1994–6	1994–6	1990s
Singapore	0.72		0.89	7					
Hong Kong	0.76		0.89	–					
Korea	0.69	0.85	0.88	–	–				31.6
Malaysia	0.61	0.77	0.78	11	16	15	22	7	49.2
Thailand	0.60	0.75	0.76	14	13	13	24	5	41.4
Philippines	0.65	0.74	0.75	15	38	37	63	27	46.2
Indonesia	0.47	0.68	0.68	19	35	27	50	15	31.7
Vietnam	–		0.69	27	51				
Lao PDR	–		0.49	39	46				
Cambodia	–		0.54	43	36				
Average	0.60	0.76	0.77	15.25	24.25	23	39.75	13.5	40.00

Sources: World Bank (2002a); United Nations (2002).

suffer significant and quasi-permanent social exclusion, including 'hill peoples', migrant workers, street children, orphans and refugees (Rigg 1997: chapter 4; World Bank 1999a: 6). Country data on poverty rates and poverty gaps reveal three patterns: low rates in Korea, medium levels in Malaysia and Thailand and persistently high levels in Indonesia and the Philippines (table 5.4). This reflects levels of economic development and inequality. The relatively egalitarian distribution in Korea and Northeast Asia is not repeated in the Southeast, notably in Malaysia and the Philippines. All these trends have been affected by the East Asian crisis discussed later on.

The regional record in improving human development is also outstanding. The average human development index for the five countries improved from 0.60 to 0.76 in the last quarter of the last century (UNDP 2002; see table 5.4). Country variations in HDI are much less than those in income poverty, notably in the Philippines where human poverty is less extensive than material poverty. To understand this we need to focus on the two non-monetary components, health and education.

Mortality, including infant mortality, has declined remarkably in the last three decades throughout the region and is low compared with countries at similar levels of development. The provision of sanitation, water and preventive health is also superior to comparator countries. Less impressive are the very high levels of maternal mortality and extensive child malnutrition, notably in Indonesia and the Philippines. These are symptomatic of a major failure to reduce further inequalities in health and access to health-related services such as immunisation, obstetric care, piped water and sanitation, together with persistent poverty. The region also faces new health threats, stemming from ageing and the epidemiological transition, urbanisation (e.g. traffic accidents) and lifestyle changes (e.g. more smoking) (World Bank 1999b). Korea and Malaysia do better on all fronts, whereas the Philippines performs worse than its income level would warrant. Since the end of the Indonesian massacres, the Vietnam War and the killings in Cambodia the region has suffered relatively little from political violence.

Illiteracy is all but eradicated in Korea, the Philippines and Thailand, but persists in Malaysia and Indonesia. Gender differences in literacy and school enrolment are very low in a comparative context. This may reflect the relatively egalitarian nature of gender relations in the region when compared with Northeast and South Asia.[3] More subtle measures of quality in education outcomes show a different pattern: Singapore and Korea are world leaders, whereas Indonesia, the Philippines and Thailand fall below the 'international mean' (Mingat 1998: 701).

In conclusion, East Asia exhibited rapidly improving levels of welfare outcomes in the last quarter of the last century, resulting in comparatively good scores on the eve of the 1997 crisis. However, the equality and sustainability of this level of human development is questioned today.

Productivist welfare regimes in East Asia

I shall argue below that these East Asian countries comprise, with one exception and some variations, a *productivist welfare regime*. There is a common pattern of institutions and outcomes which unites them and demarcates them from other countries and world regions. Unlike Africa and South Asia there are vigorous capitalist sectors and viable national states. Unlike Latin America, which resembles Southern Europe, social policy is not conceived of as an autonomous sphere of policy concerned to de-commodify and extend social rights. Rather it is part of an economic and developmental strategy to secure high growth rates and to transform national development. This proved a relatively successful strategy until the 1997 crisis (which bounds this section). The interests and institutions established by this strategy in turn generate a dynamic of development

---

[3] As evidenced by the preference ratios for a boy versus a girl child among married women awaiting a next child (Mason, cited in Rigg 1997: 222): Philippines 0.9, Indonesia 1.1, Malaysia 1.2, Thailand 1.4. Compare this with Korea 3.3, Bangladesh 3.3 and Pakistan 4.9.

which reinforces the institutions, the welfare mix and the social outcomes. It is, in other words, a recognisable regime.

I will elaborate this conception in the following stages. First, I briefly review theorisations of social policy in Northeast Asia (which sometimes includes the city-states of Hong Kong and Singapore). This contrasts culturalist explanations privileging Confucianism and political economy explanations based on the idea of developmental states. I then turn to social policy in Southeast Asia and draw out similarities and differences with Northeast Asia which are again interpreted within a similar framework. This enables regime characteristics typical of the whole region up to 1997 to be identified.

Northeast Asia: Confucianism and developmental states

Writing about Japan and the newly emerging Tiger economies of Northeast Asia and Singapore, Holliday (2000) proposes that they comprise a fourth welfare regime of *productivist welfare capitalism*. The predominant feature is that social policy is subordinated to other policy objectives, notably economic policy and the pursuit of economic growth. Within this generic welfare regime, he claims that Japan, Korea and Taiwan constitute a *developmental-universalist* mode, where the state underpins market and family provision with some universal programmes, mainly to reinforce the position of productive elements in society.[4] This is similar to Deyo's (1992) earlier view that East Asian social policy is primarily driven by the changing requirements of economic development policy (contrasted with Latin America where extra-bureaucratic political pressures have played a prominent role).

One feature of this is the existence of a genuinely 'mixed' welfare mix, and this has featured in many accounts identifying the peculiarity of welfare systems in East Asia (Kwon 1998; Jacobs 1998; cf. Esping-Andersen 1997 on Japan). The implicit argument is that these components relate to each other in a 'functional' way that is self-reinforcing, as follows.

First, the *market*: fast rising incomes plus a reasonable distribution of factor incomes permits a very high savings rate and fast rising private finance of welfare. This both reflects and contributes to low taxes and the lack of public alternatives. Put another way, equitable economic growth is Pareto-improving and there is less need for mechanisms of state redistribution (Jacobs 1998). The state has a social policy role but it is regulatory

[4] Like most students of East Asia he recognises the peculiar – and contrasting – forms of social policy in the two city-states of Hong Kong and Singapore. Again I ignore them here.

rather than fiduciary or provisioning (Kwon 1998). Second, *enterprise* social benefits, employment protection and seniority wages continue to play a substantial role. They underpin a 'male breadwinner model' of welfare, by providing good benefits for male primary-sector workers, which can only be redistributed within the family. This generates vested interests in their retention. 'Enterprises play a welfare role in a "conservative" way, by ensuring that middle-aged men, the "breadwinners" go home with decent pay' (Jacobs 1998: 79).

Third, the *family-household*: Kumagai (1986) argues that a 'modified stem family' has emerged in Japan, whereby people experience modern nuclear and traditional stem family alternatives throughout their lives, according to their working and marital status. This explains why most elderly people still live with their children, although the proportion of three-generation households is low (Jacobs 1998: 83). Income pooling within families reduces inequality between individuals resulting from the male breadwinner model. Since low earnings are concentrated among women and aged workers, 'inequality among middle-aged men is relatively lower, which must have some influence on household income inequality because most households include one middle-aged man (more so in Japan than in Western countries)' (Jacobs 1998: 95–6). This in turn reinforces the enterprise-household regime through discouraging employment opportunities for women and young people.

What has generated such a dynamic, self-reproducing yet self-limiting welfare system? Answers to this question fall into two broad schools emphasising the role of culture and of political economy respectively (White and Goodman 1998).

Jones, who first coined the term, characterised a 'Confucian welfare state' as: 'Conservative corporatism without (Western-style) worker participation; subsidiarity without the Church; solidarity without equality; laissez-faire without liberalism'. 'An alternative expression for all this might be "household economy" welfare states – run in the style of a would-be traditional, Confucian extended family' (Jones 1993: 214; cf. 1990). This is similar to Vogel's (1980) earlier characterisation of the Japanese model as 'security without entitlements'. Goodman and Peng (1996: 195) include within the 'language of Confucianism' the notions of 'respect for seniors, filial piety, paternal benevolence, the group before the individual, conflict avoidance, loyalty, dutifulness, lack of complacency, striving for learning, entrepreneurship and meritocracy'.

The most sophisticated attempt to flesh out such a culturalist explanation of (North-)East Asian social policy is that of Rieger and Leibfried (2003). They emphasise that these five countries exhibit a 'fundamentally different orientation to social policy'. It is group-based, particularistic and fragmented. Social policy is tied to the economy and gives prominence to education. Individual rights are lacking. Social policy is not an 'autonomous agent' in society posing a countervailing system of norms and ethics. Moreover, welfare state development unfolds more 'statarically' – in a slower and more restrained way. They go on to claim that 'Confucian culture can be identified as the fundamental cause of an independent path of welfare state evolution in East Asia' (Rieger and Leibfried 2003: 261). Drawing on Weber's studies of Confucianism and Protestantism they argue that the distinctive East Asian orientation to social policy is 'framed' by Confucian values, though there is no inescapable iron law at work. The view that belonging is more important than autonomy underpins the strong emphasis on familial piety and the absence of rights-based discourse. The acceptance of basic interests as the main driving force of human action (the 'utilitarian moment' of Confucianism) supports the dominance of economic and business values and the prominence given to education. The 'oikonomistic' understanding of households, firms and the state is the polar opposite of the independent role of social policy in Western societies, which are characterised by the 'perpetual, irresolvable tension between democracy, markets and the state'.

There is not the space here to engage properly with this subtle and scholarly argument, but one criticism can be made. Leibfried and Rieger rely heavily on Weber's study of Confucianism and Taoism, despite its persistent critiques, on the grounds that they are concentrating only on the links between religion and society. This is unsatisfactory, especially when competing and more recent interpretations of Christian doctrine and its social influence are counterposed to his original work on Confucianism. The result is that like is not compared with like – a static (and Western) view of Confucianism is counterposed to a historically rooted, contextual, dynamic (and Western) assessment of Christianity. But if, as they claim, Confucianism too has to pass the test of 'real world fitness' it will change, and presumably has changed.

This is illustrated by some recent work on family and care in Japan. Jacobs (1998: 84) asks whether Japanese people live with their children because they like it or because they have no alternative. He concludes, citing Kojima and Hirosima, that cultural explanations are weak and that the main reason is the lack of alternatives. In other words the lack of public services becomes an independent explanandum. Peng's (2002) recent work on gender and welfare restructuring in Japan also questions the timelessness of Confucian values. Mobilising by women's groups, both older 'housewives' and younger employed women, has been instrumental in the 1990s in expanding the state's role in providing care. In so doing these groups have challenged the notion of a 'Japanese-style welfare society' and have explicitly used the language of individual rights. Confucian values in Japan are adapting to new political (and demographic and economic) conditions. Confucianism is rather a vocabulary which enables elites to selectively mix Western and Asian values and practices. The result is an adaptive learning mechanism, not a static set of codes (Goodman and Peng 1996). The danger of all culturalist explanations is that they tend to be static and cannot explain change (White and Goodman 1998).[5]

The alternative theorisation, favoured here, is a political economy one. Putting to one side for the moment the role of external pressures, this identifies a strong link between Northeast Asian social policies and 'developmental states'. This idea has played an important part in explaining the East Asian economic miracle – from Johnson's (1982) idea of the 'developmental state' through Amsden (1989) and Wade (1990) on 'governed markets', to Weiss (1998) on the 'transformative steering state'. The core idea is that elite policy-makers set economic growth as the fundamental goal and pursue a coherent strategy to achieve it. National social policies can differ, but all of them are explicitly subordinated to economic policy and the pursuit of economic growth. It requires that state policy-makers be relatively insulated from interest groups and have a high degree of internal coherence and loyalty. Furthermore, the social ministries are subordinated to the economic planning boards and ministries (Shin 2000).

The result is a close and intentional congruence between economic and social policy. This does not rule out change. In the earlier stages of light industrialisation social policy is minimal save for education, and wages are kept low. However, the very success of this strategy pulls many more into the employed labour force, raises employment and tightens the labour market. The result is a rise in wages and the eventual necessity to shift to a higher-productivity industrial strategy which entails a more expansive social wage and/or enterprise welfare. This shift can also be fostered by forward-looking economic planning agencies.[6]

---

[5] Rieger and Leibfried's argument concerning bureaucratic patrimonialism, the integration of social policy with kin and group relations and the importance of personal relations in business is well said, but it applies to nearly all the world. This supports their argument that it is Christianity and Western social policy that is unique. As argued in part I of this book, the domains of market, kin and state are not clearly demarcated throughout the South, so the use of social policy as a 'countervailing force' has less meaning. If these features are widespread outside East Asia, the power of – and the necessity for – a Confucian explanation is weakened.

[6] On top of this economy-driven and top-down dynamic, democracy and political mobilisation from below have recently intruded in Korea and Taiwan. This will be discussed below in the post-crisis section.

Welfare regimes in Southeast Asia

To what extent does Southeast Asia replicate the welfare regime pattern of Northeast Asia? Research in this region is scarcer, though Ramesh (2000) has made an important contribution. His interpretation of the patterns of social policy is, following Crone (1993), a statist one focused on the role and interest of elites. Social policy is driven by two factors. First the industrialisation strategy of rapid export-oriented growth satisfies both accumulation and legitimation needs, in the absence of economic crisis or political turmoil. This, plus the demographics of extremely young populations, explains the emphasis on education, notably primary education. Second, in the face of political crises, regimes have launched sporadic initiatives in social security and health insurance for other strategic groups in the population.

In Southeast Asia, while the specific conditions leading to the launch of social security programmes have varied, they all stemmed from some political crisis involving outbreak of ethnic crises, civilian revolt or even expectation of losing office as a result of military coups or electoral losses. But once the programmes were established, their initial character continued to determine the programmes' future development (Ramesh 2000: 182).

This resembles Baldwin's (1990: 39) account of 'Bonapartist' social policy: 'The Bonapartist approach regards social policy in a politically functional sense as a means used by social elites of preserving the status quo, side-stepping the threat of major reform by granting modest concessions to increasingly important but still largely disenfranchised classes'. Baldwin goes on to criticise the usefulness of this explanation in Europe because it cannot explain how social policy can ever develop beyond the minimum necessary to maintain the existing order. In Southeast Asia it has largely not progressed beyond this level, so the concept has potential. We can elaborate the mechanisms as follows (Ramesh 2000: ch. 6).

First, social policy plays an important role in nation-building in post-colonial states. The region is replete with different colonial experiences: Japan in pre-war Korea, the US in the pre-war Philippines, the Netherlands in Indonesia before 1949 and the British in Malaysia until 1957. All have influenced subsequent social policies: the American educational legacy in the Philippines, the British-legislated employee provident fund in Malaysia and Japanese influence on law, bureaucracy and education in Taiwan and Korea are notable examples. Only Thailand lacks a colonial inheritance. Social policy has contributed to nation-building in the post-colonial era, certainly in the Philippines, Malaysia and Indonesia. Malaysia developed its *bumiputera* policies to strengthen ethnic solidarity through positive discrimination towards Malays. Indonesia rapidly extended national education in the post-independence years in part to develop Bahasa Indonesian as the national language (Steinberg 1971: ch. 35). In the Philippines Magsaysay adopted an almost Bismarckian policy of toughness plus concessions in the face of the Huk People's Liberation Army in the early post-war years (SarDesai 1994: ch. 19). The 1957 social security system may be seen as the culmination of this process; ever since it has imparted a different dynamic to social protection compared with the rest of the region.

Second, there is the need to secure the loyalty of the elite and of key state personnel. Such 'etatist' social policy has a long history in Europe, and is clearly evident throughout East Asia as the extent and generosity of benefits for civil servants, the military and other crucial state sector workers attest. Third, there is the role of social policies in legitimising undemocratic regimes, noted in the development of nineteenth-century European social policy. Ramesh cites here the impact of the 1950s communist insurgency and the 1969 race riots in Malaysia, and rioting against the imposition of the New Order in the late 1960s and early 1970s in Indonesia. Another piece of evidence is the well-attested time gap between legislation and implementation found throughout the region. This suits regimes that wish to give the impression of action without challenging core interests by actually delivering.

This characterisation of Southeast Asian social policies has many parallels with that of Northeast Asia. However, these policies are situated within very different socio-political contexts which modifies the nature of their welfare *regimes*. The following sketches some of these distinguishing features.

First, the role of the household differs. Southeast Asia is a resource-rich region which to a far greater extent than Northeast Asia remains a region of farmers. However, this is an agriculture which has long been semi-marketised, for several decades has been dynamic and which is now supporting 'rural industrialisation' (World Bank 1993: 32–7; Rigg 1997: 191). The interactions between the rural and urban worlds offer important clues to understanding the welfare regimes of the region. Essentially, the rich rural hinterland supports family strategies which can successfully mix different livelihoods. Growing agricultural incomes and consumption demand can finance non-farming employment which absorbs rural labour and permits further investment and productivity and income increases in agriculture. Above all, income mixes within the wider family and household transfers provide an alternative for many to state welfare – which undermines further pressures for reform.

Second, business in Southeast Asia is more internationalised than in Northeast Asia and more open to multi-national penetration. Inflows of direct investment are relatively free and substantial compared with the tightly controlled capital markets of Northeast Asia. These are not the 'group-coordinated economies' of Japan and Korea, with strong vertically and horizontally integrated *keiretsu* and *chaebol*. In addition, business in Southeast Asia has traditionally been dominated by the Chinese who enjoy economic power but suffer, to varying degrees, political exclusion. Domestic capital is developing and organising throughout the region, but it remains politically fragmented, relying on close personal links with political elites (Hawes and Liu 1993). The state, and in particular its technocrats, is less insulated from business pressures than in Northeast Asia and is as a result somewhat less autonomous, except in the case of macro-economic policy. Furthermore, the immense resource wealth of the region (oil, timber, etc.) provides alternative sources of rents which can be captured by governments. These can finance infrastructure and social investment without the need for an 'insulated pilot agency' of state technicians, or the support of domestic coalitions. According to some, this blunts governments' imperative to develop and implement national industrial strategies. Yet states in Southeast Asia continue to undertake 'substantial' industrial and economic intervention (Jomo 2001; cf. Macintyre 1994, Robison *et al.* 2000).

Businesses' interpretations of their interests are short-term, neo-liberal and anti-welfare. Southeast Asian capital is less likely to develop enterprise welfare or to support state welfare than its Northeastern counterpart. However, this does not rule out statist initiatives in social policy, since the topic (unlike trade, tax and economic policy) is generally of low salience for business. When other factors push for greater social programmes, states have not been constrained in developing them.

Third, democracy and civil society are recent growths. The dominant form of governance for the last four decades has varied between the brutal, the authoritarian and the 'semi-democratic' (Neher and Marley 1995). No country except the Philippines experienced democracy before World War II, and all have suffered military takeovers or periods of authoritarian rule in the last two decades. In addition, personalised patron–clientelist relations and a dominant party system undermine ideological politics and encourage segmental politics. This has perpetuated a weak civil society. Only in the Philippines can one identify a flourishing civil society in the pre-Marcos years and again since 1986. With the end of the Cold War, NGOs are encouraged and are expanding fast, but they remain strongly controlled in Malaysia and are fragmented in Thailand and Indonesia (Yamamoto 1995). Thus democratic pressures for social policies from outside the state remain weak.

Fourth, for the same reasons, since the late 1960s *labour* in the region has been 'weak, divided and tamed' (Deyo 1997), despite an unprecedented growth in industrialisation, wage labour, literacy and other correlates of trade union activity. Trade unions have been periodically subject to draconian measures throughout the region. Membership is low and is largely confined to state sector workers and other narrow groups. Dominant union federations are subservient to regime interests. When in the late 1980s liberalisation beckoned, unions were constrained by the new forces of globalisation. In Deyo's (1997) words, labour organisations in Southeast Asia have moved directly 'from repression to deregulation'. Compared with the West, the ability of the labour movement to win social reforms has been severely constrained.

Productivist welfare regimes

Though the form of capitalism differs between Northeast and Southeast Asia, it has achieved everywhere (at least until 1997) a high and sustained rate of growth. Though the insulation of state elites from powerful social interests is most evident in the North, all the states in the region have considerable autonomy from business and other social interests, and have prioritised economic over social policy. Throughout the region, too, the influence of labour and civil society on policy-making has been small, at least until the 1990s. Again, though the patterns of interaction of states, markets, enterprises and households vary, there is a systemic mix of welfare sources different in degree from that found in the West or Latin America.

In my view, all the countries covered in this survey (with the exception of the Philippines) can be described as *productivist welfare regimes*. These are 'welfare' regimes, first, because they are based on dynamic emerging capitalist market economies. This has driven the commodification of labour over many decades and is fostering the emergence of marketised social welfare. Second, they are unified, relatively strong states with substantial steering and infrastructural capacities. They have in turn pursued a developmental agenda with remarkable economic success. Lastly, this growth has, in the absence of seriously unequal Latin-American-style distribution, generated improving welfare outcomes.

The term *productivist* welfare regime signals that they differ from the three or four types of regime identified in the West and described in chapter 1. First, social policy is not an autonomous agent in society or even an autonomous sphere of government; rather it is subordinated to the dominant economic policy goal of maintaining high rates of economic growth. Following on from this, social policy is concentrated on social investment, notably in education and basic health rather than social protection. Third, this policy has largely been driven by the imperatives of nation-building and regime legitimation. Fourth, the state is mainly confined to regulation rather than provision and plays only a contributory role to the broader welfare mix, which is sustained by strong families and household strategies, high savings and marketised provision and, in Korea, enterprise welfare.

However, the sustainability of this regime is open to doubt because of its vulnerability. East Asian countries are vulnerable, first, to external factors and actors, due to their economic openness and geo-strategic location (below and Gough 2001a: 177–81). Second, the family component of the welfare mix is threatened by the processes of commodification, urbanisation and demographic change, among others. The very preconditions and successes of the regime undermine its longer-term sustainability. It is to these issues that I now turn.

The one exception is the Philippines. It exhibits lower growth rates, a long-established, segmented and partial social insurance tradition, high and chronic levels of unemployment, poverty and inequality, yet good access to education and a flourishing civil society. One outcome has been labour emigration, abetted by the unique Philippine Overseas Employment Administration, and high remittances which augment the role of the family. It appears closer in several respects to the Latin American regime analysed in chapter 4. The reasons for this differential development are complex and cannot be addressed here. They relate to the distinctive colonial experience (Spain until 1898, then the US until the Japanese occupation in 1942 and independence in 1946). Concentrated land ownership supports a closed oligarchy which re-emerged following the period of Marcos autarchy. The fusion of landed and political elites engenders a 'booty capitalism' removed even from the Sukarno family capitalism of Indonesia. This combination of factors has thus far blocked the emergence of a productivist welfare regime typical of the rest of the region.

The East Asian regime after the crisis

Thus far this chapter has confined itself to internal explanations of East Asian regimes. It is time now to consider their external environment. Following a general account of the global and regional setting I turn to the unprecedented crisis which shook the region in 1997–8. The impact of this on welfare outcomes is briefly traced before examining its impact on domestic policy agendas and the productivist welfare regime.

Global and regional influences

Benedict Anderson (1998) identifies four basic 'conditions-of-possibility' for the post-war East Asian 'miracle'. The first was the peculiar form of the Cold War in the region. 'Nowhere in the world was the cold war "hotter" in the third quarter of this century, and perhaps nowhere did it cool down more rapidly and dramatically, thanks to the Peking–Washington rapprochement of the middle 1970s.' As a result no world region received as much 'aid' in the third quarter of the twentieth century. The second condition-of-possibility was the propinquity of Japan, whose defeat in 1945 was followed by strong US support for its capitalist development. By the 1970s Japan had become the dominant economy in the region and its principal investor (South Korea was less welcoming). Thus 'Southeast Asia was the only region in the world in which the two most powerful capitalist national economies were deeply and on the whole cooperatively committed for four decades'. Third, the Chinese communist revolution and the Maoist autarchic project excluded it from playing a significant economic role in the region until the mid-1980s. Last, and related to this, the historic role of Chinese emigrants in the region was canalised by the newly independent states in Southeast Asia (i.e. excluding Korea and Taiwan) into business, finance and commerce. Excluded from places in the military, bureaucracy and political arenas, this 'racial' division of labour has 'made a marginalized Chinese minority the real domestic motor of the "miracle"' (Anderson 1998: 300–4).

This peculiar combination of circumstances has played an important role in the emergence of productivist social development regimes. However, Anderson goes on to doubt their continuance. The end of the Cold War has already eroded US strategic interests in the region. Japan has enduring geo-political interests but its weakened economy undermines its ability to pursue them. China is now a dominant regional power and a growing economic competitor. Its limitless supplies of cheap labour and its attraction for foreign investment threaten the traditional growth strategies of the second-tier newly industrialising countries investigated here. He concludes: 'perhaps only the overseas Chinese will remain an enduring miracle ingredient' (Anderson 1998: 304).

Others, however, consider the role of Japan to be of continuing and central importance (see Jomo 2001). Japanese private capital inflows continue to build an 'export platform' in the region. Japan is also the largest aid donor, providing one-half of ODA aid to Asia. Moreover, its government pursues a coherent regional strategy based on the model of 'flying geese'. This posits successive waves of development from the first-tier countries in the north-east, through the second-tier countries in Southeast Asia studied here, and on to a third tier comprising Vietnam, China and possibly other parts of the region. Aid is used to promote regional integration and to reproduce some elements of Japanese industrial policy in the region. The distinctive Japanese model of state capitalism cannot

Table 5.5. *Annual growth rates, 1996–2001*

	1997	1998	1999	2000	2001
Japan	1.9	−1.1	.8	1.5	−.5
Taiwan	6.7	4.6	5.4	6.0	−1.0
Korea	5.0	−6.7	10.9	8.8	2.5
Malaysia	7.3	−7.4	6.1	8.3	1.0
Thailand	−1.4	−10.8	4.2	4.4	2.0
Philippines	5.2	−0.6	3.4	4.0	2.5
Indonesia	4.5	−13.1	0.8	4.8	3.0

Source: IMF (2002).

be discounted as an important external influence on East Asian development, including its social regime. Yet this model was to be severely tested
and questioned following the crisis of 1997.

The East Asian crisis

The crisis, which began with the devaluation of the Thai baht in July
1997, was both familiar and novel. Currency values collapsed, generating higher import prices and extensive internal price changes, including
falling asset values. Output fell drastically, creating cuts in employment
and a Keynesian-style collapse in demand.[7] Real per capita GDP fell
by 16 per cent in Indonesia (an historically unprecedented collapse),
12 per cent in Thailand, 10 per cent in Malaysia, 8 per cent in Korea
and 3 per cent in the Philippines. In four of the countries, Indonesia excepted, the depression bottomed out in 1998. Yet all of these countries,
except Korea, lost at least three years of growth (table 5.5). What was
novel was the speed of transmission of the crisis and its causes. According to Higgott (2000) it was the 'first crisis of globalisation' (cf. Robison
et al. 2000, Haggard 2000).

It is beyond the scope of this chapter to analyse the causes of this
crisis in any depth. Standard explanations distinguish external and
internal factors. External factors include the instability of financial
markets, prone to over-reaction and a 'herd mentality', an instability
compounded by the combined rapid expansion and liberalisation of international capital markets in the 1990s. The internal factors stress either
macro-economic mismanagement or structural and regulatory problems.
The latter, advanced by the IMF and the World Bank, refer to 'crony

---

[7] At the same time, the Philippines, Indonesia and Thailand suffered a severe drought.

Table 5.6. *The social impacts of the crisis in East Asia (%)*

	Korea	Malaysia	Thailand	Philippines	Indonesia	Average
Change in per capita private consumption 1997–8	−10.2	−12.6	−15.1	1.3	−4.7	−8.3
Inflation 1997–8	7.5	5.3	8.1	9.7	57.6	17.6
Poverty increase, 1996–8	9.6	–	1.5	–	5.4	5.4
Unemployment 1998	6.8	3.2	4.5	10.1	5.5	6.0
Public education expenditure 1997–98	−5.8	−13.7	−1.3	+3.8	−27.7	−12.1
Public health expenditure 1997–98	−3.2	−9.7	−10.7	−7.8	−12.2	−8.7

Source: Manuelyan Atinc (2000: table 6.1).

capitalism', corruption, moral hazard and suchlike. However, this distinction between external and internal is hard to justify when the international financial institutions have played such important roles in shaping government policies in the South. According to Wade (2000), the crisis stemmed ultimately from a combination of US and Japanese-led financial capital inflows which stoked up a property and asset bubble. This inflow, and the financial opening and liberalisation which permitted it to happen, both reflected the financialisation of the US economy and the active support for the financial lobby within the US administrations. In turn, the very liberalisation of capital accounts has expanded the ability of politically connected groups to profit from their contacts: liberalisation created new avenues for cronyism (Pincus and Rami 1998). For our purposes, the important conclusion is that the very openness of the Southeast Asian economies, one source of their previous success, was deeply implicated in the crisis that afflicted them in 1997. This is supported when Korea, which had begun to liberalise its economy under pressure from the US and the Uruguay Round, is contrasted with Taiwan, which resisted such pressures: Korea was badly affected whereas Taiwan was not.

The initial social impact of the crisis is portrayed in table 5.6 (Manuelyan Atinc and Walton 1998; Manuelyan Atinc 2000). Poverty rates rose in all countries as did the depth of poverty. The demand for labour and the share of wages declined everywhere, bringing about a collapse of private consumption (yet inequality did not rise notably, partly due to the collapse of asset prices hurting the rich and middle classes). Undoubtedly many poor households coped by cutting back on nutrition, postponing healthcare, taking some children out of school and other painful adjustments. Moreover the impact differed: it was acute in Indonesia, severe in Thailand, Malaysia and Korea, and mild in the Philippines, where the preceding boom had been least. This, together with different variations in their social development regimes, resulted in different policy impacts (ADB/World Bank 2000a).

The social policy impact

In Korea, labour demand fell sharply and, though real wages fell, the major impact was on unemployment, especially among women. As part of a developed industrial economy, Korean households had fewer rural resources to fall back on. The first wave of reforms introduced by the Rho Tae-woo government in 1988 included medical insurance, the national pension programme, the minimum wage and new labour laws. Following the crisis, a second wave of reforms in 1998–9 followed, coinciding with the election of Kim Dae-jung as president. The economy was significantly liberalised and the close links between the state and the *chaebol* were loosened. This was coupled with moves towards a more Western welfare system. Expenditure on unemployment insurance, wage subsidies and public works programmes escalated, to a remarkable 4 per cent of GDP in 1999. In addition, the national health system was restructured and expanded, pension entitlements were liberalised and an expanded Labour Standard Law introduced. A 'Labour-Management-Government' Committee was established which moved away, at least in name, from state–business symbiosis to a tripartite corporatism. In brief, greater exposure to the global economy and the subsequent crisis has undermined the influence and the social provisions of the *chaebol* and required the state to develop a more autonomous Western-style social policy. The unintended consequence of globalisation and liberalisation has been to expand the role of the state in Korean social policy (Shin 2000).

In Malaysia and the Philippines the policy impact has been minimal, for related but opposite reasons. The Philippines is an outlier from the East Asian model: over the last two decades it has recorded lower growth rates (and thus less reliance on labour market income growth) coupled with chronically high poverty and unemployment rates. On the other hand, it suffered less in the 1997 crisis. It has long relied on officially encouraged emigration as a safety valve and income source. Since most Filipino emigrants are not working in crisis-affected countries, their remittances have cushioned the impact of the crisis, which may have contributed to the lack of policy innovation.

Malaysia, by contrast, has managed to cushion the domestic impact of a severe crisis by offloading its impact onto immigrant workers, who account for some 7–10 per cent of the labour force (Oberndorfer and Berndt 2000). Early on the Malaysian government announced plans to repatriate large numbers of these workers: up to 200,000 were laid off in the construction industry and the permits of another 700,000 would be denied renewal after expiry. Despite some opposition from employers, at least 200,000 illegal foreign workers, and probably many more, had left the country by August 1998 (Haggard 2000: 208–9). As a result the official unemployment rate in Malaysia barely rose from 2.5 per cent in 1996 to 3.2 per cent in 1998. In both the Philippines and Malaysia, but for opposite reasons, labour migration reduced the direct impact of the crisis and forestalled significant social policy innovation.

There has been little policy reform in Thailand and Indonesia either, but for different reasons. Both have strong rural hinterlands, where extensive smallholder agriculture has acted as a partial shock absorber, and where escalating food prices helped real incomes. The crisis led to a drastic fall in formal sector wages (by 34 per cent in Indonesia in real terms) and a shift from the formal sector back to the informal and agricultural sectors. Poor people without this fallback suffered doubly from unemployment and the mushrooming costs of food. High inflation in Indonesia also contributed to a sharp fall in real public spending on education and health, which Thailand protected more successfully. The response of both governments, with inducements from the IMF, the World Bank and the Asian Development Bank, was to instigate safety nets, expand community-based programmes and emphasise credit and savings groups.

By mid-1998, the government of Thailand had secured social loans from the Asian Development Bank and the World Bank to expand existing safety net programmes and instigate new ones. The former included scholarship and educational loan programmes, fee waivers and the free provision of uniforms to keep pupils in school, plus an expanded school lunch programme. The low-income 'health card' programme was also increased. In addition new public works and a social investment programme were introduced with funding from the World Bank. The latter, more open to patronage and 'leakage', attracted growing criticism and were soon cut back (Haggard 2000).

Indonesia followed a similar course with donor-funded safety net programmes. The OPK-subsidised rice scheme launched in July 1998 provided 20 kg of low-quality rice per household per month at a subsidised price, allocated according to an official list of poor households. A scholarship programme provided scholarships and school grants to schools in poor areas and poor households within them. A previous 'health card' programme was expanded to fund clinics and midwives in poor districts. All suffered from leakages but were adjudged relatively successful. By contrast, community social funds and public works programmes continued to be sources of patronage and corruption (Ananta and Siregar 1999). Concerns over leakage and corruption led the World Bank to pull out of many programmes from 2000, and it is unclear at present to what extent the government of Indonesia will supplement their funding. In any case spending on all social safety nets is tiny in amount, accounting for 0.25 per cent of GNP (ADB 2000; World Bank 2000a; Irawan *et al.* 2001).

Thus the record to date suggests that the regional crisis has not brought about a structural change in the regional social development regime. The one exception, Korea, is continuing with its moves towards a social insurance model. Yet the fact that Taiwan, which avoided crisis contagion, has also expanded its public social programmes suggests that democracy, rather than crisis, is the more important factor in both countries.[8] In Korea, external crisis and internal democratisation interacted in ways still not resolved. In the rest of the region, little has changed so far. Malaysia and the Philippines have been little affected, due to the cushion of immigrant labour in the former and emigrant labour in the latter. Indonesia and Thailand have relied primarily on the cushion provided by more closely integrated rural–urban households and families, but are encouraging social safety nets and community-based initiatives in a limited way. This suggests that these productivist regimes have considerable durability and adaptability. Yet path dependency in the strict sense of the term is weak.

The limits of productivist regimes

Is the productivist welfare regime sustainable? And, if not, what are the likely directions of change? I discuss first the limits of the regime outlined above, looking at each element of the welfare mix in turn.

Enterprise welfare is significant only in Northeast Asia, notably Japan and Korea. It is clear that liberalisation of capital markets and shifts in corporate functioning threaten the future of this style of corporate welfare. The rise in its share in Korea following the crisis (figure 5.3) was mainly a temporary feature due to higher levels of severance pay in response to rising unemployment. The share of enterprise welfare in Japan has been falling since the 1980s (Peng 2000). It is likely that the

---

[8] In Korea there is a problem of 'over-determination' as the election of Kim Dae-jung coincided almost exactly with the crisis impacting on Korea.

provisioning aspects of enterprise welfare will continue to diminish in the future, though state mandation on firms to fund certain cash benefits will continue.

NGOs are and will remain significant sources of mobilisation in the region and their role in social service provision is expanding in Northeast Asia encouraged by legislation. In Southeast Asia they are unlikely to emerge as important providers of welfare services. The lessons from the Philippines, with its extensive, diverse, dynamic NGOs, is not encouraging: so much progressive energy, so little to show for it in terms of poverty reduction and the alleviation of suffering!

The role of the family in the regime is also threatened, though it will remain very significant. The extensive role of families in providing security, housing and services, and in shaping livelihood strategies has been stressed above. Even in more-developed Northeast Asia a majority of elderly people live with their children, inter-household transfers are important sources of security and families fund private education and health expenses. In Southeast Asia, with large rural economies and rural–urban household strategies, the family remains the most important part of the overall welfare mix and the first source of security. Yet throughout the region a slow decline is predicted in its ability to continue performing these functions, stemming from three major features: demographic change, challenges from women's changing roles and expectations, and inherent limits in its ability to ensure acceptable levels of security.

First, in East Asia over the last thirty years, falling fertility rates and rising life expectancies have cut the share of children and raised the share of working-age adults in the population. The share of aged people rose slightly. The result has been a sharp fall in the overall dependency ratio. The prospects for the next three decades are very different, as the larger working-age cohorts enter old age and the smaller child cohorts enter working age (table 5.7). The share of those sixty-five years and over is projected to double in East Asia, and grow by two and a half times in Korea. Thus the demographic transition will accelerate and mature in East Asia in the coming period. This will place added strain on families' ability to finance and care for elderly parents.

Second, women's movements are already challenging traditional gender roles and inadequate public services in Japan and Taiwan. This is no less likely to develop in Southeast Asia, where gender inequalities are less evident and entrenched. Third, households can provide some security to their members through 'self-insurance', provided two conditions are met: a high rate of savings and a reasonably equal distribution of market incomes. Both conditions obtain (relative to the rest of the world) in the North, specifically Japan, Korea and Taiwan, but only the former holds

Table 5.7. *Demographic trends in East Asia*

	65+ dependency ratio, 2000	65+ dependency ratio, 2030	Change 2000–30	Change in total dependency ratio, 2000–30	Change in weighted dependency ratio, 1995–2030[a]
Korea	9.3	25.8	16.5	15.1	16.7
Malaysia	6.8	14.5	7.7	−16.0	−2.5
Thailand	8.4	19.6	11.2	3.1	8.3
Philippines	6.1	12.2	6.1	−19.8	−4.0
Indonesia	7.2	14.2	7.0	−8.2	0.7
Average	7.6	17.3	9.7	−5.2	3.8

[a] Persons aged 65+ years + one-third of children <15 years, expressed as percentage of persons aged 15–64.
Source: ADB (1998).

in the South. In other words, throughout much of the region high and growing levels of inequality rule out intra-household transfers as reliable and generalisable strategies for alleviating poverty. Poor people tend to have poor relations.[9]

The above amounts to a familiar 'modernisation' scenario: the ability of families to meet basic needs and guarantee security will diminish in such fast-growing economies. This is not a functionalist argument for two reasons. It recognises that East Asian families will continue to play a far greater role than in the West for a long time to come. Declines in the numbers of elderly people sharing households with their children are likely to occur but at a slow Japanese rate.[10] Furthermore, there is no necessary reasons why other welfare providers should step in and establish functional replacements for Asian families. I conclude by adumbrating two possible trajectories.

The first trajectory is towards privatisation coupled with persistent informalisation. On the one hand, the scope for marketised welfare in East Asia is large. The World Bank and other international financial agencies have traditionally pushed for privatised pensions, health provision and health insurance. Furthermore, the existing willingness and ability of upper- and middle-class families to use private schooling and health facilities, at home or abroad, forms an existing market to tap. Insofar

[9] The prospects for migration and remittances as an internationalised family strategy, pioneered in the Philippines, are also limited. Governments in the region are increasingly trying to control immigration flows, via regional agreements in ASEAN, or bilateral deals between governments.
[10] This is also a feature of Southern Europe despite extremely high levels of income in Italy.

as this 'exit' option expands, it further weakens internal political pressures to improve and extend public provision for the wider population, as Deacon (1999) and others fear. On the other hand, the pressures from dominant international financial institutions to 'de-statise' East Asian economies is remorseless. The developmental states are under pressure to liberalise and de-regulate their economies, thus weakening the productive underpinning of the East Asian miracle. Malaysia's reintroduction of capital controls is a notable but isolated counter-example. Thus both the 'economic' and the 'social' aspects of the productivist welfare regime are threatened. The most likely outcome is its transformation into a privatised and dualised regime, combining 'liberal' and informal features.

There is, however, a rival potential trajectory: towards a more universalist social investment state. This would build on another feature of the existing regime described above – its universal state provision of basic education and health services – for both economic and political reasons. Harbingers of this are evident in discussions across the region of the 'third way' and the president Kim Dae-jung's proposals for a new paradigm of 'productive welfare' in Korea (2000). This paradigm combines an equitable market system, government redistribution of wealth, with social investment for self-support and to enhance the quality of life. In the poorest of the countries studied here, Indonesia, universal school grants for all primary and junior secondary school children (at the relatively generous level of the recent targeted grants) could be provided at a cost of only 2.6 per cent of total government expenditure. For another 1 per cent of expenditure all people aged over sixty-five could receive a similar grant. Southeast Asian states have few competing fiscal commitments pre-empting this sort of social policy. They also have much of the state infrastructure in place to deliver them (Gough 2003b).

There are economic and political reasons for supposing that this is more than political rhetoric. First, the era of *extensive* economic growth based on low productivity, low wage production, already long gone in Northeast Asia, is now over in the middle-income Southeast Asian countries. China and other countries in the region offer almost unlimited supplies of far cheaper labour to attract multi-national corporations (MNCs) searching for this competitive advantage. The next row of the 'flying geese' will have to move into higher-tech higher-productivity production, requiring more public investment in secondary and tertiary education, curative health services, social protection, rural infrastructure and urban planning. In addition, globalisation paradoxically encourages state welfare, as Korea has illustrated since 1998, as investment in human development remains one of the few instruments of development intervention still open to national governments. Financial controls are strongly discouraged by the

IMF, while the 'infant industry' policies pioneered in the region are no longer permitted by WTO rules. As a result, social protection emerges even more strongly as the only functional alternative open to developmental states in a globalising world.

Second, in political terms this strategy could build on the strengths and successes of social statism in the region, which lie neither in classic European social insurance nor in targeted social assistance, but in universal state services. The very weakness of existing stratification effects among welfare recipients and of path-dependency effects in the regime as a whole may permit such a statist turn. Universal state services and demogrants (transfers to identified demographic groups) are more equitable in countries where insecurity for the majority of people is high. They are also in many respects more efficient in delivering benefits and services in countries with extensive informal sectors, which limit social insurance and complicate means-testing.

Third, democracy is belatedly emerging in East Asia, at least in the form of opposition parties and contested elections. Korea and Taiwan both witnessed democratic contestation in 1987; the result was a significant shift towards state responsibility in social welfare in the 1990s. It is not too optimistic to expect similar transformations in Southeast Asia.

The transformation of East Asian productivist welfare regimes into productivist welfare *state* regimes is thus not entirely fanciful. The older confidence in economic growth as *the* social policy is eroding. Whether these countries develop into privatised or public investment regimes is still open. One factor influencing this outside the control of regional actors will be competition between international agencies favouring the former (the WTO, the IMF, the US and still-dominant players in the World Bank, alongside multi-nationals and financial institutions with stakes in privatised welfare) and those favouring the latter (the ILO, the UNRISD, the UNDP, the EU). It will also depend on statist strategies pursued by domestic elites and, we may hope, on newly emerging democratic forces in the region.

6   The dynamics of Africa's in/security regimes

Philippa Bevan

Introduction

In this chapter I use the in/security model[1] developed in chapter 3 to analyse insecurity and welfare on the continent of Africa. The in/security model has five main components: the structural relationships and dynamics involved in the generation of insecurity; mobilisation outcomes; rectification mix; in/security outcomes; and stratification outcomes. It can be used to analyse regimes in long-term equilibrium, regimes in short-term equilibrium ('regime episodes', which can often only be identified retrospectively) and regimes in transition (often involved in 'contentious episodes' (McAdam *et al.* 2001)). As discussed in chapter 3, the model potentially allows for five 'spaces of comparison' across the five components, and a thorough analysis would make the comparison across all five spaces. However, in a chapter of this size it is not possible to do such an analysis covering all fifty-three African countries involved in processes of post-colonial transition. Furthermore, given the problems with data on welfare mix and welfare outcomes (which are discussed below), quantitative comparisons across these two spaces, of the kind made in the Latin America and East Asia chapters, would be difficult. In any case, I would argue that, in current African conditions, comparisons across the other three spaces lead to more interesting and policy-relevant conclusions.[2] As a result the structure of this chapter differs from that of chapters 4 and 5.

Tilly has suggested that understanding of 'big structures' and 'large processes' can be generated by a number of different approaches to comparison. Figure 6.1 depicts four polar ideal types, which can be used in combination. A purely individualising comparison treats each case as unique, while a purely universalising comparison identifies common

---

[1] The '/' indicates that a number of regimes can be found in Africa: a small elite minority benefit from some form of welfare regime, many rely on informal security regimes as described in Wood's chapter, while most of those involved in conflict situations are caught up in insecurity regimes.

[2] It would also be interesting and useful to make these comparisons in other parts of the world.

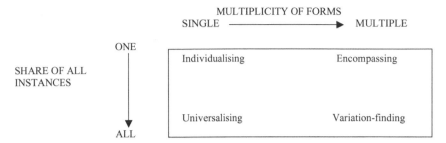

Figure 6.1. Ways of seeing and making comparisons

properties among all instances of a phenomenon. Variation-finding comparisons examine systematic differences among instances, while the encompassing approach 'places different instances at various locations within the same system, on the way to explaining their characteristics as a function of their varying relationships to the whole system' (Tilly 1984: 83).

The chapter makes use of a number of these ways of making comparisons. The first section, based on a mixture of universalising and variation-finding comparison, contains a rapid historical exploration of key elements of pre-colonial and colonial in/security regimes whose legacies are important for what is happening now, and an analysis of changes in post/colonial in/security regimes from the 1960s to the 1990s. I have included this section since it is not possible to understand the poverty, conflict and suffering currently ongoing in Africa without taking a long historical view. In the next section I use the model in combined universalising/variation-finding modes to highlight key features of current African country regime mixes, which are best viewed as a dynamic mix of informal security and insecurity regimes with very tiny welfare and productivist regime elements. The balance of these four regimes varies between countries. I then discuss some problems associated with attempts to identify country-based 'typical' regimes or regime mixes in a continent replete with state failures of various kinds, where 'no condition is permanent' (Berry 1993) and research information and effort is patchy, and suggest that, at country level, analyses in terms of regime mixes and 'episodes' (Tilly 2000) would be more fruitful. Third, I use the model in 'individualising' case analyses of a 'warlord regime' and a 'humanitarian aid regime', neither of which coincide with national borders. This leads into a discussion of the additional insights a regional perspective offers. In the conclusion I argue for a multi-level policy approach based on an 'encompassing' analysis of the ways in which different African economies and polities relate to the wider global system described in chapter 3.

Much of the material in this chapter relates to 'sub-Saharan Africa' which in many discourses is distinguished from 'Arabic' North Africa. Also a special exception is often made of South Africa as a result of the size of its modern industrial sector. A thorough analysis of all African countries across the five in/security regime spaces would currently place these countries quite near the top of an overall African regime ranking. To put it another way, a higher proportion of the populations of these countries are likely to participate in welfare regimes and a lower proportion in informal security and insecurity regimes. However, in South Africa 'there are many challenges and even threats to continued development and reconciliation' (Bradshaw and Ndegwa 2000: 4). Also Algeria is not free of conflict, there are Islamic networks linking North Africa with parts of West Africa, and Libya aspires to be a key continental actor and, as the Sierra Leone case-study shows, has historically contributed to the generation of insecurity.

African in/security regimes: an historical analysis

Application of the in/security regime model

This section is based on an analysis which uses the in/security regime categories in conjunction with empirical evidence to produce a 'quick and dirty' historical analysis of the major elements of in/security regimes in Africa from pre-colonial times to the present. In these regimes we find changing 'concatenations' (Bayart 1993) of linked, articulated and variably interpenetrating heterogeneous modes of production, political structures and cultural forms. From the fifteenth century the expansionary drives of state-based merchants, and later industrial capital, and the geo-political interests of evolving European/Western nation-state systems, played key interactive roles in the structuring and restructuring of African economies and polities, with huge consequences in terms of in/security and mobilisation and dis/continuity and in/stability. At the start of the twenty-first century a new kind of 'global capital', relatively unconfined by states or international organisations, is involved in yet another restructuring (along some familiar lines). It is not possible to understand how in/security regimes in Africa are responding to this context without taking a long historical view. 'At the heart of the sub-Saharan state the influence of a "triple history" can be seen – the pre-colonial, the colonial and the post-colonial – which had/have a concurrent effect'[3] (*ibid.*: 60).

---

[3] 'Mobutu's personality cult extends Pierre Mulele's Marxist millenarianism of the 1964–5 rebellions, the charismatic figure of Patrice Lumumba, the syncretic movements of

Since the arrival of Europeans on the continent's shores, African elites have played out their destinies at the intersection of 'historical fields of intra-continental and inter-continental interaction' (*ibid.*: 53). Within the continent 'systems of inequality and domination' (Balandier, quoted in Bayart 1993: 57) have taken diverse forms, with varying degrees of 'stateness'. Similarly, within African economies there is varying incidence of marketisation (or commodification) of material goods, labour, land, other means of production and credit; some of this marketisation is domestic (some 'formal', some 'informal'), while some is linked with wider circuits of capital, both legal and illegal, which have recently been described by Duffield (2001) as 'transborder shadow economies'. 'State' and 'market' structures, (dynamically) articulated with other political and economic structures/networks, can be usefully analysed as socially constructed by actors in a context of wider cultural constructions of meaning and value. Over the centuries these cultural constructions have entailed increasing cultural 'hybridisation': the creative intermingling of values, images and concepts from within and outside the continent. These cultures help to motivate the current 'political mobilisation' of both elites and non-elites.

The continent of Africa today: a statistical description

The African land mass (11,677,240 square miles), which is three times larger than the United States and consists of deserts, rainforests, savannahs, plateau, mountains and lakes, suffering varied climates, and in some parts containing a wealth of mineral resources, provides a huge range of livelihood opportunities and constraints for its 500 million or so inhabitants (roughly 10 per cent of the world's population). Around 70 per cent of Africans live in rural areas, although there is considerable variation in the proportion between countries (table 6.1, appendix). The continent is currently divided into fifty-three 'sovereign' states with one territory, West Sahara, still disputed. These states vary widely in size and population. Djibouti is the size of Massachusetts and Sudan is the size of Western Europe. Nigeria has a population of around 121 million while that of the Seychelles is around 79,000 (see maps 6.1 and 6.2).

In this chapter I have not been able to undertake a comparative 'rational-technical' analysis of welfare spending and welfare outcomes along the lines of the Gough and Barrientos studies of East Asia and Latin America because valid, reliable and representative information is not available. Even if it were, many dimensions of the suffering of Africans

independent churches from the colonial period and the prophetic movements of the more distant past' (*ibid.*: 60).

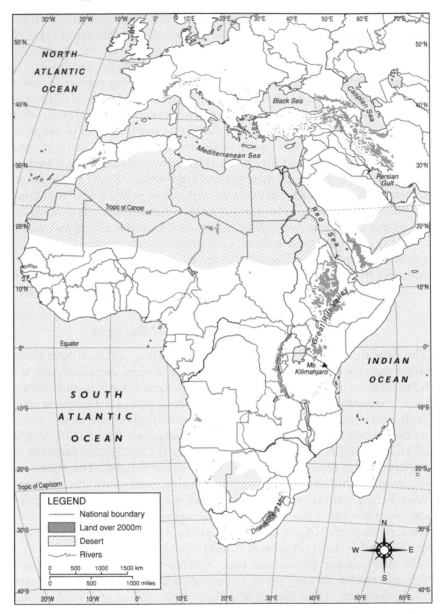

Map 6.1. Africa: physical

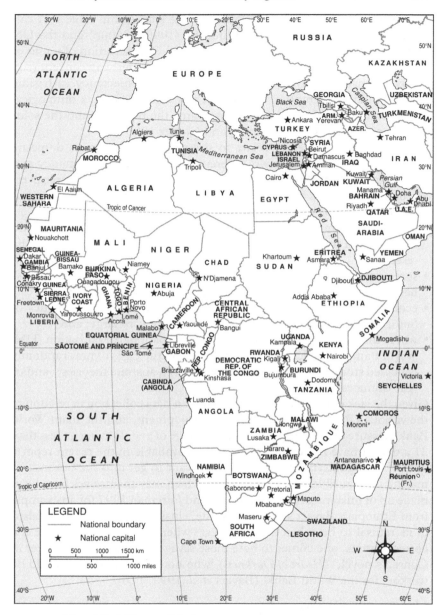

Map 6.2. Africa: political

are not reflected in the usual statistics. The statistics in table 6.1, calculated by economists at the World Bank (1999c, 2000b) and the UN
(UNDP 2000), do not 'speak for themselves'. The selection of a unit of
measurement (e.g. country or household), of an underlying concept (e.g.
survival, consumption), and of a measure (e.g. life expectancy, cash value
of household consumption in one week or month) reflects ontological
and epistemological assumptions that frame the problem (and the solution) in particular ways (Apthorpe and Gasper 1996).

The figures in table 6.1 relate to size of population, gross domestic
product per capita (using two different measures), life expectancy and
gross education enrolment. These could be seen as providing simple overall country measures of livelihood chances and in/security outcomes, but
the figures must be treated with considerable suspicion because:

- in many African countries the resources for proper data collection do
  not exist and there are big issues surrounding the actual conduct of the
  research;
- some statistics (e.g. regional populations in Nigeria, gross enrolments)
  have political repercussions and are consequently 'massaged';
- economic statistics often do not cover any or all of the activities of
  'informal sectors' which in some countries are very large; and
- where there are no incountry statistics, international organisation (UN,
  World Bank) statisticians make estimates on the basis of non-randomly
  collected studies (Bevan and Joireman 1997), abstract theories,[4] and/or
  'guesstimates'.

Given the lack of transparency about African data collection in relation to
the various UN indicators of human development, and the main World
Bank measure of country poverty (percentage of people living on less than
$1 a day), I have not included the figures available in the recent reports
of the two organisations, since I do not want to get into the business of
making up plausible stories about data which may themselves have been
made up or misrepresented (see Bevan and Joireman 1997 for an example
from Ethiopia). Bayart suggests that the 'elusiveness of Africa lies [also]
in its refusal to be subject to statistics: "when one has got to make the
correct entries, one comes to hate those savages", laments a character in
Conrad's novel,' (*Heart of Darkness*) 'who nowadays no doubt would be
working for the World Bank' (Bayart *et al.* 1999: 116).

---

[4] I once met a World Bank economist whose first job had been in a Ministry of Planning
in an African government where he was given the task of constructing a model of the
economy using government statistics. There was some surprise at the resulting model,
which suggested much more 'development' than 'old hands' thought there was. Some
years later the economist met the man who had been given the task of producing the
statistics in the first place: unable (or unwilling) to conduct first-hand research he had
used a standard American economics textbook model to generate the figures.

Assuming that the figures in table 6.1 reveal some broad similarities and differences between countries, there are a number of interesting features about the situation in the 1990s. First is the wide range of country output per capita. The North African countries (Tunisia $2,280, Algeria $1,519, Morocco $1,355, Egypt $1,120, no information for Libya), South Africa ($3,926), Botswana ($3,859 – diamonds), Namibia ($2,134), Swaziland ($1,410), and Gabon ($4,629 – oil), all produced a GDP of more than $1,000 per capita. At the other extreme a number of countries produced less than $300 per capita: Sudan $296; Mali $267; Burkina Faso $259; Nigeria $255; Madagascar $238; Chad $229; Rwanda $224; Niger $215; Mozambique $188; Eritrea $175; Tanzania $173; Malawi $167; Sierra Leone $151; Burundi $146; Congo DR $127; Ethiopia $110.

The GDP per capita figures suggest that, in terms of (measured) changes in economic output over the thirty-two years between 1966 and 1998, ten countries declined (Congo DR −68 per cent, Niger −51 per cent, Sierra Leone −45 per cent, Zambia −40 per cent, Madagascar −34 per cent, Chad −14 per cent, Senegal −11 per cent, Togo −9 per cent, Ghana −7 per cent, Mauritania −6 per cent), there was stagnation[5] in eight countries (including notably South Africa and Nigeria – from higher and lower bases), and there were some quite high growth rates (Botswana 800 per cent, Mauritius 218 per cent, the Seychelles 171 per cent, Lesotho 166 per cent, Egypt 154 per cent, Tunisia 154 per cent). There are no figures for twenty countries (almost 40 per cent).

However, the GDP PPP$ figures, whose measure is adjusted to take account of local costs of living, paint a rather different picture of changes in output in the twenty-three years between 1975 (the earliest date for figures) and 1998.[6] Using these figures, only one country, Congo DR, produced less per capita in 1998 than in 1975 (−21 per cent) and these figures do not include the output of the large parallel, and unmeasured, economy which developed increasingly through the 1970s and 1980s (McGaffey et al. 1991). Twenty-six countries have growth rates of more than 100 per cent over this period (suggesting an average rate of over 5 per cent per annum). Only one country, apart from Congo DR, has an average growth rate of less than 1 per cent per annum and that is Sierra Leone. I have been unable to establish how these data were collected, nor how the PPP$ exchange rates were calculated, and as a result I am not sure of the implications of these figures. They might suggest that, while African economies have clearly not performed as well in the 'formal sector' as

[5] Defined as an increase of less than 20 per cent over the thirty-two-year period (although this may mask rises and falls).
[6] Generally speaking, African growth rates were higher in the 1960s and early 1970s than they were in the later 1970s and 1980s.

some other developing countries, in average economic terms things may not be as desperate as sometimes portrayed.

Table 6.1 also shows a wide range of life expectancies (Sierra Leone 38; Mauritius 72) and gross primary school enrolment figures ranging from 26 per cent (Mali) to 129 per cent (Namibia). Between 1965 and 1998 all countries experienced high population growth rates and improving life expectancies. However, in some countries the HIV/AIDS pandemic has reduced both. While life expectancies in some countries, especially in southern Africa, have recently been adjusted downwards to take account of predicted HIV/AIDS deaths, the overall trend has been upwards, with some countries making greater leaps than others. The same is true of the primary school enrolment figures.[7] The remainder of this section is devoted to using the in/security regime model to provide historical reasons why African countries are currently in the situations (which may be) partially captured by these statistics.

Pre-colonial in/security regimes

Current knowledge has it that humanity originated in Africa more than 2 million years ago. Pre-colonial Africa contained extremely diverse societies that rose and adapted to change as the centuries passed. Land was generally abundant, with no private ownership, but labour was often scarce. There was a diversity of livelihood systems based on hunter-gathering, pastoralism, agro-pastoralism, settled agriculture, citimene agriculture (shifting cultivation) and mining, all involving the exploitation of commoners, women, juniors, losers, slaves and low-status ethnic groups. African political systems, and the relations between them, were marked by diversity and change. 'The perennial movements of African peoples, extending into the period of colonial conquest, led to corresponding changes in territorial control and to constant wars between advancing and retreating peoples' (Clapham 1999: 61).

Political structures varied according to the uneven distribution of resources throughout the continent. Reliable resource bases were associated with denser populations and more stable and effective political authorities. Areas with insecure bases, communication problems and sparse populations 'had correspondingly weak and fragmented political structures' (*ibid.*: 63). The major structures were (1) hierarchical 'states' and (2) segmented political systems, some of which had 'chiefs' and some of which were 'acephalous'. There were notable inter-system dependencies and relations, ranging from conquest (and rebellion) through low-intensity or

---

[7] Again I have been unable to establish how any of these figures are generated.

spasmodic conflict to peaceful, sometimes unequal, symbiosis. The nineteenth century saw widespread low-intensity conflict in which one polity or ethnicity was usually in the ascendant, attracting destruction or privileged sub-imperial status. Societies in regular conflict developed 'warrior cultures'.

Lineage (the theoretical tracing of a group to the same ancestor) and kinship dominated pre-colonial relationships (Thomson 2000: 8). Lineage associations constructed customs controlling marriage, inheritance, justice and the allocation of land and provided solidarity, security and welfare for members. However, there was considerable diversity and change as structures responded to interactions between clans, villages, age sets, and/or secret societies. Kin networks/households took a wide variety of organisational forms. While patriarchy was the rule, the status and power of women varied widely between cultures. Bridewealth, which forged bonds between lineages, was a key institution in many, but not all societies, and the same could be said of polygyny as a social ideal. In the dominant cultural model people were understood to be elements constructing many interdependent relationships existing within a supernaturally ordained order, rather than 'individuals'. There was a variety of oral traditions, rituals, witchcraft beliefs and local religions, which later adapted to Islamic and Christian influences. Elite cultures were usually marked by an 'ethic of munificence'.

Outsiders have played roles in Africa for more than two millennia. By the fifteenth century sub-Saharan Africans had built trading links with both Arabs and Europeans and the first European coastal settlements had been established. From the sixteenth century the continent became a target of European mercantilism seeking resources and slaves, and an element in wider European political competition. Arabs and Islam penetrated North and East Africa. Both Arabs and Europeans used violence, trade, political deals with local elites, and religious conversion to achieve their ends. The seventeenth and eighteenth centuries saw the height of Atlantic slavery, which was gradually replaced in the nineteenth century by commerce, exploration and informal colonisation, sometimes through companies assisted by mercenaries. Formal colonisation began in the 1880s.

Contingencies producing death, ill-health and poverty were generated by human and animal diseases in a low-science/technology context, pests, weather, and low-intensity conflict, sometimes involving genocide and rape. The 'structural poor' mainly lacked access to labour (Iliffe 1987). Elite livelihoods involved the extraction of surplus through tribute, slavery and trade. Status was the major social variable determining who suffered and who survived and prospered. Since land was not generally scarce migration was a frequent response to poor livelihoods or unacceptable suffering.

Given the lack of organisations in most contexts the main element in the social protection 'welfare mix' was the 'family', but

Africans lived in different kinds of families, from the Yoruba compound with scores of related residents to the elementary households of Buganda. Each kind of family had its particular points of weakness and excluded its particular categories of unsupported poor – orphans in one case, barren women in another, childless elders in a third. Moreover, family structure was not an immutable ethnic characteristic but could change to meet changing needs (Iliffe 1987: 7).

The second important source of welfare was the poor's own efforts, which included exploiting the resources of the bush, hawking, begging and stealing. In different societies different forms of institutional provision for poor people developed; 'their identity and means of survival were shaped by the particularity of each culture in which they were found' (*ibid.*: 94).

Lineage societies developed a range of health services including bone setting, herbalism and various forms of 'witchcraft'. These later became influenced by Christian and Islamic approaches to health, and subsequently by cosmopolitan practices. Education was performed informally in the home and community. Children acquired household, farming, herding and specialist occupation skills by copying parents and siblings. Values and traditions were learned by attending rituals and ceremonies and listening to elders. 'Formal' education often preceded rites of passage to adulthood. The earliest European schools were established by Portuguese missionaries in the sixteenth century. Qur'anic schools existed for centuries in some parts of West Africa and some nineteenth-century Christian missions started schools (Hailey 1957; Thomson 2000; Manning 1998).

Colonial in/security regimes

The partition and then conquest of sub-Saharan Africa by the colonising powers, Britain, France, Belgium, Germany (which lost its colonies following the First World War), Portugal, Spain and Italy, occupied the last quarter of the nineteenth century and was completed by 1902. A major aim of colonisation was to circumvent the African 'middlemen' and, through the establishment of efficient colonial powers, to open up Africa to the capitalist quest for raw materials. Big finance capital was attracted by mineral resources and wages below family subsistence level which depended on the peasant household to fill the gap. In the absence of minerals, colonialism and capitalism looked to agriculture for the production of wealth, via cash crops produced by settlers or the African peasantry. Exploitation involved the transfer of surplus from women to men, from young to old, from peasants and slaves to the ruling classes and merchants; conquest transferred surplus to European business and colonial administrations. Three colonial periods can be distinguished: the penetration and consolidation of colonial control (up to World War I); the exploitation and running of the colonies (up to World War II); and preparations for independence (later 1940s and 1950s) which took place during the post-war boom.

The different colonisers adopted rather different approaches to colonial government,[8] although Mamdani (1996) argues that the long-run consequences were very similar: bifurcated states where the majority were governed by a 'decentralised despotism'. One (small) segment of these states was constituted by educated urban elites and the urban formal sector: members were citizens of a 'modern' state. Initially this modern sector was overwhelmingly the domain of whites and, in some places, non-Africans who were encouraged to fill commercial positions (e.g. Asians in East Africa; Lebanese in West Africa), but as time passed, particularly in the third stage of colonialism and in non-settler countries, a growing number of educated Africans were incorporated. The second (large) segment was mainly rural although it included some 'informal sector' urban Africans; members of this segment were 'subjects' to indirect rule. Societies became racialised and sometimes ethnicised. In many areas there was a growing separation of men from women through forced labour, induced wage-labour migration and rural cash-cropping. Islam and Christian religions offered new identities and opportunities. The inferior status of stigmatised groups continued. At a cultural level people had to deal with racism, the introduction of colonial languages, and Eurocentric visions of patriarchy and individualism.

The colonial period saw huge changes in the structure of African economies, with commodification, or entry into markets, being a key feature. European industry demanded cash crops such as cotton, tobacco, coffee, cocoa, tea and palm oil, and natural resources such as timber. There was increasing mining activity, particularly of gold, diamonds and copper, and some industrialisation, particularly in settler economies, notably South Africa. This provided new economic opportunities to those who could grasp them. Colonisers looked for 'compradors' to assist in the political control of the inhabitants of the new 'states', and economic

---

[8] French and Belgians espoused 'direct rule' and the French encouraged assimilation of a few 'civilised' Africans. The theory of indirect rule governed British practices involving a smaller military and bureaucratic presence.

exploitation of labour and natural resources. Deals were struck with exist-ing political elites and where necessary new elites were created. Colonial-ism allowed a small number of cosmopolitan monopoly firms to exploit labour through mechanisms of employment and unequal exchange. In settler economies this was compounded by exclusion from land. Simul-taneously new areas of economic activity and opportunity were created including cities, transport routes and port facilities.

This economic restructuring produced huge changes in ordinary livelihoods: male migration for labour, forced labour, wage labour, the in-creasing use of cash, increasing female activity in subsistence agriculture, urbanisation, industrialisation, the generation of peasant surpluses ac-companied by increasing rural inequality, and increased opportunities for small traders. These livelihood changes were accompanied by immensely complicated changes in the nature of rural poverty. Great famines were replaced by problems of nutrition and demography. Most rural structural poverty resulted, as in the past, from lack of access to labour. However, there was land poverty in settler economies, and conjunctural poverty associated with the trade cycle became widespread and was particularly problematic during the Great Depression. Urban poverty was suffered mostly by unskilled labourers, abandoned children, the old, the disabled, and the destitute (Iliffe 1987). Africans were affected by tropical dis-eases and major endemic diseases such as tuberculosis, pneumonia, the venereal diseases, enteric fevers, and trachoma. Some, like cerebrospinal meningitis and measles, swept through populations in epidemic form.

Colonial regimes mobilised the loyalty of internal urban elites through the provision of education, and some formal employment that was often accompanied by various fringe benefits, including housing and access to health services. They mobilised the loyalty of internal rural elites by allowing them space to seek wealth, status, and power in return for main-taining order and generating the required cash crops, taxes and forced labour when required. In the British system 'chiefs' generally related to the people under their authority through the construction of patron–client relationships and the use of force where this failed. Colonial gov-ernments mobilised the political 'exit' or exclusion of most rural people through various forms of indirect rule. They attempted to minimise the mobilisation of voice against them by incorporating emerging local polit-ical elites in various ways or by force when things got out of hand, as did the Mau Mau movement in Kenya in the 1950s.

After the Second World War the Soviet Union offered an alternative model of development to nationalist movements, while the anti-colonial ideology of the United States gave heart to those seeking independence and encouraged the Europeans to provide it. At this time internal elite mobilisation involved a mixture, often at different times by the same people, of loyalty and collaboration with colonial masters, exile and diasporic political activity, and voice against the colonial masters expressed in the organisation of trade union activity and peasant resistance and 'nationalist' movements for independence. Most exploited sufferers opted for loyalty, or adverse incorporation, through participation in colonial economic activities. Some favoured the exit option and retreated into subsistence where possible. The 1940s and 1950s saw a wave of popular resistance involving labour insurgency in the towns and peasant movements in the countryside.

With the coming of the Second World War colonial governments began to acknowledge more responsibility for the welfare of all colonial inhabitants, and for the development of colonial economies, and for most the post-war boom ended a period of financial stringency. For example, in 1940 the British government enacted the first Colonial Development and Welfare Act. However, in the realm of social protection, Africans continued to rely mainly on kin and self, with the exception that colonial governments intervened to avert famines. Traditional systems of health provision and education, supported by mission activities in some areas, continued to dominate. However, governments became increasingly active in the fields of education and health. Provision of these services was generally marked by the bifurcation we have already observed, leading to the development of two- or three-tier systems in the areas of education and health services. For example, in settler countries such as Rhodesia different schools were provided for white children (government – free and compulsory from 1931), coloured and Asian children (government – free, compulsory for those living within three miles) and African (mostly mission – 65 per cent in school, 50 per cent in the two lowest classes; twenty-four Africans studying at universities). The French maintained relatively few first-class hospitals and spent comparatively little on the 'less important medical institutions' (Hailey 1957: 1106).

Colonial governments developed policies to eradicate and control diseases including programmes of vaccination, for example against smallpox. 'Most of the diseases from which the Africans suffer are either insect-borne or are due to faulty environmental sanitation (including housing and personal cleanliness) or malnutrition' (*ibid.*: 1070). Some larger industrial concerns led the way in taking measures for the promotion of health conditions among employees and their dependants (*ibid.*: 1105). There were arguments about the best way to spend 'slender resources' among those who favoured the extension of services controlled by first-class hospitals, those who supported the spread of medical centres, and those who advocated preventive and dietary approaches. '[A] really satisfactory coverage [of curative medicine] has been restricted not merely by lack of finance but in many cases also by the past failure to train a sufficient African agency for extension work' (*ibid.*: 1064). The 1950s saw a 'brief compassionate period' during which many colonial governments encouraged responsible trade unions, instituted minimum wages, and took some measures to produce skilled and better-paid labour forces.

In this colonial period of considerable structural change some social discontinuities were reduced, while others were generated. Different contexts saw diverse and interacting stratification and segmentation outcomes which varied in stability. The main stratification line was drawn between white colonial rulers and capitalists, and Africans, but also in many places stratification between internal educated elites and others intensified. Urban–rural segmentation was more pronounced in some countries than others. Differentiation within urban areas increased, as did stratification among rural peasants. The family responsibilities of women grew, particularly where men had migrated, and the contours of child labour changed, while colonial policies reduced the overall power of women by removing land rights and through the Christian marriage laws. Political segmentation and differentiation were often intensified through colonial policies: for example, army recruits often came from one ethnic group, usually one seen as a 'warlike tribe'. Processes of domination were allowed to flourish in rural areas where chiefs often ruled as they wished, while processes of destruction surfaced in the violent repression of uprisings.

Independence

Decolonisation was as quick a phase in African history as the scramble of the late nineteenth century, and at least as complex an historical process. Its causes lay partly outside Africa also, in the changing force-field of world affairs as well as the structural alterations in the needs of capital which now showed substantially less interest in the initial extractive processes that had characterised the African colonial systems in their heyday (Freund 1998: 202).

In all post-colonial African countries the post-independence period has seen a dynamic interactive and creative working out of the pre-colonial and colonial regime legacies described above, in a context of considerable and rapid global economic and political change.

Liberia and Ethiopia were never colonised and Egypt gained independence in 1922. The first general wave of independence took place in the 1950s and was led by the Arab-speaking states of Libya (1951) and Morocco, Tunisia and the Sudan (1956). Ghana gained independence from Britain in 1957, and Guinea from France in 1958. The 1960s was the major independence decade, although the Portuguese colonies had to wait until the death of Salazar in 1974, and real 'independence' came later still in the former settler colonies of Zimbabwe (1980), Namibia (1990) and South Africa (1994). A freedom movement in Western Sahara, once a Spanish colony, is still seeking independence against a claim by Morocco. The states showed a huge diversity in terms of strategic location, population, natural resources, agricultural potential, economic output, history, social structure, political inheritance, cultural mix and outside links. This diversity was of considerable importance for future national developments.

Most colonies came to independence in a world where international politics was dominated by the Cold War, and the world economy was still enjoying a post-World War II boom that was benefiting the Soviet bloc as well as Western economies. In most European states modern 'welfare regimes' were well established, accompanied by a considerable role for the state in the economy (a mixed economy model) and economic policies dominated by Keynesianism. In this context the dominant development discourse focused on 'modernisation', a process whereby 'underdeveloped' economies, societies and polities would progress through stages of growth involving various restructuring steps. It was accepted that the state had a major role to play in guiding progress, including direct involvement in the industrialisation process. There were two modernisation models on offer – the capitalist and the 'socialist' or 'communist' and, as John F. Kennedy noted in 1957, 'the perceived stakes of the Cold War contest were tied to whether the emerging leaders of Africa would "look West or East – to Moscow or to Washington – for sympathy, help, and guidance in their effort to recapitulate, in a few decades, the entire history of modern Europe and America"' (Schraeder 2000: 132).

Independence negotiations left most countries with political systems, constitutions and bureaucracies designed as copies of the particular colonial 'mother' system. In most countries these arrangements were rapidly adapted to African political realities. Independence set the stage for a new alliance between emergent indigenous ruling classes and Western business. The independence bargain contained guarantees for the property rights of Western business enterprise and strategic and military arrangements. Bargains made by different colonisers varied. At the extreme the Portuguese, under Salazar, refused even to consider independence. The French established an institutional network of cooperation, covering the franc zone, a French military presence, judicial and educational matters, and technical assistance, which provided continuity from the colonial period. The government's willingness to subsidise client states in these ways is only partially explained by French economic or strategic interests (*ibid.*: 150). The idea of a francophone Africa has always appealed to French political elites. African politicians sat in the French parliament before independence and those who inherited state command after 1960 joined a 'francophone political entity'; 'the connections made between French and African politicians in the terminal colonial period do much to explain the relative viability of Franco-African political linkages after independence'. Culture is also important: movements of political opposition 'have tended to express themselves in the various idioms of Parisian Marxism' (*ibid.*: 149). Unlike France, and partly as a result of economic difficulties, Great Britain rather soon lost interest in maintaining special ties with her ex-colonies, except for South Africa, other than through the Commonwealth of Nations, which holds a summit meeting of leaders once a year (*ibid.*: 318).

The dominant livelihood structures inherited at independence included mixes of cash crop agriculture, involving both plantation wage labour and peasant production (which sometimes involved casual wage labour), mining often based on migrating wage labour, subsistence agriculture, pastoralism, a small urban-based formal, usually public, industrial sector, an informal urban sector of petty manufacture and trade, government employment in the bureaucracy, military, police, judiciary and education and health systems, and politicians. There was a small African proletariat class, generally found in urban settings, and an unemployed or underemployed working class, the lumpenproletariat. The African peasantry was the largest class in most African countries; peasants grew food and other crops, and raised livestock for personal consumption, local sale or export. Richer peasants hired others to work on their land and participated in regional trade. Pastoralism and agro-pastoralism provided livelihoods to many in fragile environments. Most national economies were dependent on one or two major export crops for foreign exchange to provide imports for investment and consumption.

Formal institutions and organisations to help the poor were mostly created during the colonial period and thus embodied European preconceptions and concerns. They were diverse: 'independent Africa was to inherit a welfare system of baffling fragmentation and complexity' (Iliffe 1987: 193). However, most poor people who survived did so as a result of the care of their families or by their own efforts. Although educational enrolments increased rapidly in the post World War I years, colonial educational systems effectively excluded the majority of Africans. In 1960 there were only nine countries where more than 50 per cent of children of primary school age were enrolled: Cameroon, Congo/Brazzaville,

Gabon, Lesotho, Madagascar, Mauritius, Swaziland, Congo/Zaire and Zimbabwe (Chazan *et al.* 1992: 238).

By the later 1950s colonial healthcare services provided a fairly high standard of curative medicine for European expatriates to which, in some places, some Africans also had access. The remainder used patchy and variable government and mission services, and 'traditional' services. There were wide gaps between the resources available and the 'enormous healthcare needs of the population. In many African countries, diseases such as bilharzia, malaria, tuberculosis, cholera, typhoid, polio, and measles were rampant' (Chazan *et al.* 1992: 244). These diseases were exacerbated by widespread malnutrition. In 1960 public health expenditure averaged 0.6 per cent of GNP (*ibid.*: 245).

The progress of African in/security regimes: early 1960s to late 1990s

In this section, the model is applied separately to the last four decades of the twentieth century, since each of these decades is more or less marked by a set of significant changes. The detailed analysis on which the short summaries in this section are based can be found at www.bath.ac.uk/~hsspgb.

The 1960s The 1960s was a time of economic optimism as the post-war boom continued and many countries experienced economic growth. The weather was generally kind. At least one-third of the trade of most countries was with the former metropole and there was high reliance on imported capital goods. Nationalisation was accompanied by the growth of parastatals. There was increased urbanisation and high expectations about the fruits of independence. Livelihood opportunities increased as a result of growth and Africanisation. TNCs began to move into more industrially sophisticated operations. As a result of continuing demand for cash crops and the new opportunities provided by industrialisation there were increasing subsistence responsibilities for women. Metropolitan governments provided aid and technical assistance and economic links were maintained. Donors supported industrialisation and assumed the state had a leading role. There was a Cold War focus to aid provision.

The main problems of this decade were political, with movement towards one-party authoritarian patrimonial states, the destruction of autonomous organisations such as trade unions, the expansion of coercive structures, and in some countries competition for control of the state (there were eleven military coups). Metropolitan governments continued to be politically active in former colonies. A major cause of suffering in the 1960s was the Biafran civil war in which an estimated 600,000 died, mostly from famine, while 2 million were displaced. There were also civil wars in Zaire, Nigeria, Algeria, Rwanda and Burundi, uprisings in the Portuguese colonies, Eritrea and South West Africa (later Namibia), internal conflicts in Burundi, Rwanda, Chad, Tanzania and Sudan, and cross-border conflicts between Algeria/Morocco, Egypt/Israel and Somalia/Kenya, many leading to substantial refugee and displaced person populations.

Different elements of society were differentially involved in the post-independence project; the excluded tended to be rural, young, female and/or belong to ethnic groups not favoured by ex-colonial masters. Active opposition came in the form of uprisings, civil war, strikes and demonstrations. Other strategies included the search for patrons, retreat and resistance, and peasant refusal to be 'captured'. Women were mostly excluded from political and formal economic participation. There was an increase in public education but little change in the structure of health services in most countries. Public employees received welfare benefits, often including housing. Health and education services were provided by missions, and Islamic education grew. For security the vast majority of people depended on informal regimes. During contentious episodes people suffered, died and migrated; the international community became increasingly active in providing humanitarian aid and support for refugees.

The colonial legacies of the 'bifurcated state', decentralised despotism and ethnic segmentation were not dealt with in most places, leaving fertile ground for ensuing problematic state–society and intra-society relationships.

The 1970s   The 1970s, which saw the end of the world-wide post-war boom and two oil crises, was generally a decade of disillusion so far as discourses about general 'development' in Africa were concerned, although there was good economic growth accompanied by relative political stability in Botswana, Gabon, Kenya, Cameroon, Malawi, Algeria, Togo, and the Ivory Coast. Economic decline (measured by changes in GDP per capita) was recorded for ten countries. Stagnation and economic decline was often, but not always, associated with political disorder and violence. Donors focus moved to 'basic needs', but they still supported industrialisation and assumed a leading role for the state. There was some recognition of failure of industrialisation policies and an emerging fiscal crisis. However, aid was used more as a foreign policy instrument than a development tool. Governments adopted pro-US, pro-Soviet Union or non-aligned stances and accepted the role of gatekeeper between external resources and domestic processes. Despite signs of crisis, life expectancy figures for all countries, except Uganda, rose by between one year (Sierra Leone) and nine years (Libya).

Elite competition for access to, or control of, the state intensified; support was mobilised through patronage networks and/or fear of violence. There was also increasing internal surplus extraction through the state. Cold War political impacts were complicated by the problem of apartheid South Africa. There was political disorder and/or military coups in many countries and drought in the Sahel resulting in many famine deaths. Rapid population growth continued. War between Ethiopia and Somalia and civil war in Ethiopia and the ex- (as of 1974) Portuguese colonies produced thousands of refugees. War in Rhodesia/Zimbabwe, Congo DR, Chad and Namibia also led to suffering and displacement and 'citizens' experienced 'state violence' in Uganda and Equatorial Guinea; Morocco occupied West Sahara.

This decade saw the emergence of local and trans-border parallel economies and growth in 'informal sectors'. Livelihood diversification became a key strategy in many contexts. Tensions between men and women grew in situations of economic and political difficulty. In local conflict situations women often created new, generally unrecorded, modes of survival and conflict resolution. There was increasing surplus extraction via the state, part of which financed growth in public employment as one element in the construction of kin/ethnic-based patron–clientelism. There was polarisation around access to state resources. TNCs increased their search for oil and other minerals.

The 1980s The 1980s was the decade of the debt crisis and externally imposed structural adjustment programmes, and saw the end of attempts to follow socialist routes to development and to create national African economies. Continued falls in agricultural commodity prices and falling oil and mineral prices meant that only twelve countries achieved per capita GDP growth rates of 2 per cent per annum or more, and only four of these were relatively politically stable (Botswana, Mauritius, Swaziland and the Congo Republic). Three were in North Africa and most of the rest were small and 'atypical'. As a result of growing sovereign debt the Bretton Woods organisations increasingly took charge of the aid game. There was a waning of interest in 'basic needs' and loans were provided on harder terms with conditionalities related to liberalisation, stabilisation and structural adjustment. The economic decline of the Soviet Union reduced the salience of the Cold War. The decade ended in 'market triumphalism' with TNCs increasingly benefiting from mineral exploitation.

In this context many governments found it increasingly difficult to maintain patrimonial networks and in some places the vacuum was filled with the increased use of force and surveillance. There were signs of increasing political disorder, although the 'post-conflict' states of Ghana and Uganda emerged as World Bank protégés. Leaders adopted a variety of strategies to access resources to feed patrimonial networks and for personal aggrandisement including control of private long-distance trade (e.g. oil and diamonds), diversion of aid, and internal rent-seeking. There were 'complex emergencies' in Angola, Mozambique, Ethiopia, Sudan and Somalia. Many deaths in the Luwero triangle (Uganda) resulted from 'state violence'. There was death and suffering among the Tuareg (Niger) and war suffering in Chad and Namibia. The detaching of local social processes from high politics continued, resulting in a wide diversity of social patterns of autonomy and interpenetration: for example, Islamic brotherhoods in Senegal, professional and voluntary organisations in Ghana, church groups and networks in Malawi. Urban–rural linkages increased. Local cultures continued to be penetrated by a variety of external influences leading to many forms of cultural hybridisation.

There were increasing signs of mass poverty and destitution in some countries and an increasing inability in more countries to provide 'social goods' such as transport, electricity, clean water, schooling, etc. There was increasing unemployment among school leavers. The collapse or decline in what public services there were in many countries led to strains on extended family systems and increasing reliance on self for security. Students, and in some places trade unionists, demonstrated and rioted, and in Zambia there were temporarily successful food riots against structural adjustment policies. Young men, often with some education but no prospects, pursued illegal and martial livelihoods and there was increasing exit of the university-educated and professionals to Europe and the US. Donors and NGOs invested resources in the mobilisation of 'women in development', and increasing numbers of women, elderly and children entered the 'informal sectors'. The international NGO movement in both development and humanitarian fields grew stronger and NGOs, UN agencies and governments acted together to provide relief in situations of famine and conflict.

There was further polarisation between rich 'international' elites, local elites/middle classes, and poorer people in urban and rural areas, paralleled by a 'trifurcated' welfare mix (international market liberal/national conservative/informal) with the first two elements being relatively minor. There was an increase in the number of people in a fourth category (insecurity regime) without access even to informal security as a result of conflict. There was a growth in employment in 'the development industry' that included international and bilateral donors, international NGOs, international consultants, and local consultants and employees. The US began to lose interest in the 'Cold War' countries. By the end of the decade the end of apartheid was in sight.

Towards the end of the decade opportunities emerged for those not in power to press for multi-party elections. However, as the following quotation shows, practices associated with domination rather than democracy were widespread.

the space of the State is fabricated with recourse to coercion, which the postcolonial authorities are no less reluctant to use than their predecessors. Domination is exerted without disguise, especially as it is facilitated by all the technological innovations at the State's disposal. Forced labour under the pretext of human investment... the authoritarian repatriation of unemployed town dwellers into the countryside... the military 'slum clearances' from urban areas, obligatory participation at endless demonstrations of 'solidarity' and other rallies, the administration of neo-traditional rituals of political submission, *de jure* or *de facto* obligatory adhesion to the single or dominant party, the imposition of discriminatory symbolic codes – particularly related to clothing and gestures – floggings and massacres, tortures, denunciations, public executions, extra-judiciary imprisonments; through the armed forces and a network of informers the men of power exercise robust control over the populations they want to subject, to the extent of appearing to be an occupying military power (Bayart 1993: 245).

The 1990s   The world economy of the 1990s was dominated by an unregulated move to economic and financial liberation, one result of which was the increasing economic marginalisation of Africa, in a context of increasing regional economic integration around three nodes: America, Europe and East and Southeast Asia. Africa has increasingly occupied some of the dubious niches in international economic activity including drugs, illegal immigration, dumping of toxic waste, money laundering and a return of 'primitive accumulation' involving privatised unregulated exploitation of natural resources including diamonds, timber, high-value minerals and oil. A combination of aid, debt relief, political stability and IFI-supervised economic policies led to economic growth in a number of countries that had not seen it for some years (e.g. Ghana, Uganda, Mozambique). Elsewhere there was an increase in the number of internal wars. Conflict deaths and displacements increased and took on a new savagery with the Rwanda genocide and atrocities in Sierra Leone. What has been described as Africa's first 'World War' developed in the Democratic Republic of the Congo as the first decade of the twenty-first century began.

Some countries saw national conferences and/or multi-party elections, while in others there was radical privatisation of the state and criminalisation of the behaviour of power-holders. There was state collapse in Somalia, Liberia, Sierra Leone, Congo/Zaire and Angola. In some places state coercion was devolved to private foreign concerns (e.g. the South Africa-based security firm Executive Outcomes). In many countries elite land grabbing, and allocation of land to 'inward investors' for cash crop agriculture, reservoirs, oil and mineral extraction and national parks, affected the livelihoods of both pastoralists and agriculturalists.

Life expectancies fell in HIV/AIDS-afflicted countries, particularly in southern Africa. However, most countries saw an improvement in other human development statistics, and clean water, electricity, latrines and feeder roads became more generally available than at the close of the colonial era.

In this context agriculture, the informal sector, or conflict proved the main source of livelihood for most people. Livelihood strategies became increasingly 'escapist': from donor constraints and from the demands of governments and husbands. In many countries a process of de-agrarianisation was accompanied by increasing livelihood diversification, often involving 'rural–urban straddling', illegal cross-border trade and vital contributions from women, the elderly and children. Women became increasingly organised economically and politically, but still struggled to counteract national and international gender biases. As a result of information technology advances, global consumerism increasingly penetrated urban slums and remote rural areas. At the same time many countries saw a resurgence in witchcraft. Ethnic and religious mobilisation increased.

Early in the decade 'aid fatigue' led to a decline in amounts of aid and a focus on a range of conditionalities; later 'poverty' rose up the donor agenda, so that by the end of the decade conditionalities extended to poverty-reduction policies. A number of 'transitions' from socialism and war were more or less supervised by the World Bank and the IMF. There was a burgeoning of international and local development and humanitarian NGOs stimulating a growth in 'community-based organisations'.

Country trajectories through the decades   It is important to remember that, within the broad frameworks described above, each of the fifty-three countries followed their own unique path-dependent trajectory, influenced by pre-independence history, the political structure at independence, interactions with neighbours and other regional players, the ongoing modes of articulation with the changing international economy and polity, the choices made by actors at all levels, and the resultant intended and unintended consequences which set the scene for new choices. Country analysis of economic growth and political stability through the four decades reveals the non-linearity of most trajectories. Only one country, Botswana, has a history of continuous economic growth and relative political stability, which was based on a judicious use of diamond revenues. Even in this case World Bank statistics (2001a) suggest that 33.3 per cent of the population were living on less than $1 a day in 1985–6 (the latest years for which there are figures), which compares with a figure of 31.3 per cent for Ethiopia in 1995 (then the poorest country in terms of GDP per capita). Only one country, Zambia, has a history of continuous economic decline, related to the decline in world copper prices, amazingly accompanied by relative political stability (72.6 per cent living on less than $1 a day in 1996).

Current African in/security regimes

In the previous section the current African in/security regime situation is observed through a country-focused lens: I focus on factors of particular importance for 'policy'. In this section and the following section I demonstrate the advantages of adopting approaches that problematise 'state' boundaries.

Key policy-relevant features of current African in/security regimes

In/security outcomes   The widespread suffering to be found in Africa poses huge challenges for policy. While consumption poverty, poor health and lack of skills and education (the main focus of current Eurocentric social policy thinking and interventions) are big problems, they are secondary to much unacknowledged suffering generated by exploitation and opportunity hoarding, resource competition, political oppression, ideological disputes and violent conflict unregulated by any rules of war.

With regard to livelihood outcomes, African subsistence and cash crop agriculture has been in general decline for some years (Bryceson and Jamal 1997). Since the 1970s urban areas in many countries have seen declining job prospects and living standards (Francis 2000: 5), compensated to some extent by 'diversification' based on the growth of informal self-employment and employment and urban farming. Structural adjustment policies, based on economic assumptions of 'urban bias', were instrumental in processes of urban decline and increases in urban poverty, in particular reductions in public employment, the ending of food subsidies, and the abolition of minimum wages. In many countries the downturn in urban economies has produced a slowing of rural–urban migration, some return migrancy and what has been described as rural–urban straddling (there is also formal–informal sector straddling). One result of urban decline has been increased economic participation in urban areas by women, the elderly and children. This is also a feature of rural economies affected by increasing poverty, higher consumption aspirations, male migration and war. However, one consequence of the urban decline has been a fall in demand for male migrants.

Liberalisation, privatisation and other structural adjustment measures have clearly failed to produce viable economies which can generate the economic growth required for poverty reduction. There has been insufficient attention to the real structures constituting African economies and their external relations. Research shows great diversities between and within local economies.

Explaining these diverse histories requires an understanding of how large-scale social and economic changes were played out at the local level. These include the way in which localities were incorporated into colonial economies, the effects of post-colonial state policies, the operation of markets and the activities of international capital. Analysing these processes involves exploring how they have meshed with local strategies for making a living. These strategies are shaped by the opportunities people find around them, but they also reflect their values and cultural orientations (Francis 2000: 182).

The generation of insecurity   There are three major (interacting) processes of current importance: global and local economic restructuring involving large pockets of economic failure and decline, political competition for power and resources in the context of the liberalising global economy described in chapter 3, and the life processes of high population growth (producing a very high proportion of under-fifteens), epidemic diseases (particularly HIV/AIDS) and natural disasters.

The most important 'export' links that many African economies[9] have with the global economy now involve legal or illegal 'natural resource' (minerals and timber) capitalism and/or other illegal activities (Castells 1998; Bayart 1999) rather than agricultural or industrial products, most of which cannot compete in wider markets. These kinds of capitalism do not demand much 'wage labour', and therefore do not generate many livelihoods, apart from activities related to smuggling, and the creation of the disorder that allows them to flourish (Chabal and Daloz 1999). African economies have not evolved down the development paths prescribed for them by generations of development economists. The Keynesian mixed economy approach to 'development' failed to produce industrialisation. Liberalisation and structural adjustment measures

---

[9] Major exceptions are South Africa, Mauritius and the North African countries.

failed to kickstart the agricultural 'development' originally expected in no more than five years and contributed to the informalisation and diversification of economic activity. Trade liberalisation and 'inward investment' may be mainly benefiting trans-national mineral corporations and a few elite members, especially when the corporations are given 'tax holidays' to attract them. At the same time there has been a considerable growth in complex and mutable 'transborder shadow economies' (Duffield 2001: chapter 6) based on trans-national price disparities. 'Managing frontier disparities on a rent-seeking basis has become a vital component of the policy orientations of Benin, Togo, the Gambia, Niger and to a lesser extent, Chad' (Bach 1999: 5). The transborder economies of the Chad basin 'dotted with depots, hideouts, bulking and redistribution points – have become zones of economic resurgence' (Duffield 2001: 153).

On the basis of recent improvements in some countries' economic growth figures, notably those involved in 'post-conflict donor-seeking regimes' (e.g. Uganda, Mozambique, Ethiopia), some people believe that Africa is on the 'threshold of development' (Chabal and Daloz 1999: 124). However, in their exploration of why so very little development has actually been achieved, the authors suggest that, 'contrary to what has hitherto been assumed, development as we conceive it might in effect not be *the* priority for a majority of Africans' (*ibid.*: 125). The continent may be following a 'decidedly non-Western agenda': modernity without development. Bayart proposes that Africa's 'comparative advantage' lies in its capacity to host international illegality. 'Informal and illicit trade, financial fraud, the systematic evasion of rules and international agreements could turn out to be a means, among others, by which certain Africans manage to survive and stake their place in the maelstrom of globalisation' (1999: 116). It is important to note, however, that African parallel economies are based on trade not production: the parallel export of primary products and the parallel import of manufactured goods and specialised services (Duffield 2001: 158).

Cold War politics played a part in the generation of suffering and livelihood insecurity in a number of African countries on the frontiers of the competition between capitalism and socialism. They also provided mechanisms of constraint in relation to other potential conflicts. The end of the Cold War has been followed by a period of international political restructuring which is still in process. External political actors of importance for Africa's future political trajectory include the US, the former colonial powers, and Islamist movements based in Saudi Arabia and Iran. In this context most African countries are still engaged in the ongoing quest for national coherence (Chazan *et al.* 1992), with some countries, particularly the regional giants Nigeria, Ethiopia, DRC and South Africa, finding it harder than others. There is generally a preponderance of military power over other social forces. The 'state' often includes only part of society; its neo-patrimonial and military 'reach' varies between countries. Governments are presidential and dominated by Big Men. Some of these are party to political settlements with considerable numbers of residents in their countries (e.g. Botswana[10]); others have maintained power through strategic political settlements (involving patronage) with rival Big Men and/or the use of violence. At the extreme there are examples of 'state collapse'.

In all states there is a tension between the 'official face' and the patrimonial face. Resources to fuel patrimonial networks can be internally generated (through various 'taxation' processes) or externally generated (through various forms of aid and increasingly maybe through exploitation of the natural resources of neighbours[11]). 'Political settlements' depend on the successful operation of neo-patrimonial structures. When political settlements fail political elites resort to state violence. If the mass of the people are being taxed, the government is more likely to try to reach a political settlement with them, but most African fiscal systems do not tax incomes successfully. When wealth is generated by the exploitation of a resource such as oil or diamonds, then non-developmental government elites running states that lack 'administrations' are more likely to try to exclude or control 'citizens'. This process is likely to lead to the exercise of 'voice' by the excluded and disgruntled elites. In some situations this leads to problematic consequences for the mass of people who come under attack in order to move them from valuable areas, or to terrify them into acting in supportive ways. Africa's new wars involve a blurring of traditional distinctions between people, armies and government (Duffield 2001: 16).

In these contexts multi-party elections, which were widely instituted in the 1990s,[12] have been described as 'the democratisation of disempowerment' (Ake 1996, quoted in Schraeder 2000: 56); these newly established systems allow rotating and competing class fractions to continue their exploitation and exclusion activities. A number of (military) presidents who came to power as a result of coups or other violence have transformed themselves into civilian presidents via elections.

---

[10] Although the San people are derogated (described by the Tswana as 'people of the sticks' (Schraeder 2000: 65)), and have been economically and socially excluded to the point of the virtual extinction of their traditional way of life.

[11] See the recent events in the Democratic Republic of the Congo where soldiers from Zimbabwe, Uganda and Rwanda took control of natural resources.

[12] Between 1990 and 1994 more than thirty-eight countries held competitive elections (Schraeder 2000: 274).

It should not be forgotten that Taylor had unleashed such sustained violence and brutality on the population that the people decided the only way to have peace was to 'elect' him President. Thus, the people sang sardonically: 'he may have killed my pa; he may have killed my ma; but I will vote for Charles Taylor' (Abraham 2000: 15).

Mobilisation

Mobilisation by non-elites   In the context of these wider structural changes and the incidence of the life processes described above, the large proportion of Africa's population who live in or on the edge of poverty are 'desperately seeking security' (Wood 2001a) in the context of family and local structures themselves involved in processes of restructuration. As the low life expectancies show, many adults and children fail in this attempt. Some attain it (often temporarily) at the direct expense of others. Some find it through adverse incorporation into exploitative relationships of the kind described for Bangladesh (Davis, this volume). Some find it through inclusion in a local moral economy based on some form of identity and belonging (Wood, this volume). Such inclusion often involves the acceptance of inferior status and rights. Many spend their lives moving precariously from one source of livelihood to another. Some will receive temporary assistance from governments, donors and NGOs. Unfortunately there is very little research which analyses experiences of insecurity and livelihood pursuit from the longer-term perspective of poor people.

The evidence presented above shows considerable 'involuntary' exit in the form of death as a result of conflict, disease, or poverty and displacement, sometimes to refugee camps in contexts of violence and famine. Voluntary exit strategies include migration for labour to other countries, participation in informal sectors, and participation in parallel economies that often cross borders. Voice is expressed in a variety of ways including regular government-focused demonstrations and riots by urban groups such as students, taxi drivers, traders and unemployed formal sector workers. Sometimes this has led to changes in policy (e.g. the food riots in Zambia in 1987 brought the structural adjustment programme to an end) and at other times to a revolutionary change of regime (e.g. Ethiopia in 1974). Voice is also expressed in the building of new institutions/organisations, a few examples being the increase in, and reorganisation of, forms of Islamism, with their universalist agendas, and locally contextualised forms of Sufism[13] (Westerlund and Evers Rosander 1997),

---

[13] Religion is a very important source of identity, belonging and social trust for most Africans.

the growth of women's organisations, the establishment of child soldier militia units, and the spread of funeral societies (*idir*) and rotating savings groups (*equb*) in rural Ethiopia.

Mobilisation by elites   Since independence African countries have occupied a structural condition of dependence (Daloz and Chabal 1999) and African elites have mobilised to ensure that dependence has been more of a resource than a constraint. Daloz and Chabal argue that African leaders have never contemplated an economic future without dependence. Following independence, and in the context of the Cold War, developed states offered aid to 'buy' client states who negotiated political support for aid. Most sub-Saharan governments (except those of South Africa, Botswana and perhaps Gabon) maximised revenue from the export of existing resources rather than investing for future development. Also, before they were overtaken by the debt crisis, they borrowed as much and as often as they could. While these transfers had deleterious effects, they also provided African elites with the means to feed the neo-patrimonial systems in which their power resided. Since the end of the Cold War, with formal economic decline and the decline in, and increasing external control over, development aid, the neo-patrimonial reach of many elites has shrunk, forcing them to look to the international non-formal economy for sources of funds.

External mobilisation   The globalisation of markets offers huge opportunities to TNCs, smaller private businesses and organised criminals. Multi-national oil oligopolies, using capital-intensive techniques, reach deals with state elites. The oil installations are protected by private 'security' companies. The largesse is distributed along established lines of patronage to reinforce the social order and/or exported to global financial markets for personal use. Western diamond companies have played a 'devious and destructive role' in 'the massive devastation of African countries and societies' (Abraham 2000: 20). Research in Sudan (Duffield 1994), Liberia (Ellis 1999) and Sierra Leone (Reno 1995) revealed continent-wide informal trade networks involving natural resources, drugs, arms, gold, timber and imported luxuries, all financed using international currencies.

Since the end of the Cold War, and the problems the US faced as a result of their intervention in Somalia in 1993, political disorder in Africa has not generated much international political mobilisation. Unlike in the former Yugoslavia 'ethnic cleansing' in Rwanda produced no military intervention. France and Britain have been active in a minor way in some former colonies. The US has oil interests and has been involved in military training in some countries, notably Nigeria, in line with the policy of supporting regional giants. Canadian, Chinese and Malaysian oil companies are active in Sudan.

Islamism of various kinds, supported by outside networks, is a growing political and social force in North Africa and in the countries abutting North Africa (e.g. northern Nigeria) and on the eastern coast (e.g. Tanzania), which have large Muslim populations. 'In recent decades Islamist organisations have been formed in virtually all parts of Africa and their impact is felt in the religious as well as the socio-economic and political fields' (Westerlund and Evers Rosander 1997: 308). Apart from Sudan, where the Muslim Brotherhood obtained a leading role in government after the 1989 coup, Islamism in Africa is currently a force of opposition and resistance rather than government.

The IMF and the World Bank, who are in the business of lending money, have big resources to disburse on the continent. As a result of debt overhang most African countries are dependent on aid to finance the repayment of loans and varying amounts of their government budgets, which gives the IFIs considerable power in terms of setting 'formal' agendas. Aid has also been provided by an increasing number of bilateral donors, although since the end of the Cold War amounts provided have declined. In 1996 nearly $17 billion of aid went to the countries of sub-Saharan Africa, provided by at least forty major multi- and bi-lateral donors. France and the World Bank were the biggest donors, contributing $2.5 billion each (Lancaster 1999: 38).[14] In the late 1980s and 1990s there was a huge expansion of the activities (e.g. micro-credit schemes) and numbers of Western NGOs, and a related expansion of local NGOs and community-based organisations (CBOs). Very little is known about the real economic, political, social and cultural impacts of these activities.

The IFIs, whose agenda has dominated economic policy ideas for Africa since the early 1980s, tend to make the same policy recommendations for all countries regardless of livelihood structures and dynamics, of which, in particular cases, they often seem remarkably ignorant. Duffield (2001: 143) reports that while researching in Mozambique and Angola in the late 1990s Nordstrom asked aid agencies where the resources for post-war reconstruction would come from as the conventional economy was so small. 'From Angola to Mozambique most responded that non-formal economies are central to development processes' (2000: 14). However, when asked about the significance of the non-conventional economy, a senior World Bank official answered that 'we simply don't deal with those

[14] The effectiveness of aid to Africa is discussed below.

things, they are not issues we are concerned with' (*ibid.*: footnote 40). Most economic statistics collected under the aegis of the World Bank[15] do not cover activities in the criminal economy or much of the informal economy. They also ignore many economic activities and exchanges performed as part of the moral economy and the care economy (Bevan 2001b). This means that the 'African economies' that appear in many policy documents bear little resemblance to real African economies.

This is also true of African polities which are conceived of in terms of 'states' and 'civil societies'. For many countries the World Bank and bilateral donors have made multi-party elections one of the loan/aid conditionalities. Behind it lies a simple theory of accountability that is inappropriate for the authoritarian patron–client contexts in which many of these elections are held. The 'civil society' discourse usually focuses on organisations involving educated locals such as universities, the press, NGOs, trade unions, etc., ignoring many of the 'indigenous' forms of political mobilisation described above. There is a 'disconnect' (Dia 1996) between many of the Eurocentric institutions which donors seem keen to establish, and local political structures and institutions. Most of the policy-relevant social science analysis relied on by donors, particularly the World Bank, has in the past come from economists with no expertise or interest in the detailed political, social and cultural analysis[16] required to generate sensitive policies. They have developed a 'policy-messaging' (Kanbur 2001) discourse and conceptual apparatus which focuses on what it is assumed African polities and economies will become rather than what they are (see chapter 3), hence the spread of some key 'development tropes' redefined and de-politicised to remove their critical edges: 'good governance', 'social capital', 'civil society', 'empowerment', 'participation', 'pro-poor growth', etc.

Rectification   As discussed above, different 'welfare mixes' apply to different sets of Africans. There is a relatively small set of wealthy 'international' elites, who ensure personal security for themselves and their children by investing in international markets, by using the international health and education markets, and by creating family networks with branches in developed countries. There is a relatively small 'indigenous' middle class, some with links to NGOs and donors, who may have access to government and/or market social protection, and better-than-average

---

[15] Who now describe their Living Standard Measurement Study survey instrument as a 'corporate product' (www.worldbank.org/lsms).

[16] Many do not seem interested in detailed economic analysis either, relying on 'cross-country regression' analysis of the household survey data that happens to be available (Bevan 2001b).

healthcare and education. The large mass of people have to rely for personal security predominantly on the active pursuit of resources (which may harm other people or themselves) in the context of socially constructed structures involving kin, friends and patrons, and the myriad people and local organisations listed in Figure 3.1. Depending on how remote (and sometimes how poor) they are, these may have access to (usually low-quality) government education and health services, to services provided by religious organisations and other NGOs, to private pharmacies and a range of traditional healers (Bevan 2001a). There are currently few proper studies of the overall extent, quality or impact of these services.

As discussed in chapter 3, the World Bank, the IMF and bilateral donors are currently putting great pressure on African governments to 'attack poverty'. What were once called 'structural adjustment loans' are now called 'poverty reduction and growth facilities', and in order to qualify a government (or perhaps more often an international team of consultants) must have prepared a poverty reduction strategy paper, linked to the budget. There must be consultations with 'civil society' about the contents of this paper but there is also IMF scrutiny before they are accepted. There is heavy pressure to focus budget expenditure on primary education and primary healthcare. There is also growing donor interest in the area of 'social protection' as shown, for example, in the 1999 World Bank-related report on pensions and social security in sub-Saharan Africa (Barbone and Sanchez B. 1999) but, as the authors say, very little hard information. They conclude that formal social security systems 'are at present a perquisite of the middle class', except for Mauritius, Botswana, and to a certain extent South Africa, and that there is little likelihood of the extension of pension and disability cover to the informal sector, 'which represents the vast majority of the employed population in Africa' within the next generation. Even where there are formal systems they often fail to deliver due to mismanagement 'and sometimes outright pillage' (ibid.: 1).

There has been considerable variation in school enrolments: table 6.1 shows that in 1965 the gross primary enrolment rate for Niger was 11 per cent compared with 134 per cent for Gabon. The 1990 figures show improvements in all countries for which there are data, but still quite large variations between countries and regions. Providers include governments, churches, community organisations, NGOs and private entrepreneurs. In many cases even when schooling was meant to be free (before the introduction of structural-adjustment-related 'cost-sharing' in many countries), parents had to supplement inadequate or unpaid teachers' salaries, cover the costs of school uniforms, and often provide labour and bricks for the building of schools. There are many concerns about the quality and cultural appropriateness of the education available.

Governments have been less successful in providing health services. For example, Therkildsen and Semboja (1995) argue that the 'private sector' is dominant in all three East African countries. 'Services are provided by a wide range of traditional healers, private hospitals and practitioners trained in modern medicine.' In Uganda increasing numbers of government health workers provide treatment in their homes for payment (sometimes using the drugs unavailable in the government health centre). 'Pharmacists', often untrained, are important private providers of Western drugs. Voluntary agencies, especially the churches, are also important. In Kenya NGOs provide around 40 per cent of the health services. The authors conclude that the privatisation of social services in East Africa 'has taken place on a grand scale', but not in a way that fits into structural adjustment prescriptions (*ibid*.: 28). Privatisation has been to grassroots organisations rather than profit-making entrepreneurs.

The authors of a recent World Bank study of health expenditure, services and outcomes in sub-Saharan Africa (Peters *et al.* 1999) conclude that the health-related experiences of African countries are increasingly diverse. The median annual per capita expenditure was less than $6 between 1990 and 1996, but it averaged only $3 in the lowest-income countries, compared with $72 in the middle-income countries. In those years an average 1.7 per cent of GDP was spent on health, compared with 3 per cent on defence and 3.5 per cent on education. These figures are probably based on budget allocations rather than real expenditure that affects health and education. Even when these allocations turn into real disbursements it is quite possible that very little of the expenditure will impact at health centre or school level. The NGO sector plays a major role in the financing and provision of health services.

As part of its programme to 'attack poverty' and achieve the International Development Targets/Millennium Development Goals, the World Bank, in collaboration with other donors, has been pushing governments to develop 'sector-wide approaches' to the provision of (mostly primary) education and (mostly primary) healthcare. While these approaches are meant to be designed 'in partnership' with recipient governments, they are usually very much donor-driven, with the underlying models dominated by rather simplistic rational-technocratic approaches (Bevan 2001a). A government which tries, as Uganda did in the late 1980s/early 1990s, to develop a culture-sensitive curriculum in consultation with local education experts, is likely to be over-run (as the Ugandan process was) by impatient World Bank people unable to wait to get the education loan out, and with a clear idea of what primary education for rural Africans ought to look like (Bevan and Ssewaya 1995). The World Bank approach, to which African elites are signing up, has been described by Brock-Utne (2000) as a programme of intellectual recolonisation. Aid for education, defined as schooling, is often accompanied by Western curricula, developed in Western languages.[17]

Criticisms of the 'Western package of schooling' go deeper. Serpell argues that not only has the expansion of formal education provision failed to deliver economic development and autonomy, but it has 'facilitated their economic decline and increased dependency, by promoting the emergence of a national elite class whose externally oriented style of consumption drains the national economy of much of its productive energy' (1993: 4). Furthermore, most of the children going through a rural primary school leave with the feeling that they are failures; very few of them receive the certificate that will enable them to continue to secondary education, which is the criterion by which most parents, teachers and pupils judge success. This is because there are hardly any secondary school places. Serpell argues that the nature of schooling needs to be reformed so that its 'approach to cultivating children's intellectual and moral development contributes harmoniously both to the transmission of culture across generations and to the promotion of economic progress' (*ibid.*: 246).

It is also important to make the links between education and economic activity. In early post-colonial Africa completion of a secondary education usually led to a (subsidised) university degree or formal employment in government or formal private enterprises. Recent processes of de-bureaucratisation and informalisation and the withdrawal of subsidies from university education (at IFI behest) have led to a decline in these opportunities, resulting in increasing numbers of educated unemployed youth. In their search for the relatively wealthy livelihoods they were brought up to expect, many of these educated young people are turning to violence (Richards 1996) and transborder shadow economies. 'Those who once found employment in local agro-industry, the health and education sectors and development and public works projects now work as transporters, guards and carriers along the Nigerian, Cameroonian, and Chadian borders' (Roitman 2001: 4).

Stratification outcomes   In this section I focus on the activities of the development and humanitarian aid industries and the positions they occupy in the stratification outcomes related to African in/security

---

[17] Similar critiques can be made of the 'Western' economist-driven approach to health service provision (Bevan 2001a).

regimes. Developed country governments have separate and sometimes contradictory foreign policy, trade, 'international development' and 'humanitarian' agendas. It is only in the 1990s that we have seen, first, the emergence of the proposition that aid should not be used for foreign policy or trade purposes; second, the proposition that foreign policy and trade policies should take international development as one of their goals; and, third, the proposition that humanitarian aid is not something to be provided separate from development aid and conflict resolution interventions. The first two of these propositions are still to be put into effective practice. As discussed in chapter 3, Duffield has argued that the merging of development and (conflict-defined) security is one element in an emerging and complex system of global governance 'whose aim is secure stability on the borders of ordered society where the world encounters the violence of the new wars' (Duffield 2000: backpage blurb).

Whilst, in theory (and sometimes in practice), development and humanitarian aid donation are insecurity rectifiers, they can, as the Sudan case-study of humanitarian aid shows (see below), also support relationships of exploitation, exclusion, domination and destruction. This is also true of development aid, as Duffield demonstrates in his analysis of the way in which international development aid provided in the 1990s in the transition zone between North and South Sudan 'helped to reinforce the position of dominant commercial and political groups and the networks they control' while at the same time 'the poor health and economic conditions amongst most Dinka remained unchanged during the course of the 1990s' (2001: 230).

In line with the in/security regime model, development and humanitarian aid actors who become involved in African insecurity regime episodes and informal security regimes as social constructors of rectification processes (to improve livelihoods or provide social transfers) have come to occupy positions in the stratification orders of local, country, regional and global in/security regimes. These positions are associated with interests and ideologies, some of which are to do with development and welfare, but others of which are not. Furthermore, the activities generated by development industry interests and ideologies often do not have the effects anticipated in policy and project documents, since (1) the theoretical models driving much aid activity are seriously flawed; (2) interventions are conducted in cooperation and conflict with (differentially powerful) local actors, who have their own interests, ideologies and goals;[18] and (3) most processes of change in this context are non-linear.

---

[18] Porter *et al.* (1991) provide an empirical study of a development project whose main 'outcomes' were the deeper penetration of President Moi's patrimonial networks and an increase in insecurity for local people; in Ferguson's study of a Lesotho project the

The development industry is involved in the transfer of finance, technology, knowledge and ideology from developed to developing countries. The industry involves a large number of differentially powerful organisational and individual actors and networks, including international organisations such as the World Bank, the IMF and the United Nations, plus related agencies (e.g. FAO, ILO, UNICEF, UNESCO, WHO, etc.), regional organisations – for example the African Development Bank and (UN) Economic Commission for Africa – national 'donors' – for example, USAID, DFID, SIDA (Sweden), JICA (Japan), etc. – employees of these organisations and international consultants employed by them, partners in developing country governments, technocrats, bureaucrats and politicians, international NGOs (non-governmental organisations) – for example, OXFAM, national NGOs, local NGOs and CBOs – the 'beneficiaries' of the policies, programmes and projects provided by the industry, and a set of international development academics to generate the concepts, models and theories that underlie, justify or challenge[19] the practices of the different actors.

In a recent analysis of aid to Africa (subtitled *So Much to Do, So Little Done*), Lancaster (1999) concluded that aid agencies in Africa often misdiagnosed problems, could not design programmes that addressed local political environments and did not coordinate their efforts effectively. She begins with the question why, with so much aid, there has been so little development in Africa. She finds some successes, but frequently it has proved 'unsatisfactory in impact and its positive results unsustainable over the long-run' (*ibid.*: 220). Furthermore, when aid has reinforced bad policies and poor governance, 'weakening African institutions and creating dependence, more aid can buy less development' (*ibid.*: 221). While she acknowledges the contribution to aid failure made by Africans, particularly a poor policy environment and weak institutions, she argues that much of the responsibility for the ineffectiveness of aid must rest with donors (*ibid.*). One problem has been misallocation for international political reasons, and another the way aid has been designed and managed. This has three aspects. First, foreigners with little knowledge of local conditions often design complicated and experimental interventions, shaped by complicated programming processes that conflict with the experimental nature of the intervention, and frequently without the involvement of locals. Second, domestic politics and bureaucratic imperatives *within* donor countries distort aid programmes, for example pressures to spend,

---

main outcome was an increase in authoritarian penetration by the non-developmental government (1990).

[19] As discussed in chapter 3, development discourse and policy is in the process of becoming repoliticised.

the influence of political parties, private interests and government agencies themselves. Third is the huge number of poorly coordinated aid agencies operating in African countries.

The impacts of these 'big structures' (Tilly 1984) work their way through to the less powerful through diverse socially constructed, unequally 'structurated' local intermediate institutions, organisations and corporate groups (Wood's 'meso' domain, 2001a). These are a set of 'small structures' in the realm of 'society' (which does not have to be referred to as 'civil') that includes 'communities' and 'households'. There has not been room in this chapter for a serious consideration of these small structures,[20] but it is clear that they too are structurated through patriarchal processes of exploitation, exclusion, domination, destruction and rectification with serious consequences for those on the weaker end of the relationships, particularly poor women, poor children, poor old people and poor sick and disabled people.

Application of the in/security regime model

Earlier I argued that, in the context of Africa, country regime comparisons across the welfare mix/welfare outcome space were problematic for a number of reasons. Using this approach we can, in 'ideal-typical' mode, identify a quadri-furcated mix: an international elite with good outcomes reliant on international markets (in a liberal welfare regime); a middle class with relatively good outcomes reliant on a mix of government and formal markets (in a conservative welfare regime); those with uncertain outcomes who are incorporated in various societal organisations and networks, many of them adversely (in an informal security regime); and those with dreadful outcomes who are 'excluded' sometimes physically and sometimes through violence (in an insecurity regime). If the data were available, and the frequent post-colonial transitions and restructurings acknowledged, it would be possible to classify African country regimes according to the relative proportions of each of the four categories. In no cases would members of either welfare regime predominate, the majority of country cases would involve a variable set of more or less related and dynamic exclusionary and unequal informal security regimes based on some salient group identity, and it would be possible to identify a considerable number of insecurity regime episodes generated by competition and clashes between differentiated informal security regimes.

This would be a time-consuming and serious research exercise which would offer an improvement on the donor predilection for financing

---

[20] There is a short discussion in chapter 3.

endless consumption poverty analyses based on household surveys. However, it would be a 'de-politicising' exercise which would fit with the current IFI identification of the problems of poor countries as being mainly internal and with the emerging 'liberal peace' agenda discussed above and in chapter 3. Such an approach ignores the importance of the relationships between internal and external actors, goals and structures. Furthermore, static typologising approaches of this kind are less useful for understanding the complex and changing political and economic realities of post-colonial Africa than a dynamic approach focused on the insecurity generation, mobilisation and social dis/continuity and in/stability spaces. Using such an approach the following case-studies of two insecurity regimes illustrate how prolonged periods of insecurity regime equilibrium can result from the structured interactions of external players and internal players contributing to insecurity generation and/or mobilising to try to rectify it.

Case-study of a warlord insecurity regime: Sierra Leone in the 1990s

Suffering in 1990s Sierra Leone involved deaths, dismemberment and displacement, leading to the loss of loved ones and livelihoods, societal destruction, the rupture of inter-generational links, and psychological devastation. Between 1990 and 1995 estimations are that 15,000 civilians were killed, there were 100,000 mutilation victims, 40 per cent of the population were displaced, sex slavery involved girls as young as ten, many child soldiers including girls were recruited, and refugee-filled camps sprang up in which boredom and sexual and physical violence were endemic. There has been a considerable destruction of infrastructure, especially in rural areas near rebel camps and diamond areas, and in and around Freetown. Declining respectable livelihoods are indicated by a fall in GDP per capita from $277 in 1966 to $151 in 1998. Diamond smuggling has been part of the informal economy since the 'diamond rush' of the 1950s; since 1991 war has led to the destruction of many regular agricultural and urban livelihoods; many women are widows or provisioning for family needs. This is reflected in high levels of prostitution.

Sierra Leone came to independence in 1961 with a bifurcated political structure in which the colonial authorities had tended to favour the rural elite, rather than the urban creoles. Freetown became a crown colony in 1808 and was used as a refuge/dumping ground for freed/runaway British slaves and as a base for a British anti-slavery squadron. The population came to be dominated by released slaves, and there ensued a long history of opposition between creole-speaking 'town', acting as middlemen for British business interests, and 'bush', especially rainforest dwellers, with a variety of cultural groups. Much of this business involved resource extraction from the rainforest in the east of the country, which provided, among other things, including gold and diamonds, ivory and mahogany for the pianos that graced Victorian parlours. The Sierra Leone Protectorate, designed as a separate sphere of 'native administration', was established in 1896; in the 1930s economic emphasis shifted from tree crops to minerals. 'By the 1960s the country's exports were dominated by diamonds, iron ore, bauxite, and later, rutile' (Richards 1996: 40).[21] Well before independence local colonial officials encountered difficulties in imposing London's directives (Reno 1995: 27).

Nineteenth-century rural Sierra Leone was a land of numerous 'countries' containing networks of fortified settlements surrounded by satellite villages; occasionally a powerful individual would organise initiation rites for large numbers of people, thus creating personal fiefdoms which usually collapsed with the death or economic failure of the founder. In this context 'community' was constructed using various localising techniques related to patrilineal descent from the putative founder. Today in many localities such descendants still claim rights to land use, decision-making and political representation. Fanthorpe has recently argued that '[i]n much of Sierra Leone *de facto* citizenship remains a privilege for those domiciled in old villages registered for tax collection'. Young people, itinerant workers and other low-status people 'find themselves in attenuating orders of precedence in access to basic rights and properties' (2001: 363).

This is a 'mineral economy' with 70 per cent of workers involved in agriculture, 14 per cent in industry and 16 per cent in services. Syrian–Lebanese merchants have played a key economic role. The richest area lies in the east where there is rainforest, good agriculture, and gold and diamond deposits. Economic decline began in the 1970s and the economy has been in crisis since the mid-80s, seeing rising unemployment, high inflation and shortages of essentials. The polity is still bifurcated between the urban Krios and rural 'paramount chiefs'. Student protests began in the late 1970s and continued into the 80s, while 'lumpenised' youth with no rights to land or other livelihood opportunities has been easy game for party thuggery. Successive presidents tried (and failed) to balance patrimonial demands, needs for international credit, and IMF economic restructuring demands. President Momoh, who came to power in 1986, made an enemy of Charles Taylor of Liberia who promised he would make 'Sierra Leone taste the bitterness of war'. A patrimonial state fuelled by diamonds has become a 'shadow state'. The rebel war began

---

[21] This section relies heavily on research done by Richards and Reno.

in 1991. The Revolutionary United Front (RUF), founded by alienated intellectuals, is a politically motivated organisation: a 'Rambo-style social movement' (Richards 1996: 60) which uses ideas from Libyan President Qaddafi's Green Book, e.g. recognises the right of everyone to basic goods and organises 'bush schools'. The RUF invaded the eastern rainforests from Liberia; it recruited and trained child soldiers, killed notable people in villages and used civilian terror tactics to keep control of soldiers. A culture of violence was constructed, partly drawing on the American culture of violence: for example, child soldiers regularly watched Rambo videos.

A key feature of the world context that helped to shape Sierra Leone's trajectory was the unleashing of 'global' capitalism in the 1980s and 1990s, including criminal elements. Some similarities with nineteenth-century capitalism can be found: exceedingly weak trading states and opportunities for private interests to take over national natural resources. Also, with the end of the Cold War, most of Africa lost international political salience, while the 'globalisation' of culture has produced new 'creolised' local–global meanings, social networks crossing borders within and beyond Africa, and the use of guerrilla war as a show to attract outside attention. Given all these problems, damaging life processes have been much harder to deal with.

There has been a long list of external actors involved in Sierra Leone's in/security regime. From the late 1970s disaffected and exiled students were trained in Libya as Qaddafi sought to export his 'revolution'. The IMF brought in austerity programmes from 1977 and the World Bank followed with structural adjustment programmes. The eastern part of the country was occupied by the United Liberation Movement for Democracy in Liberia (ULIMO), a Liberian movement which used Sierra Leone as a base to attack Charles Taylor's forces, but later the RUF invasion was supported by Taylor, who lent Liberian and Burkinabe mercenaries. Burkina Faso supported the RUF with training bases and hundreds of soldiers from elite units. Presidents Compaoré of Burkina Faso and Eyadéma of Togo have both been involved in receiving diamonds and supplying arms to rebel factions on the continent.

An Economic Community of West African States Military Observer Group (ECOMOG) troop offensive in 1998, dominated by Nigeria, was followed by the 1999 assault on Freetown by an international cartel of criminal gangsters, including the RUF, aiming to create a satellite state directed by Charles Taylor to pillage diamonds and other resources. The international community pressured the government to negotiate with the RUF and provided United Nations Mission in Sierra Leone (UNAMSIL) forces. When these fell into difficulties the British army became involved in 2000. Private American and European businesses bought coffee, cocoa, timber, gold and principally diamonds from the RUF leader Sankoh while foreign firms provided weapons, communication systems and military training. Sankoh reached many foreign firms via Taylor in Liberia. Humanitarian NGOs have also been involved and aid stores are often looted by rebels, sobels (soldiers who behave like rebels) and bandits. 'Private security firms' or mercenaries have been involved in protecting diamond mines and supporting local civil defence militias.

Apart from some assistance from humanitarian NGOs, suffering people have largely to rely on their own efforts to survive. Many of these cause harm to other people. For example, bandits and soldiers involved in 'sell-game' (looting) disguise themselves as rebels. Local civil defence units (*kamajors*) have mobilised, and refugees have fled to Guinea, Liberia and other parts of Sierra Leone. Resources are raised through the trafficking of children and young people, and girls are sometimes forced into early marriage for bridewealth. There is also some creative informal livelihood and social protection activity including self-help schools. There is a search for patrons by war widows and orphans. Generally women and children lack voice and power; women have not been included in post-conflict negotiations.

The insecurity regime that flourished during this episode was constituted by the government plus its allies, and the RUF plus its allies, versus 'the people'. The linked conflicts in Sierra Leone and Liberia have been sustained for more than ten years as a result of the building of sophisticated international commercial and political networks: for example, rebels and the ECOMOG soldiers who were meant to be controlling them engaged in commercial cooperation to exploit diamonds. Other interests being met were those of Bulgarian arms dealers, South African mercenary companies, Belgian diamond dealers, Asian timber importers, the UK army, French business, the presidents of Burkina Faso and Togo, the UN, Nigeria, ECOMOG and humanitarian NGOs.

There are other regimes in Africa, apart from Sierra Leone and Liberia, where 'warlord' politics dominate, including the Democratic Republic of the Congo, Angola and arguably Nigeria. All of these states are rich in mineral resources. Warlord insecurity regimes are marked by a transition from neo-patrimonial politics to 'the market-based tactics and nonbureaucratic organisation of warlord politics' (Reno 1999: 218). These tactics and organisations are not confined within state borders. For some years Charles Taylor was excluded by ECOMOG from taking formal power; he responded by setting up a parallel government in the area under his control which he called 'Greater Liberia', and established relationships with leading Ivorian, French and Lebanese business people.

Elites and others from neighbouring countries are attracted to the mineral resources 'honeypot', as the series of conflicts in the DRC has shown. Here, in 2001 the warring factions included the DRC 'government', at least three rebel Congolese groups, and representatives of 'the neighbouring' governments of Angola, Namibia, Rwanda, Uganda and Zimbabwe. Some of these governments have regional security interests, since an ungoverned DRC can provide a base for their rebel movements. But the war yielded profits to any group that could take control of an area with valuable mineral resources.

Governments and 'rebels' in warlord regimes will, whenever possible, try to access the resources that go with IFI, UN and bilateral donor aid. If this means jumping through some hoops, like the production of a poverty reduction strategy paper, they are likely to cooperate. But these are not leaders looking for any kind of political settlement with the people living in the territories that they control, least of all 'the poor'.

Case-study of a humanitarian aid insecurity regime: Sudan in the 1980s

In the 1980s Western donor governments increasingly directed humanitarian aid through international NGOs; this gave them a new status as sub-contractors, which in turn led to new interests and made it more likely that they would become unwitting elements in insecurity regimes that benefited the powerful more than their putative 'clients'. An example of this which has been well documented (Keen 1994b, de Waal 1997) can be found in the civil war/famine emergency in southern Sudan in the 1980s.

In 1988 the death rates among famine victims (mostly Dinka) were among the highest ever recorded anywhere in the world. Raiding for cattle and slaves, often combined with a government scorched-earth policy, left communities without the cattle and grain stores they needed to survive. Between 1984 and spring 1986, before the worst of the raiding, an estimated 340,000 head of cattle were stolen in the eastern part of Bahr el Ghazal. The context for these disasters was a country with over 570 ethnic groups in which much of the south is occupied by African agro-pastoralist groups practising traditional religions, while the north and west have a dominant Arab population following Islamic religions. As a result of a politically constructed 'split' between the Arab/Islamic north and the African/Bantu south the second civil war began in 1983, followed in 1989 by a fundamentalist-backed coup. Since independence the south has suffered economic neglect and exploitation, and what is experienced as sexual repression and religious indoctrination.

One key aspect of the wider context for the suffering of poor and powerless people in southern Sudan was that in the 1980s Sudan was an important strategic ally for the West in relation to next-door Libya, although by 1989 the Cold War tensions were easing. Media interest in 'famines' leading to pressure on donors from their citizens changed donor calculations in 1988. One 'life process' feature of this scenario was that among starving people diseases such as diarrhoea, measles and malaria spread rapidly and killed easily.

The Sudan government is dominated by *riverain* elites from the centre-east. They used the manipulation of hunger as an important tactic in the civil war. In 1983 they faced pressures and restlessness among the increasingly well-armed Arab Baggara, who, as a result of renewed rebellion in the south, lacked access to the labour previously provided by southern migration. They also faced escalating international debt and balance of payments problems. The solution was to enlist Baggara militias in organised attacks on the Dinka by providing arms, ammunition, intelligence and freedom from prosecution. This would simultaneously enable them to gain access to unexploited oil and channel Baggara frustrations including allowing slavery to provide labour. The rebel Sudan People's Liberation Army (SPLA) started the civil war supported by many groups in the south, notably the Dinka. They advocated a 'new Sudan' based on economic justice and cultural and religious tolerance, but they also used the manipulation of hunger as an important tactic.

Famine victims tried to sell assets, including labour, and to buy grain, which raised prices sharply; price movements were shaped by raiding, intimidation, collusion in the marketplace and the blocking of relief. Non-market strategies, such as collecting wild food and moving to places where there were relatives, were stopped by government soldiers, officials and government-supported militias. Donor relief came little and late; deliveries were inadequate in relation to the very severe needs, and they were blocked by a range of politically influential groups with vested interests in the success of the famine processes. For example, merchants paid railway workers not to load relief grain on trains and the army was slow to provide military escorts. Donor-provided grain was often not delivered to the south and Western agencies were kept out of the area by the Sudan government. Donors did not explore the considerable 'room for manouevre' that existed until the peak of the famine mortality in 1988 was revealed in media coverage.

The limited donor agendas before 1989 helped to produce the severe famine. They did not tackle the underlying causes of famine but concentrated on reacting with nutritional interventions in the final stages when mortality was high. They intervened too late as a result of their models of famine which defined it in terms of daily death rates rather than the earlier distress linked to sales of livestock. They did not use the leverage resulting from the fact that they were providing around half of government recurrent expenditures and did not consider channelling relief direct to rebel-held areas. They accepted government definitions of 'accessibility', and while there was concern about the allocation of relief no steps were taken to ensure it was actually received by famine victims.

In this regime famine promised, and to some extent delivered, economic and military benefits to the Sudan government, the Baggara, livestock merchants exporting to the north, who benefited from low livestock prices and high grain prices, and army personnel who had an incentive to restrict the provision of grain to keep prices high. Famine victims were exploited through artificially high grain prices. The limited agendas of the donors allowed them to present an image of successful relief operations 'and maintain relatively good diplomatic relations with a Sudanese government that was actually promoting the famine' (Keen 1994a: 120). Victim groups were exposed to famine because they could not get 'effective representation within the Sudanese state'; the assets controlled by the Dinka (land, livestock, newly discovered oil) exposed them to exclusionary and exploitative processes.

Keen emphasises the continuities with the colonial regime.

The use of famine as a cheap counterinsurgency tactic was a technique of long standing in Sudan, as was the device of buying the loyalty of potentially rebellious groups (like the Baggara) by granting them a licence to plunder. Both techniques had been used in the early years of the British condominium administration, as colonial officials sought, on the basis of meagre central-government resources, to bring Sudanese civil society under control (*ibid.*: 114).

He concludes that '[u]nless donors address themselves to the underlying processes creating famine, to the local power structures that shape famine and famine relief, their interventions may serve merely to reinforce these power structures and exacerbate famine' (*ibid.*: 121).

'Humanitarian aid regimes' which seem to benefit recipient governments, international and bilateral donors and NGOs more than the aid 'victims' which is their ostensible purpose, have been identified in a range of places and times. The use of international relief aid for military and political purposes by the Ethiopian government in 1984/5 is described by Hendrie as being supported by 'an almost unbelievable naivety on the part of the international community concerning the government's use of food aid in the region'. The consequence was the 'de facto exclusion of some two to three million people from access to the world's food aid until it was too late' (1994a: 137). Duffield (1994) argues that in a number of 1980s conflicts (Angola, Mozambique, Ethiopia, Sudan and Somalia) famine was not a consequence of conflict, but rather its goal.

'Complex emergencies' are usually highly politicised and 'frequently associated with non-conventional warfare, regional insecurity or situations of contested governance' (Duffield 1994: 50). These regimes often cross international boundaries and involve a range of players, including aid agencies and NGOs. Duffield regards famine as one outcome of a process of impoverishment resulting from the transfer of assets from weak to strong (other possible outcomes are large-scale migration, rapid expansion of urban slums or a refugee exodus). Methods of asset transfer can range from market pressure to violent appropriation. The more coercive the transfer the more likely it is that the winners have mobilised some form of cultural justification (e.g. ethnic, religious, national sectarianism). Increasing Islamisation in the north of Sudan allowed processes of asset transfer in the south that have weakened or destroyed a number of distinct semi-independent socio-economic groups including the Dinka, the Fur, the Nuba, the Maban, the Uduk, the Anuak, the Chai, the Murle, the Toposa and the Mundari (*ibid.*: 55). The Sudanese asset transfers are part of a wider parallel economy linked to

national level extra-legal mercantile activity. In turn, this articulates with higher-level political and state relations together with regional and international parallel networks which trade in commodities and hard currency. It is this level that provides the initial site for the integration of international aid and relief assistance with the parallel economy. As assets flow upwards and outward, culminating in capital flight, international assistance flows downwards through the same or related systems of power (*ibid.*: 56).

While disaster relief has often provided indirect and appropriated benefits to the politically strong, it has been estimated that it rarely provides more than around 10 per cent of the food needs of the 'victims' (*ibid.*: 63). In/security regimes based on humanitarian aid take the form of 'permanent emergencies' requiring permanent humanitarian intervention which 'has tended to favour and support the politically strong to the detriment of the weak' (*ibid.*: 64). Donors and NGOs are key players in these regimes.

Regional features of African in/security regimes

The two insecurity regime episodes just described did not take place within the territory of a 'state'. Such 'diversification of state–society relations ... goes along with the development of new patterns of regional interaction which undermine territorial control and the efficiency of institutional attempts to promote regional integration' (Bach 1999: 5). Clapham (1999: 54) distinguishes between two broad kinds of relationship between a state and its boundaries: 'between boundaries which are created by states and states which are created by boundaries'. For most Africans the boundaries preceded the state; the effect of this is the mutual recognition by African rulers that their boundaries provide one part of the legitimacy for their rule. The boundaries 'defined and legitimated the particular kind of power structure which grew up within post-colonial African states, and provided the framework for the politics of patronage and allocation through which those who controlled these states sought to survive'. One thing they did was to define the revenue base which depended on customs duties and state manipulation of markets for agricultural produce. Today, while it is possible to identify a number of 'normal' states which control their national territories, effectively maintain their boundaries, and have made some progress towards an indigenous sense of nationhood (Clapham 1999: 56), there are also a significant number of states with declining capacity to control their territories, mainly as a result of the failure of African economies and the related IFI interventions which, at least in the short run, have accelerated the process of state decay (*ibid.*: 58). The demand for multi-party democratisation may also 'weaken or destroy the state since a system of government which depends on popular election must ultimately be prepared to recognise the right to secession of any community which does not wish to remain within the existing frontiers of the state'.

As described above, there are informal processes of regionalisation to be found in Africa. At the same time 'the results achieved by the numerous IGOs [inter-governmental organisations] meant to promote regional co-operation or integration are a far cry from the objectives assigned to them in their founding charters' (Bach 1999: 5). One solution might seem to be the creation of effective systems of regional integration around potential regional leaders, but this is problematic since all the larger states have experienced some form of civil war:

In several regions of the world, the regionalisation process goes hand in hand with institutional strategies which constitute a political response of the member states to the globalisation of economies... In sub-Saharan Africa, regionalisation proceeds mostly from interactions initiated by non-state actors and interpersonal networks, faced with decaying states unable or unwilling to assert their sovereignty. The continentalisation of trade and financial flows is happening, but as a paradoxical outcome of the preservation of market segmentation and interstate disparities. Trans-state integration is stimulated by market distortions as opposed to trade liberalisation, a situation which accounts for the overall failure of the IGO's programmes towards market integration (Bach 1999: 12–13).

Implications for 'global social policy' in relation to Africa

African in/security regimes, country regime mixes, regime episodes and transitions occupy a range of niches in the structures and dynamics of the wider global in/security regime described in chapter 3. Within this global regime most of Africa occupies a position of increasing marginalisation in the 'legal' global economy, its major involvement relating to natural resource exploitation. However, its role in the criminal global economy has been growing. These two features of Africa's niches are having important effects on livelihood and in/security outcomes for Africans. In this context, insofar as there has been a 'global social policy' for the rectification of insecurity in Africa, it is one that has been theorised, financed and implemented by outsiders, using concepts, methodologies and theories developed out of the Western 'Enlightenment' project, which often seem to bear little relationship to realities on the ground. As shown above, post-colonial aid expenditure in Africa has not been 'value for money'.

A major factor in the failure of the development in Africa lies in the ontological, epistemological, theoretical, value and praxis assumptions that have guided the development (1950s–70s), neo-liberal (1980s/early 90s), and 'poverty' (later 1990s) agendas of aid donors. These assumptions resonate with the values and interests of the 'development industry' and the governments financing it, but cannot provide a proper social scientific understanding of insecurity in Africa, which cannot be understood using concepts developed in relation to 'Western' realities. Most current 'development' research in Africa is conducted through the lenses of such concepts and feeds into dominant 'policy narratives' based on the implicit assumption that 'development' means 'modernisation' and 'modernisation' means continued pursuit of the Western Enlightenment project. In the African context these value assumptions, and related conceptual, theoretical and methodological approaches, and, most importantly, empirical and policy conclusions, are being increasingly challenged by academic researchers, particularly those in the fields of social anthropology (e.g. Leach and Mearns 1996), social history (e.g. Moore and Vaughan 1994), and political science (e.g. Bayart *et al.* 1999; Chabal and Daloz 1999; Duffield 2001).

'States' and financial 'markets' for land, labour and finance were violently introduced to Africa by the European colonisers, and modern state and market forms are in some ways well entrenched in many parts. Modern states construct 'citizens' with duties and rights and a bifurcation between 'public' and 'private'; modern markets construct people as individual owners of property and cash, and sellers of labour, and a bifurcation between collective and individual goods. 'Africans are resisting, criticising and reinflecting these dichotomies in a variety of idioms' (Karlstrom 1999: 117) including political witchcraft, politics of the belly, presidential patriarchy, and local appropriations of 'democracy' and electoral practices. International donors to Africa are still trying to build Western-style states, markets and, more recently, 'civil societies', on the basis of Eurocentric assumptions about 'communities' and 'households', without seeming to know very much about how modern African polities, economies, societies and cultures actually work in the context of globalisation, or to consider all the possible consequences of their interventions. The in/security regime model offers the 'development discourse', particularly the 'social development discourse', a way into the Africanist academic discourses in social anthropology, political science, history and sociology which could inform a more responsible approach to aid and 'global social policy' for Africa. This would involve recognition of the roles which Northern economic and political interests play in the generation of African insecurity and illfare, action to control these interests, and a search 'for ways of assisting in the social re/construction of culturally appropriate and politically viable institutions[22] which meet universal human and social needs for security' (Bevan, Chapter 3 this volume).

[22] In relation to African states Clapham has argued that '[w]here the state is unable to create an effective political authority within the frontiers it has inherited, then whatever authority does emerge must eventually create its own frontiers, no matter how long it takes the publishers of maps or the allocators of seats at the United Nations General Assembly to recognise them' (1999: 61).

Appendix

Table 6.1. *Some statistics comparing the 1960s and the late 1990s*

	Population 1965 millions	Population 1998 millions	Urban %	GDP US$ (1995) per capita 1966	1998	% change	GDP PPP$ per capita 1975	1998	% change	Life expectancy 1967	1997	1998	Gross enrolment 1965	1990
West Africa														
Nigeria/B	46	121	43	228	255	12	441	922	109	42	54	50	32	91
Ghana/B	8	18	38	427	399	−7	693	1,661	140	48	60	60	69	75
Ivory Coast/F	4.5	14.5	46	765	825	8	964	1,881	95	43	47	47	60	67
Burkina Faso/F	5	11	18	175	259	48	312	1,035	232	38	44	45	12	33
Mali/F	5	10.5	29	n.a.	267	n.a.	294	739	151	36	50	54	24	26
Niger/F	4	10	20	438	215	−51	493	842	71	38	47	49	11	28
Senegal/F	3.5	9	47	657	584	−11	750	1,768	136	40	52	53	40	59
Guinea/F	3.5	7	32	n.a.	594	n.a.	n.a.	1,838	n.a.	36	46	47	31	37
Benin/F	2	6	42	364	393	8	431	1,276	196	36	53	54	34	58
Sierra Leone/B	2.5	5	36	277	151	−45	346	401	16	33	37	38	29	50
Togo/F	1.5	4.5	33	365	333	−9	714	1,421	99	43	49	49	55	109
Mauritania/F	1	2.5	56	507	478	−6	697	1,746	151	41	53	54	13	49
Liberia	1	3	n.a.	n.a.	n.a.	n.a.	n.a.	n.a.	n.a.	45	47	n.a.	41	n.a.
Gambia/B	0.5	1.2	n.a.	n.a.	n.a.	17	603	1,459	142	35	53	47	21	64
Western Sahara/S	n.a.	n.a.	n.a.	n.a.	n.a.	n.a.	n.a.	n.a.	n.a.	n.a.	n.a.	n.a.	n.a.	n.a.
Guinea-Bissau/P	0.5	1	n.a.	n.a.	n.a.	n.a.	421	810	92	35	44	45	26	n.a.
Central Africa														
Congo DR/Be	18	48	30	397	127	−68	1,069	847	−21	44	51	51	70	70
Cameroon/F+B	5	14.5	48	545	644	18	746	1,929	159	43	57	54	94	101
Rwanda/Be	3	8	6	222	224	1	292	696	138	44	40	41	53	70

	Population 1965 millions	Population 1998 millions	Urban %	GDP US$ (1995) per capita 1966	1998	% change	GDP PPP$ per capita 1975	1998	% change	Life expectancy 1967	1997	1998	Gross enrolment 1965	1990
Burundi/Be	3	6.5	9	128	146	14	286	636	122	43	42	43	26	73
Chad/F	3	7.5	23	265	229	−14	444	n.a.	n.a.	37	49	48	34	54
C.A.Rep/F	1.5	3.5	41	427	644	51	713	1,320	85	41	45	45	56	65
Congo/Be	1	3	62	486	825	70	573	1,641	186	45	48	49	114	132
Gabon/F	0.5	1	n.a.	2,770	4,629	67	4,286	7,556	76	43	52	52	134	n.a.
Eq Guinea/F	0.27	0.43	n.a.	n.a.	n.a.	n.a.	n.a.	n.a.	n.a.	39	50	50	65	n.a.
Southern African														
South Africa	20	41	52	3,463	3,926	13	3,382	7,187	113	52	65	53	90	121
Mozambique/P	8	17	39	n.a.	188	n.a.	n.a.	913	n.a.	41	45	44	37	67
Madagascar/F	6	14.5	29	359	238	−34	577	927	61	44	57	58	65	103
Angola/P	5	12	34	n.a.	487	n.a.	n.a.	1,334	n.a.	36	46	47	39	91
Zimbabwe/B	4.5	11.5	35	469	687	46	948	2,325	145	49	55	44	110	116
Malawi/B	4	10.5	24	125	167	34	266	695	161	40	43	40	44	68
Zambia/B	3.5	9.5	40	650	388	−40	613	910	48	45	43	41	53	99
Namibia/SA	0.7	1.6	30	n.a.	2,134	n.a.	n.a.	4,932	n.a.	46	56	50	n.a.	129
Lesotho/B	1	2	27	182	485	166	335	1,827	445	47	56	55	94	111
Botswana/B	0.5	1.5	50	429	3,859	800	1,028	8,547	731	50	47	46	65	113
Swaziland/B	0.37	1	n.a.	n.a.	1,410	n.a.	1,026	3,313	223	44	60	61	74	111
East Africa														
Tanzania/B	12	32	32	n.a.	173	n.a.	n.a.	513	n.a.	44	48	48	32	70
Kenya/B	10	29	32	225	334	48	428	1,168	173	48	52	51	54	95
Uganda/B	8	21	14	n.a.	332	n.a.	n.a.	1,183	n.a.	48	42	41	67	74
The Horn of Africa														
Ethiopia	25	61	17	n.a.	110	n.a.	n.a.	517	n.a.	39	43	43	11	33
Sudan/B	12	28	n.a.	215	296	38	535	1,640	207	42	55	55	29	53

(continued)

Table 6.1 (*cont.*).

	Population 1965 millions	Population 1998 millions	Urban %	GDP US$ (1995) per capita			GDP PPP$ per capita			Life expectancy			Gross enrolment	
				1966	1998	% change	1975	1998	% change	1967	1997	1998	1965	1990
Somalia/I	3	9	n.a.	n.a.	n.a.	n.a.	n.a.	n.a.	n.a.	39	47	n.a.	10	n.a.
Eritrea/I	1.5	4	18	n.a.	175	n.a.	n.a.	813	n.a.	42	51	51	n.a.	n.a.
Djibouti/F	0.1	0.6	n.a.	n.a.	n.a.	n.a.	n.a.	n.a.	n.a.	39	50	51	n.a.	38
North Africa														
Egypt/B	29	61	45	441	1,120	154	571	3,120	446	50	66	67	75	94
Algeria/F	11	30	60	1,008	1,519	51	1,768	4,540	157	51	70	69	68	100
Morocco/F	13	28	55	691	1,355	96	919	3,357	265	50	67	67	57	67
Tunisia/F	4.5	9	65	897	2,280	154	1,334	5,453	309	52	70	70	91	113
Libya/I	1.5	5.5	n.a.	n.a.	n.a.	n.a.	n.a.	n.a.	n.a.	50	70	70	78	105
The small islands														
Mauritius/B	0.75	1.5	n.a.	1,257	3,993	218	1,490	9,629	546	62	71	72	101	109
Seychelles/B	0.05	0.09	n.a.	2,667	2,852	171	2,261	11,188	395	n.a.	71	71	n.a.	n.a.
Comoros/B	n.a.	0.5	n.a.	n.a.	407	n.a.	n.a.	1,488	n.a.	45	60	59	24	75
São Tomé/P	0.07	0.14	n.a.	n.a.	337	n.a.	n.a.	1,536	n.a.	n.a.	64	64	n.a.	n.a.
Cape Verde/S	0.2	0.4	n.a.	n.a.	1,138	n.a.	n.a.	2,999	n.a.	55	68	69	n.a.	121

SA = South Africa

B = British

F = French

Be = Belgian

P = Portuguese

S = Spanish

I = Italian

Sources: World Bank (2001a, 2000d); UNDP (2000).

Part III

Regimes in global context

7   Rethinking the welfare regime approach in the context of Bangladesh

Peter Davis

Introduction

The study of welfare regimes in 'developed countries' has proved to be a particularly useful tool in understanding the connecting logic underlying different attributes of welfare states. Over the last decade the approach has generated a wide literature within the field of social policy and formed the basis for conceptual schemas used in empirical research examining the dynamic relationship between societal values, group interests and emerging welfare systems (Esping-Andersen 1999; Goodin *et al.* 1999). It has also generated its own share of criticism (Castles and Mitchell 1993; O'Connor, Orloff and Shaver 1999; Room 2000a).

However, the approach has rarely been applied in developing contexts. This chapter[1] explores welfare regime theory using the case of Bangladesh to highlight its strengths and weaknesses in a wider context. I begin by summarising the relevant features of the welfare regime approach for such a task. I then reflect on the usefulness of these for the Bangladesh context, exploring the strengths and weaknesses of the conceptual apparatus in such a setting. My approach is sympathetic to the overall dynamic and political economy focus of the original welfare regime approach, especially due to their relative neglect in current development discourse. The chapter also aims to use the Bangladesh experience to contribute to a wider discussion on more broadly applicable schemas for understanding and analysing social policy in a less state-centric way so as to be relevant in developing contexts. The chapter concludes by suggesting a research agenda for low-income countries, examining the relationship between a wider range of social policy inputs and their related welfare, stratification and political mobilisation outcomes, at local, national and global levels.

---

[1] Thanks to Lyla Mehta, IDS Sussex, for valuable comments. Useful comments and ideas arising from discussions with the Social Policy in Development Contexts team at the University of Bath and with staff at IDPAA, PROSHIKA are also gratefully acknowledged. Some material in this chapter was previously published in Davis (2001), and is reproduced with the permission of the publishers.

A welfare regime approach?

The welfare regime approach shows that there is not one kind of welfare state in OECD countries but a small number of different styles or 'worlds' of welfare capitalism. These are seen as ideal types which combine distinct social values with particular programmes and policies (Esping-Andersen 1990; Goodin *et al.* 1999). In Esping-Andersen's seminal work he examined distinct social policy regimes, seen as a product of the historical relationship between political and social coalitions, the organisations and institutions in society they form, and the social policy mix they create and maintain (Esping-Andersen 1990). Thus a welfare regime refers to a particular political settlement in society as a whole, rather than merely the mix of social policy measures carried out by the state. This evolving settlement reflects an ongoing struggle between political coalitions and classes displaying differing interests and values. In different clusters of countries, distinct systems (or regimes) of welfare provision are created, which apportion responsibility in various combinations among institutional spheres in society, particularly the state, market and, in some cases, the family. The use of the term 'regime' is seen to draw attention to the relationship between norms and values and the evolution of a fairly resilient path-dependent constellation of institutions. The approach tends towards a social democratic, political-economy approach to comparative social policy, concentrating particularly on the state–market nexus.

The approach also builds on thinking in social policy – starting with that of T. H. Marshall – which attempts to understand the dynamic relationship between social policies and social stratification and mobilisation (Marshall 1950). Social policies are seen not only in terms of ameliorating the inequality and alienation produced by the industrial mode of production, but also in terms of the contribution they make to social stratification and political mobilisation, both positively and negatively. Esping-Andersen's work shows that the development of group interests, social stratification and political mobilisation produce – and continue to reproduce – distinct patterns of welfare provision. These patterns positively feed back to reinforce the political coalitions and class configurations that created them. Using the language of 'path dependency' to describe this process, Esping-Andersen suggested that distinct trajectories of welfare state formation have led to three patterns (or worlds) of welfare provision: the liberal, conservative (or corporatist), and social democratic, clustered according to their differing levels of what he calls 'de-commodification'.

Esping-Andersen draws from Marx and Polanyi in describing de-commodification as the degree of protection received by people from the vulnerability and alienation produced by dependence on the labour market. The social democratic regime (e.g. Sweden) is seen to be the most de-commodifying and the liberal regime (e.g. the USA), the least. The conservative regime is intermediate and is seen as more strongly retaining vestiges of a precommodified past in the form of corporatist (e.g. Italy) or etatist (e.g. Germany) structures.

The approach depends on an idealised conception of industrialised societies, and assumes that the main engine producing inequality and vulnerability is the 'pure cash nexus', as in the labour–capital relationship in classical Marxism. The modern industrial society is seen as having largely moved on (in differing extents) from its pre-commodified past, characterised by traditional status relations. De-commodifying social policy ameliorates vulnerability and insecurity (welfare outcomes), influences inequality and class formation (stratification outcomes) and generates configurations of political mobilisation (political mobilisation outcomes). Welfare, stratification and political mobilisation outcomes are distinguishable but are all related to the level of de-commodification achieved by a particular regime.

Bringing the welfare regime approach into the Bangladesh context

What value then, would such an approach have in a low-income context like Bangladesh?

First, it must be kept in mind that since 1990 the welfare regime approach has been subjected to vigorous criticism on a number of fronts. Many of these have been reviewed by Esping-Andersen himself (Esping-Andersen 1999; see also Gough 1999). It has been suggested that some countries have been misplaced in the schema (e.g. Castles and Mitchell 1993), the possibility of alternative or additional regime types has often been raised, and the use of de-commodification as the predominant dependent variable has come under strong criticism, especially from feminist writers (e.g. O'Connor et al. 1999). Esping-Andersen himself draws attention to the fact that his 1990 typology reflects the prevailing economic conditions of welfare states up until their climax in the 1970s and 1980s. This was 'an economy dominated by industrial mass production; a class structure in which the male, manual worker constituted the prototypical citizen; and a society in which the prototypical household was of the stable one earner kind' (Esping-Andersen 1999: 74). Now, however, contemporary Organisation for Economic Cooperation and Development (OECD) countries show markedly different characteristics. Emerging social and economic configurations are displacing those previously experienced and call for new theoretical concepts and methods to explain them.

When the welfare regime approach is brought into the Bangladesh context, many of these criticisms are reinforced, and a few more are introduced. Even though such societies are often referred to as 'pre-industrial', we cannot assume that Bangladesh is merely pre-destined to follow one of the already well-trodden paths to industrialisation, the commodification of labour and the formation of one of the three welfare regimes. Bangladesh has its own particular path dependence, positioned within a particular global and historical context.

At a more abstract level the emphasis on the iterative relationship between social and political coalitions and the policy regimes they create and maintain is certainly welcome. However, international and non-state actors must be included in the mix of interested groups. The inherent critique, albeit limited, of teleological determinism and national convergence built into the approach is also welcome. Development discourse is too often predicated on an assumed 'developed' end towards which developing countries are directed. Emphasising diverse and continuing 'development' processes within the so-called 'developed' world helps to undermine simplistic teleological approaches for poorer countries. The position adopted in this chapter is that the basic principles of welfare regime theory outlined do have analytical value in the Bangladesh context but only with substantial modification.

These areas of modification are grouped as follows:[2]

1. A much wider range of actors and organisations contributing to social policy inputs needs to be examined than in the conventional welfare regime approach. These must include non-state (NGOs and informal community-level institutions) and supra-national organisations (IFIs and international donors).
2. A wider range of formal and informal welfare strategies and institutions contributing to welfare needs to be recognised, rather than the conventional narrow focus on state provision of income maintenance and labour market policies.
3. A more comprehensive set of concepts (in place of indices of de-commodification) needs to be developed, to explore: (a) structural patterns of disadvantage and ill-being; (b) how these patterns are produced, maintained and changed; and (c) how the ameliorative impact of 'social policy' – defined widely – can be measured and analysed in a way that is useful for critical approaches to social policy.

---

[2] Comments made by Graham Room, University of Bath, helped clarify these three general areas of discussion.

A wider range of actors and organisations

Our wider definition of social policy (see chapter 1) created a new set of problems for social policy analysis.[3] How can ameliorative social policy be distinguished from other processes of social change which are the product of people's agency but do not necessarily fall within the definition of 'intentional action within the public sphere oriented towards welfare goals'? And if the focus of social policy analysis is on the relationship between causes of systemic social problems/disadvantage (epitomised as commodification by Esping-Andersen) and the ability of public action to ameliorate them (de-commodification in Esping-Andersen), and such public action includes the activities of not just states, but also markets, families and communities at local, national and global levels, how is it possible to distinguish between beneficial social processes (social policy) that mitigate and those that are being mitigated against (social problems)? In this chapter I retain the idea that social policy is about the intentional amelioration of social problems, but would argue that the central social policy actor should be seen as the citizen rather than the government agency. 'Social policy in development contexts' should therefore be citizen-centred and defined more as a *perspective* focusing on the amelioration of social problems, by citizens organised in various ways, rather than in terms of well-defined social policy sectors, associated with the state and ameliorating the excesses of the market, as has been the case in Western social policy. At the supra-national level citizenship (or membership) should be seen as multi-tiered.

An example of the problematic universal applicability of the framework is that, in 'developed' societies, Esping-Andersen regards the 'third sector' of non-state, non-market organisations as peripheral and shies away from considering it as a distinct welfare-providing arena within a welfare mix, due to either its insignificant contribution to welfare or what he sees as its 'semi-public' nature (Esping-Andersen 1999). Other Western social policy commentators also tend to see the welfare mix divided between the welfare state, the (labour) market and the family (see, for example, O'Connor et al. 1999) and generally ignore the contribution made by NGOs and voluntary or community-based organisations. In Bangladesh, however, it is impossible to ignore the contribution made to public welfare by such organisations.

The conventional focus on the nation-state as the defining unit of analysis in Western social policy is weakening due to the rising interest in globalisation (Deacon et al. 1997; Mishra 1999). The interest in

---

[3] This definition of social policy was helpfully formulated by Ian Gough, University of Bath.

European social integration and its potential multiple sovereignties, the impact of occupational mobility, the rise of network enterprises, company-based welfare, international pension schemes, and health and education-related travel, all challenge the state focus in Western social policy. There is also lively debate about the influence of globalisation on present stresses and future crises of the welfare state (Pierson 1998). However, social policy analysts would be compelled to move away from a state-centric focus far more quickly if low-income countries like Bangladesh took more prominence in their field of study. Unfortunately the OECD focus in social policy studies supports the problematic assumption that low-income countries are merely destined to become one of the Western welfare state models. This underestimates the importance of the relationship between supra-national actors and national-level coalitions of interests which shape policy at national and local levels. It also encourages the inappropriate transplantation of state-centric social policy approaches based in the formal sector which are largely the product of nineteenth-century political struggle in industrialised non-colonised countries.

The examination of a context like Bangladesh contributes to a critique of the OECD state-centric focus found in Western social policy. An adequate analysis of social policy without a recognition of the wider range of social policy actors has always been inconceivable in Bangladesh, as it is now becoming increasingly untenable in Western societies. Unfortunately for analysts, this makes the task of assembling data to describe such complex welfare mixes more difficult. Many non-state actors operate completely within national boundaries, others involve actors and institutions (transfers, networks – including kinship networks – and pressure groups) which span national borders in various ways. Since the state is becoming an increasingly problematic unit of analysis in social policy studies, new approaches are needed that seek to understand welfare regime inputs and outputs (welfare, stratification and mobilisation) combining local, national and global levels of analysis.

Development NGOs as social policy actors

In Bangladesh the most visible example of the shortcomings of the conventional welfare regime approach is in its lack of emphasis on development-oriented non-governmental organisations (NGOs). In Bangladesh there are over 1,600 NGOs actively providing various forms of welfare, funded largely, but not exclusively, by foreign aid. The majority of these are locally based NGOs which have come to form a particularly significant part of the non-state welfare mix, but do not fit easily into any conventional sector division. They are to differing extents semi-community, semi-public and semi-market organisations and are largely dependent on bilateral and multi-lateral funding for their 'welfare' operations. Many operate in contracts with the Bangladesh government to supply welfare services and some have commercial wings devoted to development-oriented business ventures (Davis and McGregor 2000).[4] The Bangladesh Rural Advancement Committee (BRAC), Proshika Manobik Unnayan Kendra (PROSHIKA), the Grameen Bank (now not officially an NGO) and the Association for Rural Advancement (ASA) are examples of the largest of these locally based but (initially at least) foreign-funded NGOs.

In the past, weak state provision of welfare, low levels of private foreign investment and high levels of readily available bilateral and multi-lateral donor funding created the political and economic space in Bangladesh for the spectacular growth of these locally based welfare-providing organisations. As donors channelled more and more funds directly through them, their size, number and scale of operation rapidly increased. There are presently over 1,600 development NGOs registered with the NGO Affairs Bureau of the government of Bangladesh. Registration is a prerequisite for receiving foreign funding and does not account for the much larger number of organisations not receiving foreign funding but still involved in a wide range of community activities. NGOs have had a particularly prominent role in anti-poverty programmes, with the scale of their activities increasing as donors considered them to be more effective channels for poverty reduction objectives. Data from the Bangladesh government's NGO Affairs Bureau illustrates how this funding increased over the 1990s (see table 7.1).

NGOs have played a prominent role in the post-independence social and political history of Bangladesh and now some of these organisations are among the largest southern-based NGOs in the world. Most were founded in the aftermath of the Bangladesh independence war in 1971 and many began with radical agendas based on a political reflection of deep-seated structural causes of poverty in Bangladesh. Some of the first NGO activists had been previously linked to student left-wing and Maoist groups, but after the independence struggle there was a degree of disillusionment with the failure of radical political parties. Many of these activists, instead, chose to channel their social concern into mobilisation of the poor through NGO groups in order to combat what they saw as the structural causes of poverty.

---

[4] It should be noted that the same phenomenal growth is not seen across the border in West Bengal where state-sponsored organisations have tended to occupy an equivalent niche.

Table 7.1. *Growth in NGO funding in the 1990s*

Financial year	Number of active NGOs		Projects financed	Foreign grants (US$ million)		Percentage of total aid
	Local	Foreign		Approved	Released	
1990/1	395	99	464	158.5	106.6	6.15
1991/2	521	111	549	287.1	121.6	7.55
1992/3	596	126	626	391.4	195.7	11.68
1993/4	684	122	581	314.0	171.0	10.97
1994/5	792	127	579	440.7	210.3	12.09
1995/6	830	128	702	182.3	156.8	10.85
1996/7	830	128	746	182.3	156.8	10.58
1997/8	1,096	143	705	188.3	206.9	16.53
				2,145.2	1,331.0	

Source: ERD (1999).

In the early years many NGOs framed their activities in the language of 'conscientisation' (following Paulo Freire) and generally had a much stronger social mobilisation agenda than is found today. NGO leaders emphasised the importance of understanding subordination in terms of patron–clientelism – linking poor clients to richer patrons within individual vertically aligned relationships – as the main mechanism maintaining and generating inequality in Bangladeshi society. Patrons were landlords, moneylenders or employers (often in combination), and the major 'class' of clients were poor landowners, sharecropping tenants and landless labourers (Kramsjo and Wood 1992).

Kramsjo and Wood's observations were consistent with a number of works emerging from this period of analysis, including BRAC (1983) and Hartmann and Boyce (1983). Vertical networks of 'clientelism' are distinguished from collective exploitation. The individual alignment and loyalty required of clients to patrons contributes to the weakness of horizontal class solidarity among the poor, while at the same time creating a system of social cohesion based on vertical relationships, with the lack of horizontal class solidarity undermining the possibility of mass movements among the poor against the interests of the rich.

Into the 1980s, however, many of these NGOs, under the influence of the major bilateral and multi-lateral donor organisations, began to move away from their somewhat radical mobilisation agenda – based on the social analysis above – and at the same time began to 'scale up' in a more technocratic service-delivery-type role, focusing particularly on the provision of micro-credit (Hashemi and Hassan 1999). In the

1990s these large organisations also faced continued pressure to raise a larger portion of their own running costs. A number, in practice, became providers of micro-finance services from which they generated their own running costs, with very little of their original radical mobilisation agenda remaining.

Over this period, NGOs in Bangladesh made a significant impact on poverty through the provision of credit and other financial services, health services, primary and non-formal education, housing, public works schemes, the organisation of poor people's (especially women's) groups, family planning, agricultural extension, immunisation and a number of other activities. Their impact on welfare outcomes is considerable, rivalling government welfare activities. However, their long-term impact on stratification and political mobilisation have to be seen less favourably. While a small number of NGOs do still act to empower and organise poor groups to enhance their 'voice' in policy processes, most NGOs operate within socially embedded structures of patronage relations which undergird particularly resilient hierarchies (see, for example, Devine 1999). The dependence of NGOs on foreign funding and their weak channels of accountability to their poor local clientele continue to undermine their ability to catalyse genuine social mobilisation, establish social rights, and effectively change prevailing power structures at local or national levels.

The prominence of NGO activity in Bangladesh draws attention to the need for social policy analysts to find concepts to describe and explain their stratification and political mobilisation impact within the prevailing welfare system. NGO activity needs to be evaluated with regard to the quality of social citizenship rights achieved for citizens in terms of coverage, enforceability, universalism and reliability, and with regard to their impact on structures and processes of clientelism, exploitation and exclusion. Questions also need to be asked about the significance for welfare regime variables of local versus foreign funding arrangements, contractual relationships with government agencies (e.g. in the Vulnerable Group Development programme) and of NGOs evolving into businesses.

In the absence of aggregate empirical data on welfare, stratification and political mobilisation outcomes and of realistic counterfactuals (although the West Bengal case provides an interesting comparison), it is difficult to evaluate the overall impact of the NGO component on the political economy of welfare in Bangladesh. The development of an appropriate conceptual framework and the formulation of appropriate indicators of welfare (e.g. poverty reduction), stratification (e.g. inequality) and political mobilisation (e.g. substantive achievement of wider sets of citizenship rights through political action) outcomes would be an obvious way to start.

International organisations shaping the welfare regime

The emphasis on the underlying principle of path dependence and the recognition of the political 'stickiness' (Pierson 2000) or resilience of social policies in Western comparative social policy studies provides a corrective to the present study of social policy in development contexts where analysis still tends to be more synchronic and apolitical.

The Indian sub-continent has a long history of welfare. It would be a mistake to view the countries of South Asia as only recently emerging welfare regimes in some new context of globalisation and with no historical antecedents. In the Bangladesh case the present state is only thirty-two years old, but its relevant history in terms of welfare institutions or the impact of globalisation began long before the independence war in 1971. Bengal itself has been a beneficiary and victim of globalisation at least since the Middle Ages, and very strongly so since the beginnings of the activities of the East India Company in the eighteenth century. Welfare institutions in turn have also developed over a long history. For example, the word used to describe the group formed in the ubiquitous and celebrated micro-finance programmes in present Bangladesh – the *samiti* – has a recorded usage in governance systems of the Vedic age (before 1000 BC). Present social policy is influenced by ancient systems of reciprocity and approaches to famine relief and public works that existed long before the arrival of the British. Thus the welfare regime has a prehistory shaped by a pre-imperial, imperial and post-imperial (yet donor-dominated) past which has shaped institutions, intervention strategies, labels and values concerning social policy in the region.

Even a cursory examination of the history of the Indian sub-continent in general, and of the region now known as Bangladesh in particular, provides valuable insights into the historical antecedents of the present system. Just as in Esping-Andersen's evaluation of Western systems of social policy, the influence of values and interest groups over imperial and post-imperial history can provide key insights. There is much scope for further research into the historical antecedents of present social policy in the region. Here it is worth drawing attention to some key influences.

Recent historiography has helped to undermine the largely negative impression made of the Mughals as prime examples of 'oriental despots'. According to Bose and Jalal 'the Mughal empire is beginning to be viewed as a complex, nuanced and loose form of hegemony over a diverse, differentiated and dynamic economy and society' (Bose and Jalal 1997).

In Mughal India, government remitted land revenue, gave loans, imported foodgrains from surplus zones and opened government shops and free kitchens for afflicted people during famine. While the extent of famine relief and tax exemption depended on the whims of the rulers, there was a firm respect for the subsistence needs of the peasantry and an expectation that rulers would not extract revenue during times of famine. Such values resonate with James C. Scott's description of the moral economy of the peasant (Scott 1976). In Bengal itself, there is evidence of extensive public works programmes, including the construction of roads, large ponds, mosques, bridges, embankments, rest houses and alms houses by the Muslim rulers who ruled with varying autonomy from Delhi from 1203 to 1757 (Ali 1985).

The Mughals also made various attempts to mitigate the impact of famine through the importation of food, price controls – with punishment and torture of offending grain dealers – and remission of taxes. Under Akbar (1556–1605), in times of drought or crop failure, revenue collectors were ordered to remit taxes, which in usual times generally came to about one-third of the annual harvest.

Such relief also occurred in areas that remained under Indian administration during the British period. Davis (2001) points out that in the 1791–2 famine the Mahratta rulers intervened with grain relief, and the Poligars also imported grain. Later, during the South Indian famine of 1876–7, large numbers of villagers migrated into the territory of the Nizam of Hyderabad in order to access relief not accorded by the British administration, leaving large areas depopulated, before British officials managed to organise relief after extensive loss of life (Davis 2001).

During the British period, the eighteenth- and nineteenth-century classical political economists, many of whom were actively involved in the East India Company, left an enduring legacy of their approach to welfare (Ambirajan 1978). Under this particular external hegemony, moral economy norms were weakened and the limits of legitimate extraction by colonial and national elites were extended. Highest priority was given to the principle of non-interference with grain markets, even in the face of widespread starvation, and rights to the land in Bengal became more exclusive under the terms of the Permanent Settlement. British famine policy was dominated by the free trade theorists, particularly from the 1806–7 famine in the Madras Presidency until the aftermath of the 1865–6 Orissa famine (Ambirajan 1978). This emphasis culminated in the great famine of 1876–7, presided over by Viceroy Lord Lytton (see Davis 2001).

The classical attitude of the early political economists towards the role of government in the alleviation of the distress of the poor was based more on the principle of non-interference of markets, combined with Malthusian population theory that stressed that interference in the inexorable laws of nature would lead to increased misery in the long run

(Ambirajan 1978). Public works schemes for famine relief were seen as acceptable but viewed with apprehension due to possible interference with markets and the encouragement of laziness and dependence. The same arguments were used by the classical economists of the eighteenth and nineteenth centuries against the Poor Laws. They were seen to encourage paupers to depend on state charity and place a burden on the hardworking sections of society. The prevailing view was that the market alone should allocate scarce resources.

Many of these colonial values embedded in social policy in Bangladesh have not substantially changed in the formal public sphere, and have been subsumed within a dominant neo-liberal development paradigm. In the informal sphere, 'moral economy' values and associated informal forms of social protection persist. Even social policy in neighbouring India, which had more opportunity to move away from her colonial past during seventeen years under essentially Fabian Nehru, with more effective domestic mobilisation and interest group formation, the colonial logic of non-interference in markets and an excessive fear of encouraging dependency in social policy formulation has not been substantially dislodged. Bangladesh, in contrast, has suffered from predominantly external (western-wing) martial control in the East Pakistan era, followed by the post-1971 era characterised by fifteen years of military government ('cantonment raj' as Rehman Sobhan aptly calls it) and neo-liberal foreign-donor policy cultivating a dominant national elite with no interest in redistributive social policies (Sobhan 2000).

According to Sobhan (1982), at independence Bangladesh had a severe deficit of foodgrains, very low levels of internal savings and a high proportion of the population below the poverty line (over 80 per cent). At the same time, the configuration of prevailing class coalitions made it extremely difficult to enforce redistributive mechanisms of extraction through taxation or pricing policies from any of the dominant social groups. The ruling elite and the powerful urban business families were largely the same people, and were net consumers of public resources. In rural areas, local elites commanded the votes of the rural masses through complex vertical hierarchies – as they continue to do today – also hindering the possibility of substantive redistribution or pricing policies which did anything but subsidise elite activities (Sobhan 1982).

In 1971, following independence, foreign donors dramatically stepped up aid flows. In the first six months after independence donors increased external assistance with US$612 million committed for the first six months, followed by US$886 million committed for 1972/3. This commitment constituted about a 150 per cent increase in aid compared with previous years, and came to about 9.5 per cent of GDP and 76 per cent of imports. At the time, the amount of disbursed aid was greater than the annual development budget.[5] Although aid has decreased as a proportion of government expenditure in the years since 1971, a regime has been created which is characterised by a host of resilient elite strategies which appropriate and hoard aid resources, coupled with a persistent unwillingness to shoulder the fiscal burden of protecting the poorest – which continues to be seen as the role of foreign aid. Many of the elite strategies are outlined by Sobhan (1982, 1998).

By the end of the 1990s, although the proportion of foreign aid in government spending decreased significantly over three decades, it left a defining influence on the shape of the welfare regime in Bangladesh, drawing attention again to the importance of path dependence.[6] Many observers (including prominent Bangladeshi specialists) of trends in the impact of foreign development assistance, present strong arguments that aid has inhibited domestic resource mobilisation, leading to the reinforcement of political coalitions which in turn perpetuate external dependence (Sobhan 1982, 1998). The relatively recent reduction of donor funding, and therefore influence, in Bangladesh corresponds with a time of unprecedented influence in the form of global capital also linked to well-established local elites. It remains to be seen whether significant coalitions of the subordinate potential beneficiaries of social policies will emerge from their long history of disenfranchisement in this new environment. Table 7.2 gives an indication of the scale of aid in welfare regime formation over the two decades from 1977/8 until 1997/8.

The long history of foreign influence in the welfare regime problematises Esping-Andersen's state-focused approach to regime formation. The implicit bargain between outsiders (where the balance of power has historically been with a neo-liberal ideology) and coalitions of elites (who

---

[5] The national budget of Bangladesh consists of the revenue budget and the development budget. Revenue consists of taxes and fees, and non-tax receipts such as dividends from state-owned enterprises and banks, and the sale of assets. Revenue expenditures are seen as recurrent costs plus interest on domestic and foreign loans. The development budget finances development projects out of revenue surplus and foreign loans and grants. For the first six years after independence actual disbursements not only exceeded the development budget but also financed some of the revenue budget as well. From independence until 1986/7 the development budget was larger than the revenue budget.

[6] In the current Fifth Five-Year Plan (1997–2002), 39 per cent of proposed development expenditure will still be met from foreign aid. From independence in 1971, up until 30 June 1998, Bangladesh received about US$40 billion of official development assistance (ODA). Of this, 14 per cent was food aid, 25 per cent commodity aid and 61 per cent project aid. Now, three decades after independence, ODA is equivalent to about 4 per cent of GDP and food aid has declined as a proportion of total aid over the years. In the 1971–3 period food aid was 38 per cent of all aid; in 1996–8 it was 7.1 per cent (Planning Commission 1998).

Table 7.2. *External resources in the Bangladesh welfare regime*

	Population (millions)	Total government expenditure (US$ million)	Aid disbursed (US$ million)	Tex revenue (US$ million)	Worker remittances (US$ million)	Foreign grants released through NGOs (US$ million)
1977/8	83.68	1,417.71 (56% ADP) (44% Rev.)	833.86 (59% of TGE)	684.90 (48% of TGE)	102	
1982/3	94.32	2,156.86 (63% ADP) (47% Rev.)	1,177.38 (55% of TGE)	909.00 (42% of TGE)	617	
1987/8	105.30	3,001.80 (50% ADP) (50% Rev.)	1,640.38 (55% of TGE)	1,397.10 (47% of TGE)	737	
1992/3	113.20	4,425.32 (42% ADP) (68% Rev.)	1,675.00 (38% of TGE)	2,313.59 (52% of TGE)	944	$195m through 722 NGOs (596 local and 126 foreign)
1997/8	126.50	5,945.93 (41% ADP) (59% Rev.)	1,251.30 (21% of TGE)	3,519.86 (59% of TGE)	1475	$207m through 1,239 NGOs (1,096 local and 143 foreign)

Source: Economic Relations Division (1999).
Notes: TGE = total government expenditure
ADP = annual development programme

have vested interests in hindering the emergence of universal social citizenship rights) has created a system where there is no substantive political connection between welfare funding and the potential coalitions of interests which should be the main beneficiaries of welfare.

In welfare state studies, the welfare regime argument holds that path dependence occurs due to positive feedback mechanisms within national political configurations. However, the Bangladesh case shows welfare funding decisions largely made outside the domestic political system, which result in weak (or non-existent) positive feedback mechanisms. Such low-income countries dominated by globalised social policy will therefore tend to be vulnerable to trajectory shifts and have less resiliently established sets of social rights – in the Marshallian sense. A political challenge within global social policy is to foster channels to force international donors to find new political connections between the formulators of international and national social policy and the coalitions of interests who should benefit from it. No amount of rhetoric about participation will compensate for a failure to allow a progressively widening array of social rights to emerge in this way. In such contexts there is therefore an urgent need in social policy formulation to consider how politically empowered coalitions of interests based around particular sets of policies – for example, old-age pensioners – can be fostered in order for progressive feedback mechanisms to emerge. The mobilisation potential of social policy has been neglected in developing countries and is one of the main lessons that can be taken from the welfare regimes approach.

Informal and community-based welfare

In addition to the relatively recent NGO phenomenon, customary cultural institutions of welfare provision also continue to provide the most important social safety net for millions of poor Bangladeshis (see, for example, Indra and Buchignani 1997). Informal social institutions that contribute to the survival of the very poor are observed in sociological and anthropological studies but are rarely analysed in policy terms. There is an urgent need to analyse further the significance of indigenous, informal, community-based welfare for poor people operating in the absence of formal welfare provision. In Bangladesh various social group memberships – such as kinship (*bangsho/gosti*) and community (*samaj*) – accord a range of informal entitlements, which provide the most significant source of social protection in times of crisis. Poor people receive *zakat, fitra*, gifts, loans, employment, meals, help with dowry and medical costs, hospitality, land, help with disputes and physical security from a range of actors in local communities and in accordance with recognised and 'routinised'

social institutions. The influence of socio-economic change on such social institutions, and their impact on welfare, social stratification and
mobilisation, is little understood even though they are vital for the survival of millions. There is evidence also that with socio-economic change
(urbanisation, migration, increased landlessness, improved infrastructure
and the formation of a stronger urban middle class) the levels of support
providing protection to the very poor in times of crisis by community and
extended kinship channels will decline. The decline in such support is associated with the presently emerging recognition of a 'very poor' category
in Bangladesh for whom the language of social exclusion is applicable.
There is therefore an urgent need to understand further the dynamics of
such forms of support.

In Bangladesh informal social relationships that provide security to
poor people are of a double-edged nature. Those who have the power resources at their disposal to provide economic security for others (often official and unofficial community leaders) utilise the loyalty and power they
derive to buttress their own power resources. Local vertical hierarchies
and factions are formed which help perpetuate the prevailing modes of
articulation of power resources. Official welfare and anti-poverty programmes (particularly those which rely on the distribution of grain) become embedded in this system. Local leaders (particularly elected Union
Parishad chairmen and members) play the role of intermediaries and are
able to manage, and to some extent legitimate, widespread looting of food
aid programmes due to their positions of power in local communities.
While these processes need to be acknowledged, they lead to a problem
for analysts if they are seen as part of the social policy mix within a simple
ameliorative model of social policy. Informal and yet 'structural' routes
to social protection both create and ameliorate disadvantage and can be
seen therefore as both social policy and social problem.

Customary modes of support are also augmented by more recently
evolving strategies of local and international occupational mobility with
expectations of support. For example, over the two decades covered in
table 7.2, worker remittances from abroad to Bangladesh have increased
more than tenfold. While migrant worker remittance data are notoriously
unreliable, they are now at least over 25 per cent of total government
expenditure and exceed total ODA. Wages earned by migrant workers in
the Middle East and Southeast Asia support and build up the assets of
groups of close relatives and help workers build up the capital to set up
businesses on their return to Bangladesh.

There has been little research done into the role of informal welfare
strategies involving the variety of relationship support networks and such
transfers from one location to another. Research would require both a

conventional quantitative economic analysis and a sociological exploration of norms and expectations associated with membership of networks and the quality of informal entitlements (or informal rights) flowing from them. Since a large proportion of international remittances come from employment in the Gulf region, these sources are vulnerable to the vicissitudes of international politics. Creative international social policy solutions, such as international pension schemes, health insurance and micro-finance services, are needed to help protect those groups whose livelihoods span international borders.

A wider range of welfare strategies contributing to social policy outcomes

In addition to the wider range of actors highlighted in the Bangladesh case there is also a need to recognise a much wider range of welfare strategies and institutions contributing to social policy outcomes. Such inputs include many functional equivalents to aspects of welfare found in Northern welfare regimes (using the idea of 'functional equivalence' without taking on the problematic teleological or convergence fallacies of old-fashioned functionalism). This widens the scope of what can be seen as the welfare mix. These include formal strategies, such as government and NGO-mediated health, education, housing, land, micro-finance provision and public works programmes, and also the 'informal', community-based forms of welfare provision which are arguably of greater significance in countries with rudimentary public welfare systems.[7] Development studies research on livelihood strategies highlights the importance of complex portfolios of resources that poor people draw from in managing risk and maintaining their livelihoods (Carney 1998; Ellis 2000; Bebbington 1999). Social policy analysis in developing contexts will also have to acknowledge such diversity and move beyond the limited focus on income maintenance and formal labour market practices found in Western social policy.

Official social policy strategies in Bangladesh are also difficult to track due to multiple sources and destinations leading to a high degree of complexity in funding and implementation. 'Welfare' strategies are usually nested within wider 'development' programmes and historically it is development discourse, driven by international donors, which shapes the nature of the welfare component of these development programmes. Donors have in the past tended to shy away from the language of 'welfare',

---

[7] See Indra and Buchignani (1997) for an example of extended traditional community/kinship sources of entitlement and social protection in Bangladesh.

with its associated connotations of unsustainable relief, handouts and poor people's dependency, and prefer the language of 'sustainable development'. Sustainability often includes the need to avoid welfare dependency, reflecting attitudes reminiscent of the neo-classical economists of an earlier time and the present 'anti-politics machine' (Ferguson 1994; Harriss 2002) tendencies of mainstream development discourse. To conform to donor concerns, welfare investments are often referred to as investments in human capital, emphasising the instrumental role of welfare in contributing to economic development, rather than seeing welfare provision as a development end in itself. Development discourse, with its focus on measuring poverty levels, also tends to overemphasise the immediate welfare outputs of development interventions, overlooking the stratification and political mobilisation outputs, which are arguably more important in fostering durable social rights.

The importance of health and education within the welfare regime

The Bangladesh context underlines the need to include health and education (along with housing, land and financial service) policies in what is understood by 'welfare', as opposed to Esping-Andersen's more narrow definition. These sectors have a direct influence on welfare and stratification in society. Public social sector spending in Bangladesh on health, education and safety net programmes has increased rapidly in recent years with education spending increasing the most, followed by public health. Education, health, social welfare and family planning expenditure increased from 10 per cent in 1989/90 to 24 per cent of the ADP in 1995/6. According to the Fifth Five-Year Plan, by 2001 this should increase to 30 per cent: a planned increase higher than any of the other South Asian countries.

Unfortunately Esping-Andersen's approach tends to sideline the role of health, education and many other policies within the welfare regime. His original work focuses on income maintenance and labour market practices. In Bangladesh, however, the range of health, education, housing, land policy and financial services has a greater impact on poor people's livelihoods than the meagre cash transfers or regulation of the formal labour market. For example, elite-driven and ruthless housing policies, leading to slum clearances, drastically undermine the rights of urban poor *bustee* dwellers and demonstrate how poor people lack political clout when it comes to securing access to land.

Although the increasing levels of government spending on social services like health and education can be expected to improve welfare outcomes, the impacts on stratification and political mobilisation outcomes are more complex. There are wide differences in service quality and in the ability of different groups of people to access public services. In addition, as official and de facto yet unofficial privatisation of public resources takes place, anti-rural, anti-poor and anti-female biases in the provision of health and education services are exacerbated. Private spending is concentrated in urban areas and is accessed predominantly by the richer segments of the population.[8] Rural public health facilities are poorly resourced and crippled by corruption, yet provide disproportionately for the poor, those remotely situated, and women.

The World Bank estimates total health spending at about US$6 per capita, with about 49 per cent of this public expenditure. Although expenditures are now relatively high in Bangladesh (1.2 per cent of GDP compared with 0.7 per cent for India, 0.8 per cent for Pakistan, and 1.4 per cent for Sri Lanka), poor quality of service and poor targeting of expenditure to benefit the poorest continue to inhibit improvements in health outcomes (World Bank 1999c).

Even in spending terms public health inputs are not redistributive (although they are less regressive than education expenditure). MOHFW expenditure is about equally divided between the poor and the non-poor. The bottom half of the population receives 57 per cent of health expenditure compared to the bottom half of the population receiving only 38.4 per cent of education expenditure (Chowdhury and Sen 1998). When non-MOHFW health spending is taken into account, the redistributive impact of health spending declines further. Heavy spending on health by the Ministry of Defence on hospitals and other non-health-sector ministries skew government spending on health towards the rich and the urban areas. In addition, public spending on health for women is about the same as for men, while private spending is much higher for men than for women (NHA 1998).

An ongoing cause for concern in patterns of health spending is that rural residents (85 per cent of the total population and 89 per cent of the poor) receive less than half the public spending on health compared to urban residents while only 12 per cent of the total population have access to public health (NHA 1998). This is exacerbated by the widespread practice of government-employed doctors in rural areas devoting time

---

[8] The Bangladesh National Health Accounts (NHA) estimate that a total of about US$10.6 per capita was spent on health, including non-Ministry of Health and Family Welfare (MOHFW) government spending, NGO, private and household expenditures. This came to about 3.9 per cent of GDP in 1996/7. Of this, government health expenditure contributed 34 per cent, households and private sources 64 per cent and NGOs 1 per cent.

to more lucrative private clinics, usually located in towns, rather than in more remote and poorly equipped government clinics and hospitals.

Health crises are among the most common causes of impoverishment among the rural poor in Bangladesh. Treatment and medicine costs routinely form a large proportion of the household budget of poor people, particularly when household members are old or infirm. In times of health crisis, the sale of productive assets to pay for medical treatment commonly leads to an irreversible catastrophic downward trajectory, pushing families from 'just getting by' into complete destitution. The provision of cheap effective healthcare for the poor must therefore be seen in the wider welfare context as a way of mitigating processes leading to impoverishment, increased inequality and powerlessness.

Patterns in education policy broadly follow health policy but tend to be even more regressive. Even though in recent years public expenditure on education has increased steadily,[9] public expenditure on education in Bangladesh stood at about 2.9 per cent of GNP in 1999 – well below the average of about 4 per cent for low-income countries. The legacy of neglect of public primary and secondary education, found across South Asia, associated with continued high rates of illiteracy in the region, are especially marked in the case of Bangladesh. At present about 60 per cent of the population are still illiterate and women lag behind men with about 73 per cent being illiterate. Illiteracy rates are also much higher in rural areas and among the poorest.

As in the case of India described by Drèze and Sen, the lack of investment in Bangladesh to improve basic levels of education can be related to the biased impact of political activism and pressures from elites (Drèze and Sen 1995). Past biases in educational priorities, and in the allocation of limited government resources to the rich have both reflected existing social inequalities and, in typical path-dependent fashion, have also tended to reinforce those inequalities.

Revenue and development expenditure in primary education in Bangladesh have increased considerably in recent years (i.e., Tk1,050 million total in 1981–2 to Tk17,795 million in 1995–6) (Ahmad 1997). However, with 60 per cent of the development budget for primary education financed by foreign donors, much of the impetus for increasing education expenditure has originated in shifting foreign-donor fashions rather than through domestic pressure to increase funding. Much of this increase in expenditure has gone into new school buildings (from the development budget) and teacher remuneration (from the recurrent

---

[9] From 1985/6 to 1994 benefits from public education spending as a proportion of household income increased from 0.7 per cent to 1.3 per cent.

budget). Teacher training, textbook expenses and repair and maintenance have remained relatively neglected. Teacher remuneration has increased to some extent through a combination of the increased qualification of many non-governmental primary schools to receive government funds and to some extent through the increased political muscle of unionised teachers. Thus poor quality of education remains a real area of concern limiting the benefits accrued, especially to the rural poor. This is reflected in high drop-out rates and low learning achievements. While net enrolment stands at about 75 per cent for primary-aged children, for secondary-aged children, net enrolment is a dismally low 22 per cent compared to the 60 per cent average for all developing countries (UNDP 1999). The number of children not attending secondary school reflects both the poor quality of secondary schooling and the high drop-out rates from primary schools. There are large inequalities in educational achievements between males and females, rural and urban areas and between the poor and non-poor.

According to Chowdhury and Sen (1998), the poorest 20 per cent of households receive about 14 per cent of public expenditure on education compared to the richest 20 per cent who receive 29 per cent. Skewed allocation is mainly due to the effect of secondary and tertiary education. Poor households receive only about 15 per cent of public expenditure on higher education and the poorest 20 per cent of the population receive 1 per cent of tertiary education and 6 per cent of secondary education. In contrast, the bottom 20 per cent receives 19.4 per cent of primary education expenditure compared to 21 per cent for the top 20 per cent of the population. The gross primary enrolment rate in rural areas is around 80 per cent overall, but for the very poor it is only about 30 per cent (Chowdhury and Sen 1998).

To include health and education services in a regime analysis requires further investigation of service quality and structure vis-à-vis class coalitions and political mobilisation. Privileged access to quality health and education services for groups such as the military and urban upper classes draws attention to the political clout of these groups. Limited access for the rural poor (especially women) reflects the relative political strength of the urban elite and the middle classes and the continued lack of a rural political voice, particularly from women.

Functional equivalents of social security

In addition to giving more attention to health and education within the welfare regime, a wide range of functional equivalents to 'social security' need to be included in a regime analysis. Functional equivalents of social security and social protection in Bangladesh are implemented through an extremely wide array of government departments, directorates and boards, with NGOs increasingly incorporated into the mix. Large formal poverty alleviation programmes, implemented by both government and NGOs, all have a large welfare component. Such programmes receive significant support from external donors, and government and non-government programmes are not easily separated in their expenditure, their administration or their implementation. The ministries of Agriculture, Women and Children's Affairs, Livestock and Fisheries, Youth and Sports, Social Welfare, Disaster Management and Relief, Environment and Forests, Water Resources, Local Government and Cooperatives, and agencies such as the Bangladesh Rural Development Board (BRDB) and the Local Government Engineering Department (LGED) all have their own poverty alleviation programmes.

Adding to the complexity, many of the large poverty alleviation programmes are administered across multiple government departments and implemented by a combination of local government representatives, at different levels, and in combination with NGOs. In Bangladesh there has been a long tradition of using external food aid as a safety net for the poorest and as relief during times of catastrophe. Large public works programmes are an essential part of this system. These programmes had their origin in England's workhouses under the 1834 Poor Law Amendment Act as did the massive anti-famine programmes of nineteenth-century India. In terms of numbers of person days employed, programmes in India and Bangladesh are still the largest in the world.

In the 1970s and early 1980s Bangladesh was one of the largest recipients of food aid. The majority of this aid is referred to as the Public Food Distribution System (PFDS), which had its origins in the 1943 Bengal famine and was seen initially as an instrument of price stabilisation in order to control speculative foodgrain trading which could result in widespread food shortages. Control was achieved mainly through rationing, price-stabilising interventions and stockholding.

In the 1970s only 5 per cent of food distributed through government channels was used in directly targeted distribution programmes. By the late 1980s this had increased to 45 per cent of all food aid and 60 per cent of cereals food aid. The difficulties experienced in effective targeting and leakage to the non-poor in the famine of 1974 were a major factor in shifting the strategy towards self-targeted project food aid. This trend was seen in a major expansion of Food-for-Work programmes in the late 1970s. More recently the targeted Vulnerable Group Development programme and the Food-for-Education programme have also become major channels of distribution for targeted food aid.

Public food distribution now consists mainly of food-assisted programmes which make a contribution to social protection for the poor. The largest of these are: Food-for-Work (FFW), Vulnerable Group Development (VGD), and Food-for-Education (FFE). Other smaller programmes which continue as vestiges of the past are: Vulnerable Group Feeding (VGF), Test Relief (TR)[10] and Gratuitous Relief (GR). In addition to the grain-based programmes the government widow's benefit (*bidhoba bhata*) and old-age pension (*boyosko bhata*) provide small monthly sums (100Tk, or about US$2 per month) to a small proportion of potentially eligible people (for the old-age pension less than 10 per cent of people over sixty). In addition the NGO, CARE, implements the cash-waged Rural Maintenance Programme (RMP). These programmes together combine to provide some social protection, in addition to developing rural infrastructure and human capital.

The FFW project has evolved into the present Rural Development Project and is a particularly complex set of public works interventions. What is usually referred to as Food-for-Work (*kajer binimoy khaddo*) is now really a cluster of different food-assisted public works programmes. Together these programmes aim to provide immediate relief to rural poor people and also help to build and maintain rural infrastructure (mainly maintenance and construction of rural roads, river embankments and irrigation channels) in the water, roads, forestry and fisheries sectors. Wages are usually given in wheat (sometimes rice) rather than cash. FFW programmes are usually referred to as 'self-targeting', since targeting is achieved by the requirement to participate in manual labour at low enough rates of remuneration (ideally close to the prevailing market wage for unskilled labour) to exclude the non-poor.

FFW in Bangladesh was started in 1975 in the wake of the 1974 famine. At that time, as with most other similar programmes, its focus was more on relief rather than 'development', as is the case now. It runs mainly over the dry season between November and April when earthworks are possible. Historically this period was a season of slack employment in rural areas. More recently, however, this period coincides less with seasonal patterns of want in rural areas, which usually occur from late September to early November and late March to early May. Green revolution technology and other developments have moved seasonal patterns of want away from the winter season, making FFW programmes less effective forms of social protection in these periods of crisis.

---

[10] In the colonial period 'test relief' referred to the tests – such as the requirement to travel or labour for food aid – used to indicate an impending famine.

In 1994/5 US$62.2 million worth of food was allocated to the RD project by the World Food Programme (WFP) and bilateral donors. Organisations involved include the WFP, bilateral and multi-lateral donors, Bangladesh Water Development Board (BWDB), the Department of Public Health Engineering (DPHE), the Local Government Engineering Department (LGED), the Bangladesh Agricultural Development Corporation (BADC), the Ministry of Land, the Forest Department, the Department of Fisheries, the Bangladesh Rural Development Board (BRDB) and various implementing NGOs.

In rural areas FFW programmes are notorious for enhancing power struggles and collusive practices between local power-brokers. Wheat is nearly always appropriated by local government officials, local leaders or gang leaders. While the positive development of infrastructure and the increased supply of employment is beneficial for poor labourers, the social impact of such programmes on local configurations of power should be more critically examined. These programmes certainly enhance the power and economic resources of a number of actors at local levels. These people are usually local labour gang leaders (*sardars*), community leaders (*matobars*), gang leaders (*mastaans*), Union Parishad chairmen and members, *upazilla* (sub-district) level officials and other departmental government officials.

The VGD programme, which reaches about 500,000 destitute women with a food aid and development package, is supported by the WFP and other bilateral donors, is managed through the joint responsibility of the Department of Women's Affairs and the Directorate of Relief and Rehabilitation, and is implemented by local governments and NGOs (BRAC and Jagoroni Chakra). The VGD programme started in 1986 and evolved from the VGF programme which started in 1975. VGF continues as a short-term relief programme during times of natural calamity. The VGD programme targets destitute women in rural areas and is one of the most successful programmes at reaching the 'very poor' in Bangladesh. The present programme reaches about 500,000 women and runs over an eighteen-month cycle. Previous cycles ran for two years. From the early 1980s the programme focus moved from relief to development with increasing emphasis on enhancing the self-reliance of disadvantaged women. At present the programme runs under three sub-projects: income generation; women's training centres; and group leader extension workers.

Even though the WFP now prefer to use the language of 'sustainable development' rather than 'welfare' to describe this programme, for most of the destitute target group the 30 kilograms of wheat made available to them for eighteen months is the only form of official welfare available.

Unfortunately the number of beneficiary cards available for distribution by local (union-level) government officials is much smaller than the number of eligible beneficiaries. As with most other welfare-type programmes in Bangladesh, this discretion gives local officials the ability to buttress their own local power resources, which in turn undermines the ameliorative impact of the programme on social stratification or mobilisation. Beneficiary cards tend to go to families where greater numbers of votes can be reaped, and 2 or 3 kilograms per beneficiary per month are usually skimmed off for sale by the local government members and other workers in the programme. The discretion of local government officers and their strong local power resources preclude any effective protest by beneficiaries.

Food-for-Education was launched in 1993, in what were seen as 460 'backward' unions in 460 *upazillas*, to address the problem of poor children not attending school because their families could not afford either the direct schooling costs or the opportunity costs of children's help in the home or outside the home. In 1996/7 the programme expanded to 1,243 unions providing 2.3 million students with grain. Its objectives are to increase attendance rates and to reduce drop-out rates. Participating children receive monthly rations of wheat or rice if they attend at least 85 per cent of their primary school classes. It is a rapidly growing programme which accounts for half of the ADP's primary education budget (Tk4.05 billion in fiscal year 1998–9). Unfortunately this programme has also been marked by leakage and illicit sale of grain by local committee members, grain dealers, officials and power-brokers. This includes the practice of fabricating false numbers of students receiving grain at schools. Profits from the excess grain are then shared amongst colluding officials.

The RMP was started in 1983 using Canadian food aid. Phases I and II of the programme were implemented by the Ministry of Relief and Rehabilitation in collaboration with the international NGO, CARE. In July 1995, phase III of the RMP was transferred to the LGED. In 1997–8 about 41,000 destitute women were expected to be participating in the programme from 4,100 unions in 435 *upazillas* in sixty-one districts. The RMP uses a lottery system to choose the small number of women labourers who can participate in the programme and, like the widow's benefit and old-age pension, wages are paid directly into bank accounts. This mode of operation reduces some of the discretionary power of local officials and power-brokers and reduces the opportunity for 'leakage'.

In general, complexity is a major feature of public works and relief programmes, producing high transaction costs, inefficient information flows and wide scope for rent-seeking, strengthening the power bases of elites, and leakage. Complexity is created by weak donor coordination combined with the local scramble of various government departments for donor resources (see Sobhan 1998). The dependence of such programmes on external donor funding, the high levels of rent-seeking and corruption and the excess discretionary power given to local elites calls into question redistributive stratification outcomes and the consolidation of social rights. From a welfare regime perspective, positive feedback mechanisms are also undermined by the lack of political connection between the dominant players (foreign donors) and the intended recipients (the poor). Instead a psychology of plunder prevails where unholy alliances of de facto illicit beneficiaries get away with as much as donors will let them. The reluctance of bilateral donors to replace these problematic grain-based programmes with cash has to be seen within in the wider context of their own domestic political interests.

In addition to public works and relief programmes, financial services for the poor in Bangladesh, predominantly in the form of credit programmes, have received considerable attention in the development literature. Although small loans are intended for use in starting up small businesses, many loans are also used by the very poor to smooth consumption in times of crisis and must therefore be seen as part of an overall social protection system. These programmes are implemented by government (e.g. the BRDB) and well over a thousand NGOs. Services are usually targeted at landless and near landless households. Credit is usually provided to small groups of borrowers without collateral but with some basis of joint liability and denial of further loans if a group member defaults. Loans are often also associated with training activities and contributions are often made to emergency funds.

Prominent NGOs running credit programmes include BRAC, PROSHIKA, the Association for Social Advancement (ASA) and many others. The Grameen Bank falls into a category of its own as it now displays more of the features of a commercial bank. The significance for a regime analysis is that although credit programmes have been shown to have a significant impact on poverty alleviation and empowerment for millions of people, conventional measures of welfare regime performance are not appropriate for analysing their impact on welfare and in terms of the establishment of citizenship rights. There is also increasing evidence in Bangladesh that a section of the 'very poor' and destitute people tend to be excluded from the benefits of micro-credit. Mohammed Yunus, the founder of the Grameen Bank, has advocated for many years that credit for the poor should be seen as a basic 'human right'. How then can such a right be conceptualised in welfare regime terms? Measures of de-commodification are certainly not sufficient. As is proposed below, concepts of de-clientalisation, inclusion–exclusion, and women's empowerment (analogous to Esping-Andersen's de-familialisation) may be more appropriate conceptual tools to use to evaluate the performance of such programmes. This leads to the need for a research agenda developing concepts which may capture such impacts.

New concepts to explain stratification systems and the generation of disadvantage

Poverty and inequality in Bangladesh

Present analyses of poverty and inequality in Bangladesh show us that there was a slight increase in the incidence of poverty in percentage terms from the mid-1980s through to about 1991–2, followed by a modest decline in poverty since then. Poverty reduction in percentage terms seems to have been much greater in urban areas than in rural areas, and over all years the incidence of rural poverty has been greater than that of urban poverty. Poverty is very much a rural phenomenon, with 93 per cent of the 'very poor' and 89 per cent of the 'poor' living in rural areas in 1996. According to World Bank sources, between 1983–4 and 1991–2, 30 per cent of the decline in poverty (measured as 'cost of basic needs' (CBN)) came from urban areas, even though only 15 per cent of the total population live in urban areas.[11]

At the same time inequality is increasing in both rural and urban areas. Urban inequality is much higher than rural inequality and is increasing much more rapidly. Inequality between rural and urban areas has also increased. Between 1983–4 and 1991–2, urban real mean consumption increased from 24 per cent higher than the rural rate to 40 per cent above the rural rate.[12]

---

[11] Some differences arise in poverty trends when alternative methods are used to determine the national poverty lines. When poverty is measured using indices of direct calorie intake, rather than cost of basic needs (CBN), the levels of urban and rural poverty are more similar, and poverty is not shown to decline during the 1990s. In fact, in urban areas it tends to increase slightly and rural poverty does not change significantly. At present most argue for the use of the more realistic CBN method. The Bangladesh Bureau of Statistics has recently adopted this method (starting from the 1995/6 household expenditure survey (HES)) for its household expenditure survey in conjunction with the World Bank. A number of independent surveys also seem to support the conclusion that poverty increased slightly (or at least remained roughly constant) from the mid-1980s and began to decline modestly in the 1990s (e.g. the Bangladesh Institute of Development Studies (BIDS) Analysis of Poverty Trends Project).

[12] Ravillion and Sen also estimate that at population growth rates of about 2 to 2.5 per cent per year and 1996 levels of inequality, national income would have to grow at about 3 to

Present data can show broad trends in poverty and inequality in Bangladesh but there are presently insufficient concepts to explain the stratification and political mobilisation effects of the welfare system. The Bangladesh context highlights a wide range of welfare organisations and welfare strategies that render the task of welfare regime analysis based on existing conceptual tools particularly problematic. As I have argued, the concept of commodification as a tool for exploring T. H. Marshall's notion of social citizenship rights is clearly insufficient (Esping-Andersen 1990: ch. 2).

To summarise:

- Non-governmental development organisations funded predominantly (but not exclusively) by overseas development assistance supply a significant proportion of the welfare mix.
- Informal (family, kinship, community, patron–clientelistic) mechanisms of coping with risks and shocks are significant but only partially understood.
- Remittances from overseas workers make a major, and increasing, contribution to the social security of relatives at home.
- The persistence of widespread poverty along with increasing inequality (particularly in rural areas), despite almost three decades of considerable foreign development assistance (about US$40 billion between December 1971 and June 1998),[13] raises questions about the de-politicising influence of foreign aid and the role it plays in the consolidation of elite interests.

A broad conceptual outline

One challenge posed by exploring the welfare regime approach in such contexts is to further develop more appropriate concepts and indices of the ameliorative performance of the welfare system than de-commodification. Here I go no further than presenting preliminary discussion based on the Bangladesh context. Alternative measures need to recognise prevailing social mechanisms which generate and maintain poverty and inequality and aid the formulation of indicators of their amelioration in an environment where informal relationships of asymmetric reciprocity outside the formal labour market are crucial for the survival

4 per cent per year to prevent an increase in the total number of poor people. If the trend of rising inequality continues, a growth in national income of 5 to 6 per cent per year would be required to prevent an increase in absolute numbers of poor people (Ravillion and Sen 1996).

[13] See Economic Relations Division (ERD) (1999).

of most poor people. In the Bangladesh context a schema that recognises a combination of 'ideal-type' processes (as in Max Weber's definition of an ideal type) of exploitation and exclusion would capture these social processes more effectively.

Exploitation can be best distinguished from exclusion, as it is a process that involves the extraction of some kind of 'surplus value', within an asymmetric relationship, where the dominant party draws disproportionate benefit from the relationship. In contrast, exclusion, as an ideal type, does not involve such extraction – it is more a process of shutting people out from access to power resources. Exploitation may occur via the labour–capital relationship in a simple commodification sense, or through the use of symbolic or coercive resources in more 'pre-commodified' relationships (e.g. gender-related exploitation, family labour, patron–clientelistic exploitation or the requirement to participate in violence for the benefit of others). Exploitation does not capture all types of inequality-producing social processes. The notion of exclusion describes the social processes of 'shutting out' certain categories of people from the benefits of participation available to others, based, not on the ownership of capital or the possession of the means of violence, but on other forms of identity. In practice most inequality-generating relationships consist of a combination of the ideal types of exploitation and exclusion (Tilly 1999).

As noted in what are sometimes referred to as pre-industrial societies, patron–client relationships are significant in creating and maintaining structured inequality. These relationships are often inclusive but usually display a high degree of exploitation. The term 'adverse incorporation' can be used to highlight the difference between this detrimental inclusion and notions of social exclusion. However, such societies also create disadvantage through a host of closure, monopolisation and opportunity-hoarding practices, which combine to create patterns of exclusion. The task of social policy here is to identify recurring exclusionary processes and design ameliorative interventions to mitigate their effects.

It may also be possible to evaluate to what extent social policy strategies ameliorate dependence on adverse exploitative and clientelistic relationships through policies that lead to 'de-clientelisation' – in an analogy to Esping-Andersen's de-commodification. For example, micro-credit programmes, which function to undermine dependency on patrons for consumption-smoothing credit, could be evaluated in terms of their varying de-clientelisation capacity. In contrast, a food-based programme which (de facto) relies on poor people's connections to local elites who hold discretionary powers over beneficiary selection may score lower in terms of de-clientelisation (e.g. the VGD programme).

In more urban, industrialised (and therefore commodified) settings, notions of de-commodification (Esping-Andersen 1990) and de-familialisation (Esping-Andersen 1999) may continue to have analytical purchase. The limitations of de-commodification in the Bangladesh context have been outlined. De-familialisation refers to the impact of social policies on reliance on family and kinship structures, especially women's unpaid labour. The provision of childcare would be considered as a de-familialising strategy allowing women in particular to enter the labour market.

In addition, there is also a need to conceptualise inequality-generating social dynamics that do not include exploitative clientelism, commodification or reliance on unpaid (women's) labour. Here measures of exclusion associated with Weberian social closure (Weber 1922; Parkin 1979), and more recently Charles Tilly (1999), would be useful. These recognise that not all inequality is generated by exploitation. The rise of 'post-industrial' network structures draws increasing attention to those left outside markets, support networks and welfare benefits. The mutually reinforcing effects of multiple exclusions leading to the *state* of 'social exclusion' has been of particular concern in European social policy. However, it should be noted that *processes* of exclusion (as opposed to the *state* of social exclusion, which may only occur in some cases) occur at all levels of society and in all societies. An evaluation of social policy needs to include some indicator of beneficial inclusion and the mitigation of harmful exclusion.

As an example, credit programmes that may perform well in terms of 'de-clientelisation' may not score so well in terms of undermining socially embedded processes of exclusion. There is increasing evidence in Bangladesh that the 'very poor' are not well catered for in micro-finance programmes and that group behaviour leading to processes of exclusion contributes significantly to this. Such processes could be analysed in terms of group strategies of social closure or the monopolisation of scarce resources by organised groups.

Social closure theory, or in Tilly's terms 'resource hoarding', also provides the conceptual underpinnings for exploring processes related to forms of ascribed identity and difference (Tilly 1999). Inequality generated by group dynamics based on ethnicity, age, regional origin, religion or caste usually involve processes of shutting out access to benefits, with or without the exploitative extraction of surplus value. Segmented markets based on ethnicity are a good example.

Conclusion

The Bangladesh context throws considerable light on the welfare regime approach. In its favour the approach may allow a more systemic and political description and evaluation of social policies. In developing countries, such political-economy thinking about welfare is normally subsumed within development discourse which has been plagued by the 'antipolitics machine' tendencies of the development industry (Ferguson 1994; Harriss 2002). Adapting a conceptual framework from one discourse to the subject matter of another allows new questions to arise that may be obscured within conventional paradigms.[14]

Analysing welfare using a welfare regime approach presents an opportunity to go beyond entrenched and opposing positions towards an analysis of the actual matrix of welfare, its history, its organisations, institutions and coalitions of interests, and its impact on human well-being and social inequality. Here the development establishment can be included as one cluster of the wider group of varied social institutions and organisations supported and maintained by political and economic interests. Thus the approach takes into account issues of power and avoids depoliticising social policies. On the other hand, it also avoids high levels of abstraction associated with radical emphases on 'interests' which fail to recognise the complexity of societal groups, organisations or institutions to which these are seen to be attached. The approach attempts to steer a path between teleological or functionalist (both modernisation and evolutionary Marxist) approaches on the one hand and post-modern approaches emphasising national uniqueness and divergence on the other (Gough 1999).

However, the Bangladesh case has drawn attention to the limited focus of social policy studies on the state–market nexus, leading to a lack of emphasis on family, kinship, community and 'civil society' forms of welfare, as well as those mediated by bilateral and global actors. It also draws

---

[14] Much development discourse falls victim to competing paradigms between unrealistic alternatives, usually either between naïvely optimistic accounts of welfare benefits accrued in developing societies resulting from the activities of the development industry on the one hand, and ideologically sustained radical criticisms of its detrimental effects on the other (Ferguson 1994). The former are underwritten by foreign aid donors, and largely buttressed by a neo-liberal ideology that has traditionally emphasised economic growth as a development 'end' and improved human welfare as its by-product. The latter usually represent critical responses that a priori assume that the process of development is ultimately detrimental for welfare because it represents the abstract 'interests' of imperial capital. In the language of welfare regimes, the former views tend to emphasise welfare outcomes while ignoring stratification outcomes; the latter do the opposite.

attention to the wider range of relevant public welfare strategies, which can be seen as functionally equivalent to social security in industrialised countries.

Thus an initial research agenda emerges consisting of:

1. the need further to understand the complex social processes which affect well-being and inequality in developing countries;
2. the need to develop concepts to help clarify the societal characteristics that social policies would attempt to influence; and
3. the need to formulate sets of indicators to measure their impact.

To remain relevant these would have to take into account the role of local, informal or customary strategies of managing welfare and insecurity, on the one hand, and global or international strategies, on the other.

The application of a welfare regime approach to development contexts also reinforces the need for supra-national organisations and international financial institutions to evaluate the relationship between aid policy and welfare regime formation. These organisations should be encouraged to recognise the role they play in the formation of various welfare regimes, and the particular problems created when political connections between the recipients of welfare and those funding it are weak. Positive political feedback has been shown to build resilience and resistance to the attempts at cutting back the welfare state in the West (Pearson 1998) and has therefore helped to foster firmly established sets of social citizenship rights. Those who tend towards a social democratic ideology would justifiably be concerned by the weak stratification and mobilisation outcomes of donor-influenced welfare systems in development contexts, and the resulting lack of the progressive emergence of social citizenship rights. In order to strengthen ameliorative social policy in such settings, political connections will have to be forged in the future. This constitutes a challenging political agenda within social policy in developing countries.

8   Multi-tiered international welfare systems

Graham Room

Introduction

The research programme from which this book derives has a number of conceptual roots. One is the notion of a 'welfare regime', made fashionable by writers such as Esping-Andersen, in the context of his analysis of OECD countries in general, Western Europe in particular (Esping-Andersen 1990). Previous chapters of this book have taken this concept and explored its applicability to a range of developing countries, in South Asia, sub-Saharan Africa, East Asia and Latin America. They demonstrate that the concept of a welfare regime can be applied fruitfully to many of those countries, even if in some important respects it must be revised.

Here I want to start from that same point of reference – the analysis by social policy scholars of the welfare regimes of Western Europe – but I want to take off in a different if complementary direction. I want to consider not the national welfare regimes of Western Europe, but the dynamic relationships of those regimes to their international environment. The foregoing chapters have examined how far an analysis of European welfare regimes provides specific insights into the national welfare regimes of the developing world: I want now to ask whether an analysis of the European welfare regimes in relation to their international environment also provides insights, but now into the corresponding relationships between the welfare regimes of the developing world and *their* international environment.

In the preceding chapters of this book, one of the central concerns has been the capacity of the state, in the developing world, to manage the welfare regime of the country concerned, taking into account the domestic and international political and economic stakeholders with whom it must deal. This chapter will consider the extent to which in Europe the state is similarly constrained. However, what it will also examine is the extent to which sovereignty in relation to social welfare has been pooled in a regional welfare regime, and whether this then offers a model for the developing world, the international order and global social policy.

The chapter concludes that the analysis of welfare regimes has for too long focused on the nation-state, even in those parts of the world where publicly provided welfare was until relatively recently a key element of statecraft. In Europe the nation-state is no longer the autonomous and sovereign source of imperative coordination: nation-states are, rather, creating institutions of supra-national coordination which, slowly but surely, are becoming instruments of policy transformation in their own right. The analytical and political task has now shifted its focus, from the domestic political settlements that underpin national welfare regimes, to the interdependencies between these domestic arrangements and the architecture of the international arena. It follows that to analyse these interdependencies between the international and national levels, and to elaborate corresponding programmes of political and institutional reform, is now the critical task. Missing this means dissipating energies in an analytical and political cul-de-sac.

Welfare and nation-building

In Western Europe, welfare systems organised by the public authorities have long been an important tool of nation-building. In some cases – the Elizabethan Poor Law of 1601, for example – they consolidated the claims of the central state, and undermined the claims of the feudal baron or the church, to be the principal focus of protection and loyalty. In other cases – the introduction of social insurance by Bismarck, for example – they were an instrument not only for heading off working-class insurrection, but also for binding together the workforce of a Germany only recently united into a single state (Rimlinger 1971).

The development of national welfare systems continued to be a core tool of European statecraft throughout the twentieth century. These welfare systems generally involved two elements: protection against interruptions to consumption and investment in citizens' human capital. They aimed to secure livelihoods – and hence social peace – and to promote national efficiency. Many welfare developments were also the result of war or the preparation for war; and warfare and welfare proved in turn to be the most powerful engines for the development of the administrative apparatus of the modern state (Titmuss 1963: ch. 4). This apparatus gave government the tools it needed to manage and steer the lives and the energies of both the civilian and the military population; and it gave this population a degree of security and predictability in dealing with the austerities which they faced, sufficient to preserve popular morale and good order, or at least acquiescence. Even in the Axis and Communist blocks, where good order was preserved by terror as much as by social protection, the latter played no small part in securing mass commitment to the purposes of the state (Rimlinger 1971). Indeed, the European nation-states of the mid-twentieth century proved so successful in mobilising and organising their populations that they brought each other to the verge of mutual annihilation. But the consequence was that, in Western Europe at least, political elites could no longer regard the nation-state as capable of securing the well-being of its citizens, if the governance of the international environment was left unreformed.

Formal systems of welfare had a quite different path of development in other parts of the world. In many cases they were part of a colonial regime, whose aim was to secure the predictable administration of a dependent territory. One instrument was the creation of a local administrative cadre whose security and loyalty depended on the colonial power and which was, in some degree at least, extricated from the informal networks of the wider society which they administered. Social benefits for such strata, aimed at ensuring a formal rationality of administration on the Western model, had few links with the welfare offered to the society at large, in the form of humanitarian efforts to establish basic education and healthcare in rural areas and for the growing urban populations (see, for example, the discussion of Africa offered by Bevan, chapter 6 above).

In many cases these various elements were at no stage brought together into any coherent national welfare regime, for reasons that are well stated in the foregoing chapters. The state apparatus bequeathed by the colonial authorities was weak in relation to the objectives of the emerging national elites, if not in relation to those of the departing colonial powers. The nation was in many cases an artefact of the colonial power and ill suited as the source of social and political obligation. On the one hand, the welfare needs of the mass of the population continued to be determined principally by informal community networks, often with strong hierarchical, clientelistic and oppressive elements. On the other hand, those in public administration, along with the more affluent sections of the urban population, enjoyed welfare systems modelled on those of the erstwhile colonial powers, and in many cases also had access to specialist facilities in those advanced countries.

Elsewhere, in countries which had escaped thoroughgoing colonisation, or had made an early escape, a more coherent state purpose proved possible. In many Latin American countries, welfare programmes were established during the nineteenth and twentieth centuries which drew on the Bismarckian model of social protection (Barrientos, chapter 4 above). In East Asia, programmes which focused on human investment more than social protection were established in the second half of the twentieth century (Gough, chapter 5 above). Indeed, so successful did these prove, that they became the envy of the countries of Western Europe, whose welfare regimes by the 1980s were looking increasingly obsolete.

European welfare regimes in the international arena

In analysing the European welfare regimes, it is common to treat each of them as though its historical development was shaped overwhelmingly by socio-political factors endogenous to the country concerned (Esping-Andersen 1990). However, as seen earlier, the welfare regimes of the nineteenth and twentieth centuries were powerfully shaped by the international arena in which these countries found themselves, and the goals which these states set themselves within this arena. I have already referred to war and the preparation for war as important drivers of welfare advance. In other ways also, challenges and developments in the international arena shaped domestic welfare policy. International working-class solidarity threatened to import political insurrection and provided the spur for welfare developments, for example in Bismarck's Germany (Rimlinger 1971). 'Beggar my neighbour' economic policies in the 1920s and 1930s, involving a progressive collapse of international economic co-operation, forced attention to the inadequacies of support for the unemployed (Mommsen 1981: part 2). International migration created ethnically diverse societies in Western Europe during the 1960s and 1970s and tested the boundaries of national social citizenship (Castles and Kosack 1973).

In the late 1940s, two of these challenges were particularly obvious to the political leaders of Western Europe. First, it was evident that the anarchic international political environment, in which nation-states were impelled to mutual destruction, needed to be collectively managed for the common good. Second, collective management of the international economy was needed if the political destabilisation of high unemployment was not to recur, with all the unpleasant consequences of which the interwar experience had warned.

The first challenge was addressed by pooling the instruments of war – the coal and steel industries – in the European Coal and Steel Community (Collins 1975). The possibility that social welfare, that other instrument of war, should also be pooled, did not occur to those establishing what was to become the European Community. On the contrary, it was in relation to social policy that the rhetoric of national sovereignty persisted longest. The same applied to the second challenge, that of unemployment: the creation of a common market was embraced as a collective project, but employment policies remained lodged at national level. Only under competitive pressure from the dynamic economies of North America and East Asia were there moves during the 1990s to coordinate employment policies and to focus on policies of human investment. Social policy was now defined, to an increasing extent, as a dynamic investment in human skills and productive capacity, rather than as a means of protecting against interruptions to consumption (Room 2002). In the new era of global economic competition, government would be judged by its effectiveness in raising the productivity of its people in the global struggle for markets.

It was still possible during the 1980s to view the European Community as a common market, in which enterprises based in independent national states could compete with minimal cross-border barriers. On this view, the development of world-wide free trade, under the auspices of GATT and subsequently the WTO, was to be welcomed as a logical extension of the European market and might, indeed, one day subsume the regional arrangement. By the end of the 1990s, however, such a view was no longer tenable. The countries of the EU were building collective institutions which involved concerted action in the employment and social fields and, at long last, pooling of responsibility for social welfare. Henceforth it was incontrovertible not only that national welfare strategies had to take international developments into account – that had long been obvious – but also that collective supra-national and international strategies in respect of social welfare were developing *sui generis*. The jealously protected boundary to national social citizenship was dissolving, as European welfare states became enmeshed in the collective institutional arena of the EU: although the nation-state and national welfare regimes were not redundant, it was these European institutional developments that would increasingly shape them.

It is to a deeper analysis of this European experience that I now turn, in order to consider the specific insights it may provide for understanding the dynamics of the relationships between the welfare regimes of the developing world and their international environment. Writing a decade after Esping-Andersen, Ferrera, Hemerijck and Rhodes (2000) take stock of the challenges which face the welfare systems of Western Europe, including those rooted in globalisation, and assess the ways in which they are responding to these challenges. Their findings are threefold:
• Welfare regimes differ in the trade-offs they have traditionally made between income security and employment: liberal welfare regimes such as that of the UK have prioritised employment over poverty reduction; conservative regimes such as Germany have protected their income maintenance schemes but have then seen unemployment remain high;

the Scandinavian countries have done relatively well on both fronts, although they remain heavily dependent on public sector employment.

• National prosperity under conditions of intensified global competition depends on welfare systems shifting towards 'flexicurity', involving a closer linkage between income security on the one hand and activation policies on the other, designed to enable and encourage people to participate within a dynamic labour market.

• While each welfare regime imposes certain institutional constraints to such adjustment, there is still scope for distinctive policy initiatives and each welfare regime offers examples of countries which are adjusting well to these new challenges.

However, as Ferrera and his colleagues recognise, national policy-makers are, to an increasing extent, making their social policy choices within a new European welfare architecture, which involves several key elements:

• policy targets to which member states commit themselves in the employment and social fields: not only minimum social standards but also, and to an increasing extent, benchmarks of best practice;

• support to countries in raising their policy performance, involving:
  • resource transfers for investment in declining industries, infrastructure and rural development and adaptation to new industrial opportunities;
  • capacity building and skill development, in part through the EU Structural Funds (although the small scale of their resources – much less than 1 per cent of EU GDP – should be noted);

• cross-national policy learning and the exchange of good practice;

• new institutional arrangements for shared governance, with multilateral surveillance and peer review by the EU institutions and the member states, but also involving civil society.

In general, therefore, while national governments retain responsibility for welfare policy, they discharge this responsibility within a collectively managed and rule-based European system. The pursuit of agreed social policy targets may not be legally prescribed, as are the rules governing the European market, and penalties for non-performance may be moral rather than financial, as in the case of monetary disciplines. Nevertheless, the above elements form, in combination, an impressive array of incentives to policy coordination and performance enhancement through mutual learning and support (de la Porte *et al.* 2001).

These recent developments are, however, concerned only with the coordination of national welfare policies: they do not therefore address the governance of trans-national welfare in the EU. In contrast, the single market means that those economic actors who shape the patterns of need to which welfare services respond are, to an increasing extent, trans-national in their scope: multi-national corporations in particular, taking decisions on the employment and remuneration of workers, the health and safety of the products which consumers purchase, etc. The single market has also brought increasing opportunities for public and private suppliers of welfare – private pension funds, educational institutions, health and social care services – to move beyond their national arenas and to develop trans-national operations, even if this is as yet only limited in scale. In short, at the same time as national policy-makers have locked themselves into new systems for coordinating national public policies in relation to welfare, the determination of welfare is, to an increasing extent, escaping their control, and is being shaped by trans-national rather than national actors (Leibfried 1996: 195–7).

There has, of course, been some EU regulation of these trans-national operations, notably by reference to the minimum social standards which enterprises in all member states must meet. The political impetus has been the wish to discourage regime shopping, whereby enterprises locate to the least onerous regime, promoting 'social dumping'. These standards include legislation on health and safety at work (including the length of the working week), expedited by qualified majority voting under the Single European Act. EU legislation on information and consultation aims to ensure that workers who are affected by enterprise closure or removal to another member state are given adequate notice and explanation. Nevertheless, EU legislation has been geared primarily to removing national obstacles to a single market.

Behind these concerns with a level playing field and minimum standards lay a more general fear: that footloose capital would increasingly opt out of national welfare regimes and the national political settlements they embody, and that the costs of welfare would increasingly fall on immobile workers and consumers. During the second half of the 1990s, however, the EU policy concern shifted, from a fear that footloose capital would opt out if social costs and regulation were too onerous, to the goal of attracting mobile capital by offering a high-skills labour force, made available through energetic policies of human investment (Room 2002). Social protection policies are being re-engineered in support of this shift. This is the rhetoric, at least, of the EU, notably as expressed at the Lisbon Summit of March 2000, where the EU set itself the goal of becoming 'the most competitive and dynamic knowledge-based economy in the world, capable of sustainable economic growth with more and better jobs and greater social cohesion'.

This goal now provides the focus for coordination of national social and employment policies and their benchmarking by reference to best practice. It also informs the EU-level social dialogue with employers and trade unions, aimed at inducing capital to opt into a new welfare pact at European if not at national level, trading the social responsibility of business for the availability of a highly skilled labour force and an innovation-friendly institutional hinterland (Room 2002). Nevertheless, the governance of this new regime is still inchoate. Employers, unions, professional associations and social NGOs have become organised as trans-European actors, but as yet there is no coherent and constitutional forum within which they can, jointly with governments and the EU institutions, address these issues of trans-national welfare.

The European model and its rivals

These developments in European welfare regimes are of interest here not for their own sake, but as possible models for the developing world, the international order and global social policy. This relevance to the wider world can be treated as three separate if related questions. First, the European Union is not the only experiment in regional integration: from the standpoint of the questions to which this book is addressed, what, if anything, is distinctive about the European model and what are the principal alternatives suggested by its rivals? Second, how far can the European model serve as a model for the international order more generally and for global social policy? Third, in constructing an international order modelled on the European experience, how important are regional blocks as part of the new structure of international social governance? These three questions structure the remaining three sections of this chapter.

The European exit from the nation-state, dissolving national boundaries and developing new systems of multi-tiered policy-making which straddle national and international arenas, does not go unchallenged by other experiments in regional integration. In particular, the system of supra-national social governance which is emerging in the EU is only one of several models of post-national welfare. Many of the other and more recent experiments in regional integration, in different parts of the world, are self-consciously defining their own paths of development by reference to this European model of multi-tiered policy-making in general, and its social dimension in particular: in some cases adopting and adapting the European model, in others rejecting some of its key elements, but unable to ignore it.

Two other models are, or have been, particularly important. Alongside the European model, they provide points of reference for other regional integration initiatives that are in progress. The Council for Mutual Economic Cooperation (COMECON) is the 'failed' model, the model to be avoided, the model of 'socialist planning' whose spectre can be invoked by those opposed to attempts to regulate the market by reference to social goals. Although socialist paths to modernisation may be highly unfashionable, COMECON's attempt to withdraw from the international trading system and to create a social and economic order based on distributive principles other than those of the market still finds some echoes in present-day debates, notably among the anti-globalisation lobby. Nevertheless, these echoes are weak and attract little support from national governments or any of the existing international organisations.

The North American Free Trade Agreement (NAFTA) is the free market model, purporting to promote citizens' welfare by expanding international markets, not least in welfare services themselves. Except in relation to trade, NAFTA does not offer a framework for supra-national policy-making, least of all in the field of social governance. What NAFTA purports to provide is an arena in which economic actors can range freely across national boundaries, untrammelled by local regulations. The nation-state is put in question not by supra-national institutions, but by its reduced control over the economic actors who shape its prosperity (and who, indeed, largely shaped the NAFTA treaty itself: Marchand, 2001). Social goals are assumed to be sufficiently met by the free operation of the trans-national market and the rigorous application of domestic social legislation: infringements of such legislation can be prosecuted through the courts of another member state, but beyond this they are of no interest to NAFTA (Compa 1999).

How are these differences between the EU and NAFTA to be explained? They are in part ideological. Within the European context, markets are seen as political creations: political and economic projects are unavoidably entwined. In contrast, NAFTA has been constructed by actors whose ideological assumptions treat the market as an autonomous arena which wise politicians will set free; COMECON was constructed by actors whose ideological assumptions treated the market as an arena which could and should be subjected to hegemonic political control.[1]

The contrast is also historical. NAFTA extended a bilateral free trade agreement between the USA and Canada to Mexico. It had no political agenda for the three countries, beyond creating a free trade area, and such supra-national administrative organs as were established focused almost exclusively on the policing of this trading arena. Not that politics have been absent from the development of NAFTA, of course. Within

---

[1] It is worth recalling such classical accounts of the sociological tradition as those by Nisbet (1970) and Giddens (1971): both stress that whereas the Anglo-Saxon tradition was to treat the market system as though it was, or could be, an autonomous apolitical order, the continental vision was of the market as an unavoidably political and social device.

each of the countries concerned, the NAFTA negotiations provoked conflict among domestic stakeholders, as it became clearer who would be the winners and who the losers; and once NAFTA was in force, some new cross-border political alliances developed among these stakeholders (Marchand 2001: 204–7; Compa 1999). However, the explicit aims of NAFTA were economic not political (save inasmuch as the Mexican government sought through NAFTA to lock Mexico into neo-liberal economic policies by treaty: Marchand 2001: 201).

In contrast, as we have seen, a strong thrust towards political union underpinned the European project from its earliest days. The successive political projects which have driven European integration – and which have left as their residue the system of multi-tiered policy-making described above – have been threefold. The first was to secure a settlement among the erstwhile combatants. This involved the industries on which warfare was based being placed under supra-national control and active social policies being instituted for those of their workers made redundant. The second project was to expand the Community, in part to incorporate potentially unstable countries on its margins. Successive waves of expansion from 1973 onwards involved political bargains with the newcomers, to sugar the pill of the *acquis communautaire*: these bargains commonly involved new initiatives in social and regional policy, to help the transition to membership. The third project, during the 1980s and 1990s, was to catch up economically and technologically with the United States and the East Asian tigers: this involved the move towards economic and monetary union, accompanied by concerted policies of human capital investment, social dialogue and labour market reform.

Each of these political projects involved the EU in redefining the rivalries between states; and each involved new social bargains among domestic stakeholders across the countries of the EU. Indeed, part of the importance of the EU is that it has provided an institutional framework within which stakeholders with different interests and loyalties could thrash out a new political settlement. At the heart of this settlement – although not necessarily always seen as such – has been the construction and reconfiguration of a multi-tiered welfare regime.[2] Increasingly, this has involved a whole range of actors of civil society – the social partners, but also the

---

[2] There is a growing literature concerned with multi-tiered social policy-making in the EU. Leibfried, for example, shows that even though much of social policy is still seen by EU national governments as their own preserve, the discharge of their supposed autonomy in this policy area in fact depends heavily on other national and supra-national actors in the EU. The result is that social policy is today determined by various complicated patterns of joint decision-making at national and EU levels (Leibfried 1994; Leibfried 1996; Leibfried and Pierson 1995: ch. 2).

regions and a wide variety of NGOs – in a new civil dialogue. This is quite different from NAFTA, whose agenda of debate is set by what is ostensibly just an economic project.

It follows that each of these experiments in regional integration produces a distinctive institutional residue which shapes the governance of the experiment, according legitimate roles to some actors but withholding such legitimacy from others. They define the conditions under which particular political and economic actors are entitled to intervene in the domestic affairs of a member state, and the conditions under which such a member state is entitled to make use of the resources, institutions and other opportunities which the regional block has placed at its members' disposal. They set the terms of the 'two-level games' in which political actors become involved, pursuing interlocking strategies at domestic and regional levels (see, for example, Evans *et al.* 1993). They also set the terms on which new members may seek accession.

Both the EU and NAFTA have become powerful models in wider international debates on global social governance. There are, of course, a number of other attempts at regional integration, most of which build upon either shared concerns about security, or the wish to create a free trade area (Compa 1999; Deacon 2001; Schulz *et al.* 2001), although none is as well developed as the EU or NAFTA. Some (for example, the South African Development Community (SADC)) derive from shared histories of violent struggle and conflict, the legacies of colonialism and the break-up of empire. Some, because they include countries at very different levels of social and economic development, have had to address the relationship between free trade and development. These regional blocks vary in the extent to which they embody a social dimension (this is greater in Mercusor, for example, than in the Association of Southeast Asian Nations (ASEAN)). The more that they make free trade their *raison d'être*, however, and the less they have a social and political purpose that transcends the creation of a common market, the more likely it would seem that they will one day be subsumed within the arrangements for worldwide free trade that are developing under the auspices of the WTO (Deacon 2001).

Developing countries and their welfare regimes in the international arena

What are the implications of the foregoing for the analysis of welfare in developing countries? How far can the European experience serve as a model for the international order more generally and for global social policy?

The international arena within which developing countries find themselves has been shaped by the projects which have been pursued by the world's most powerful economic and political actors. These include:

- the imperial systems of the great powers of the nineteenth century, which continue to define spheres of cultural influence (see, for example, the discussion of French Africa in Bevan above, chapter 6; see also Room 2000c);
- the United Nations system, including the ILO, established as those great powers withdrew from empire, exhausted by their world wars, but leaving hope of a better world;
- the Bretton Woods system, centred on the IMF and the World Bank, set up under American hegemony after the Second World War, flowering in the 'Washington consensus' of the post-Cold War period, and complemented in the 1990s by the WTO;
- the efforts of MNCs in the late twentieth century to establish global production chains (Marchand 2001), consolidate their 'structural power' vis-à-vis labour and the nation-state (Gough and Farnsworth 2000) and secure a light regulatory regime for themselves world-wide;
- international social NGOs, developing strongly in the 1990s, in part in reaction to the NAFTA and WTO agreements, which were seen as unduly dominated by the interests of MNCs (Marchand 2001; O'Brien *et al.* 2000).

These successive political projects, through their institutional residues, shape the way that international markets work, the international governance of social policy and the basic assumptions which shape the international social division of welfare. They determine which international actors and institutions are stakeholders in the development of a country's welfare regime, and the terms on which they become such. They determine the conditions under which individual countries are beholden to these international stakeholders and the conditions under which they can take advantage of the opportunities which these stakeholders provide. They also determine the terms on which individual countries are able to participate in thrashing out a new international political and welfare settlement.

Economic globalisation and its social impact

The globalisation of the world economy has been conducted under the auspices of the Bretton Woods institutions and under the strong impetus of MNCs. The world economic order embodies many of the same neo-liberal assumptions as those underlying NAFTA. The policy prescription is simple: free trade for those who can compete, conditional aid and structural adjustment for those who cannot. The preceding chapters of this book have considered the welfare regimes of various parts of the developing world, and the ways they are being reshaped, not least in response to economic globalisation. In the light of these studies, and related literature, what evaluation can be made of the neo-liberal prescription? More particularly, how far does the international architecture bring forth the national responses which the neo-liberal prescription expects?

The analysis of East Asia which is offered by Gough (see chapter 5 above) underlines the vulnerability of national economies to the volatility of the global economy and the insecurity which households in consequence experience. The financial crisis of 1997 revealed that neither national economies nor households had sufficient 'buffers' available to protect them against this volatility. South Korea is the paradigm case. Rapid economic transformation since the 1970s, based on state-led programmes of industrial and human capital investment, had dramatically raised standards of living and created a modern urban-industrial society (Torres 2001: 75–8). These radical changes had also, however, undermined the extended family as a system of informal support in adversity: when adversity struck, the population suffered. Korea has responded by putting in place public social protection systems not unlike those in Western Europe.

If, therefore, the Asian crisis drew attention to the need to reduce the volatility of the international financial system, so as to buffer individual national economies from its shocks, it also drew attention to the importance of buffers to protect households. Supply-side measures to provide skills and human capital may be necessary if countries are to prosper in the global economy: but giving people ladders to opportunity is insufficient if the opportunities disappear. This argument is consistent with that of Rieger and Leibfried (1998). They argue that as far as domestic populations are concerned, national social protection systems provide buffers against external shocks in the international economy: they are therefore more necessary the more that trade barriers are removed and a national economy is exposed to these shocks.

Bangladesh has made some economic progress during the 1990s, opening up to the international economy, but at the price of increasing inequality (Torres 2001: 69–71). In human investment and in social protection, South Korea has chosen universalistic provision; Bangladesh, in contrast, with its more limited resources, has concentrated public sector support on the better-off, leaving social development and welfare for the mass of the population heavily dependent upon the informal sector. Extended family networks are important and, along with patron–client relations, provide an informal safety net for many poor Bangladeshis. These networks have in recent years evolved strategies of international occupational mobility, to diversify and strengthen the sources of income upon which the family network can rely: worker remittances from abroad are now a quarter the size of total government expenditure in value (Davis, chapter 7 above). Similar developments are evident in many of the other countries of East Asia (Gough, chapter 5 above).

Non-governmental social development organisations also play a major role in Bangladesh. They draw on substantial funding from foreign donors, but they also operate on contracts from the Bangladesh government (some of these contracts themselves being funded through the government by foreign aid). Indeed, they now represent a substantial set of interests in their own right, arguably limiting the scope for major shifts in the balance between state and NGO activities, and many of them are enmeshed in the clientelist power structures of Bangladeshi society. The foreign aid (including food aid) which is being disbursed, while it may serve to meet certain population needs, may also provide 'rents' and supports to patrons and secure thereby the 'adverse incorporation' of the population into these clientelist structures.[3]

While state capacity may be low, it is not of course non-existent. As Davis shows, government programmes connected with welfare and human capital investment have been growing rapidly, relative to other South Asian countries. However, private spending on health is as large as public spending and is geared to the richer sections of the urban population. As for education, the majority of primary education is financed by foreign donors: higher education is supported by domestic funds, but as the preserve of the better-off (Torres 2001: 71).

The experience of Bangladesh suggests two conclusions by reference to the neo-liberal prescription. First, a comparison with South Korea suggests that even where free trade and open economies encourage economic growth, the fruits of this growth may be distributed more or less evenly, depending on the institutions and policies operating domestically. (This is also a major conclusion of the ILO studies on the social dimensions of globalisation coordinated by Torres: see Torres, 2001: part III.) Second, where a country is heavily dependent on outside aid, this is unlikely to solve the problem of state incapacity and may well worsen it, by creating interests – both domestic and foreign – that benefit from that incapacity.

---

[3] The proliferation of NGOs tapping foreign aid is not the necessary consequence of low levels of development. In chapter 7, Davis contrasts the Bangladeshi situation with that of neighbouring West Bengal, where state-sponsored organisations predominate.

The challenges faced by many of the countries of sub-Saharan Africa include many of those faced by Bangladesh – the marginalisation of their economies, the vulnerability of livelihoods and the low level of state capacity – but compounded by high levels of warfare and conflict (Bevan, chapter 3 above). International indebtedness and poverty together render these countries the most heavily dependent on the World Bank and other international donors. In many cases, state capacity is even lower than in Bangladesh; the state has little or no commitment to welfare; and the state finds its major legitimation in the international political system rather than the inhabitants. Life chances and 'welfare' are therefore shaped by a wide range of social organisations, formal and informal, associated with the extended family, the clan, and the ethnic or religious community. In many sub-Saharan countries, it is only through foreign NGOs that some welfare services are offered on a less particularistic basis.

As Bevan argues, this hardly augurs well for African participation in a world of neo-liberal prosperity. This is, however, not only because some of the policy prescriptions offered by international donors – including poverty reduction strategies – take insufficient account of local conditions and are driven too much by domestic political and bureaucratic interests in the donor countries. It is also because these local conditions are themselves being reshaped by international actors who, often in concert with the public authorities, are engaged in predatory looting to which international donors pay insufficient attention. Bevan refers, on the one hand, to international criminal gangs, and, on the other, to international commercial interests concerned with extracting Africa's mineral wealth, whose only obligation to the host country is to furnish 'rents' to those in power. Where prosperity is available only to those who are predatory, and the surveillance of such activity is weak, we must expect these illegitimate means to be pursued: they will then themselves create sets of interests, extending to the public authorities, which will resist moves to the sorts of governance which Western neo-liberalism normally assumes. Indeed, in pursuit of such interests, state capacity may be quite high.

National welfare and international social governance

In the earlier discussion of EU developments, I argued that national welfare reforms are being made within an emergent, collectively managed and rule-based European system. I now consider whether anything analogous is developing at the global level, modifying the neo-liberal order described above. The desirability of such a development is central to the 'anti-globalisation' arguments propounded by some of the international social NGOs. It has also recently been stressed by Juan Somavia, director-general of the ILO.[4]

A rule-based international system, he argues, would build upon – but go beyond – the rules that already exist for trade and finance. It would encompass the ILO core labour standards, which would apply to the developing and not just the developed countries; it would also include rules governing resource transfers from the advanced countries to support development. By implication, the ILO director-general criticises the arbitrary and often inconsistent way in which the most vulnerable of the developing countries are currently treated in the international arena. This sort of rule-based bargain is very evident within the EU, where capacity building, the opening of markets and the pursuit of agreed social standards by national authorities march hand in hand. At first glance, there would seem no reason why such a system could not also be established globally.[5]

The collectively managed and rule-based system, by means of which national social policy-making in the EU is coordinated, has four main elements. First, as seen earlier, it involves policy targets and disciplines, to which the member states commit themselves in the employment and social fields. Such targets and disciplines are variously evident in the international arenas with which developing countries have to deal: they include the conventions espoused by the International Labour Organisation and, more particularly, the 1998 core labour standards; they also include the targets and conditions laid down by the World Bank and the IMF when offering financial support; and the trade rules and sanctions involved in the WTO. However, the treatment meted out by these various regulatory bodies differs considerably between countries at different levels of development.

Second, the coordination of national policy-making in the EU involves support to countries in raising their policy performance, by means of resource transfers for investment, capacity building and skill development. Such transfers exist in the international realm and they are, of course, the ostensible *raison d'être* of international aid. There is, however, one crucial difference. In the EU, funds are allocated for such cross-national transfers on the basis of Community-wide taxation; the criteria on which they are to be distributed are decided by the member states together;

[4] See his keynote address to the EU seminar 'The European Social Agenda and the EU's International Partners', held in November 2001 (European Commission 2001).

[5] See, for example, the 'Marshall Plan for Africa' agreed in Nigeria in October 2001, envisaging that African governments would improve domestic governance and ensure respect for human rights, while the rich world would provide aid for development and access to their markets for African exports.

and to receive such funds, if the criteria are satisfied, is an entitlement rather than charity. Resource transfers to the developing world, far from being rule-based, can perhaps best be described as fragmented charity, in many cases being driven by the domestic agendas of donors from the rich world.[6]

Third, processes of national policy coordination in the EU include mechanisms for cross-national policy learning and the exchange of good practice. This is intended to enable different countries – and specific actors within them – to define and assess more efficiently than hitherto the range of policy options which they might deploy in their local circumstances, drawing upon the models of intervention to be found in their fellow member states. Preceding chapters of this book provide warnings of the one-sided nature of this transfer internationally and the inappropriate use of Western models of welfare in developing countries. Bevan (see chapter 6) documents the donor-driven educational programmes which are developing in Africa, with the encouragement of the World Bank in particular, but with insufficient regard to the primary educational needs of rural Africans. Moreover, both Bevan and Davis (chapter 7) point to the ways in which Western schooling then becomes an additional factor in social stratification within the developing countries concerned, used by local elites to consolidate privileges for their kin (see also Room 2000c).

Finally, joint policy-making in the EU involves new institutional arrangements for shared governance. These include multi-lateral surveillance and peer review by the EU institutions and the member states; they also involve civil society. However, when we compare the situation of developing countries with that of the poorer members of the EU, two differences are immediately apparent: first, their much smaller voice in the global arena in determining the targets and disciplines to which they are then subjected; second, the fragmented and dispersed nature of these different regulatory instruments. In consequence, poorer countries have much less scope for engaging in the sort of political negotiation and trade-off with their richer neighbours that is commonplace in the functioning of the EU. In EU policy-making, each member state can insist on being heard, by virtue of its veto capacity: the treaties assert the sovereign equality of solvent partners.[7] Charity for debt defaulters, and the consequent muting of their voice, is no substitute for this.

---

[6] See, for example, the critique of such aid offered in the UK White Paper on international development: DFID (2000: ch. 7). For a recent overview of debt relief to heavily indebted poor countries (HIPC), see DFID (2001: ch. 1).

[7] Such a status for developing countries was demanded by the representative of the ACP countries at the conference cited in footnote 4: see European Commission (2001).

Trans-national need and welfare

Much of the contemporary debate on the social dimension of globalisation – for example, the concern with respect for core labour standards – is focused on the relationship of individual national regimes to the institutions of the international environment. This was also the focus of the preceding discussion, concerned with the extent to which international social governance already involves the sort of collectively managed and rule-based system that characterises the EU. However, as in the discussion of European developments, at least as important is the governance of trans-national welfare: on the one hand, of those trans-national actors who shape the patterns of need to which welfare services respond; on the other hand, the trans-national provision of welfare itself. (Note, in particular, the growing intrusion of internationally organised health and education services, for example in Indonesia, which will from 2003 permit unrestricted foreign investment in all healthcare (Gough, 2000b: 11); and the market for overseas health treatment and education of more privileged strata, encouraged by the entrepreneurial strategies of public and private sector providers in the West.)

As in the EU, global regulation of these trans-national operations is driven principally by trade rules which require that producers from different countries should enjoy a level playing field. Discrimination against foreign producers is proscribed. Under the auspices of the WTO, this is being progressively extended beyond goods to services (GATS – the General Agreement on Trade in Services) and capital, although restrictions on the movement of persons remain as dependent as ever on the discretion of potential host countries.

At the same time (and again as in our discussion of the EU), trans-national operators are being required to respect minimum international standards, in order to ensure that globalisation does not produce socially unsustainable consequences, and to avoid enterprises relocating in a 'race to the bottom'. Nevertheless, as systems for regulating these trans-national actors, such standards are not entirely robust, in that they are indirect: they depend on the national authorities of the countries where these trans-national actors operate being signatory to the standards in question, and able and willing to enforce them. Neither the WTO nor the ILO has any mandate to regulate multi-national corporations, even though it is these corporations who play a major role in shaping – through national governments – the architecture of the international arena (Madeley 2001). Even less do they have any mandate to regulate the 'underside' of international transactions: the international criminal gangs which figure strongly in Bevan's account of Africa, along with the international commercial interests which, by furnishing 'rents' to those in power, reinforce the continent's misery.

Consumer pressure in the advanced countries has led to various social and environmental codes of practice that trans-national enterprises are enjoined to follow in their dealings with developing countries. The UN secretary-general's Global Social Compact also represents an attempt to engage international business directly in a social and environmental pact. Nevertheless, it is as yet only a modest initiative. Global governance of trans-national operators remains highly fragmented.

Regional blocks and international social governance

This chapter is concerned with the relevance of European welfare developments, bringing together national and supra-national elements in a regional welfare regime, for the developing world, the international order and global social policy. This relevance to the wider world has been treated as three separate, if related, questions. First, we have considered what is distinctive about the European model when compared with its principal rivals, in particular NAFTA. We proceeded in the preceding section to consider how far the European model – and its rivals – serve as models for the international order more generally, and for global social policy in particular. We now turn to the third question: the potential significance of regional blocks modelled on the European experience, as part of the new structure of international social governance.

Many experiments in regional integration began as local attempts to build free trade areas, which were less ambitious than a global free trading system. They could therefore be viewed as transitional arrangements, pending the establishment of such a global system. Deacon argues that there will be strong pressures for the dissolution of many existing regional groupings in the face of the neo-liberal global trading system that is now emerging (Deacon 2001). Even if this has a social dimension, it is not self-evident that such a global trading system presupposes regional blocks for its effective operation, if the social dimension consists first and foremost in establishing a level playing field for trans-national economic actors and ensuring that they respect certain minimum social standards. On the contrary, such trans-national economic actors are likely to view regional blocks as a potential impediment to the global trading system. Against this, Schirm (2002) argues that it has been precisely the pressures of global markets that have encouraged efforts at regional integration, as a means by which national governments could seek – cooperatively – to maintain some scope for policy initiative.

There are two possible reasons for believing that the existence of regional blocks within the system of international social governance will
have major implications for the nature of that global system. The first
is political and cultural. Regional confederations of nations will, other
things being equal, enable their member states to speak more powerfully in global arenas than they can individually, and to secure attention
for their view of what this international social governance should involve
(Öjendal 2001: 164). The previous section drew attention to the lack of
voice which much of the developing world enjoys, compared with the situation of the poorer member states within the EU: regional blocks within
the developing world may be crucial for this voice.

The second reason why the existence of regional blocks is of significance for international social governance is economic and social. The
neo-liberal global trading system that is now emerging, under the spon-
sorship of the United States in particular, and as an extrapolation from its
experience of NAFTA, looks to the market to develop prosperity for all.
The social dimension of such a neo-liberal system involves, at most, respect for certain basic social standards, to secure a level playing field for
market competitors. However, long-established critiques of neo-liberal
thought suggest dire economic and social consequences of such a limited
social dimension.

Differential market power in the international trading system is likely to
push poorer countries into low-technology, labour-intensive, low-value-
added production, while advanced countries consolidate their hold on
high-tech, high-value-added products. Neo-liberal theory can appeal to
the classical analysis of comparative advantage in international trade, in
justifying such an outcome, as yielding the greatest benefit – if not prosperity – for all. However, long-established critiques of this analysis of
comparative advantage point out that it neglects the opportunity for countries to invest in their physical and human capital resources. Countries
which are induced to concentrate on low-technology, labour-intensive
production will have less incentive and less opportunity to make such investments and they may get locked into a downward spiral of cumulative
comparative disadvantage.[8]

As our earlier discussion suggested, these developments are likely to be
accompanied by widening inequalities within developing countries, with
elites prospering from the global trading environment, but the mass of

---

[8] It is not only the incentives which are created by free trade that put these investments
under threat. In developing countries, a large share of government tax receipts typically
comes from trade tariffs: a free trade regime tends to diminish these receipts and therefore
the resources for public investment, with no assurance that greater national prosperity
will provide an alternative fiscal base (Deacon 2001; Torres 2001: 40–4).

the population sharing in this progress only if there are vigorous policies of human investment and social protection for all. In many developing countries, the extended family has traditionally supported its members in times of both adversity and opportunity: this is unlikely to suffice under the conditions of dynamic social and economic change that economic globalisation is unleashing.

How does this establish a role for regional blocks? First, such regional blocks may represent additional buffers or cushions for their populations in times of global economic adversity, if they can create the conditions for regional economic interdependence. Many developing countries are vulnerable to volatility in the global economic environment because of their specialisation in particular sectors, a specialisation which is, however, imperative if they are to survive in global markets: regionally integrated economies may help to pool these risks.

This is not all. As argued above, vigorous policies of human investment are necessary on the part of developing countries, both to avoid a downward spiral of cumulative comparative disadvantage, and to avoid growing social polarisation (see also Torres 2001: 54–6). In face of the same challenge, the countries of the EU have in recent years found it necessary to work in concert, if they are to develop a competitive and dynamic knowledge-based economy, able to attract high-tech capital by offering a highly skilled labour force and infrastructures supportive of innovation. In the case of the smaller developing countries, the case for regional approaches is likely to be even stronger. This is, indeed, the central lesson that can be drawn from the European experience, especially when contrasted with the neo-liberalism of NAFTA: the development of human capital through concerted action at regional level is a precondition for prosperity in the global economy (Room 2002).[9]

Whether, therefore, regional blocks are seen by reference to their role in pooling risks of economic insecurity, or by reference to the base they provide for common efforts to promote human investment, the motivation

---

[9] The importance of a regional approach to human investment can be argued at various levels. One is in terms of the readiness of individuals, employers and public authorities to invest in skills development. Crouch, Soskice and others have argued that unless there are strong institutional inducements to collective action, employers and countries are likely to free-ride and poach, and will end up in a low skills equilibrium (Crouch et al. 1999). A high skills equilibrium presupposes a pact at the level of the sector and the nation, and increasingly at the level of the region: a new political settlement around a human investment regime.

It is worth adding that, according to Soskice and his colleagues, the readiness of individuals to invest in their skills can depend in part on the income security which they enjoy: and this depends in part on the income maintenance systems that are in place. Such safety nets then appear as not just a means of preventing destitution, but also a tool in a policy of skill development (Estevez-Abe et al. 2001).

to develop regional blocks arises from the increasingly competitive environment with which global markets confront national actors (Schirm 2002). Moreover, as the preceding argument demonstrates, this incentive to regional cooperation focuses less on measures of 'negative integration' and market-making and more on moves to 'positive integration', with common policies and institutions.

Conclusion

Those who offer neo-liberal market prescriptions for economic and social progress are in the political ascendancy. Nevertheless, such prescriptions must be judged critically by reference to their consequences and they cannot claim any a priori privileged status.

Neo-liberal economics tends to make two assumptions about the functioning of competitive market economies. First, they have an inherent tendency towards equilibrium. Second, they tend towards Pareto optimality, providing a level of benefits to the population which could not be improved for some, except by imposing a cost on others. Both of these assumptions are put in question, at least, by the studies of the developing world that have been offered in this collection. Indeed, our work strongly suggests that the neo-liberal world order that is being built is liable to generate growing inequality and polarisation between and within countries, even if it brings prosperity to some. This is liable, in turn, to undermine social cohesion and to generate growing dissent, from whose costs it is unlikely that the 'haves' can entirely insulate themselves.

These empirical developments lend credence to the critique of these neo-liberal assumptions offered by the new political economy. Market economies are inherently unstable and 'they tend to exert a constant destabilising effect on the societies within which they operate' (Goldthorpe 1984: 3). Not least, by continuously rendering skills obsolete and by changing the balance of power in labour markets, they destabilise and generate permanent insecurity in livelihoods, and thereby provoke endemic social conflict. From this standpoint, what is needed if such market economies are to function efficiently is a political settlement, within which these conflicts and sources of instability can be managed.

The champions of a neo-liberal trading system – intellectuals, business leaders and politicians – do not appear disposed to address the terms of such a political settlement for the international arena. For them, the merits of markets are self-evident: political agreement is needed only on the extension and liberation of such markets. However, the European experience recounted in this chapter builds on a different set of assumptions. The social and economic order is politically constructed, as part of a 'settlement' between countries, between classes and between social institutions. The development of international markets, while it can serve the political task of creating common interests between formerly antagonistic states and opening up new opportunities for producing economic wealth, can also produce instability and conflict, both nationally and internationally. Political management of these developments is a precondition for economic efficiency as well as social equity.

In the project of European integration, progress has depended on a readiness to address these political challenges. Much of the time, this progress has therefore been slow. This chapter suggests, nevertheless, that a similarly bold effort is now needed at global level, with a view to establishing a new international political settlement concerned with governance of the global market. Drawing on the European experience, our discussion has suggested that this settlement must include six key elements:

1. Human capital investment must be central to the social dimension of globalisation, if all are to have the opportunity of being included in the prosperity of which it holds promise.
2. There must be a commitment by national governments to social standards and policy targets agreed internationally, with regular monitoring of progress.
3. There must be support to countries in raising their economic, social and policy performance, involving resource transfers for investment in infrastructure, rural development, adaptation to new industrial opportunities, capacity-building and skill development: these resource transfers must be based on entitlement rather than the discretionary charity of rich donors. Their funding will, therefore, need to have a secure fiscal base, rather than depending on appeals to the generosity of the rich: whether this takes the form of a tax on capital movements (the Tobin tax) or internet transactions, charges for exploitation of the seabed or pollution of the commons, or a national levy in proportion to GDP, goes beyond the scope of this chapter.
4. There must be improved scope for cross-national policy learning and the exchange of good practice, but with developing countries participating fully in the definition of what is appropriate to their needs, and being regarded, indeed, as potential sources of good practice themselves.
5. Building on the consumer-driven codes of conduct to which MNCs are increasingly subject, and the UN's Global Compact and Global Reporting Initiative, there must be an international social audit and benchmarking regime for MNCs no less robust than that which is here being proposed for governments.

6. There must be new institutional arrangements for shared governance, involving national governments but also representatives of regional blocks, the social partners and civil society, all having a degree of voice that can command general agreement. These governance arrangements must, moreover, be sufficiently coherent to enable political negotiation and trade-offs across a broad front.

How far would such an international system render regions and nations obsolete? The preceding section of this chapter set out some of the reasons why regional groupings could be an important element of international governance. But what is the role of the nation-state in this global arena? And what is needed to ensure that it is in a position to play this role effectively? This was, of course, the question posed at the outset of this chapter: the extent to which national sovereignty in relation to social welfare is now more appropriately pooled in regional and maybe global welfare regimes.

One view is that the task of the nation-state is simply to support the functioning of the international neo-liberal market order. This it can do by opening up its domestic markets and withdrawing special treatment from domestic producers. It also has a role to play in supporting the casualties of market turbulence: Michael Moore, as director of the WTO, envisages that this turbulence will drive citizens to demand safety net support from their national authorities, and therefore also to exert pressure for urgently needed reforms to state capacity (Moore 1999). He is less open to the possibility that international markets may themselves tend to undermine state capacity, by reducing the fiscal base or encouraging illicit activity. Nor does he envisage a role for states in modifying market distributions of life chances or in managing development.

The argument of this chapter does not, however, make the nation-state the privileged manager of welfare and politics. Nor does it therefore infer that for developing countries the path to social citizenship must consist of imitating their European forebears and constructing a high-quality national welfare regime for national social citizenship. Nevertheless, national governments have a crucial role to play, both as participants in the global regulation of welfare and as brokers bringing together national and international actors in a mutually supportive framework for social welfare.

European experience as yet offers only limited guidance as to the content and organisation of a global welfare regime, operating within such a mutually supportive framework. As we have seen, it suggests some of the forms of joint governance that might be applied globally, including the approval of national policy targets, policy learning, resource transfers and the sovereign equality of solvent partners. What it leaves still to be addressed is the extent and substance of the public realm as far as welfare is concerned. Is the European social space to consist of no more than the coordination of national public policies, coupled with the more effective supra-national social regulation of trans-national market actors, all underpinned by some system of European social governance involving major stakeholders? Or is the European social space to consist of European-level public policies for European citizens, enlarging and Europeanising the commons?

It is perhaps unsurprising that these questions have not yet been addressed. The project of European integration has, since the mid-1980s, been driven by the single-market project and by economic and monetary union. The public space has been on the retreat in all the member states: the public are viewed increasingly as consumers rather than as citizens. In consequence, EU proposals for giving greater content to European citizenship – a key element of larger debates on EU governance – are very emaciated. In social and employment policies, the European public space – apart from supporting the coordination of national policies and undertaking some regulation of market actors – remains very limited. It consists primarily of support to cross-European networking (among students, universities, public sector professionals, etc.) and the exchange of good practice; European agencies concerned with the provision of Europe-wide statistics; and the monitoring of standards.

As seen at the start of this chapter, welfare systems organised by the public authorities have long been an important instrument of statecraft, securing popular loyalty and maintaining commitment in times of adversity. Nation-states may now, to an increasing extent, have to work out their destinies within systems of pooled international sovereignty: nevertheless, the need to secure popular loyalty to this – international as well as national   welfare regime remains undiminished. A competitive arena of trans-national market actors, even if they are socially regulated, may attract the approval of consumers but seems unlikely to secure the political obligation of citizens. Without a European public space, what is likely to happen is that the more affluent sections of the population will make increasing use of international market provision, while national public authorities are left to look after the less affluent. To build an international welfare regime, working in conjunction with national institutions, and serving as a focus for citizenship and political obligation embracing all sections of society, is a political task which is in danger of being ignored. If this is true at the European level, it is also fundamental to any discussion of global social welfare.

Conclusion   Rethinking social policy in development contexts

Geof Wood and Ian Gough

This conclusion is in four parts. The first part clarifies the intellectual and normative foundations of the welfare regime approach developed in this book. The second part summarises and situates our findings about welfare regimes in Asia, Africa and Latin America. In the third part we outline in some detail the implications of our approach for thinking about social policy in development contexts. Finally, we consider recent arguments about the globalisation of welfare provision and the scope for a global welfare regime.

Foundations of our approach

This volume begins from a widely held concern to improve global human welfare and progressively reduce poverty. Based on an empirical core, it also has an unashamedly conceptual and theoretical purpose. It seeks to convince readers of the need for a wide range of institutions to contribute to secure welfare under contemporary global conditions. Notwithstanding the unifying and converging forces of global capitalism, we emphasise the variegated and path-dependent patterns of development or lack of development across different zones of the world. This builds on our middle-range theory of welfare regimes, which opposes both teleological or functionalist approaches (both modernisation and Marxist) on the one hand, and post-modern approaches emphasising uniqueness and diversity on the other hand. The political upshot is a distinction between universal goals and context-specific means. It leads us to reject 'one-size-fits-all' policy solutions to poverty eradication, whether from the right (unregulated market capitalism), the left (basic income) or the fashionable reformist centre (participation and 'good governance'). Social policies must reflect the welfare regime.

In accepting certain facts about globalisation, we are essentially settling for a principle of social capitalism, or mixed economy capitalism. Neither markets, nor states, nor communities alone can provide an adequate framework for meeting human needs. Political economies which mix these three principles within a democratically governed polity provide a more sustainable and flexible framework for enhancing human well-being (Gough 2001a; Wood 2000). Accepting global reality for the foreseeable future entails that this mix will operate within a framework with extensive private property: in other words a capitalist framework. However, capitalism needs to be regulated in order to achieve equitable social objectives and secure welfare outcomes for all. This is a major rationale for Western social policy and Western 'welfare states'.

Yet how well does this apply under conditions of peripheral capitalism, low levels of development and partial commodification? This question represents our key point of departure for analysing the relationships between the institutional options for poverty eradication in different sets of socio-economic conditions within the global political economy.

In order to capture these different sets of conditions, we have modified Esping-Andersen's concept of welfare regimes. We have generalised the relationship between different institutional domains into a series of distinctive welfare regimes. Thus 'welfare regime' is at the apex of our conceptual hierarchy. At the next level, we identify three distinct regime 'genuses': Esping-Andersen's original welfare state regimes, informal security regimes and insecurity regimes. Within each of these there is the possibility of identifying different 'species'. Within welfare state regimes, Esping-Andersen distinguishes three: liberal, conservative-corporatist and social democratic. In addition, we have two mixed variants combining informal security elements: liberal-informal welfare regimes in Latin America (Barrientos), and productivist welfare regimes in East Asia (Gough). The concept of informal security regimes per se is derived from Wood's work in South Asia, and is here exemplified by Davis on Bangladesh. Lastly, Bevan identifies insecurity regimes in parts of sub-Saharan Africa and elsewhere. This is as far as we go for a typology in this volume. Of course, further study of other areas of the world may well yield other regime types.

In moving beyond welfare state regimes, premised on political settlements between conflicting group-based power resources, we also develop a more general conceptualisation of welfare regimes as the relationship between rights and correlative duties. The manner in which that relationship is specified is a product of history, and especially a history reflecting the interrelations in different epochs between domestic institutions and the global economy. Those interrelations circumscribe the relative autonomy and legitimacy of the state, and bring a range of non-state actors at global as well as local level into our generalised account of social policy. Thus, for many societies, rights cannot only be understood in a strict statutory sense, and correlative duties will come, if at all, from domains other than the domestic state.

This variation has been crucial for our analysis. The social conditions of many societies in the South do not mimic those in the North. Their histories are different, and incomes in poorer countries continue to reflect combinations of subsistence production, informal casual employment, petty trade, remittances, sinecures, monopoly rents, and corruption alongside formal sector employment and regulated trading. In other words the subsumption of labour under capital remains to a significant extent formal rather than real. The relations of production, while serving the interests of capital locally and globally, have not been fully commoditised and have not yet attracted regulation. We might also observe that the world-wide evidence of increasing casualisation and flexibilisation of labour undermines any sense of secular trend towards the organised, formal labour markets of industrial and post-industrial societies (Standing 1999).

Welfare regimes in Asia, Africa and Latin America

Chapters 4 to 7 of this book explore the welfare regimes in three regions of the world – Latin America, East Asia (excluding China) and Africa – and in Bangladesh, part of South Asia. We thus ignore several world regions outside the OECD: the degrading statist welfare regimes of the ex-Soviet Union and Eastern Europe, the emerging regime in China, as well as the Middle East and the remainder of South Asia. This section summarises our findings and sketches their situation in terms of their histories, economies and polities. The approach used is that of historical political economy which gives due weight to external and internal factors in their evolution (see also Cammack *et al.* 1993: chs. 1, 2).

Latin America: from conservative-informal to liberal-informal regimes

According to Barrientos, there is enough commonality across Latin America to identify a single welfare regime, and one with similarities to those in developed capitalist societies.[1] The early de-colonisation and political independence in the region, and the development of export economies plus partial industrialisation, developed a capitalist class and

---

[1] This does not apply to most of the Caribbean countries, which gained independence only after World War II, and which are more influenced by their colonial inheritance. This book is concerned with the Spanish-speaking countries of Central and South America, plus Brazil.

an urban proletariat alongside the landowning class. The devastating inter-war crisis brought about a switch from export economies to import substitution strategies. This fostered the emergence of social insurance and employment protection schemes for formal sector workers, which gained an institutional autonomy. On this basis an alliance of industry, public sector workers and urban industrial workers emerged which acted to protect and extend these incipient welfare institutions.

As a result, a welfare regime emerged in post-war Latin America, most clearly in the more developed Southern Cone, not unlike that of Southern Europe. There were aspirations towards universal access in health and education. Social insurance and employment protection institutions provided a substantial degree of protection against risk for formal sector workers and their dependants. However, the dualised economy left the mass of informal sector workers unprotected and reliant on unregulated labour markets, residual public assistance programmes and above all their own resources. Throughout the region, household provision and livelihood mixing was important, and the private sector was not clearly distinguished from the public.

Barrientos characterises this as a *conservative-informal welfare regime*. It was a *welfare state* regime along European lines in that there was a conscious attempt to mitigate market forces in sectors important for welfare and security. It was a *conservative* welfare regime because of the segmented nature of the social protection (education and health provision aspired to be universal but in practice was not). It was conservative-*informal* due to the absence of protection and the high insecurity of the millions of peasants, landless labourers, urban unemployed and marginal workers.

This welfare regime has been transformed in the last decade, Barrientos argues. The import substitution strategy was fatally undermined by the neo-liberal redirection of global economic governance in the 1970s and the crisis this induced. High interest rates and debt crises led to the imposition of structural adjustment programmes in the early 1980s. The import substitution model, increasingly ill-adapted to the liberalisation of trade, investment and finance, was replaced by export-oriented growth models. At the same time, from the mid-1970s to the mid-1980s, military-authoritarian-bureaucratic rule spread across the continent. In the face of this combined onslaught the political constituency of industry, public sector workers and formal sector workers crumbled.

As a result the welfare regime began to shift to a *liberal-informal* one in the 1990s. Employment protection withered in the face of labour market de-regulation, social insurance began to be replaced by individual saving and market provision, and private financing and provision of health and education was encouraged. 'The change in development model undermined support for social insurance from the state and employers, while at the same time reducing the political influence of urban industrial workers and public sector workers.' At the same time, the resurgence of political democracy across the region offers opportunities for new, perhaps more inclusive, social programmes and forms of social development to emerge.

East Asia: productivist welfare regimes

All East Asian countries except Siam were colonised but by a variety of different powers: Portugal, Spain, the Netherlands, France, Britain, the US and Japan. The atomic end of the Japanese attempt to build an East Asian imperium ushered in a period of political instability, paradoxically coupled with unprecedented economic development. According to Anderson (1998), there were four external 'conditions-of-possibility' for the post-war East Asian miracle: first, the Cold War and contested US hegemony; second, propinquity to the extraordinarily dynamic Japanese economy which fostered trade, then investment; third, the isolation of China for four decades; and, fourth, the role of the overseas Chinese in developing entrepreneurial networks which were yet barred from political power.

These external circumstances impacted upon relatively large states with different colonial and pre-colonial institutional and cultural legacies. Due to the Japanese occupation, revolutionary movements and authoritarian responses to these movements, landowners and capitalists have been relatively weak as a class. On the other hand, states have periodically been able to raise themselves as an independent force above society. East Asian states are relatively autonomous and have been despotically powerful, if not always infrastructurally strong. In the countries of Northeast Asia most influenced by Japan (Korea and Taiwan), strong group-coordinated economies emerged guided by developmental states wherein elite policy-makers set economic growth as the fundamental goal and pursued coherent strategies to achieve it. In the city-states of Hong Kong and Singapore different forms of state-guided development took place. The second wave of emerging market economies in Southeast Asia (Malaysia, Thailand, the Philippines and Indonesia) also exhibit relatively strong states but with fewer policy levers. Compared with Northeast Asia, business is more internationalised and more in the control of a separate Chinese business class. State policies are more reactive, to secure state legitimacy or elite loyalty.

According to Gough (chapter 5), all the middle-income countries in East Asia (with the exception of the Philippines) can be described as *productivist welfare regimes.* These regimes are based on dynamic emerging capitalist market economies, which have driven the commodification of labour over many decades and are fostering the emergence of marketised social welfare. Moreover, they are governed by unified, relatively strong states with substantial steering and infrastructural capacities. They have in turn pursued a developmental agenda with remarkable economic success. Lastly, this growth has, in the absence of seriously unequal Latin-American-style distribution, generated improving welfare outcomes.

The term *productivist* welfare regime signals that the East Asian countries differ from the types of welfare state regime identified in the West. First, social policy is not an autonomous agent in society or even an autonomous sphere of government; rather it is subordinated to the dominant economic policy goal of maintaining high rates of economic growth. Following on from this, social policy is concentrated on social investment, notably in education and basic health rather than social protection. Third, this policy has largely been driven by the imperatives of nation-building and regime legitimation. Fourth, the state is mainly confined to regulation rather than provision and plays only a contributory role in the broader welfare mix, which is sustained by strong families and household strategies, high savings and marketised provision and, in Korea, enterprise welfare.

However, the sustainability of this regime is open to doubt because of its vulnerability exemplified in the East Asian financial crisis of 1997. The open economies of the region were exposed to short-term inflows of hot money from the US and Japan which financed unsustainable bank lending and investment projects. The ultimate collapse of the Thai baht triggered a currency and banking crisis with major impacts upon incomes, poverty and living standards. As a result, the absence of social protection measures and the lack of social investment in higher education was exposed. It remains to be seen whether this transforms the productivist social development regimes in the region.

Bangladesh and South Asia: informal security

Chapter 7 presents a detailed study of Bangladesh, which though distinct in significant ways offers some pointers to the rest of South Asia. The extreme poverty of the region and relative absence of sustained economic development until recent years has parallels with Africa. Development discourses dominate and 'welfare' strategies are nested within wider 'development' programmes. Yet, by contrast with many parts of Africa, the British colonial legacy bequeathed to several states recognisable territories and competences. A formal system of law and, within

India, liberal-democratic practices are also well established. This combination of 'stateness' alongside absent or uneven capitalist development and rural poverty enables us to identify distinct welfare regimes in South Asia which reley heavily on informal mechanisms of security.

The dominant political economy of Bangladesh is of rural class relations based on land-holding, coupled with elite control over resources and opportunities at both national and local levels. A history of state monopolies has fostered widespread rent-seeking and corruption. As a result, reliance on networks, linkages, informal rules, personal favours and discretion is pervasive. Political parties are segmental, factional and non-ideological. Despite recent growth and some flourishing export sectors the dominant policy environment is one of poverty and over-population. 'In a context where the emerging capitalist system does not enjoy political stability and general acceptance, where the state is not strong enough to enforce order by force and where civil society is failing to create the ideological support for the emergence of capitalism, patron–client networks which organise payoffs to the most vociferous opponents of the system are an effective if costly way of maintaining political stability' (Khan 1998: 115).

The Bangladeshi regime, according to Davis, is an informal security regime with contradictory results. It is characterised by a bewildering range of actors: over 1,200 officially registered NGOs; a large number of international donor organisations (who also provide much of the finance for the domestic NGOs); informal, community-based welfare and development organisations; and burgeoning labour migration to the Middle East and elsewhere generating growing household remittances. An integral feature of this regime is the interrelation between the international donors and actors and internal elites and patrons. All operate within, adapt to, and in turn influence the vertical patron–client relationships that structure interest representation in Bangladesh. Foreign aid can improve welfare outcomes but at the same time can harm the potential for poor people to participate and organise for longer-term social development. 'A psychology of plunder prevails where unholy alliances of *de facto* illicit beneficiaries get away with as much as donors will let them.' The lack of a citizenship link between the funding of programmes and their disbursement prevents the emergence of a positive feedback link characteristic of Western welfare regimes. It is unclear how the recent economic upsurge, rapid socio-economic change and modernisation will affect this regime of informal security. In the absence of more institutionalised official programmes, it may well result in new forms of social exclusion and extreme poverty. In these circumstances, the prime task of social policy is *de-clientelisation*.

Sub-Saharan Africa: a regional insecurity regime

The dominant historical legacy in Africa south of the Sahara is of European colonialism – late, brief and rivalrous – superimposed on an earlier system of kingdoms and stateless societies. The prime motive for the establishment of colonies was economic, and the colonies became dependent on foreign capital and trading companies. The colonial legacies of the British, French, Belgians, Portuguese and others differed, but a common factor was a lack of both sustained economic development and investment in education and human services. Significant European settlement in southern and eastern Africa modified this legacy and introduced later bifurcated and racialist forms of development, notably in South Africa.

De-colonisation occurred late – mainly in the 1960s – and nowhere was political independence prepared for in a sustained and meaningful way. Many small states were created, superimposed on a mosaic of livelihood systems. The new states emerged in a continent dominated by the Cold War and external players. Discourses of modernisation and industrialisation dominated in the early years and there was a significant effort to improve and widen education provision. However, the openness to international forces, the predominantly pre-industrial social formations and the lack of state capacities engendered unbalanced development alongside rapid urbanisation. Patron–clientelist political relations flourished in place of class movements. Above all, a harsher economic climate in the 1970s (for all but oil-producing countries) engendered disillusionment and crisis. The IMF and other powerful players imposed structural adjustment programmes in the 1980s which stalled economic development and began to reverse aspects of social development.

At the present time, according to Bevan, much of the continent of Africa constitutes a generalised *insecurity regime*. The dominant forms of livelihood are agriculture and informal urban activities. The two main ways of mitigating risks are the efforts of individuals within families, households and clans and patrimonial relations. The importance of the latter leads to a continuing investment in social networks and the role of 'Big Men' in offering some security, if at the price of 'adverse incorporation' into hierarchical and disempowering relationships. Above all, a wide range of external agencies increasingly intervene in the welfare mix: supra-national governmental organisations (the World Bank, the IMF, the United Nations and its related agencies), regional associations, powerful Western governments, international donors of many kinds and international NGOs. These may alleviate suffering but can also reinforce dependency relations, inequality and domination. The outcomes have been deteriorating health and rising poverty in many areas. Superimposed on this, in many parts of the continent, the HIV/AIDS pandemic or/and war and civil conflict have generated extreme levels of suffering. The result is an unplanned insecurity regime.

Moreover, the regime label can only in certain respects be applied at the national level, according to Bevan. Major areas of Africa resemble more an open field of play for powerful external interests: governments, multi-national corporations, development agencies and criminal gangs, among others. Many states are 'incoherent' in two senses: they are not institutionally differentiated from the societies within which they are embedded, and they lack meaningful territorial borders. As a result, the external players intrude into and enmesh with domestic elites in a novel and menacing way. This can enhance the power of the military, criminals and informal elites in ways which establish a perverted form of path dependency. The World Bank and the IMF, recently converted to pro-poor growth, now earnestly wish to reverse this downward spiral, but this entails confronting the results of past international involvements. Pockets of social development and African success stories qualify but do not alter this conclusion.

We have thus demonstrated that there are critical differences between welfare regimes across the developing world (and this still excludes China, the transitional countries of Eastern Europe and Central Asia, and significant other parts of the South). It makes no sense to apply a 'one-size-fits-all' model to analyse the nature of social development across these countries and regions, let alone to conceive and promote alternative social policies.

Social policy in development contexts

What then are the implications of our analysis for social policy in the South? If social policy is the public pursuit of secure welfare, we must first dwell upon the meaning of public action. Social policy in the West can be understood as the product of a dual movement: pressures from below and reforms from above (Gough 1979: ch. 1). Let us consider each in turn before considering the implications for social reforms in development contexts.

It is no coincidence that welfare state regimes in Western industrial societies evolved alongside the proletarianisation of labour. As we learn from Marx, mature capitalism brings about the social conditions under which alienation becomes a shared experience and labour can be organised to confront or remedy that alienation. Thus the forms of public action that brought about the 'welfare state' involved the struggles of the increasingly organised labour movement. In many northern European countries, these developments were linked to a range of other class mobilisations, notably by agricultural workers and later the 'service class', other social movements (such as the temperance movement in Scandinavia), and self-help institutions, such as friendly societies in Britain. Thus concessions were progressively wrung from the bourgeois state through public action.

On the other hand, social policies have also been introduced from the top down by far-sighted elites recognising the various 'functions' that social policies can perform and the beneficial results of accumulation, legitimacy and stability for the pursuit of their own interests. Stable inequality can only be achieved if poverty is somehow managed either through meaningful chances of upward mobility or through moderated exploitation. This is also a 'public goods' argument for social reform, whether public health measures to control epidemics, social programmes (alongside social control) to prevent runaway crime and physical insecurity, schooling for skills and citizenship, or housing and town planning to counter the social costs of unplanned urbanisation. Concessionary capitalism has to formalise some public goods as social rights in order for stable inequality to persist.

What are the chances of similar mechanisms taking hold in the poorer parts of the South and transforming informal into formal welfare regimes? First, can we expect serious, sustained and effective bottom-up pressure from organised labour? Outside a few areas, no; so we have to search for public action in other quarters. As we have previously argued, such public action takes two essential forms: action which provides immediate welfare, though usually at the price of loyalty to degraded arrangements and other forms of adverse incorporation; and action which seeks to improve the quality of institutions through which welfare might be secured. The former action can be broadly summed up as clientelism; the latter as social development, when it is not revolution.

Our conceptualisation of informal security regimes establishes a proposition: social policy as the public pursuit of secure welfare requires *de-clientelisation*. There is a need to disestablish clientelist forms of representation and provisioning and establish more formal rights to welfare and security. The immediate qualification that needs to be made is that since clientelism does perform significant short-term welfare functions, a policy of de-clientelisation can only be ethically contemplated if the processes that achieve this outcome also offer alternative welfare functions. This is a tall order. However, such a proposition is consistent with our distinction above between the pursuit of universalist goals and needs and the use of context-dependent means to achieve them.

What is the realistic basis of public action, which might deliver this agenda? Having rejected a critical role for organised labour, how do we assess the claims made across the world for a *civil society* alternative? We certainly need to be wary of much rhetoric from the official bilateral agencies and the IFIs. In this rhetoric, the good governance agenda is combined with optimism about participatory social action as the means to improve public institutional performance, poverty-focused policy implementation, and community-based social development.

Yet there is some contrast of judgement between gloomy academics on the one hand (Wood, 2000; Cooke and Kothari 2001) and the evidence of widespread NGO/civil society movements operating at local, national and global levels with increasing sophistication as lobbyists and pressure groups. Obviously the 'de Tocqueville' understanding of civil society as critical and independent, able to exert restraining pressure upon the state, has to be tempered by the arguments of hegemonic pessimists.[2] At the same time, the preoccupation with hegemony does not sit easily with the many small gains made by civil society action, social movements and collective action. With some finite exceptions, states cannot rule for long by coercion alone. Concessions to struggle are made, rights do get extended, policies do get changed, reforms do happen. Perhaps the hegemonic pessimists have simply been too impatient and have not attributed enough significance to small victories. In examining the hegemonic implications of authoritative labelling, Wood (1985) also points out that 'targets strike back'. In other words, the ways in which the state might seek to organise and reorganise its population for convenient, limited policy concessions can itself produce new solidarities and social bases for critical social action. One way or another, the achievement has been to organise solidarities outside the category of organised labour. Post-modernist analysis has drawn our attention to these possibilities, as identities and interest groups outside the historic capital–labour confrontation have emerged as significant. This has been reinforced by the evidence from transforming, recently agrarian, societies where peasants, quasi-peasants, tenants, landless agricultural labour, informal sector workers, migrants and women from these categories have been mobilised in the 'reformist' era following the great 'peasant' revolutions associated with Russia, China, Mexico and Vietnam *inter alia*.

Turning to top-down reforms, elites in the South typically surround the state and have contradictory relationships to it. Some are definitely

---

[2] Thus Gramscian arguments about civil society incorporated into the state's project; in the 1970s, Althusser's 'ideological state apparatuses'; and the critical theory of Habermas, Marcuse and others associated with the Frankfurt School.

part of the problem of the state, while others lament its irresponsibility. From experience in South Asia and Latin America, it is clear that even well-connected elites have insufficient trust in the state to commit to it wholeheartedly. Typically, a desire for public goods co-exists with an unwillingness collectively to invest in them, resulting in widespread tax avoidance and evasion. It also results in public squalor alongside private wealth, privately protected. A social policy agenda in poor countries clearly has to include converting the elite's objective interest in, and frequent desire for, public goods into corresponding public action to deliver them. In other words, a regime change in which their correlative duties are expanded in response to rights claimed by others. In this sense, civil society action has to embrace the middle classes far more than hitherto, and beyond narrow professional or neighbourhood associations. Of course the threat of unstable inequality can be an incentive, as perhaps has been the case recently in Venezuela. In a nutshell, the transformation of informal security regimes into welfare state regimes entails a subtle and complex process of de-clientelisation.

The transformation of insecurity regimes into even informal security regimes requires more basic preconditions: stable, legitimate states with some minimal jurisdiction over their territories; international curbs on the actions of threatening outside actors and regulation of global markets; and moves to enhance civil society and norms of governance. Some of this agenda is now embraced by the World Bank and aid agencies, but as Gore (2000) argues, this paradigm is contradictory and thus naïve. The discourse of normative standards at the international level (such as the Millennium Goals) do not displace the responsibilities of national governments. Yet the severe and intensifying international constraints on nation states are barely recognised. If, however, as we argue, international factors and actors must be fully integrated into the analysis, then the prospects for countries in unstable zones to improve on their insecurity regimes are dependent on changes in the global architecture of nations and institutions.

All of this implies a moral hierarchy of regime types on a continuum from insecurity to informal security to formal security. There can be no doubt that such a formulation poses a theoretical dilemma for us. Are we simply repeating a modernisation mantra and in effect unfavourably contrasting traditional with modern social arrangements? Not really. On the one hand, we have indicated that we are sensitive to history, colonialism and neo-colonialism, and persistent conditions of unequal exchange in the global political economy. We are acknowledging path dependency, and not assuming that globalisation produces the homogeneity of modern social systems. On the other hand, we do claim that formal security of welfare (in the sense of individual, guaranteed, non-personal and justiciable rights independent of birth, wealth, gender, status or other ascribed characteristics) is the most satisfactory way of meeting the universal human need for security and well-being. That condition must be better for most people than persistent instability; insecurity; violence; threats of anarchic, arbitrary rulings; zero-sum game conflict; high-level vulnerability; and little room to manoeuvre for survival.

Yet we are not suggesting a global programme of catching up. We are not suggesting for the foreseeable future (i.e. at least during the lifetime of the Millennium Development Goals) that the welfare regimes of poor countries can somehow be transformed into the welfare state ones of the West, or even that this would be desirable. That would be to deny path dependency and to be insensitive to the different historical ways in which societies are represented within globalisation. Improvements towards formal security have to be judged in each situation according to its particular circumstances, and we have to be realistic rather than utopian.

The regime approach enables us to retain a universalism about ends while being relativist about means. This relativism essentially reflects the basic ways in which poverty needs to be understood in different sets of societies, and thus constitutes the conceptual basis for defining appropriate security of welfare, and the institutional room for manoeuvre in any meaningful timeframe. This relativism certainly requires us to box more clever in considering the repertoire of social policy initiatives by a wider range of actors in the public domain, not confined to the state. This is the basic contrast to Western social policy. The relationships between rights and correlative duties have to be found more subtly and supported in ways which do not presume the absolute authority of the state and which respect the sustainable contribution of other agencies.

The globalisation of welfare regimes?

Despite our emphasis on difference, there remain critical commonalities that distinguish the countries and states of the developing and transitional world from the OECD world. One recurring theme is their vulnerability to external forces. This power inequality is of two sorts, based on exit and voice. First, the structural power of capital has grown over the last two decades as a result of liberalisation of trade, foreign exchange and capital markets. Capital can now more easily 'exit' from any jurisdiction if it considers an alternative one more favourable to its profitability, security and growth (Gough and Farnsworth 2000). This enhances its power relative to nation-states and national actors such as trade unions, NGOs and social movements. Second, and related to this, the 'voice' and political leverage of external actors has strengthened, notably the US government and other powerful states and the IMF, World Bank, World Trade Organisation and other international financial institutions. Both forms of trans-national power impinge on Northern states, but there is little doubt that they are far more constraining on Southern states.

The very idea of welfare states and welfare state regimes entails the conscious imposition by public actors of collective values and choices on unplanned market outcomes. Thus, it might be concluded, 'globalisation' fatally undermines the prospects for further welfare regime development across the world. And indeed this is a recurring theme in much contemporary literature. Yet, as regards the North, evidence to back up this assertion is remarkably thin. On the contrary, the conclusion of comparative studies of OECD countries is that global pressures are effectively mediated by the different welfare state regimes: common pressures generate distinct policy reactions according to the domestic pattern of institutions, interests and ideas. National welfare regimes appear to be quite resilient in the face of trans-national forces (Gough 2001a).

Does the same apply in the South? Here many, such as Deacon (1999), are pessimistic. The preconditions to build cross-class political coalitions are fatally weakened, he concludes, by the opportunities available to Southern elites and middle classes to 'exit' from national social policies and programmes. Medical care and education can be sought abroad or bought privately; private or company pensions substitute for public; cheap domestic care labour can be purchased on the open market. This undermines the chances that elites will recognise the public goods aspect of social provision and thus add their powerful voices to support universal public alternatives. At the same time, multi-nationals buy up medical facilities or administer pension funds and thus undermine national control. The chances of developing a political settlement on which to base national social citizenship were always restricted in the South and are now vanishingly small.

The obvious corollary to this position is that the battle for social citizenship is increasingly to be played out on the international and global stage. This would entail far more than the 'pro-poor growth' now advocated by the World Bank. It would necessitate the replication at global or regional level of the full panoply of social regulation, investment, protection and redistribution currently the preserve of Western states. This is the subject of Room's chapter. Using the European Union as his model of a multi-tiered welfare system, he considers what this would entail for an international welfare regime. The list of requirements is substantial: a commitment by national governments to the regular monitoring of social standards and policy targets; greater resource transfers from rich to poor countries and world regions financed by earmarked taxes; an auditing and benchmarking regime for multi-national corporations; new forms of cross-national social policy learning in which Southern countries play a major role; and new and more equitable forms of international governance with better representation for regional blocks and civil society. And even this would not take us across the threshold from nationally-based to supra-nationally-based social citizenship. The European Union has not yet made that leap – though, as we write, it is the subject of a profound debate.

As Room recognises, a multi-tiered welfare strategy may be no more politically achievable than a nationally-based one in today's world. But it would at least recognise two opposing features of the modern world: on the one hand, the growing importance of global economic power and trans-national and external institutions in shaping insecurities and diswelfares in the South; on the other hand, the lessons of emerging multi-tiered economic and social regulation that is such a feature of the world today, including at the regional level. If the EU is a model for other regional associations, then economic integration will slowly foster pressures for social interventions which may presage regional welfare regimes. If not, then the prospects for stable informal, let alone welfare state regimes, look bleak. Either way, the nation-state is no longer the sole frame of reference for analysing welfare, nor for proposing alternative social policies.

References

Abraham, A. 2000, 'Sierra Leone and Liberia: The Misery of Civil War and Social Decay', mimeo, Oxford.

Adam, H. M. 1995, 'Somalia: A Terrible Beauty Being Born?', in Zartman, I. W. (ed.) *Collapsed States: The Disintegration and Restoration of Legitimate Authority*, Boulder: Lynne Rienner.

Adedeji, A. (ed.) 1999, *Comprehending and Mastering African Conflicts: The Search for Sustainable Peace and Good Governance*, London: Zed Books.

African Rights 1997, *Food and Power in Sudan: A Critique of Humanitarianism*, London: African Rights.

Aguilar, M. I. (ed.) 1998, *The Politics of Age and Gerontocracy in Africa*, Eritrea: Africa World Press.

Ahmad, M. 1997, 'Financing of Primary Education', in Jalaluddin, A. K. and Chowdhury, A. M. R. (eds.), *Getting Started: Universalising Primary Education in Bangladesh*, Dhaka: University Press, pp. 148–67.

Alber, Jens and Standing, Guy (eds.) 2000a, 'Special Issue: Europe in a Comparative Global Context', *Journal of European Social Policy*, 10 (2): 99–203.

2000b, 'Social Dumping, Catch-up or Convergence? Europe in a Comparative Global Context', *Journal of European Social Policy*, 10 (2): 99–119.

Alcock, P., Erskine, A. and May, M. (eds.) 1998, *The Student's Companion to Social Policy*, Oxford: SPA and Blackwell.

Ali, Muhammad Mohar 1985, *History of the Muslims of Bengal*, Riyadh: Imam Muhammad ibn Saud Islamic University.

Allen, T. (ed.) 1996, *In Search of Cool Ground: War, Flight and Homecoming in Northeast Africa*, London: James Currey.

Altimir, O. 1997, 'Desigualdad, empleo y pobreza en America Latina: efectos del ajuste y del cambio en el estilo de desarrollo', *Desarrollo Económico*, 37 (145): 3–29.

Ambirajan, S. 1978, *Classical Political Economy and British Policy in India*, Cambridge: Cambridge University Press.

Amsden, Alice H. 1989, *Asia's Next Giant: South Korea and Late Industrialization*, Oxford: Oxford University Press.

Ananta, Aris and Siregar, Reza 1999, 'Social Safety Net Policies in Indonesia', *ASEAN Economic Bulletin*, 16 (3): 344–59.

Anderson, Benedict 1983, *Imagined Communities*, London: Verso.

1998, *The Spectre of Comparisons: Nationalism, Southeast Asia and the World*. London: Verso.

Anderson, D. M. and Broch-Due, V. 1999, *The Poor Are Not Us: Poverty and Pastoralism*, Oxford: James Currey.

Anderson, M. B. 1999, *Do No Harm: How Aid Can Support Peace – Or War*, Boulder: Lynne Rienner.

Apthorpe, R. and Gasper, D. (eds.) 1996, *Arguing Development Policy: Frames and Discourses*, London: Frank Cass.

Arts, Wil and Gellisen, John 2002, 'Three Worlds of Welfare Capitalism or More? A State-of-the-Art Report', *Journal of European Social Policy*, 12 (2): 137–58.

Asher, Mukul 1998, 'The Future of Retirement Protection in Southeast Asia', *International Social Security Review*, 51 (1): 3–30.

Asian Development Bank 1998, *Pension Systems and Policy in the APEC Economies*, 3 volumes, prepared by Stanton, D. and Whiteford, P., Manila: ADB.

2000, 'Assessment of Poverty in Indonesia', Manila, October.

Asian Development Bank and World Bank 2000, *The New Social Policy Agenda in Asia*, Proceedings of the Manila Social Forum, Manila: ADB.

Atkinson, A. B. 1995, 'Social Insurance', in Atkinson, A. B. (ed.) *Incomes and the Welfare State: Essays on Britain and Europe*, Cambridge: Cambridge University Press, pp. 205–19.

1997, 'Bringing Income Distribution Back from the Cold', *Economic Journal*, 107 (441): 297–321.

Attiyeh, G. 1999, *Africa in Chaos*, Basingstoke: Macmillan.

Bach, D. C. (ed.) 1999, *Regionalisation in Africa: Integration and Disintegration*, Oxford: James Currey.

Bailey, F. G. 1966, 'The Peasant View of the Bad Life', reprinted in Shanin, T. (ed.) 1971, *Peasants and Peasant Societies*, Harmondsworth: Penguin.

Baldwin, Peter 1990, *The Politics of Social Solidarity*, Cambridge: Cambridge University Press.

Banerjee, A. V. and Newman, A. F. 1998, 'Information, the Dual Economy and Development', *Review of Economic Studies*, 65: 631–53.

Banfield, E. 1958, *The Moral Basis of a Backward Society*, New York: Free Press.

Banuri, T. and Amadeo, E. J. 1992, 'Mundos dentro del Tercer Mundo: Instituciones del Mercado de Trabajo en Asia y América Latina', *Trimestre Económico*, 59 (4): 657–723.

Barbone, L. and L.-A. Sanchez, B. 1999, 'Pensions and Social Security Options in Sub-Saharan Africa: Issues and Options', paper presented at the XIIIth International Social Security Association African Regional Conference, Accra.

Barrientos, A. 1996, 'Pension Reform and Pension Coverage in Chile: Lessons for Other Countries', *Bulletin of Latin American Research*, 5 (3): 309–22.

1998, *Pension Reform in Latin America*, Aldershot: Ashgate.

1999, 'The Emerging Pension Fund Management Market in Latin America', *Journal of Pensions Management*, 5 (1): 60–8.

2000, 'Work, Retirement, and Vulnerability of Older Workers in Latin America. What Are the Lessons for Pension Design?', *Journal of International Development*, 12: 495–506.

2002, 'Health Policy in Chile: The Return of the Public Sector?', *Bulletin of Latin American Research*, 21 (3): 442–59.

Barrientos, A. and Lloyd-Sherlock, P. 2000, 'Reforming Health Insurance in Argentina and Chile', *Health Policy and Planning*, 15 (4): 417–23.

2002, 'Health Insurance Reforms in Latin America: Cream Skimming, Equity and Cost Containment', in Haagh, L. and Helgo, C. T. (eds.), *Social Policy Reform and Market Governance in Latin America*, Basingstoke: Palgrave.

Bayart, J.-F. 1993, *The State in Africa: The Politics of the Belly*, London: Longman.

Bayart, J.-F., Ellis, S. and Hibou, B. 1999, *The Criminalisation of the State in Africa*, Oxford: James Currey.

Bebbington, A. 1999, 'Capitals and Capabilities: A Framework for Analysing Peasant Viability, Rural Livelihoods and Poverty', *World Development*, 27: 2021–44.

Berger, I. and White, E. F. 1999, *Women in Sub-Saharan Africa*, Bloomington: Indiana University Press.

Berman, B. J. and Leys, C. 1994, *African Capitalists in African Development*, London: Lynne Rienner.

Berry, S. 1993, *No Condition is Permanent: The Social Dynamics of Agrarian Change in Sub-Saharan Africa*, Madison: University of Wisconsin.

Besteman, C. 1999, *Unraveling Somalia: Race, Violence and the Legacy of Slavery*, Philadelphia: University of Pennsylvania Press.

Bevan, P. 1993, 'Household Structures in Africa', mimeo, Oxford: CSAE.

2000a, 'Who's a Goody? Demythologising the PRA Agenda', *Journal of International Development*, 12 (5): 751–9.

2000b, 'The Successful Use of Consultancies in Aid-Financed Public Sector Management Reform: A Consultant's Eye View of Some Things Which Matter', *Public Administration and Development*, 20 (4): 289–304.

2001a, 'Illness, Prevention and Cure in Rural Ethiopia: The Macro-Micro Interface', Bath: CDS Working Paper.

2001b, 'Microeconomic Approaches to Growth and Poverty: A Sociological Comment', paper prepared for Sida Seminar on Economic Growth and Poverty Reduction, Stockholm: www.bath.ac.uk/~hsspgb.

2001c, 'Dynamics of African (In)security Regimes and Some Implications for Global Social Policy', SPDC Working Paper, mimeo, University of Bath.

Bevan, P. and Joireman, S. 1997, 'The Perils of Measuring Poverty: Identifying the Poor in Rural Ethiopia', *Oxford Development Studies*, 25 (3): 315–44.

Bevan, P. and Pankhurst, A. 1996, 'Ethiopian Village Studies', Addis Ababa and Oxford: Department of Social Anthropology and CSAE.

Bevan, P. and Sseweya, A. 1995, 'Understanding Poverty in Uganda: Adding a Sociological Dimension', Working Paper, Oxford: Centre for the Study of African Economies.

Birdsall, N. and Sabot, R. H. 1996, *Opportunity Foregone. Education in Brazil*, Washington: Inter-American Development Bank.

Booth, A. 1999, 'Initial Conditions and Miraculous Growth: Why Is Southeast Asia Different from Taiwan and South Korea?' in Jomo, K. S. (ed.) 2001.

Booth, D. 1985, 'Marxism and Development Sociology: Interpreting the Impasse', *World Development*, 13 (7): 761–87.

Booth, D. (ed.) 1994, *Rethinking Social Development*, Harlow: Longman.

Bose, Sugata and Jalal, Ayesha 1998, *Modern South Asia: History, Culture, and Political Economy*, New York: Routledge.

BRAC 1983, *The Net: Power Structure in Ten Villages*, Dhaka: BRAC Prokashana.

Bradshaw, Y. and Ndegwa, S. N. 2000, *The Uncertain Promise of Southern Africa*, Bloomington: Indiana University Press.

Bravo, J. 1992, 'Demographic Consequences of Structural Adjustment in Chile', in IUSSP, *The Demographic Consequences in Structural Adjustment in Latin America*, Liège: International Union for the Scientific Study of Population, Centro de Desenvolvimento e Planejamento Regional, pp. 1–22.

Brock-Utne, B. 2000, *Whose Education for All? The Recolonisation of the African Mind*, London: Falmer Press.

Brooks, S. and James, E. 1999, 'The Political Economy of Pension Reform', mimeo, Washington: World Bank.

Bryceson, D. F. (ed.) 1995, *Women Wielding the Hoe*, Oxford: Berg.

Bryceson, D. F. and Jamal, V. (eds.) 1997, *Farewell to Farms: De-agrarianisation and Employment in Africa*, Aldershot: Ashgate.

Buttel, F. H. and McMichael, P. 1994, 'Reconsidering the Explanandum and Scope of Development Studies: Toward a Comparative Sociology of State-Economy Relations' in Booth, D. (ed.) 1994.

Byrne, D. 1998, *Complexity Theory and the Social Sciences: An Introduction*, London: Routledge.

Callaghy, T. 1987, 'The State as Lame Leviathan: The Patrimonial Administrative State in Africa', in Ergas, Z. (ed.) *The African State in Transition*, New York: St Martin's Press.

Callaghy, T. and Ravenhill, J. (eds.) 1993, *Hemmed In: Responses to Africa's Economic Decline*, New York: Columbia University Press.

Cammack, P., Pool, D. and Tordoff, W. 1993, *Third World Politics: A Comparative Introduction*, Basingstoke: Macmillan.

Caplan, P. 1997, *African Voices, African Lives: Personal Narratives from a Swahili Village*, London: Routledge.

Carney, D. (ed.) 1998, *Sustainable Rural Livelihoods: What Contribution Can We Make?* London: Department for International Development.

Castells, M. 1996, *The Rise of the Network Society*, Oxford: Blackwell.

  1997, *The Power of Identity*, Oxford: Blackwell.

  1998, *End of Millennium*, Oxford: Blackwell.

Castles, F. 1998, *Comparative Public Policy: Patterns of Post-War Transformation*, Cheltenham: Edward Elgar.

Castles, F. and Mitchell, D. 1993, 'Worlds of Welfare and Families of Nations', in Castles, F. (ed.), *Families of Nations*, Dartmouth: Aldershot, pp. 93–128.

Castles, S. and Kosack, G. 1973, *Immigrant Workers and Class Structure in Western Europe*, Oxford: Oxford University Press.

CELADE 1996, 'Patrones reproductivos, estructura familiar y trabajo femenino en América Latina y el Caribe: resultado de investigaciones', Report LC/DEM/R.265, Santiago: Centro Latinoamericano de Demografía, CEPAL.

Chabal, P. 1992, *Power in Africa: An Essay in Political Interpretation*, Basingstoke: Macmillan.

Chabal, P. and Daloz, J.-P. 1999, *Africa Works: Disorder as Political Instrument*, Oxford: James Currey.

Chakravarty, S. P. and Hojman, D. E. 1999, 'Voting, Collective Action, and Liberalisation in Latin America: The Rise and Fall of the Hillinger Paradox', *Public Choice*, 101: 215–33.

Chambers, R. 1983, *Rural Development: Putting the Last First*, Harlow: Longman.

Chazan, N., Mortimer, R., Ravenhill, J. and Rothchild, D. 1992, *Politics and Society in Contemporary Africa*, Boulder: Lynne Rienner.

Cheyre, H. 1991, *La previsión en Chile ayer y hoy*, Santiago: Centro de Estudios Públicos.

Chowdhury, O. H. and Sen, B. 1998, *Public Expenditure and Social Development in Bangladesh*, Dhaka: CIRDAP.

CIEDESS 1994, *Modernización de la seguridad social en Chile. Resultados y tendencias*, Santiago: Corporación de Investigación, Estudio y Desarrollo de la Seguridad Social.

1998, *La administración de los seguros de salud en Latinoamérica*, Santiago: Corporación de Investigación, Estudio y Desarrollo de la Seguridad Social.

CLAISS 1999, *Síntesis de estudios de caso de microseguros y otras modalidades de protección de salud en América Latina y el Caribe*, Estudio RRMEX-PS/EST.4s, Mexico: Centro Latinoamericano de Investigaciones de Sistemas de Salud.

Clapham, C. 1996, *Africa and the International System: The Politics of State Survival*, Cambridge: Cambridge University Press.

1998, *African Guerillas*, Oxford: James Currey.

1999, 'Boundaries and States in the New African Order', in Bach, D. C. (ed.) 1999, pp. 53–66.

Clayton, A. 1999, *Frontiersmen: Warfare in Africa since 1950*, London: UCL Press.

Collard, D. A. 2000, 'Generational Transfers and the Generational Bargain', *Journal of International Development*, 12 (4): 453–62.

2001, 'The Generational Bargain', *International Journal of Social Welfare*, 10 (1): 54–65.

Collins, D. 1975, *The European Communities: The Social Policy of the First Phase*, vol I: *The European Coal and Steel Community, 1951–70*, London: Martin Robertson.

Comaroff, J. L. and Comaroff, J. 1999, *Civil Society and the Political Imagination in Africa*, London: University of Chicago Press.

Compa, L. 1999, 'Works in Progress: Constructing the Social Dimension of Trade in the Americas', paper presented to EU-US Seminar on the Social Dimension of Economic Integration, Washington, October 1999.

Conference on Promoting Women's Capabilities: Examining Nussbaum's Capabilities Approach, St Edmund's College, Cambridge, 9–12 September 2002.

Conway, T., de Haan, A. and Norton, A. (eds.) 2000, 'Social Protection: New Directions of Donor Agencies', DFID, Social Development Department, June.

Cooke, B. and Kothari, U. (eds.) 2001, *Participation: The New Tyranny?* London: Zed Books.

Coquery-Vidrovitch, C. 1997, *African Women: A Modern History*, Boulder: Westview Press.

Cox, D. and Jimenez, E. 1998, 'Risk Sharing and Private Transfers: What about Urban Households?', *Economic Development and Cultural Change*, 46 (3): 621–37.

Crone, Donald 1993, 'States, Elites and Social Welfare in Southeast Asia', *World Development*, 21 (1): 55–66.

Cross, N. 1992, *At the Desert's Edge: Oral Histories from the Sahel*, London: Panos/SOS Sahel.

Crouch, C., Finegold, D. and Sako, M. 1999, *Are Skills the Answer?*, Oxford: Oxford University Press.

Cummins, R. and Nistico, H. 2002, 'Maintaining Life Satisfaction: The Role of Positive Cognitive Bias', *Journal of Happiness Studies*, 3: 37–69.

Cutler, D. M., Knaul, F., Lozano, R., Méndez, O. and Zurita, B. 2000, 'Financial Crisis, Health Outcomes and Aging: Mexico in the 1980s and 1990s', Working Paper 7746, Cambridge, MA: National Bureau of Economic Research.

Dasgupta, B. 1998, *Structural Adjustment, Global Trade and the New Political Economy of Development*, London: Zed Books.

Davis, Mike 2001, *Late Victorian Holocausts: El Niño Famines and the Making of the Third World*, London: Verso.

Davis, P. 1997, 'The Concept of Social Exclusion as an Approach to Poverty in Bangladesh: New Problematic of Eurocentric Imposition?', M.Sc. Development Studies Dissertation, University of Bath.

2001, 'Rethinking the Welfare Regime Approach: The Case of Bangladesh', *Global Social Policy*, 1 (1): 79–107.

Davis, P. R. and McGregor, J. A. 2000, 'Civil Society, International Donors and Poverty in Bangladesh', *Commonwealth and Comparative Politics*, 38: 47–64.

De la Porte, C., Pochet, P. and Room, G. 2001, 'Social Benchmarking, Policy-Making and Governance in the EU', *Journal of European Social Policy*, 11 (4): 291–307.

De Waal, A. 1989, *Famine that Kills: Darfur, Sudan, 1984–1985*, Oxford: Clarendon Press.

1997, *Famine Crimes: Politics and the Disaster Relief Industry in Africa*, Oxford: James Currey.

Deacon, B. 1999, 'Globalisation, Social Policy and Social Development at the End of the 1990s', Presented to IDS Conference on Social Policy, October.

2001, 'The Social Dimension of Regionalism: A Constructive Alternative to Neo-Liberal Globalisation?', Globalism and Social Policy Programme occasional paper no. 8, Helsinki: STAKES.

Deacon, B., Hulse, M. and Stubbs, P. 1997, *Global Social Policy: International Organizations and the Future of Welfare*, London: Sage.

Deery, S. and Mitchell, R. 1993, 'Introduction', in Deery and Mitchell (eds.) *Labour Law and Industrial Relations in Asia*, Melbourne: Longman Cheshire Pty Ltd.

Devine, J. 1999, 'One Foot in Each Boat: The Macro Politics and Micro Sociology of NGOs in Bangladesh', Ph.D. thesis, Bath: University of Bath.

Deyo, Frederic 1992, 'The Political Economy of Social Policy Formation: East Asia's Newly Industrialized Countries', in Appelbaum, R. and

Henderson, J. (eds.) *States and Development in the Asian Pacific Rim*, London: Sage.

1997, 'Labour and Industrial Restructuring in Southeast Asia', in Rodan *et al.* (eds.) 1997.

DFID 2000, *Eliminating World Poverty: Making Globalisation Work for the Poor*, White Paper on International Development (Cm 5006), London: HMSO.

2001, 'Departmental Report 2001', London: The Stationery Office.

Dia, M. 1996, *Africa's Management in the 1990s and Beyond: Reconciling Indigenous and Transplanted Institutions*, Washington: World Bank.

Dicken, P. 1998, *Global Shift: Transforming the World Economy*, London: Chapman.

Downes, A. S., Mamingi, N. and Antoine, R.-M. B. 2000, 'Labour Market Regulation and Employment in the Caribbean', Research Networks Working Paper R-388, Washington: Inter-American Development Bank.

Doyal, Len and Gough, Ian 1991, *A Theory of Human Need*, Basingstoke and London: Macmillan.

Drèze, J. and Sen, A. 1995, *India: Economic Development and Social Opportunity*. Oxford: Oxford University Press.

Duffield, M. 1994, 'The Political Economy of Internal War: Asset Transfer, Complex Emergencies and International Aid', in Macrae, J. and Zwi, A. (eds.) 1994.

2001, *Global Governance and the New Wars: The Merging of Development and Security*, London: Zed Books.

Duryea, S. and Székely, M. 1998, 'Labour Markets in Latin America: A Supply Side Story', Working Paper WP374, Washington: Inter-American Development Bank.

ECLAC 1995, *Family and Future. A Regional Programme in Latin America and the Caribbean*, Santiago: Economic Commission for Latin America and the Caribbean.

1997a, *La brecha de la equidad. América Latina, el Caribe y la cumbre social*, Santiago: Economic Commission for Latin America and the Caribbean.

1997b, *The Equity Trap. Latin America and the Caribbean and the Social Summit*, Santiago: Economic Commission for Latin America and the Caribbean.

1998, *Social Panorama of Latin America 1997*, Santiago: Economic Commission for Latin America and the Caribbean.

2000, *La brecha de la equidad: una segunda evaluación*, Santiago: Economic Commission for Latin America and the Caribbean.

Economic Relations Division 1999, *Flow of External Resources into Bangladesh*, Dhaka: Ministry of Finance, Government of the People's Republic of Bangladesh, March.

Economist Intelligence Unit 1999, *Healthcare Global Outlook*, 2000 edition, edited by Haresnape, J., London: EIU.

Edwards, S. 1995, *Crisis and Reform in Latin America: From Despair to Hope*, New York: Oxford University Press.

Eisenstadt, S. N. and Roniger, L. 1984, *Patrons, Clients and Friends: Interpersonal Relations and the Structure of Trust in Society*, Cambridge: Cambridge University Press.

Ellis, S. (ed.) 1996, *Africa Now: People, Policies and Institutions*, London: James Currey.

Ellis, F. 2000, *Rural Livelihoods and Diversity in Developing Countries*, Oxford and New York: Oxford University Press.

Ellis, S. 1999, *The Mask of Anarchy*, London: Hurst & Co.

Elster, Jon 1979, *Ulysses and the Sirens: Studies in Rationality and Irrationality*, Cambridge: Cambridge University Press.

Ensminger, J. 1996, *Making a Market: The Institutional Transformation of an African Society*, Cambridge: Cambridge University Press.

Erskine, Angus 1998, 'The Approaches and Methods of Social Policy', in Alcock *et al.* (eds.) 1998.

Esping-Andersen, Gøsta 1990, *The Three Worlds of Welfare Capitalism*, Cambridge and Oxford: Polity Press.

(ed.) 1996, *Welfare States in Transition: National Adaptations in Global Economies*, London: Sage.

1997, 'Hybrid or Unique? The Japanese Welfare State between Europe and America', *Journal of European Social Policy* 7 (3): 179–89.

1999, *Social Foundations of Postindustrial Economies*, Oxford: Oxford University Press.

2000, 'Two Societies, One Sociology, and No Theory', *British Journal of Sociology* 51: 59–77.

Estevez-Abe, M., Iversen, T. and Soskice, D. 2001, 'Social Protection and the Formation of Skills', in Hall, P. and Soskice, D. (eds.), *Varieties of Capitalism*, Oxford: Oxford University Press.

European Commission 2001, 'The European Social Agenda and the EU's International Partners', report of an international conference, 20–1 November 2001, Brussels.

Evans, P. B., Jacobson, H. K. and Putnam, R. D. (eds.) 1993, *Double-Edged Diplomacy: International Bargaining and Domestic Politics*, Berkeley: University of California Press.

Eve, R. A., Horsfall, S. and Lee, M. E. (eds.) 1997, *Chaos, Complexity and Sociology: Myths, Models and Theories*, London: Sage.

Fanthorpe, R. 2001, 'Neither Citizen nor Subject? "Lumpen" Agency and the Legacy of Native Administration in Sierra Leone', *African Affairs*, 100 (400): 363–86.

Ferguson, J. 1990, *The Anti-Politics Machine: 'Development', Depoliticisation, and Bureaucratic Power in Lesotho*, Cambridge: Cambridge University Press.

1994, *The Antipolitics Machine: 'Development', Depoliticisation and Bureaucratic Power in Lesotho*, London: University of Minnesota Press.

1999, *Expectations of Modernity: Myths and Meanings of Urban Life on the Zambian Copperbelt*, London: University of California Press.

Ferrera, M., Hemerick, A. and Rhodes, M. 2000, 'The Future of the European Welfare States', report for the Portuguese Presidency of the European Union.

Folster, S. 1999, 'Social Insurance Based on Personal Savings', *Economic Record*, 75 (228): 5–18.

Foltz, W. J. 1995, 'Reconstructing the State of Chad', in Zartman, I. W. (ed.) 1995, pp. 15–31.

Francis, E. 2000, *Making a Living: Changing Livelihoods in Rural Africa*, London: Routledge.

Freeman, R. B. 1993, 'Labor Market Institutions and Policies: Help or Hindrance to Economic Development', *World Bank Economic Review*, 7 (3): 117–44.

Freund, B. 1998, *The Making of Contemporary Africa: The Development of African Society since 1800*, Basingstoke: Macmillan.

Fukuyama, F. 1995, *Trust: The Social Virtues and the Creation of Prosperity*, London: Penguin.

Gajardo, M. 1999, 'Reformas educativas en América Latina. Balance de una década', Working Paper 15, Santiago: PREAL.

Garrett, Geoffrey 1998, *Partisan Politics in the Global Economy*, Cambridge: Cambridge University Press.

Ghazali, Aidit bin 1991, 'Zakat Administration in Malaysia', in Ariff, M. (ed.) *The Islamic Voluntary Sector in Southeast Asia*, Singapore: Institute of Southeast Asian Studies.

Ghilarducci, T. and Ledesma, P. L. 2000, 'Union's Role in Argentine and Chilean Pension Reform', *World Development*, 28 (4): 753–62.

Giddens, Anthony, 1971, *Capitalism and Modern Social Theory*, Cambridge: Cambridge University Press.

1984, *The Constitution of Society*, Cambridge: Polity Press.

Godement, François 2000, 'Models and Politics for Asian Social Policies', World Bank, May.

Goldin, C. 1994, 'The U-Shaped Labour Force Function in Economic Development and Economic History', Working Paper 4707, Washington DC: National Bureau of Economic Research.

Goldthorpe, J. H. 1984, *Order and Conflict in Contemporary Capitalism*, Oxford: Oxford University Press.

Goldthorpe, J. H. and Bevan, P. 1977, 'The Study of Social Stratification in Great Britain: 1946–76', *Social Science Information*, 16 (3/4): 270–334.

Goodin, R. E., Heady, B., Muffels, R. and Dirven, H. 1999, *The Real Worlds of Welfare Capitalism*, Cambridge: Cambridge University Press.

Goodman, R. and Peng, I. 1996, 'The East Asian Welfare States: Peripatetic Learning, Adaptive Change and Nation-Building', in Esping-Andersen, Gøsta (ed.) *Welfare States in Transition: National Adaptations in Global Economies*, London: Sage, pp. 192–224.

Goodman, R., White, G. and Kwon, H. (eds.) 1998, *The East Asian Welfare Model: Welfare Orientalism and the State*, London: Routledge.

Gore, Charles 2000, 'The Rise and Fall of the Washington Consensus', *World Development*, 28 (5): 789–804.

Gough, Ian 1979, *The Political Economy of the Welfare State*, London: Macmillan.

1999, 'Welfare Regimes: On Adapting the Framework to Developing Countries', *Discourse: A Journal of Policy Studies* (Dhaka: PROSHIKA), 3 (1): 1–18.

2000a, *Global Capital, Human Needs and Social Policies*, Basingstoke: Palgrave Macmillan.

2000b, 'Welfare Regimes in East Asia and Europe', SPDC Working Paper, University of Bath (presented to Annual World Bank Conference on Development Economics, Europe 2000 (Paris, June)), mimeo.

2001a, 'Globalization and Regional Welfare Regimes: the East Asian Case', *Global Social Policy*, 1 (2): 163–189.

2001b, 'Social Assistance Regimes: A Cluster Analysis', *Journal of European Social Policy*, 11 (2): 165–70.

2003a, 'Lists and Thresholds: Comparing our Theory of Human Need with Nussbaum's Capabilities Approach', WeD Working Paper 1, University of Bath.

2003b, 'Securing Social Protection in Indonesia', ILO InFocus Programme on Socio-Economic Security.

2003c, 'Welfare Regimes in East Asia', in Marshall, K. and Butzbach, O. (eds.) *New Social Policy Agendas for Europe and East Asia*, Washington: World Bank, pp. 499–512.

2003d (forthcoming), 'Social Policy Regimes in the Developing World', in *Handbook on Social Policy*, Aldershot: Edward Elgar.

Gough, Ian and Farnsworth, Kevin 2000, 'The Enhanced Structural Power of Capital: A Review and Assessment', in Gough, Ian 2000a, pp. 77–102.

Gough, Ian and Kim, Jin-wook 2000, 'Tracking the Welfare Mix in Korea', University of Bath, unpublished paper.

Gough, Ian and Olafsson, Gunnar (eds.) 1999, *Capitalism and Social Cohesion: Essays on Exclusion and Integration*, Basingstoke: Macmillan.

Gough, Ian and Thomas, Theo 1994, 'Why Do Levels of Human Welfare Vary Across Nations?' *International Journal of Health Services*, 24 (2): 715–48.

Gough, Ian and Wood, Geof 2000, 'Regimes, Mixes and Ground Realities: A Synthesis Paper', SPDC Working Paper presented to Social Policy in S. Asia Conference, Dhaka, Bangladesh, March.

Gouveia, M. 1997, 'Majority Rule and the Public Provision of a Private Good', *Public Choice*, 93: 221–44.

Gramsci, A. 1976, *Selections from the Prison Notebooks*, edited by Hoare, Q. and Smith, G. N., London: Lawrence and Wishart.

Granovetter, M. 1985, 'Economic Action and Social Structure: The Problem of Embeddedness', *American Journal of Sociology*, 91 (3): 481–510.

Gray-Molina, G. 1999, 'La economía política de reformas institucionales en Bolivia', Working Paper R-350, Washington: Inter-American Development Bank.

Green, D. 1999, *Gender Violence in Africa: African Women's Responses*, Basingstoke: Macmillan.

Grindle, M. 2001, 'Despite the Odds: The Political Economy of Social Sector Reform in Latin America', Faculty Research Working Paper RWP01–021, Washington: J. F. Kennedy School of Government.

Haggard, Stephan 2000, *The Political Economy of the Asian Financial Crisis*, Washington: Institute for International Economics.

Hailey, Lord, 1957, *An African Survey: Revised 1956*, London: Oxford University Press.

Harbeson, J. and Rothchild, D. (eds.) 1991, *Africa in World Politics*, Oxford: Westview Press.

Harriss, J. 2000, 'The Second "Great Transformation"? Capitalism at the End of the Twentieth Century', in Allen, T. and Thomas, A. (eds.) *Poverty and*

Development into the 21st Century, Oxford: Oxford University Press, pp. 325–42.

2002, *Depoliticizing Development: The World Bank and Social Capital*, London: Anthem.

Hartmann, Betsy and Boyce, James K. 1983, *A Quiet Violence: View from a Bangladesh Village*, London: Zed.

Hashemi, S. and Hassan, M. 1999, 'Building NGO Legitmacy in Bangladesh: The Contested Domain', in Lewis, D. (ed.) *International Perspectives on Voluntary Action Reshaping the Third Sector*, London: Earthscan, pp. 124–31.

Haugerud, A. 1995, *The Culture of Politics in Modern Kenya*, Cambridge: Cambridge University Press.

Hawes, G. and Liu, H. 1993, 'Explaining the Dynamics of Southeast Asian Political Economies', *World Politics* 45.

Heidenheimer, Arnold J. 1981, 'Education and Social Security Entitlements in Europe and America', in Flora, Peter and Heidenheimer, A. J. (eds.) *The Development of Welfare States in Europe and America*, New Brunswick and London: Transaction, pp. 269–306.

Herbst, J. 2000, *States and Power in Africa: Comparative Lessons in Authority and Control*, Princeton: Princeton University Press.

Higgott, Richard 2000, 'The International Relations of the Asian Economic Crisis: A Study in the Politics of Resentment', in Richard Robison *et al.* (eds.) 2000.

Hirschman, A. O. 1970, *Exit, Voice and Loyalty*, Cambridge, MA: Harvard University Press.

Holliday, Ian 2000, 'Productivist Welfare Capitalism: Social Policy in East Asia', *Political Studies*, 48 (4): 706–23.

Hope, K. R. (Sr) 2000, *Corruption and Development in Africa: Lessons from Country Case-Studies*, Basingstoke: Macmillan.

Huber, E. 1996, 'Options for Social Policy in Latin America: Neoliberal versus Social Democratic Models', in Esping-Andersen, G. (ed.), *Welfare States in Transition. National Adaptations in Global Economies*, London: Sage, pp. 141–91.

Hyden, G. 1980, *Beyond Ujamaa in Tanzania: Underdevelopment and an Uncaptured Peasantry*, London: Heinemann.

Hyden, G. and Bratton, M. (eds.) 1992, *Governance and Politics in Africa*, London: Lynne Rienner.

IADB 1996, *Economic and Social Progress Report 1996*, Washington: Inter-American Development Bank.

1998, *Economic and Social Progress in Latin America 1998–1999 Report: Facing up to Inequality in Latin America*, Washington: Inter-American Development Bank.

Ignatieff, Michael 1998, *Isaiah Berlin: A Life*, London: Vintage.

Iliffe, J. 1987, *The African Poor: A History*, Cambridge: Cambridge University Press.

ILO 1995, *World Employment*, Geneva: International Labour Office.

1999a, *Key Indicators of the Labour Market*, Geneva: International Labour Office.

1999b, 'Panorama Laboral 1999', *Informa 6*, Lima: International Labour Office.

2000a, *World Labour Report 2000*, Geneva: International Labour Office.

2000b, 'Migrant Worker Remittances, Micro-Finance and the Informal Economy: Prospects and Issues', Social Finance Unit Working Paper 21, International Labour Office: www.ilo.org/public/english/employment/ent/papers/wpap21.htm.

IMF 2002, *World Economic Outlook*: www.imf.org/external/pubs/ft/weo/2002/02/

Indra, D. M. and Buchignani, N. 1997, 'Rural Landlessness, Extended Entitlements and Inter-Household Relations in South Asia: A Bangladesh Case', *Journal of Peasant Studies* 24: 25–64.

Ippolito, R. A. 1997, *Pension Plans and Employee Performance. Evidence, Analysis and Policy*, Chicago and London: University of Chicago Press.

Irawan, P., Rahman, E., Romdiati, H. and Suhaimi, U. 2001, 'Social Safety Nets Analysis and Recommendations: Prospects in Indonesia', paper presented at Regional Seminar on Strengthening Safety Nets, Bangkok, May.

ISSA 1995, 'Social Security in the Caribbean', *International Social Security Review*, 48 (2/95): 73–116.

1996, 'Social Security in the Caribbean (2)', *International Social Security Review*, 49 (1/96): 73–88.

Jackson, R. H. and Rosberg, C. G. 1989, *Why Africa's Weak States Persist*, Basingstoke: Macmillan.

Jacobs, Didier 1998, 'Social Welfare Systems in East Asia', CASE Paper no. 10, London: Centre for the Analysis of Social Exclusion, London School of Economics.

Janoski, T. and Hicks, A. M. 1994, *The Comparative Political Economy of the Welfare State*, Cambridge: Cambridge University Press.

Jesmin, S. and Salway, S. 2000, 'Marriage among the Urban Poor of Dhaka: Instability and Uncertainty', *Journal of International Development*, 12 (5): 689–705.

Johnson, Chalmers 1982, *MITI and the Japanese Miracle: The Growth of Industrial Policy 1925–1975*, Stanford: Stanford University Press.

Jomo, K. S. (ed.) 2001, *Southeast Asia's Industrialization: Industrial Policy, Capabilities and Sustainability*, Basingstoke: Palgrave.

Jones, Catherine 1990, 'Hong Kong, Singapore, South Korea and Taiwan: Oikonomic Welfare States', *Government and Opposition*, 25: 446–62.

1993, 'The Pacific Challenge: Confucian Welfare States', in Jones, C. (ed.) *New Perspectives on the Welfare State in Europe*, London: Routledge.

Jones, Margaret 2002, 'Infant and Maternal Health Services in Ceylon, 1900–1948: Imperialism or Welfare?', *Social History of Medicine*, 15 (2): 263–89.

(forthcoming 2003), *Health Policy in Britain's Model Colony: Ceylon 1900–1948*, Hyderabad: Orient Longman.

Jorgensen, S. and Holzmann, R. 2000, 'Emerging Directions for a Social Protection Sector Strategy: From Safety Net to Spring Board', chapter 2 in Conway, T. *et al.* (eds.) 2000.

Joseph, R. (ed.) 1999, *State, Conflict and Democracy in Africa*, Boulder: Lynne Rienner.

Jost, T. S. 1999, 'Managed Care Regulation: Can We Learn from Others? The Chilean Experience', *University of Michigan Journal of Law Reform*, 32 (4): 863–98.

Journal of International Development 2000, 'The Inter-Generational Bargain: Special Conference Issues', *Journal of International Development* 12 (4) May (See papers by Collard; McGregor, Copestake and Wood; and Kabeer).

Kanbur, R. 2001, 'Economic Policy, Distribution and Poverty: The Nature of Disagreements', *World Development*, 29 (6): 1083–94.

Karlstrom, M. 1999, 'Civil Society and its Presuppositions: Lessons from Uganda', in J. L. Comaroff and J. Comaroff, *Civil Society and the Political Imagination in Africa: Critical Perspectives*, London: University of Chicago Press.

Kasza, Gregory 2002, 'The Illusion of Welfare "Regimes"', *Journal of Social Policy*, 31 (2): 271–87.

Kay, S. J. 1999, 'Unexpected Privatizations. Politics and Social Security Reform in the Southern Cone', *Comparative Politics*, 31 (4): 403–22.

Kearney, M. 1996, *Reconceptualising the Peasantry*, Boulder: Westview.

Keen, D. 1994a, 'The Functions of Famine in Southwestern Sudan: Implications for Relief', in Macrae, J. and Zwi, A. (eds.) 1994.

1994b, *The Benefits of Famine: A Political Economy of Famine and Relief in Southwestern Sudan, 1983–1989*, Princeton: Princeton University Press.

Khadiagala, G. M. 1995, 'State Collapse and Reconstruction in Uganda', in Zartman, I. W. (ed.) 1995.

Khan, M. 1998, 'The Role of Civil Society and Patron–Client Networks in the Analysis of Corruption', in *Corruption and Integrity Improvement Initiatives in Developing Countries*, New York: UNDP/OECD Development Center.

Khan, M. I. A. 2000, 'Struggle for Survival: Networks and Relationships in a Bangladesh Slum', Ph.D. thesis, University of Bath.

King, K. 1996, *Jua Kali Kenya: Change and Development in the Informal Economy 1970–1995*, London: James Currey.

King, K. and McGrath, S. (ed.) 1999, *Enterprise in Africa: Between Poverty and Growth*, London: Intermediate Technology Publications.

Kleinman, A., Das, V. and Lock, M. (eds.) 1997, *Social Suffering*, London: University of California Press.

Kochar, A. 1999, 'Evaluating Family Support for the Elderly: The Intrahousehold Allocation of Medical Expenditures in Rural Pakistan', *Economic Development and Cultural Change*, 47 (3): 621–56.

Kramsjo, B. and Wood, G. D. 1992, *Breaking the Chains*, London: IT Publications.

Krasner, Stephen D. (ed.) 1983, *International Regimes*, Ithaca: Cornell University Press.

Kumagai, Fumie 1986, 'Modernisation and the Family in Japan', *Journal of Family History*, 11 (4): 371–82.

Kwon, Huck-ju 1998, 'Democracy and the Politics of Social Welfare: A Comparative Analysis of Welfare Systems in East Asia', in Goodman, R. *et al.* (eds.) 1998.

Labrousse, A. 1999, 'The Production and Distribution of Illicit Drugs', in Bach, D. C. (ed.) *Regionalisation in Africa: Integration and Disintegration*, Oxford: James Currey.

Lan, D. 1985, *Guns and Rain: Guerrillas and Spirit Mediums in Zimbabwe*, London: James Currey.

Lancaster, C. 1999, *Aid to Africa: So Much to Do, So Little Done*, London: University of Chicago Press.

Lanjouw, P. and Ravallion, M. 1995, 'Poverty and Household Size', *Economic Journal*, 105 (433): 1415–34.

Leach, M. and Mearns, R. 1996, *The Lie of the Land: Challenging Received Wisdom on the African Environment*, Oxford: James Currey.

Lee, H. K. 1999, 'Globalization and the Emerging Welfare State: The Experience of South Korea', *International Journal of Social Welfare*, 8 (1): 23–39.

Leibfried, S. 1993, 'Towards a European Welfare State?', in Jones, C. (ed.), *New Perspectives on the Welfare State in Europe*, London: Routledge, pp. 133–56.

    1994, 'The Social Dimension of the European Union: En Route to Positively Joint Sovereignty?', *Journal of European Social Policy*, 4 (4): 239–62.

    1996, 'Social Policy', in Wallace, H. and Wallace, W. (eds.), *Policy-Making in the European Union*, Oxford: Oxford University Press.

Leibfried, S. and Pierson, P. 1995, *European Social Policy*, Washington: Brookings.

Lewis, D., Glaser, M., McGregor, J. A., White, S. and Wood, G. 1992, 'Going it Alone: Female Headed Households in Bangladesh', CDS Occasional Paper, University of Bath.

Lewis, J. 2000, *Empire State-Building: War and Welfare in Kenya 1925–1952*, Oxford: James Currey.

Leys, C. 1996, *The Rise and Fall of Development Theory*, London: James Currey.

Lipton, M. 1968, 'Theory of the Optimising Peasant', *Journal of Development Studies*, April.

Ljungqvist, L. 1995, 'Wage Structure as Implicit Insurance on Human Capital in Developed versus Underdeveloped Countries', *Journal of Development Economics*, 46: 35–50.

Lloyd-Sherlock, P. (ed.) 2000, *Healthcare Reform and Poverty in Latin America*, London: ILAS.

Lo Vuolo, R. M. 1997, 'The Retrenchment of the Welfare State in Latin America: The Case of Argentina', *Social Policy and Administration*, 31 (4): 390–409.

Londoño, J. L. and Frenk, J. 1997, 'Structured Pluralism: Towards an Innovative Model for Health System Reform in Latin America', *Health Policy*, 41: 1–36.

Long, N. and van der Ploeg, J. D. 1994, 'Heterogeneity, Actor and Structure: Towards a Reconstitution of the Concept of Structure', in Booth, D. (ed.) 1994, pp. 62–89.

Lora, E. and Pages, C. 1996, 'La legislación laboral en el proceso de reformas estructurales de América Latina', mimeo, Washington: IADB.

Loughhead, S., Mittal, O. and Wood, G. 2000, 'Urban Poverty and Vulnerability in India: DfID's Experiences from a Social Policy Perspective', DFID, mimeo, September.

Louis, W. Roger 1999, 'Foreword', in Brown, J. and Louis, W. R. (eds.) *Oxford History of the British Empire: The Twentieth Century*, Oxford: Oxford University Press.

Luna, Emmanuel 2000, *NGO Natural Disaster Mitigation and Preparedness: The Philippines Case Study*, Research report for DFID.

Lund, F. 2001, 'South Africa: Transition Under Pressure', in Alcock, P. and Craig, G. (eds.) *International Social Policy*, Basingstoke: Palgrave.

Lustig, N. and Deutsch, R. 1998, 'The Inter-American Development Bank and Poverty Reduction: An Overview', Mimeo POV-101-R, Washington: IADB.

McAdam, D., Tarrow, S. and Tilly, C. 2001, *Dynamics of Contention*, Cambridge: Cambridge University Press.

MacGaffey, J. *et al.* 1991, *The Real Economy of Zaire: The Contribution of Smuggling and Other Unofficial Activities to National Wealth*, London: James Currey.

MacGaffey, J. and Bazenguissa-Ganga, R. 2000, *Congo–Paris: Transnational Traders on the Margins of the Law*, Oxford: James Currey.

McGregor, Allister 1989, 'Towards a Better Understanding of Credit in Rural Development. The Case of Bangladesh: The Patron State', *Journal of International Development*, 1 (4): 467–86.

Macintyre, A. (ed.) 1994, *Business and Government in Industrialising Asia*, Ithaca: Cornell University Press.

Macrae, J. and Zwi, A. (eds.) 1994, *War and Hunger: Rethinking Responses to Complex Emergencies*, London: Zed Books.

Madeley, J. 2001, 'Trade – What Kind of Organisation?', *Developments*, 15: 12.

Mair, Lucy 1944, *Welfare in the British Colonies*, London: Royal Institute of International Affairs.

Malkki, L. H. 1995, *Purity and Exile: Violence, Memory, and National Cosmology among Hutu Refugees in Tanzania*, London: University of Chicago Press.

Mamdani, M. 1996, *Citizen and Subject: Contemporary Africa and the Legacy of Late Colonialism*, Kampala, Princeton, London, Cape Town: Fountain Publishers, Princeton University Press, James Currey, David Philip Publishers.

Manderson, Lenore 1987, 'Health Services and the Legitimisation of the Colonial State: British Malaya 1786–1941', *International Journal of Health Services*, 17: 91–112.

Manning, P. 1998, *Francophone Sub-Saharan Africa: 1880–1995*, Cambridge: Cambridge University Press.

Manor, J. (ed.) 1991, *Rethinking Third World Politics*, London: Longman.

Manuelyan Atinc, Tamar 2000, 'Coping with Crises: Social Policy and the Poor', paper presented to World Bank seminar 'Lessons towards the new social policy agenda in East Asia', Paris, 27 June.

Manuelyan Atinc, Tamar and Walton, Michael 1998, *Social Consequences of the East Asian Financial Crisis*, World Bank.

Marchand, M. H. 2001, 'North American Regionalisms and Regionalization', in Schulz, M. *et al.* (eds.) 2001.

Márquez, G. 1998, 'El desempleo en America Latina y el Caribe a mediados de los años 90', Working Paper 377, Washington: Inter-American Development Bank.

Márquez, G. and Pagés, C. 1998, 'Ties that Bind: Employment Protection and Labour Market Outcomes in Latin America', Working Paper WP 373, Washington: IADB.

Marshall, A. 1996, 'Weakening Employment Protection in Latin America: Incentive to Employment Creation or to Increasing Stability?', *International Contributions to Labour Studies*, 6: 29–48.

Marshall, G. 1998, *The Oxford Dictionary of Sociology*, 2nd edn, Oxford: Oxford University Press.

Marshall, T. H. 1950, *Citizenship and Social Class and Other Essays*, Cambridge: Cambridge University Press.

1981, *The Right to Welfare and Other Essays*, London: Heinemann.

May, R. J. 2002, 'Governance and Social Safety Nets in the Philippines', in OECD 2002.

Mbembe, A. 1992, 'Provisional Notes on the Postcolony', *Africa*, 62 (1): 3–37.

Medard, J.-F. (ed.) 1992, *Etats d'Afrique Noire: formations, mécanismes et crises*, Paris: Karthala.

Mehrotra, Santosh 2002, 'The Capabilities and Human Rights of Women: Towards an Alternative Framework for Development', Conference on Promoting Women's Capabilities, St Edmund's College, Cambridge, 9–12 September 2002.

Mesa-Lago, C. 1989, *Ascent to Bankruptcy: Financing Social Security in Latin America*, Pittsburgh: University of Pittsburgh Press.

1991, 'Social Security in Latin America and the Caribbean: A Comparative Assessment', in Ahmad, E., Dreze, J., Hills, J. and Sen, A. (eds.), *Social Security in Developing Countries*, Oxford: Clarendon Press, pp. 357–94.

1994, *Changing Social Security in Latin America: Toward Alleviating the Social Costs of Economic Reform*, Boulder: Lynne Rienner.

1999, 'Política y reforma de la seguridad social en América Latina', *Nueva Sociedad*, 160: 133–50.

Mesa-Lago, C. and Bertranou, F. 1998, *Manual de economía de la seguridad social*, Montevideo: Centro Latinoamericano de Economía Humana.

Mesa-Lago, C., Cruz-Saco, M. A. and Zamalloa, L. 1993, 'Determinants of Social Insurance/Security Costs and Coverage: An International Comparison with a Focus on Latin America', in Abel, C. and Lewis, C. M. (eds.), *Welfare, Poverty and Development in Latin America*, London: Macmillan, pp. 49–74.

Meyer, Birgit and Geshiere, Peter (eds.) 1999, *Globalisation and Identity: Dialectics of Flow and Closure*, Oxford: Blackwell.

Mikell, G. (ed.) 1997, *African Feminism: The Politics of Survival in Sub-Saharan Africa*, Philadelphia: University of Pennsylvania Press.

Mingat, Alan 1998, 'The Strategy Used by High-Performing Asian Economies in Education', *World Development*, 26 (4): 695–715.

Mishra, R. 1999, *Globalisation and the Welfare State*, Cheltenham: Edward Elgar.

Mommsen, W. (ed.) 1981, *The Emergence of the Welfare State in Britain and Germany*, London: Croom Helm.

Moore, H. and Vaughan, M. 1994, *Cutting Down Trees: Gender, Nutrition, and Agricultural Change in the Northern Province of Zambia, 1890–1990*, London: James Currey.

Moore, M. 1999, 'States, Social Policies and Globalisation: Arguing on the Right Terrain?', paper presented to IDS/DFID conference, Brighton, October.

Moran, Michael 1999, *Governing the Health Care State: A Comparative Study of the United Kingdom, the United States and Germany*, Manchester: Manchester University Press.

Moser, C. 1998, 'The Asset Vulnerabilty Framework: Reassessing Urban Poverty Reduction Strategies', *World Development*, 26 (1): 1–19.

Mostajo, R. 2000, 'Gasto social y distribución del ingreso: caracterización e impact redistributivo en países seleccionados de América Latina y el Caribe', Working Paper LC/L 1376, Santiago: CEPAL.

Muller, K. 2001, 'La reforma de pensiones en Bolivia: una aproximaciòn', mimeo, Frankfurt: European University Viadrina.

Murdoch, J. 1998, 'Between the State and the Market: Can Informal Insurance Patch the Safety Net?', *World Bank Research Observer*, 14 (2): 187–207.

Musah, A.-F. and Fayemi, J.'K. 2000, *Mercenaries: An African Security Dilemma*, London: Pluto Press.

Myrdal, A. 1944, *Nations and Family: The Swedish Experiment in Democratic Family and Population Policy*, London: Kegan Paul, Trench, Trubner and Co.

Neher, Clark and Marley, Ross 1995, *Democracy and Development in Southeast Asia*, Oxford: Westview Press.

NHA 1998, *Bangladesh National Health Accounts*, Dhaka: Data International, Ministry of Health and Family Welfare.

Nisbet, R. 1970, *The Sociological Tradition*, London: Heinemann.

Nordstrom, C. 2001, 'Out of the Shadows', in Callaghy, T., Kassimir, R. and Latham, R. (eds.) *Authority and Intervention in Africa*, Cambridge: Cambridge University Press.

North, Douglass 1990, *Institutions, Institutional Change and Economic Performance*, Cambridge: Cambridge University Press.

Nussbaum, M. 2000, *Women and Human Development: The Capabilities Approach*, Cambridge: Cambridge University Press.

Oberndorfer, Dieter and Berndt, Uwe 2000, 'The 1997–99 East Asian Crisis: Implications for Policies Affecting Migrants', paper presented to ASEM-World Bank Workshop, October.

O'Brien, R., Goetz, A. M., Scholte, J. A. and Williams, M. 2000, *Contesting Global Governance*, Cambridge: Cambridge University Press.

O'Connor, Julia, Orloff, Ann Shola and Shaver, Sheila 1999, *States, Markets, Families: Gender, Liberalism and Social Policy in Australia, Canada, Great Britain and the United States*, Cambridge: Cambridge University Press.

OECD 2001, *Social Expenditure Database 1980–1998*, 2nd edn, Paris: OECD.

    2002, *Towards Asia's Sustainable Development: The Role of Social Protection*, Paris: OECD.

Öjendal, J. 2001, 'South East Asia at the Constant Crossroads', in Schulz, M. *et al.* (eds.), 2001.

Opel, A. E. O. 2000, 'The Social Context of Labour Markets in Dhaka Slums', *Journal of International Development*, 12 (5): 735–50.

PAHO 2000, *Health Expenditures for Latin America and the Caribbean*, Public Policy and Health Program, Division of Health and Human Development.

Parkin, F. 1979, *Marxism and Class Theory: A Bourgeois Critique*, London: Tavistock.

Peng, Ito 2000, 'A Fresh Look at the Japanese Welfare State', *Social Policy and Administration*, 34 (1): 87–114.

    2002, 'Social Care in Crisis: Gender, Demography and Welfare State Restructuring in Japan', *Social Politics*, 9 (3): 411–43.

Peters, D. H., Kandola, K., Elmendorf, A. E. and Chellaraj, G. 1999, 'Health Expenditures, Services and Outcomes in Africa: Basic Data and Cross-National

Comparisons 1990–1996', Washington: World Bank Health, Nutrition and Population Publication Series.

Phananiramai, Mathana and Hewison, Kevin 2002, 'Governance and Social Policy in Thailand', in OECD 2002.

Pierson, P. 1998, *The New Politics of the Welfare State*, Oxford: Oxford University Press.

  2000, 'Increasing Returns, Path Dependence, and the Study of Politics', *American Political Science Review*, 94: 251–67.

Pincus, Jonathan and Ramli, Rizal 1998, 'Indonesia: From Showcase to Basket Case', *Cambridge Journal of Economics*, 22: 723–34.

Piñera, J. 1991, *El cascabel al gato: La batalla por la reforma previsional*, Santiago: Zig-Zag.

Pitruzzello, S. 1999, 'Decommodification and the Worlds of Welfare Capitalism. A Cluster Analysis', mimeo, Florence: European University Institute.

Planning Commission 1998, *Fifth Five-Year Plan 1997–2002*, Dhaka: Ministry of Planning, Government of the People's Republic of Bangladesh, March.

Platteau, J. 1991, 'The Free Market is not Readily Transferable: Reflections on the Links between Market, Social Relations and Moral Norms', paper presented at the twenty-fifth Jubilee of IDS, Sussex University.

Polanyi, K. 1944, *The Great Transformation*, New York: Rinehart; republished 1957, Boston: Beacon Press.

Porter, D. 1991, *Development in Practice: Paved with Good Intentions*, London: Routledge.

Prunier, G. 1995, *The Rwanda Crisis: The History of a Genocide*, London: Hurst and Co.

Psacharopoulos, G. and Patrinos, H. A. 1994, *Indigenous People and Poverty in Latin America*, Washington: World Bank.

Puryear, J. 1997, 'La educación en América Latina: problemas y desafíos', Working Paper 7, Santiago: PREAL.

Putnam, R. 1993, *Making Democracy Work: Civic Traditions in Modern Italy*, Princeton: Princeton University Press.

Queisser, M. 1995, 'Chile and Beyond: The Second Generation Pension Reform in Latin America', *International Social Security Review*, 48 (3): 23–39.

  1998, 'The Second-Generation Pension Reforms in Latin America', Working Paper AWP 5.4, Paris: OECD.

Ramesh, Mishra, with Asher, Mukul 2000, *Welfare Capitalism in Southeast Asia*, Basingstoke: Macmillan.

Ravillion, M. and Sen, B. 1996, 'When Method Matters: Toward a Resolution of the Debate about Bangladesh's Poverty Measures', *Economic Development and Cultural Change*, 44: 761–92.

Reno, W. 1995, *Corruption and State Politics in Sierra Leone*, Cambridge: Cambridge University Press.

  1998, *Warlord Politics and the African States*, London: Lynne Rienner.

Richards, P. 1996, *Fighting for the Rain Forest: War, Youth and Resources in Sierra Leone*, Oxford: James Currey.

Rieger, E. and Leibfried, S. 1998, 'Welfare State Limits to Globalisation', *Politics and Society*, 26 (4): 363–90.

2003, *Limits to Globalization: Welfare States and the World Economy*, Cambridge: Polity Press.

Rigg, Jonathan 1997, *Southeast Asia: The Human Landscape of Modernization and Development*, London: Routledge.

Rimlinger, G. 1971, *Welfare Policy and Industrialisation in Europe, America and Russia*, New York: John Wiley.

Robbins, D. 1994, 'Relative Wage Structure in Chile, 1957–1992: Changes in the Structure of Demand for Schooling', *Estudios de Economía*, 21: 49–78, special issue on Labor Economics in Developing Countries.

Roberts, B. 1978, *Cities of Peasants*, London: Edward Arnold (reprinted subsequently).

Robison, R., Beeson, M., Jayasuriya, K. and Kim, H. (eds.) 2000, *Politics and Markets in the Wake of the Asian Crisis*, London and New York: Routledge.

Rodan, G. 1997, 'The Prospects for Civil Society in Southeast Asia', Eastern Asia Policy Papers 18, University of Toronto.

Rodan, G., Hewison, K. and Robison R. (eds.) 1997, *Political Economy of Southeast Asia: An Introduction*, Oxford: Oxford University Press.

Rodrik, Dani 1998, 'Why Do More Open Economies Have Bigger Governments?' *Journal of Political Economy*, 106 (5): 997–1032.

Roemer, Milton 1991, *National Health Systems of the World*, vol. I: *The Countries*. Oxford: Oxford University Press.

Roitman, J. 2001, 'The Frontiers of Wealth Creation and Regulatory Authority in the Chad Basin', in Callaghy, T., Kassimir, R. and Latham, R. (eds.) *Authority and Intervention in Africa*, Cambridge: Cambridge University Press.

Room, G. 1999, 'Social Exclusion', mimeo, Bath: SPDC.

2000a, 'Commodification and Decommodification: A Developmental Critique', *Policy and Politics*, 28 (3): 331–51.

2000b, 'Trajectories of Social Exclusion: The Wider Context', in Gordon, David and Townsend, Peter (eds.), *Breadline Europe: The Measurement of Poverty*, Bristol: Policy Press.

2000c, 'Globalisation, Social Policy and International Standard-Setting: The Case of Higher Education Credentials', *International Journal of Social Welfare*, 9 (2): 103–19.

2001, 'Response to Deacon – Stage 2', SPDC Working Paper, University of Bath, mimeo.

2002, 'Education and Welfare: Recalibrating the European Debate', *Policy Studies*, 23 (1): 37–50.

Rothchild, D. 1995, 'Rawlings and the Engineering of Legitimacy in Ghana', in Zartman, I. W. (ed.) *Collapsed States: The Disintegration and Restoration of Legitimate Authority*, Boulder: Lynne Rienner.

Rothchild, D. and Chazan, N. (eds.) 1988, *The Precarious Balance: State and Society in Africa*, London: Westview Press.

Sadoulet, E., de Janvry, A. and Benjamin, C. 1998, 'Household Behavior with Imperfect Labor Markets', *Industrial Relations*, 37 (1): 85–108.

Sandbrook, R. 1985, *The Politics of Africa's Economic Stagnation*, Cambridge: Cambridge University Press.

Sayer, A. 2000, *Realism and Social Science*, London: Sage.

Sbragia, A. M. 1992, *Euro-Politics*, Washington: The Brookings Institution.

Schaffer, B. B. and Lamb, G. 1981, *Can Equity be Organised?* Farnborough: Gower.

Schirm, S. A. 2002, *Globalization and the New Regionalism*, Oxford: Polity.

Schlemmer, B. 2000, *The Exploited Child*, London: Zed Books.

Schraeder, P. 2000, *African Politics and Society: A Mosaic in Transformation*, Boston: Bedford/St Martin's Press.

Schulthess, W. and Demarco, G. 1993, *Argentina: Evolución del sistema nacional de previsión social y propuesta de reforma*, Santiago: CEPAL/PNUD.

Schulz, M., Söderbaum, F. and Öjendal, J. (eds.) 2001, *Regionalization in a Globalizing World*, London: Zed Books.

Schutz, B. 1995, 'The Heritage of Revolution and the Struggle for Governmental Legitimacy in Mozambique', in Zartman, I. W. (ed.) 1995.

Scott, James C. 1976, *The Moral Economy of the Peasant: Rebellion and Subsistence in Southeast Asia*, New Haven: Yale University Press.

Sen, A. 1981, *Poverty and Famines*, Oxford: Clarendon Press.

1985, *Commodities and Capabilities*, Oxford: Elsevier Science.

2002, 'How to Judge Globalism', *American Prospect*, 13 (1).

Seppala, P. and Koda, B. (eds.) 1998, *The Making of a Periphery: Economic Development and Cultural Encounters in Southern Tanzania*, Dar es Salaam: Mkuki na Nyota.

Serpell, R. 1993, *The Significance of Schooling: Life-Journeys in an African Society*, Cambridge: Cambridge University Press.

Shalev, M. 1999, 'Limits of and Alternatives to Multiple Regression in Macro-Comparative Research', mimeo, Florence: European University Institute.

Sharif, I. and Wood, G. (eds.) 2001, *Second Generation Microfinance: Supervision, Regulation and New Challenges*, Dhaka: University Press and Oxford: Oxford University Press.

Shin, Dong-myeon 2000, 'Financial Crisis and Social Security: The Paradox of South Korea', *International Social Security Review*, 53 (3): 83–107.

Simons, A. 1995, *Networks of Dissolution*, Boulder: Westview Press.

Sobhan, R. 1982, *The Crisis of External Dependence*, Dhaka: University Press.

1998, 'How Bad Governance Impedes Poverty Alleviation in Bangladesh', OECD Paper: http://www.oecd.org/dev/pub/tp1a.htm.

2000, 'Building a Responsible Civil Society: Challenges and Prospects', in Jahan, Rounaq (ed.) *Bangladesh: Promise and Performance*, Dhaka: University Press.

Sorrentino, C. 1990, 'The Changing Family in International Perspective', *Monthly Labor Review*, 113 (3): 41–58.

Standing, Guy 1999, *Global Labour Flexibility: Seeking Distributive Justice*, London: Macmillan.

2000, background paper prepared for the ILO InFocus Programe on Socio-Economic Security: http://www.ilo.org/public/english/protection/ses/index.htm.

Stanton, D. and Whiteford, P. 1998, *Pension Systems and Policy in APEC Countries*, Manila: Asian Development Bank.

Stewart, F. 2000, *Income Distribution and Development*, QEH Working Paper 37, Queen Elizabeth House: Oxford.

Stiglitz, J. E. 1974, 'The Demand for Education in Public and Private Schools Systems', *Journal of Public Economics*, 3: 349–85.

Stocker, K.,Waitzkin, H. and Iriart, C. 1999, 'The Exportation of Managed Care to Latin America', *New England Journal of Medicine*, 340: 1131–36.

Swift, J. 1989, 'Why are Rural People Vulnerable to Famine?', *IDS Bulletin*, 20 (2): 9–15.

Székely, M. and Hilgert, M. 1999, 'The 1990s in Latin America: Another Decade of Persistent Inequality', Working Paper 410, Washington: IADB.

Tamale, S. 1999, *When Hens Begin to Crow: Gender and Patliamentary Politics in Uganda*, Boulder: Westview Press.

Therborn, Goran 1983, 'When, How and Why Does a State Become a Welfare State?', presented at the ECPR Joint Workshops in Freiburg, 20–5 March.

1992, 'The Right to Vote and the Four World Routes to/through Modernity', in R. Thorstendahl (ed.) *State Theory and State History*, London: Sage.

Therkildsen, Ole and Semboja, Joseph 1995, *Service Provision under Stress in East Africa*, London: James Currey.

Thomson, A. 2000, *An Introduction to African Politics*, New York: Routledge.

Tilly, C. 1984, *Big Structures, Large Processes, Huge Comparisons*, New York: Russell Sage Foundation.

1999, *Durable Inequality*, London and Los Angeles: University of California Press.

2000, 'Mechanisms in Political Processes', mimeo, Columbia University.

Titmuss, R. M. 1958 and 1963 (2nd edition), *Essays on the Welfare State*, London: Allen and Unwin.

Torres, R. 2001, *Towards a Socially Sustainable World Economy*, Geneva: ILO.

Townsend, Peter 1979, *Poverty in the United Kingdom: A Survey of Household Resources and Standards of Living*, London: Allen Lane.

Tripp, A. M. 1997, *Changing the Rules: the Politics of Liberalisation and the Urban Informal Economy in Tanzania*, London: University of California Press.

2000, *Women and Politics in Uganda*, Kampala, Oxford, Madison: Fountain Publishers, James Currey, The University of Wisconsin Press.

UDAPE 1997, 'Pension Reform in Bolivia', mimeo, La Paz: UDAPE.

UNDP 1999, *Human Development Report 1999*, Oxford: Oxford University Press.

2000, *Human Development Report 2000*, Oxford: Oxford University Press.

2001, *Human Development Report 2001*, Oxford: Oxford University Press.

2002, *Human Development Report 2002*, Oxford: Oxford University Press.

US Social Security Administration 1999, *Social Security Programs Throughout the World 1997*, US Social Security Administration.

Uthoff, A. 1999, 'Trends in Social Security Reform and the Uninsured', conference paper, Washington: Inter-American Development Bank.

Van Binsbergen, W., Reyntjens, F. and Hesseling, G. 1986, *State and Local Community in Africa*, Brussels: Centre d'Etude et de Documentation Africaines.

Villalon, L. A. 1995, *Islamic Society and State Power in Senegal: Disciples and Citizens in Fatick*, Cambridge: Cambridge University Press.

Vogel, Ezra 1980, *Japan as Number One: Lessons for America*, Princeton: Princeton University Press.

Von Gersdorff, H. 1997, 'The Bolivian Pension Reform', Working Paper 1832, Washington: World Bank.

Wade, Robert 1990, *Governing the Market: Economic Theory and the Role of Government in East Asian Industrialization*, Princeton: Princeton University Press.

2000, 'International Institutions and the US Role in the Long Asian Crisis of 1990–2000', unpublished paper.

Waldrop, M. M. 1992, *Complexity: The Emerging Science at the Edge of Order and Chaos*, Harmondsworth, Penguin.

Wallman, S. 1996, *Kampala Women Getting By: Wellbeing in the Time of AIDS*, London: James Currey.

Weber, M. 1922, 'Wirtschaft und Gesellschaft', in Roth, G. and Wittich, C. (eds.) 1978, *Economy and Society: An Outline of Interpretive Sociology*, Berkeley: University of California Press.

Weiss, Linda 1998, *The Myth of the Powerless State*, Cambridge: Polity Press.

Westerlund, D. and Evers Rosander, E. 1997, *African Islam and Islam in Africa*, London: Hurst and Co.

White, Gordon and Goodman, Roger 1998, 'Welfare Orientalism and the Search for an East Asian Welfare Model', in R. Goodman *et al.* (eds.) 1998, pp. 3–24.

Wincott, Daniel 2001, 'Reassessing the Foundations of Welfare (State) Regimes', *New Political Economy*, 6 (3): 409–25.

Wood, G. 1985, 'The Politics of Development Policy Labelling', *Development and Change*, 16 (3): 347–73.

1994, *Bangladesh: Whose Ideas, Whose Interests?*, London: IT Publications.

1996, 'Avoiding the Totem and Developing the Art: Rural Development in Northern Pakistan', Working Paper for Aga Khan Rural Support Programme, Gilgit and Bath.

1999a, 'Adverse Incorporation: Another Dark Side of Social Capital', GSP Working Paper.

1999b, 'Prisoners and Escapees: Towards Political and Administrative Improvement', draft for World Bank.

2000, 'Prisoners and Escapees: Improving the Institutional Responsibility Square in Bangladesh', *Public Administration and Development*, 20: 221–37.

2001a, 'Governance and the Common Man!: Embedding Social Policy in the Search for Security', SPDC Workshop.

2001b, 'Desperately Seeking Security', *Journal of International Development*, 13: 523–34.

2003a, 'Environment and Collective Action under Threat: Tales from the Hindukush', chapter 11 in Winnett, A. and Warhurst, A. (eds.), *Towards an Environment Research Agenda*, vol. II, Basingstoke: Palgrave Macmillan.

2003b, 'Staying Secure, Staying Poor: The Faustian Bargain', *World Development*, 31 (3): 455–71.

Wood, G. and Salway, S. 2000, 'Introduction: Securing Livelihoods in Dhaka Slums', *Journal of International Development*, 12 (5): 669–88.

Woodiwiss, A. 1998, *Globalisation, Human Rights and Labour Law in Pacific Asia*, Cambridge: Cambridge University Press.

World Bank 1984, *World Development Report 1984*, Washington: World Bank.

1993, *The East Asian Miracle: Economic Growth and Public Policy*, Oxford: Oxford University Press.

1994, *Averting the Old Age Crisis*, London: Oxford University Press.

1997, *World Bank Indicators 1997*, CD-ROM Query Database.

1999a, 'East Asia Health Nutrition and Population Strategy', Human Development Sector Unit, East Asia and Pacific Region, IBRD, draft, October.

1999b, 'Towards an East Asian Social Protection Strategy', Human Development Unit, East Asia and Pacific Region, IBRD, draft, September.

1999c, *World Development Indicators*, Washington: World Bank.

2000a, 'Poverty Reduction in Indonesia: Constructing a New Strategy', draft report, October.

2000b, *Word Development Report 1999*, Washington: World Bank.

2000c, *World Development Indicators*, Washington: World Bank.

2000d, *Africa Database 2000*, CD-ROM, Washington: World Bank.

2001a, *World Development Report 2000/1: Attacking Poverty*, Oxford: Oxford University Press.

2001b, *African Poverty at the Millennium: Causes, Complexities, and Challenges*, Washington: World Bank Strategic Partnership with Africa.

2002a, *World Development Indicators*, Washington: World Bank.

2002b, *Taming the Leviathan – Reforming Governance in Bangladesh: An Institutional Review*, Washington: World Bank.

The World Guide 2001/2, *An Alternative Reference to the Countries of our Planet*, Oxford: New Internationalist.

World Health Organisation 2000, *World Health Report 2000*.

Yamamoto, T. 1995, 'Integrative Report', in Yamamoto, T. (ed.) *Emerging Civil Society in the Asia Pacific Community*, Singapore: Institute of Southeast Asian Studies, and Tokyo: Japan Center for International Exchange.

Yermo, J. 2000, 'Institutional Investors in Latin America: Recent Trends and Regulatory Challenges', in OECD (ed.) *Institutional Investors in Latin America*, Paris: OECD, pp. 23–120.

Zartman, I. W. (ed.) 1995, *Collapsed States: The Disintegration and Restoration of Legitimate Authority*, London: Lynne Rienner.

Index

Lightning Source UK Ltd.
Milton Keynes UK
UKOW06f1156190816

281050UK00009B/234/P